Sustainability Management in the Oil and Gas Industry

The oil and gas industry is a complex sector with significant reach in terms of providing the energy needs of the global economy and the security, environmental, and development consequences thereof. In particular, the sector is extremely important for the economic growth of emerging markets and developing countries. Furthermore, the lifespan of oil and gas resources is limited, with high health and safety risks and substantial environmental costs, which require careful management and sustainability practices to ensure optimal extraction and utilisation of these resources. This book examines the challenges and opportunities in the oil and gas industry, in the context of emerging markets and developing economies.

The book provides comprehensive coverage of the management and sustainability practices of the sector, the environmental impact, and sustainability of resources as well as the businesses that operate in the sector across the entire value chain. It addresses the current discourse on topics such as the sustainable development goals, the green economy, the Paris agreement, and Glasgow climate pact and concludes with a chapter on the future of the oil and gas industry. The discussions around energy and energy transitions, in particular, continue to gain momentum with a wide-reaching and up-to-date overview of the industry.

The book introduces readers to the concepts and formal models of analysis in the oil and gas sector and will serve as a useful resource for students, scholars, and researchers in operations, marketing, procurement and supply chain management, project management, health and safety management, environmental economics, natural resource economics, development finance, and development studies. Researchers and practitioners working in these areas will also find the book a useful reference material.

Joshua Yindenaba Abor is a Financial Economist, Professor of Finance, and former Dean of the University of Ghana Business School. He is an External Fellow at the Centre for Global Finance, SOAS University of London, UK, and Adjunct Professor of Development Finance at the University of Stellenbosch Business School, South Africa.

Amin Karimu is an Associate Professor in Economics at the School of Economics, University of Cape Town, South Africa and Visiting Scholar at the Centre for Environmental and Resource Economics at Umeå University, Sweden.

Routledge Studies in the Economics of Business and Industry

A Market Process Theory of the Firm
An Alternative to the Neoclassical Model
Mateusz Machaj

The Rural Enterprise Economy
Edited by Birgit Leick, Susanne Gretzinger and Teemu Makkonen

The Evolution of Contemporary Arts Markets
Aesthetics, Money and Turbulence
Andrés Solimano

The Economics of Corporate Trade Credit in Europe
Julia Koralun-Bereźnicka and Dawid Szramowski

The Economics of the Global Oil and Gas Industry
Emerging Markets and Developing Economies
Edited by Joshua Yindenaba Abor, Amin Karimu and Runar Brännlund

The Professional Standards of Executive Remuneration Consultants
Calvin Jackson

International Trade and the Music Industry
Live Music Services from the Caribbean
Lisa Gordon

Sustainability Management in the Oil and Gas Industry
Emerging and Developing Country Perspectives
Edited by Joshua Yindenaba Abor and Amin Karimu

For more information about this series, please visit www.routledge.com/Routledge-Studies-in-the-Economics-of-Business-and-Industry/book-series/RSEBI

Sustainability Management in the Oil and Gas Industry

Emerging and Developing Country Perspectives

Edited by
Joshua Yindenaba Abor
Amin Karimu

LONDON AND NEW YORK

First published 2023
by Routledge
4 Park Square, Milton Park, Abingdon, Oxon OX14 4RN

and by Routledge
605 Third Avenue, New York, NY 10158

Routledge is an imprint of the Taylor & Francis Group, an informa business

© 2023 selection and editorial matter, Joshua Yindenaba Abor and Amin Karimu; individual chapters, the contributors

The right of Joshua Yindenaba Abor and Amin Karimu to be identified as the author[/s] of the editorial material, and of the authors for their individual chapters, has been asserted in accordance with sections 77 and 78 of the Copyright, Designs and Patents Act 1988.

All rights reserved. No part of this book may be reprinted or reproduced or utilised in any form or by any electronic, mechanical, or other means, now known or hereafter invented, including photocopying and recording, or in any information storage or retrieval system, without permission in writing from the publishers.

Trademark notice: Product or corporate names may be trademarks or registered trademarks, and are used only for identification and explanation without intent to infringe.

British Library Cataloguing-in-Publication Data
A catalogue record for this book is available from the British Library

Library of Congress Cataloging-in-Publication Data
Names: Abor, Joshua Yindenaba, editor. | Karimu, Amin, editor.
Title: Sustainability management in the oil and gas industry : emerging and developing country perspectives / edited by Joshua Yindenaba Abor and Amin Karimu.
Description: 1 Edition. | New York, NY : Routledge, 2023. | Series: Routledge studies in the economics of business and industry | Includes bibliographical references and index.
Identifiers: LCCN 2022059349 (print) | LCCN 2022059350 (ebook) | ISBN 9781032314617 (hardback) | ISBN 9781032314624 (paperback) | ISBN 9781003309864 (ebook)
Subjects: LCSH: Oil industries--Developing countries. | Gas industry--Developing countries. | Renewable energy sources--Developing countries.
Classification: LCC HD9490.D442 S87 2023 (print) | LCC HD9490.D442 (ebook) | DDC 338.2/7282/091724--dc23/eng/20221209
LC record available at https://lccn.loc.gov/2022059349
LC ebook record available at https://lccn.loc.gov/2022059350

ISBN: 978-1-032-31461-7 (hbk)
ISBN: 978-1-032-31462-4 (pbk)
ISBN: 978-1-003-30986-4 (ebk)

DOI: 10.4324/9781003309864

Typeset in Bembo Std
by KnowledgeWorks Global Ltd.

Contents

List of Tables	viii
List of Figures	ix
List of Contributors	xi
Acknowledgements	xvi

PART I
Overview   1

1 Introduction to Sustainability Management in the Oil and Gas Industry   3
   JOSHUA YINDENABA ABOR AND AMIN KARIMU

PART II
Oil and Gas Management   13

2 Oil and Gas Storage Management: Evidence from a Developing Country   15
   JOHN B. DRAMANI, EDWIN PROVENCAL, SENYO HOSI, AND BENJAMIN SARFO

3 The Business of Oil Refining in Africa   30
   GEORGE ACHEAMPONG, ISHMAEL ACKAH, AND AMIN KARIMU

4 Downstream Petroleum Sector in Ghana: Mapping the Key Marketing Issues   48
   KOBBY MENSAH, ERNEST YAW TWENEBOAH-KODUAH, BEATRICE BOATENG, AND CHRIS ATADIKA

5 Oil and Gas Operations, Transportation, and Logistics Management   60
   ANTHONY AFFUL-DADZIE, IDDRISU AWUDU, AND BRIGHT ANSAH OWUSU

6 Procurement and Supply Chain Management in the Oil and Gas Industry 73
JOSHUA OFORI-AMANFO, PROSPER BIAKA KONLAN, AND FLORENCE NEWMAN

7 Digital Technology and Innovations in the Oil and Gas Industry 86
ERIC AFFUL-DADZIE, EMMANUEL AWUNI KOLOG, JOHN EFFAH, VINCENT OMWENGA, AND SULEMANA B. EGALA

8 Oil and Gas Project Management 99
KWASI DARTEY-BAAH, SAVIOUR AYERTEY NUBUOR, PAUL GBAHABO, AND KWESI AMPONSAH-TAWIAH

9 Human Resource Management Practices in the Oil and Gas Industry 111
JAMES B. ABUGRE, YVONNE LAMPTEY, SIMEON IFERE, AND RICHARD NYUUR

10 Strategic Management in the Oil and Gas Industry 124
OBI BERKO O. DAMOAH AND EMMANUEL KWESI BOON

11 Corporate Governance in the Oil and Gas Sector 138
DANIEL OFORI-SASU, PATIENCE ASEWEH ABOR, COLLINS NTIM, AND TEEROOVEN SOOBAROYEN

12 Implementing Total Quality Management in the Oil and Gas Industry 159
DANIEL AGYAPONG, EVELYN LAMISI ASUAH, AND EDMOND YEBOAH NYAMAH

13 Performance Management in the Oil and Gas Industry 174
TEDDY O. KWAKYE, RITA A. BEKOE, KINGSLEY O. APPIAH, AND ROBERT O. NYAMORI

PART III
Sustainability Management in the Oil and Gas Industry 189

14 Occupational Health and Safety in the Oil and Gas Industry 191
PATIENCE A. ABOR, FLORENCE NAAB, ANITA A. DANIELS, AND AARON A. ABUOSI

15 Corporate Social Responsibility of Multinational
   Corporations in the Oil and Gas Sector: Evidence from
   Sub-Saharan Africa   208
   LWANGA ELIZABETH NANZIRI AND GIFTY ABBAN

16 Environmental and Sustainability Management in the Oil
   and Gas Industry   223
   ALBERT AHENKAN, MAWUENA A. CUDJOE, AMIN KARIMU,
   AND GORDON ABEKAH-NKRUMAH

17 Natural Gas and Liquefied Natural Gas Resource
   Management   240
   AMIN KARIMU, JOHN BOSCO DRAMANI, AND ISHMAEL ACKAH

18 Petrochemical Resource Management   256
   STEPHEN M. BRAIMAH AND JUSTICE T. MENSAH

19 The Role of Oil and Gas in Sustainable Development
   in the Global South   267
   ASAAH SUMAILA MOHAMMED AND JOSHUA YINDENABA ABOR

20 The Future of the Oil and Gas Industry in Emerging
   and Developing Countries   280
   JOSHUA YINDENABA ABOR, JAMES ATAMBILLA ABUGRE,
   GEORGE NANA AGYEKUM DONKOR, AND AMIN KARIMU

   Index   294

Tables

3.1	Oil refineries in Africa	39
5.1	List of major final products from natural gas and crude oil and their usage	62
5.2	Refineries proposed or under construction in some selected African Countries	65
5.3	Some selected oil and gas pipelines in Africa	67
10.1	Sample SWOT matrix for an oil & gas company	132
11.1	2017 RGI country ranking of the oil and gas governance	143
11.2	Performance shift	144
11.3	Implementation gap of governance in oil and gas economies	145
11.4	Government stability index	147
13.1	Implementing the AHP and BSC PM framework in the petroleum industry	184
14.1	Ratification of ILO convention by country and date	197
14.2	Measures of dealing with the challenges of OHS	203
17.1	Production of natural gas in billion cubic metres	243
17.2	Consumption of natural gas in cubic million metres	244
17.3	Export trade value for natural gas for the top 20 exporting countries	248
19.1	The list of the millennium development goals (MDGs) and the sustainable development goals (SDGs)	270

Figures

2.1	Storage capacity of Ghana's BOST	23
3.1	A diagram with the four categories of petroleum products in a refinery process	34
3.2	Schematic flow of oil refining	35
3.3	Import volumes of petroleum products from 2010 to 2020	37
3.4	Import volumes of petroleum products in Africa, 2020	37
3.5	Oil demand in Africa as of 2020, by petroleum products (1,000/day)	37
3.6	Total outputs of refineries in Africa from 2014 to 2019 (1,000 metric tons)	40
3.7	Regional refining margins (first quarter 2000 to fourth quarter 2020)	42
4.1	Petroleum industry value chain framework	49
4.2	Marketing factors in the petroleum downstream sector	49
4.3	Ghana's OMC Market Share Statistics (NPA, 2021)	50
4.4	Petroleum consumption in Nigeria	52
4.5	Retail outlets of key players, 2018	52
4.6	Petroleum industry revenue share among firms (2021)	53
4.7	Kenyan petroleum downstream	54
5.1	A depiction of oil and gas operations	61
5.2	The oil refinery status of African countries	64
6.1	The value chain of the oil and gas industry	75
6.2	Procurement risk management framework	78
6.3	The supply chain efficiency framework	81
9.1	Strategies and criteria for technology transfer	118
9.2	Total reward perspective in the oil & gas sector	120
11.1	Resource governance scores of emerging oil and gas countries	142
11.2	State-owned oil and gas corporate governance practice	142
11.3	Oil and gas shareholder governance	143
11.4	Governance and institutional framework across different oil and gas producing regions	146

11.5	Oil and gas governance and institutional framework across different income brackets	148
11.6	Impact of shareholder governance and institutional arrangements	153
11.7	Impacts of institutional arrangements	154
13.1	Strategy map	178
13.2	Firms' health and performance key performance indicators (KPIs)	179
14.1	WHO healthy workplace model	198
16.1	Oil production in million metric tons in Africa by country 2020	224
17.1	Global proven reserves of natural gas	241
17.2	Relationship between natural gas export value, real GDP, and employment for top gas-exporting countries in the developing and emerging economies	249
17.3	Transparency and accountability index	252
17.4	Distribution of Natural Gas and Liquefied Petroleum Revenue in Ghana	253
18.1	Value chain of the petrochemical industry	257
18.2	Value chain of the petrochemical industry	259

Contributors

Gifty Abban is a Postgraduate Research Student and an Associate Lecturer with the Centre for Research in Accounting, Accountability and Governance of University of Southampton Business School, United Kingdom.

Gordon Abekah-Nkrumah is an Associate Professor of Health Policy and Management in the Department of Public Administration and Health Services Management, University of Ghana Business School.

Joshua Yindenaba Abor is a Financial Economist, Professor of Finance, and former Dean, University of Ghana Business School; he is an External Fellow at the Centre for Global Finance, SOAS University of London, UK, and Adjunct Professor of Development Finance at the University of Stellenbosch Business School, South Africa.

Patience Aseweh Abor is a Senior Lecturer in the Department of Public Administration and Health Services Management, University of Ghana Business School.

James Atambilla Abugre is a Doctoral Researcher at the Department of Finance, University of Ghana Business School, and a Senior Economic Development Planner, Ministry of Finance, Ghana.

James B. Abugre is Associate Professor of Human Resource Management at the Department of Organisation & Human Resource Management, University of Ghana Business School, and on the editorial boards of the *Journal of African Business* and *International Journal of Cross-Cultural Management*.

Aaron A. Abuosi is an Associate Professor of Health Policy and Management in the Department of Public Administration and Health Services Management, University of Ghana Business School.

George Acheampong is a Senior Lecture in the Department of Marketing and Entrepreneurship at the University of Ghana Business School.

Ishmael Ackah is an Energy Economist, and Executive Secretary, Public Utilities Regulatory Commission, Ghana.

Anthony Afful-Dadzie is an Associate Professor of Management Science and Head of the Department Operations and Management Information Systems (OMIS) at the University of Ghana Business School, University of Ghana.

Eric Afful-Dadzie is an Information Systems and Decision Science Researcher at University of Ghana Business School and CEO of MData Consult Ltd, a data analytics firm providing wide-ranging data solutions to firms in Africa.

Daniel Agyapong is a Professor in Finance and Entrepreneurship at the School of Business, University of Cape Coast, Ghana, and Director of the Directorate of Academic Planning and Quality Assurance at the University of Cape Coast.

George Nana Agyekum Donkor is the President of the ECOWAS Bank for Investment and Development, Lomé, Togo.

Albert Ahenkan is an Associate Professor and Head of the Department of Public Administration and Health Services Management, University of Ghana Business School.

Kwesi Amponsah-Tawiah is an Associate Professor in the Department of Organisation and Human Resource Management at the University of Ghana Business School.

Kingsley O. Appiah is an Associate Professor in Accounting and Corporate Governance at the School of Business, Kwame Nkrumah University of Science and Technology, Kumasi.

Evelyn Lamisi Asuah is a Lecturer in the Department of Business Administration at the University of Professional Studies, Ghana.

Chris Atadika is a Teaching and Research Assistant in the Department of Marketing and Entrepreneurship at the University of Ghana Business School. He is currently on the PhD Marketing programme at the same institution and his research interests include political marketing, consumer behaviour and psychology studies and marketing analytics.

Iddrisu Awudu is an Associate Professor of Management at Quinnipiac University, USA.

Rita A. Bekoe is a Senior Lecturer in the Department of Accounting, University of Ghana Business School, University of Ghana.

Beatrice Boateng is a Master of Philosophy postgraduate student from the University of Ghana Business School. She obtained a Bachelor of Technology in marketing at the Kumasi Technical University with first-class honours. She has served as Graduate and Research Assistant at the Department of Marketing and Entrepreneurship, University of Ghana Business School.

Emmanuel Kwesi Boon is a retired Professor of Environmental Management and Sustainable Development of Vrije Universiteit Brussel (VUB) in Brussels, Belgium, and Chairman of International Centre for Enterprise and Sustainable Development (ICED) in Ghana.

Stephen M. Braimah is a Senior Lecturer with the Department of Marketing and Entrepreneurship at the University of Ghana Business School.

Mawuena A. Cudjoe is a Lecturer in Accounting and Sustainability in the Department of Accounting at the University of Ghana Business School.

Obi Berko O. Damoah is an Associate Professor of Strategic Management and the Head of Department of the Department of Organisation and Human Resource Management, University of Ghana Business School.

Anita A. Daniels is an Assistant Lecturer in the Department of Public Administration and Health Services Management, University of Ghana Business School.

Kwasi Dartey-Baah is an Associate Professor in the Department of Organisation and Human Resource Management at the University of Ghana Business School.

John Bosco Dramani is a Senior Lecturer at the Department of Economics and a Research Fellow of the Brew Hammond Energy Centre, Kwame Nkrumah University of Science and Technology, Kumasi, Ghana.

John Effah is an Associate Professor of Information Systems at the University of Ghana Business School, and serves on the editorial board of the *Electronic Journal of Information Systems in Developing Countries* and Deputy Editor-in-Chief of the *African Journal of Information Systems*.

Sulemana B. Egala is a Doctoral Researcher at the School of Management and Economics, UESTC, China, and an Assistant Lecturer at the Department of Informatics, Faculty of ICT, SD Dombo University of Business and Integrated Development Studies, Wa, Ghana.

Paul Gbahabo is a Private Research Consultant and completed his PhD dissertation in Development Finance at the Stellenbosch Business School, South Africa.

Senyo Hosi is the Executive Chairman of Kleeve & Tove, and he also served as CEO of the Ghana Chamber of Bulk Oil Distributors.

Simeon Ifere is a Senior Lecturer and Director of the Doctor of Business Administration (DBA) Programme at the University of Lagos Business School; and Ifere was a Fellow at Swansea University, UK.

Emmanuel Awuni Kolog is a Senior Lecturer at the University of Ghana Business School, an Adjunct Professor at the Malawi University of Science and Technology, and a Research Fellow at the University of Turku in Finland.

Amin Karimu is an Associate Professor in Economics at the School of Economics & Senior Research Fellow at the Environmental Policy Research Unit (EPRU), University of Cape Town, South Africa, and Visiting Scholar at the Centre for Environmental and Resource Economics at Umeå University, Sweden.

Prosper Biaka Konlan is a recent graduate of the University of Ghana Business School where he pursued an MPhil in operations management from the Department of Operations and Management Information Systems, and is currently the MD of KB Supplies, the key distributor for Accra Breweries Ltd in the north-east region of Ghana.

Teddy O. Kwakye is a Senior Lecturer in Accounting at the University of Ghana Business School, University of Ghana.

Yvonne Lamptey is a Senior Lecturer in the Department of Organisation and Human Resource Management at the University of Ghana.

Asaah Sumaila Mohammed is a Senior Lecturer at the Department of Environmental Science at the C.K. Tedam University of Technology and Applied Sciences in Navrongo, Ghana, and Executive Director of the Nature and People Trust, a Ghanaian Natural Resources and Environmental Governance and Conservation NGO.

Justice T. Mensah is an Economist at the World Bank, Washington DC, USA.

Kobby Mensah is a Senior Lecturer at the University of Ghana Business School, and Editor of the book *Political Marketing and Management in Ghana: A New Architecture*.

Florence Naab is an Associate Professor in the School of Nursing, University of Ghana, and a Researcher and an Expert in the area of psychosocial health problems associated with infertility.

Lwanga Elizabeth Nanziri is the Head of the African Centre for Development Finance, and a Senior Lecturer with the Development Finance Programme at the Stellenbosch University Business School, South Africa.

Florence Newman is a recent graduate of the University of Ghana Business School with an MPhil in operations management from the Department of Operations and Management Information Systems, and is currently a Market Researcher for a Telecommunications Company based in Accra.

Collins Ntim is a Professor of Accounting at the Centre for Research in Accounting, Accountability and Governance (CRAAG), Department of Accounting, Southampton Business School, University of Southampton, UK.

Saviour Ayertey Nubuor is a Lecturer in the Department of Organisation and Human Resource Management at the University of Ghana Business School.

Edmond Yeboah Nyamah is a Lecturer in the Department of Marketing and Supply Chain Management at School of Business, University of Cape Coast, Ghana. His areas of expertise include supply chain management, risk and sustainable management, and project management.

Robert O. Nyamori is an Associate Professor of Accounting at the UAE University in the United Arab Emirates.

Richard Nyuur is an Associate Professor (Reader) of Strategic Management and International Business at the Newcastle Business School, Northumbria University, UK, and is currently on the editorial boards of the *Journal of African Business*, *Critical Perspectives on International Business*, and the *European Journal of Economics and Management*.

Joshua Ofori-Amanfo is a faculty of the Department of Operations and Management Information Systems, University of Ghana Business School.

Daniel Ofori-Sasu is a Lecturer in Finance at the Department of Finance, Central University, Ghana. His areas of expertise include banking, finance, investment, insurance and risk management, corporate governance and regulations, monetary economics, and sustainability issues.

Bright Ansah Owusu holds an MPhil degree in operations management from University of Ghana. His research interest is in the area of oil and gas planning and management and energy policy and analysis.

Edwin Alfred Provencal is the Managing Director of BOST and former Managing Director of the Bulk Oil Transportation (BOST) Company Limited and Technical Advisor at the Minister of Energy.

Benjamin Sarfo is a Teaching Assistant at the Department of Finance, University of Ghana Business School.

Teerooven Soobaroyen is a Professor of Accounting at Essex Business School, University of Essex, UK, and previously held academic positions at the University of Mauritius, Aberystwyth University and the University of Southampton.

Ernest Yaw Tweneboah-Koduah is an Associate Professor of Marketing in the Department of Marketing and Entrepreneurship at the University of Ghana Business School.

Acknowledgements

Joshua Yindenaba Abor
To my wonderful wife, Dr. Patience Aseweh Abor and our lovely children, Ivana, Bastien, and Venka for their love, support, and encouragement. Also, to my parents, Mr. Abor Ndobire and Madam Amina Tobga for their inspiration and commitment throughout my education. I also wish to appreciate my co-editor, Amin, and co-authors of the various chapters.

Amin Karimu
I am eternally grateful to my awesome wife, Nasum and my lovely children, Zaeem and Afnan for the love and support throughout the entire process of the book. A special thanks goes to the entire members of the N-yo family for their wonderful support and encouragement. I would also like to appreciate the cooperation and support from my co-editor and co-authors of the various chapters contained in the book.

General
We the editors would like to thank all contributing authors for the high quality of their chapters. We wish to thank the Dr. Charles Asante, University of Ghana, for the excellent work in proofreading and language editing. We also thank all the reviewers of the various chapters as well as Dr. Daniel Ofori-Sasu, and Bright Oduro for providing editorial assistance.

We wish to specially appreciate the financial support provided by Petrosol Ghana Limited and Ghana Chamber of Bulk Oil Distribution in completing this book project.

Part I
Overview

1 Introduction to Sustainability Management in the Oil and Gas Industry

Joshua Yindenaba Abor and Amin Karimu

1.1 Introduction

The world, since the industrial revolution, has relied significantly on oil and gas (O&G) resources to fuel, especially for its industrial and transportation activities. The major consuming block for oil before 2012 was always the Organization for Economic Cooperation and Development (OECD) countries, which are more industrialised relative to countries in the non-OECD block. Data from British Petroleum (2020) suggests consumption from the non-OECD block for the first time surpassed that of the OECD countries in 2012 and has continued to do so since then. The high consumption of oil by the non-OECD block in recent decades is due to two key reasons: increased industrialisation, a rising middle class in some OECD countries, and improvements in energy-efficient technologies in OECD countries.

The transition of a significant number of people into the middle class in countries such as India and China, coupled with the efforts towards industrialisation to promote growth and reduce poverty in these countries, has contributed to the high consumption of oil in the non-OECD countries since 2012. OECD countries, on the other hand, due to climate change and energy security concerns, are implementing strict environmental regulations which, among other things, have promoted the development of energy-efficient technologies, leading to more efficient energy utilisation, especially in the European Union countries.

Natural-resource-endowed developing countries tend to be overly dependent on these resources for national development. This suggests that if these resources are not well managed, growth and development will suffer significantly, especially in countries such as Nigeria, Saudi Arabia, Venezuela, Angola, and Iran. Oil exports as a share of merchandise exports for each of the listed countries exceed 80%, highlighting the level of over-dependence on oil incomes. In these countries, there is a need to optimally add value from the value chain of the O&G industry and to obtain the maximum return from the resource.

A high dependence on natural resources exposes countries to the 'resource curse' phenomenon (a situation where high dependence on a natural resource

DOI: 10.4324/9781003309864-2

leads to poor economic growth and development relative to countries with less dependence on natural resources), especially those with weak institutions and a significant alight capture. Norway is a classic example of a country rich in oil resource but has over the years managed to achieve impressive growth and development compared to Nigeria, an oil-rich country which ironically experiences poor growth and development outcomes. Why are both Norway and Nigeria rich in oil resources, but exhibit stark differences in the realisation of growth and development outcomes? A simple answer to that is the way in which these resources are managed over time, value addition along the value chain of the oil industry, diversification of the economy, and the quality of institutions in the two countries.

In most emerging and developing countries (EDCs), when O&G resources are discovered, they are often quick to extract these resources with the aim of rapidly growing the economy, reducing poverty, and gaining some political capital without a careful management plan. A carefully devised management plan could, among other things, aid in deriving the maximum benefit from the value chain of the O&G industry. Moreover, due to the lack of both domestic technology and funds to extract the O&G resources, governments of these countries are quick to accept poorly designed contracts with international O&G companies, which in the long run are to the disadvantage of the oil-rich EDCs.

Furthermore, these resources are non-renewable, suggesting the need to carefully manage them in a way that the future generations will also benefit from them. Moreover, both production and utilisation of these resources involve major health and safety issues resulting from heavy pollution that contributes significantly to global climate change. Therefore, from the perspective of sustainability, management of these resources must incorporate both environmental sustainability and health and safety aspects.

Transition to a low-carbon economy is progressively being promoted, especially in the developed countries, where the focus is on transforming the world economy and redirecting it away from fossil fuels. In this transformation, renewable energies, energy efficiency, and technological developments such as carbon capture are being promoted.

Though the transition to renewables will not be done overnight, the prospects for renewables and other clean energy technologies are very promising from an investment perspective. Such prospects for clean energy sources will create significant risks in investing in the O&G industry and likely drive investment away from the sector. For instance, in a net-zero carbon scenario, the IEA (2021) estimates the market size of a clean-energy technology industry (technological equipment) to be 1.2 trillion US dollars in 2050, and that of oil to be 182 billion US dollars. Such a market prospect for clean fuels will create problems for the O&G industry, especially in countries that overly depend on O&G resources for revenue generation.

Despite the transition to low carbon economy being underway along with the associated increased interest in renewable energy sources globally, especially among policymakers and investors in developed countries, demand for O&G resources will continue to surge due to growing demand from EDCs such as China, India, South Africa, and Brazil. Most developing countries will still depend heavily on O&G resources in the short-to-medium term as the existing infrastructure will need to be transformed to become compliant with clean energy sources. Moreover, in the medium term, demand for gas resources will surge due to its low carbon content and relative stability, to complement intermittent renewable energies such as solar and wind.

These developments in the world due to climate change effects as a result of human activities, especially in the area of transport, manufacturing, agriculture, and thermal energy generation, make it imperative for countries with O&G resources, especially EDCs, to carefully plan and manage their reserves. They must sustainably extract optimal value along the value chain of their O&G resources to avoid the resource curse. They must also carefully manage the risk of excessive investment and dependence on the O&G industry, keeping in mind the prospects of the clean energy transition. This book provides a comprehensive resource on the management, environmental sustainability, and health and safety issues of the O&G industry in EDCs.

1.2 Purpose of the Book

As mentioned above, O&G resources will continue to play a key role in the global economy, at least in the short-to-medium term, especially in EDCs alongside the gradual transition into renewables. The industry is complex, and the lifespan of O&G resources is finite. There are high health and safety risks and a significant environmental consequences that require careful management, marketing, and sustainability practices to ensure optimal extraction and utilisation of these resources. Such a complex but important sector is generally not well understood both in academia and in policy circles in relation to efficient and effective management of the resources to support the sustainability of these resources.

This edited book seeks to contribute to the understanding of the O&G industry from a management and sustainability perspective. It will serve as a comprehensive material on the management and sustainability aspects of the O&G sector with a focus on EDCs, for academia, policymakers, and practitioners. It provides a comprehensive coverage on the management and sustainability of O&G resources and the industries that operate in the sector across the value chain in EDCs.

The book is made up of contributions from scholars and practitioners in the O&G industry across the value chain. It will serve as a useful resource for students, scholars, and researchers in the operations, marketing, procurement and supply chain management, health and safety management, environmental economics, natural resource economics, development finance, and development studies. Researchers and practitioners working in these areas will also find the book a useful reference material.

1.3 Overview of the Chapters

This book is composed of 20 chapters, and we provide an overview of the remaining chapters.

In Chapter 2, John B. Dramani, Edwin Provencal, Senyo Hosi, and Benjamin Sarfo discuss the effects of O&G storage on energy security and the O&G storage infrastructure in emerging economies. They further discuss the O&G infrastructure investment gap and the business potential for closing the gap in EDCs. The authors use the Bulk Oil Storage and Transportation Company Limited (BOST) in Ghana as a case study and examine how it has ensured optimal management of Ghana's O&G storage.

Chapter 3 presents the business of oil refining with a focus on emerging and developing economies. In this chapter, George Acheampong, Ishmael Ackah, and Amin Karimu analyse the business of oil refining by focusing on factors to consider in siting a refinery, the supply chain of a refinery, infrastructure requirements, the input-output of a refinery, demand for refined products, refining margins for the industry, trends in the refining business, as well as health, safety, and environmental concerns of the refining industry. The authors further highlight the constraints and opportunities in Africa's oil refining industry.

In Chapter 4, Kobby Mensah, Ernest Yaw Tweneboah-Koduah, Beatrice Boateng, and Chris Atadika explore key issues in downstream petroleum marketing in emerging economies. They find that the petroleum downstream sector in emerging markets offers key products and services such as gasoline, vehicle maintenance, and convenience stores. The most prevalent factors of public discourse are pricing, policy, the stakeholder, and operational incidents in the sector. On policy, it is noted that all case countries have a mixed regulatory petroleum downstream sector that is partly regulated and partly deregulated. In the selected study countries, evidence shows a good mix of both global and local supplier brands. As a marketing strategy, players in the sector make claims of serving customers with high-quality fuel and lubricants at the most competitive prices, as well as world-class customer service standards such as checking for leaks, easy mobile payment methods, a lube bay, a quick-shopping option, and places of convenience at service stations.

In Chapter 5, Anthony Afful-Dadzie, Iddrisu Awudu, and Bright Ansah Owusu look at the operations, transportation, and logistics management (OTLM) in the O&G industry in EDCs. The authors provide an overview of OTLM in the O&G industry in general while highlighting some of the situational challenges faced by EDCs in an African context. They find that the major challenges faced by the O&G industry in the EDCs are lack of financial resources, refinery capacity, regulatory compliance monitoring, investment in state-of-the-art technology, and political instability. The authors further discuss how improvements in the OTLM can help address some of these challenges, including feasible solutions that can be adopted by EDCs to realise an immediate impact on the management of O&G industries.

In Chapter 6, Joshua Ofori-Amanfo, Prosper Biaka Konlan, and Florence Newman present the value and the practical relevance of effectively managing the procurement and supply chain function of O&G industry in EDCs. The authors provide a detailed exposition of the nature of the O&G supply chains and provide an analysis of procurement as a critical risk factor in O&G projects. Further, the authors examine how procurement and supply chain risks can be managed. They further explore the avenues for leveraging supply chain efficiencies in the O&G industry. The findings of the chapter show that in many EDCs the industry is characterised by a drastic shortage of domestic skills and expertise with minimal regard for sustainability initiatives. The consequence is low profitability and citizens' low perceived benefits from the industry resulting in frequent agitations, uprisings, and sabotage.

In Chapter 7, Eric Afful-Dadzie, Emmanuel Awuni Kolog, John Effah, Vincent Omwenga, and Sulemana B. Egala review and discuss existing and potential technologies that present opportunities for the O&G industry towards a full uptake in the fourth industrial revolution, especially in Africa. Notable technologies discussed in the chapter include artificial intelligence, blockchain technology, remote sensing, and big data analytics in the O&G sector. Despite the tremendous opportunities that digital technology presents in the O&G sector, there exist some challenges that hinder the full realisation of the fourth industrial revolution, especially in Africa. One of such challenges is the drain of such technologies on the O&G industry's capital.

In Chapter 8, Kwasi Dartey-Baah, Saviour Ayertey Nubuor, Paul Gbahabo, and Kwesi Amponsah-Tawiah examine ways in which the O&G sector creates opportunities for employment, drives technology and research, and boosts local businesses. Additionally, project success is crucial in the O&G sector to make the necessary impact, to cope with a fast-changing world, and to satisfy the increasing demand for O&G products. However, in many less industrialised countries, project management in the public O&G sector is ineffective because project managers in these organisations lack the requisite project management competencies. Findings indicate that projects related challenges are compounded in the O&G sectors due to their large size and political characterisation. The authors recommend requirement engineering in dealing with the challenge of stakeholder management and scarce resources in the O&G industry.

In Chapter 9, James B. Abugre, Yvonne Lamptey, Simeon E. Ifere, and Richard Nyuur provide an overview of human resource management (HRM) practices in the O&G industry in developing countries. They explore HR practices, concepts, and designs and how these are utilised in the supply chain operations associated with the exploration, extraction, production, and consumption of O&G resources in the upstream, mid-stream, and downstream processes. The authors suggest the need for a significant bundle of human resource practices required in the O&G industry, which should include recruitment and selection of employees; contracting and local content for manpower; strategic training and development; technological transfer; empowerment of personnel; and rewarding of employees.

In Chapter 10, Obi Berko O. Damoah and Emmanuel Kwesi Boon discuss strategic management of O&G firms in emerging and developing markets. The authors argue that because of the complex and constant changing trends from the external environment, strategic management principles which aim to manage the influences from external changes and complexities are a panacea for O&G firms that desire to be profitable and remain sustainable. The authors further apply the strategic management process, also known in the field as the strategic management framework to the O&G sector in developing and emerging economies.

In Chapter 11, Daniel Ofori-Sasu, Patience Aseweh Abor, Collins Ntim, and Teerooven Soobaroyen explore the key issues related to governance in the O&G industry from the perspective of emerging markets and developing economies. The authors provide evidence that several countries within different contextual settings have demonstrated good governance and realised that weak or poor governance systems can be avoided with the right structural reforms, knowledge, institutions, regulations, and policies. Thus, there is reason for cautious optimism that more countries within the region might have learnt hard lessons from weak governance system in the past. Consequently, these countries will pursue strategies and policies that will allow them to fully reap the benefits of good governance practices in the future. The authors provide a strong justification for countries with a low O&G governance index to follow countries with best governance practices and institutional arrangements as their benchmark to achieve a stable governance system.

In Chapter 12, Daniel Agyapong, Evelyn Lamisi Asuah, and Edmond Yeboah Nyamah provide a new insight into the implementation of total quality management (TQM) in developing economies in O&G industries. The authors stress that any offshore project implementing a TQM system is expected to become more productive and cost-effective. With TQM, businesses could save money through effective management framework and activities. Consequently, management time is freed up to focus on increasing production, expanding product variety, and improving existing offerings. The authors conclude that to achieve a sustained competitive advantage and ensure compliance with industrial and regulatory requirements, there is a need to implement the TQM philosophy efficiently.

In Chapter 13, Teddy O. Kwakye, Rita A. Bekoe, Kingsley O. Appiah, and Robert O. Nyamori investigate performance management in the O&G industry. The authors present various theories and practices underpinning performance management systems and advance the balanced score card (BSC) as the industry's most widely used performance management tool. They further advance two primary performance improvement processes – lean accounting and benchmarking – and highlight how these processes help O&G companies to attain operational excellence. The authors explain that lean accounting ensures improved performance through meeting customer needs, reducing inventory, and ensuring employee satisfaction. Benchmarking

Introduction to Sustainability Management in the O&G Industry 9

in the O&G industry involves learning from others regarding environmental management (EM), environmental impact (EI), and disclosure and transparency (D&T) to improve the businesses of the O&G sector.

In Chapter 14, Patience A. Abor, Florence Naab, Anita A. Daniels, and Aaron A. Abuosi discuss the occupational health and safety (OHS) in the O&G industry in developing countries. The authors further review ILO standards, legal frameworks, the WHO healthy workplace model, and empirical literature relating to OHS. The study shows that apart from physical hazards, issues with the ratification of the conventions and poor implementation have led to the failure of the O&G industries in developing countries to achieve the ILO standards. Despite the specific challenges identified in the OHS of the O&G industry, the authors show that there are no rigorous measures to resolve the challenges given the diverse conventions. Thus, constructive actions are required to curb the challenges workers in the industry encounter.

In Chapter 15, Lwanga Elizabeth Nanziri and Gifty Abban focus on the CSR activities of MNCs for the socio-economic development and well-being of local communities in the sub-Saharan African economies. The authors identify positive impacts of CSR activities on the socio-economic well-being of the local communities within the study area. The authors conclude by discussing cases of MNCs suffering negative publicity and reputational damage within the O&G sector in Africa and provide some policy recommendations for the governments of oil-and-gas-rich countries in Africa.

In Chapter 16, Albert Ahenkan, Mawuena A. Cudjoe, Amin Karimu, and Gordon Abekah-Nkrumah present an overview of environmental and sustainability management in the O&G industry in EDCs. The authors specifically discuss the environmental governance, ethics, management of EIs in the industry, pollution prevention, and greening of the O&G industry. The authors reveal that although the O&G sector has improved the economies of most developing countries over the years, its activities have had significant EIs. They stress that although enacted regulations are the ways to ensure that the effects of the activities of the O&G sector are brought under control, these laws have not done much in the developing economies because they are almost nonexistent. However, the authors conclude that the sense of duty towards the environment has helped mitigate the effect of the activities of the industry.

In Chapter 17, Amin Karimu, John Bosco Dramani, and Ishmael Ackah provide an overview of the natural gas (NG) and liquefied NG resource management in EDCs, as well as the challenges faced by the industry. The authors show that NG reserves in EDCs have the potential to promote growth, promote exports of NG and to contribute significantly to revenue and employment generation. Thus, policy measures should be designed to help to create forward and backward linkages in the NG sector in EDCs. In addition, the authors conclude that EDCs should continue to use a fiscal partnership regime and the adoption of a sovereign wealth fund approach for sustainable management of NG resources.

In Chapter 18, Stephen M. Braimah and Justice T. Mensah present an exploration into the concept of petrochemical resource management of the O&G industry. The authors show that petrochemical feedstock accounts for over 12% of the global oil demand and it is expected to increase in the future, especially in developing economies. They conclude that assessing the relative price of natural gas manifests the competitiveness of US petrochemical companies and that the wider the promulgation, the greater the merits the world will realise from ethane.

In Chapter 19, Asaah Sumaila Mohammed and Joshua Yindenaba Abor provide novel insights into the role of O&G in sustainable development in the Global South. They provide evidence that achieving the Sustainable Development Goals (SDGs) in the Global South is largely dependent on domestic revenue mobilisation capacities and deliberate efforts to prioritise specific planned and targeted indicators. Despite increased spending on national priorities, Ghana and Nigeria, in particular, have not demonstrated enough targeted spending of oil revenue to achieve the SDGs. Nigeria has the Sovereign Wealth Fund and Ghana has the Heritage Fund, and both funds are aimed at investing oil revenue for future generations. They show that implementation is however challenged by mismanagement, misappropriation, and in some cases of corruption. Oil revenue is thinly distributed across several areas with no clear targets or lines of progressive tracking. The authors conclude that it is imperative to provide deliberate and progressive planning and utilisation of oil revenues for accelerated growth and sustainable development in the Global South.

In Chapter 20, Joshua Yindenaba Abor, James Atambilla Abugre, George Nana Agyekum Donkor, and Amin Karimu explore the future of the O&G industry in EDCs. The chapter discusses the exploration of O&G, how the environment is being impacted by the activities, and the role of market players along the value chain of the O&G sector. It highlights how the world is transitioning to renewable energy use through the analysis of demand trends and challenges confronting the O&G industry. The authors assert that despite the immeasurable contributions to the development of the global economy, there have been systemic shifts in their demand in recent times. They demonstrate that the high cost of capital requirements in O&G production, climate change effects of global warming, deprivation and community conflicts, and technological advancements account for these shifts in the demand trends of O&G.

1.4 Conclusion

The O&G sector is an important global industry and, as this book demonstrates, can have both positive and negative impacts on a range of areas covered by the SDGs. With careful management, planning, marketing, implementation, and sustainability practices, the O&G industry has the opportunity to contribute across all SDGs, either by enhancing its positive contributions or by avoiding or mitigating negative impacts. The industry is complex, while the life span of O&G resources is finite. Yet emerging and important concepts within the sector are generally not well-understood both in academia and in policy circles in relation to the efficient and effective management of the resources to support their sustainability. For that reason, this book provides a comprehensive insight into the sustainability management of the O&G industry in EDCs. It includes a holistic overview and discussion of the concepts of management and sustainability of O&G resources and the industries that operate in the sector across the value chain in EDCs. Given that sustainability has long been a key consideration for the O&G industry, the book offers a general understanding that adherence to health, safety, and environmental regulations in the management strategies and increasing contributions to the societies and economies in which they operate around the world, form the core of the existing sustainability management of the industry. In general, the book serves as a useful resource for researchers and policymakers based on the contributions and policy implications made by the scholars and practitioners in the O&G industry across the value chain.

References

British Petroleum. (2020, July). Statistical review. https://www.bp.com/en/global/corporate/energy-economics/statistical-review-of-world-energy.html

IEA. (2021). World energy outlook. https://iea.blob.core.windows.net/assets/4ed140c1-c3f3-4fd9-acae-789a4e14a23c/WorldEnergyOutlook2021.pdf

Part II
Oil and Gas Management

2 Oil and Gas Storage Management
Evidence from a Developing Country

John B. Dramani, Edwin Alfred Provencal, Senyo Hosi, and Benjamin Sarfo

2.1 Introduction

Crude oil and natural gas are the dominant energy sources in the global energy market. Oil and gas storage plays an essential role in the global supply of primary energy. Since 1974, both developed and developing countries have built strategic petroleum reserves (SPRs) in extensive underground storage facilities to address supply and demand imbalances and energy security considerations to insulate themselves from supply disruptions. The storage facilities for crude oil include salt caverns, rock caverns, and tanks, whereas those for natural gas storage, salt caverns, deep aquifers, depleted reservoirs, and tanks have been adopted. The establishment of SPRs and other forms of stock did not only serve to insulate countries from supply disruption but also dampened and moderated price fluctuations. However, storage entails opportunity cost as current production or consumption resources are instead spent on energy storage.

This chapter examines the effects of oil and gas storage on energy security and the oil and gas storage infrastructure in emerging economies. We use Bulk Oil Storage and Transportation Company Limited (BOST) in Ghana as the case study and examine how it has ensured optimal management of Ghana's oil and gas storage.

The chapter is structured as follows. Section 2.2 presents global crude oil and gas storage and energy security. It highlights the merits of building strategic reserves and discusses African countries' strategies to stockpile oil and gas resources. Section 2.3 discusses the oil and gas infrastructure investment gap and the business potential for closing the gap in emerging and developing countries. It also deals with the evolution of oil and gas storage in Ghana with special reference to the role of BOST in managing strategic reserve stocks and developing a national network of oil pipelines. In Section 2.4, issues on financing oil and gas strategic reserves in Ghana are discussed, while Section 2.5 provides a case study on how oil and gas are stored in Ghana. Section 2.6 gives insight into the various LPG programmes Ghana has implemented. Finally, Section 2.7 concludes the chapter.

DOI: 10.4324/9781003309864-4

2.2 Global Crude Oil and Gas Storage and Energy Security

Storage has become an integral part of crude oil and gas markets as it helps deal with the reliability of supply required to meet consumers' demands. Establishing an SPR is essential for domestic security to tackle market supply disruptions. It is envisioned as an insurance policy against any significant oil supply interruption and ensures energy security in net-importing countries.

2.2.1 The Evolution of Strategic Petroleum Reserves and Natural Gas Strategic Reserves

The first global oil crisis occurred in 1973 when the Organization of Petroleum Exporting Countries (OPEC), led by Saudi Arabia, placed an embargo on the U.S. and its allies for supporting Israel in the Yom Kippur War. This crisis caused the price of a barrel of crude oil to rise by about 400% globally (Corbett, 2013), causing an economic recession in the U.S. and consequently influencing its energy policy direction for over 40 years. The Department of Energy (DOE) created an emergency underground reservoir in 1975 to stockpile crude oil to mitigate future supply shocks from oil cartels. By the close of September 2021, the inventory was about 621.3 million barrels, occupying a space of 98,780,000 m^3. This amount of oil can cover about 31 days of the current oil consumption pattern (2019 daily U.S. consumption of 20.54 million barrels per day) and offers 65 days of import protection (9.141 million barrels per day). However, the maximum withdrawal capacity from the SPR is about 4.4 million barrels per day, which extends its exhaustion capacity by about 59 days of import protection. At present, the SPR and the private sector inventory offer an estimated amount of 115 days of import protection from external supply shocks to the U.S.

According to the US Department of Energy, withdrawal from the SPR is based on conditions agreed upon and written in the 1975 Energy Policy and Conservation (EPCA) to mitigate significant supply disruption. Over the years, the principal objective of the SPR has changed from the initial intention of reducing the risks associated with supply interruptions to combating the effects of natural disasters such as hurricanes on oil markets. Again, the recent increase in U.S. domestic oil production has reduced its reliance on oil imports. Based on this, some policymakers think the SPR has outlived its original aim and envisaged it as a tool for providing financial support to legislations such as health care.

In 2005, some policymakers in the U.S., motivated by a similar threat to natural gas supply disruptions after the shut-in of natural gas in the Gulf of Mexico during the hurricane season, considered putting forward a proposal to build a natural gas strategic reserve. Hurricanes Katrina and Rita shut down natural gas production by 800 Bcf, representing about 22% of yearly Gulf production. This caused the price of natural gas to rise significantly to more than US$15.00 per million Btu (MMBtu) and made residential consumers pay the highest prices for natural gas heating in the winter. Nevertheless, there was no shortage as the market efficiently allocated the amount produced among consumers. Again, in September 2021, staggering natural gas prices caused fear in Europe, and policymakers started looking around for sustainable solutions. European leaders realised that solutions such as bailing out natural gas suppliers, providing subsidies to poor and vulnerable consumers, and pleading with Russia to increase supply are not sustainable. The construction of strategic gas reserves appears to be the best long-term solution to the instability of gas prices.

There is currently a high gas storage level equivalent to about 77 billion cubic meters. However, this does not serve the purpose of a strategic gas reserve since it is handled by private investors who are driven by a profit motive to draw down these reserves anytime prices are rising, not necessarily by shortages. This implies that distribution firms can intentionally deplete their stocks for high rewards even before a crisis. The European Union draft directive recognises the importance of natural gas storage and thus believes in creating a strategic natural gas reserve. This recognition comes from the background that natural gas storage is fundamental to preventing supply disruption during political and natural disasters in the producing nations.

Several African countries have implemented strategic oil and gas storage programmes over the years. In the context of Ghana, the government established BOST Company Limited in 1993 with the principal objective of stockpiling oil to combat any supply-side interruptions. BOST has been mandated to establish and keep a national network of facilities for bulk storage, transportation, and distribution of petroleum products to achieve at least six weeks of national consumption coverage. In Nigeria, the Nigeria Pipeline and Storage Company Limited (NPSC) has the mandate of building and maintaining pipelines and bulk storage infrastructure across Nigeria. It is also responsible for managing petroleum products' bulk transportation and storage and initiating plans to maximise pipelines and the revenues of storage assets. In South Africa, the government set up the strategic fuel fund (SFF) which has the duty of procuring, maintaining, and managing a strategic oil stockpile for the government. The SFF owns two storage facilities at Saldanha, holding about 45 million barrels, and Milnerton, holding about 7.8 million barrels, located in the Western Cape.

2.2.2 The Strategic Petroleum Reserve and Oil Price Volatility

Oil price volatility may be defined as the sharp rise or fall in oil prices. Oil price volatility can destroy economies through a high cost of living and political instability. Fundamentally, oil price volatility can be caused by a disruption in the supply of the commodity through the activities of OPEC, particularly when a consuming country holds an insignificant surplus to cushion the effect of sudden price increases in the event of global supply curtailment. These volatilities are expected to intensify if the role played by shale in addressing the oil supply deficit remains uncertain in the global oil supply. Based on this, economists and oil market traders suggest that strategic oil reserves should be applied to smoothen out price fluctuations in the event of supply disruption.

A supply shock arising from a strategic decision by OPEC to curtail supplies will cause domestic prices in almost all economies to rise regardless of whether or not a particular country imports from the affected supply areas. The negative consequences of such a supply shock can be moderated by releasing additional supplies from the strategic stocks of countries with spare capacity. However, oil purchases for strategic storage when prices are stable do not cause fluctuations, thus leading to optimal management strategies. The role of SPR in price moderation ensures that governments and international energy agencies do not curtail demand for oil by introducing unpopular tools such as quotas, taxes, or tariffs. In addition, helping to stabilise oil prices using the SPR can avert economic recessions that most countries are likely to suffer due to the volatility of oil prices (Stevens, 2014).

In addition, SPR is expected to play the role of expectation management of the oil market. The oil market responds very fast to expected variations in supply and demand, which can sharply influence price changes. For instance, in 2012, the sanctions on Iranian oil exports along with other important geopolitical shocks could have significantly impacted oil prices. However, this effect was moderated by an expectation that oil from U.S. SPR and other International Energy Agency (IEA) countries could be released to dampen any price rise. Immediately after the sanctions were announced, both the G-20 and G-7 members issued statements to release oil from their strategic reserves when the situation demanded it.

2.2.3 Managing Strategic Petroleum Reserves and Energy Security

Energy security is when a country experiences a guaranteed energy supply at an affordable price, with easy access and with lower risks of harm to the environment. Natural disasters and supply disruptions have significant adverse effects on the global energy supply. Except for the IEA members, most developing countries have oil stocks capable of lasting for only a guaranteed 20 continuous days. Based on this, these countries cannot survive any form of energy crisis since they do have guaranteed energy security beyond 20 days. A strategic oil reserve has the potential to ensure a sustained supply of energy during periods of supply disruptions as it reduces dependence on imports and tames oil inflationary pressures.

SPR reduces an economy's risks of oil price shocks due to supply disruptions. Generally, any significant shock in oil supply causes a drawdown of oil which increases supply and ensures easy access to energy, while domestic oil is affordable as its prices are controlled. This helps to reduce the negative effect on the economic welfare of the population. However, there is a significant opportunity cost associated with keeping SPR to promote energy security. For instance, it reduces the amount of resources available to produce goods and services, leading to less consumption in the future. Thus, there is a trade-off in resources between establishing an SPR and general welfare in the long run.

Lynch (1997) indicates that the problem of energy security is a short-term issue rather than a long-term one. Thus, the fundamentals of supply interruptions are driven by economics and price rather than supply shortages.[1] Therefore, the most appropriate approach to address supply disruptions is the SPR along with a few alternative sources. Tolley and Wilman (1997) suggest that oil-importing countries can minimise the risks of supply disruptions, primarily through embargos, by managing the release rate against the accumulation rate. By this approach, SPR will be most effective when released at a fixed rate when the duration of an embargo is known. Also, the SPR should be drawn down at a decreasing rate if traders are uncertain about the duration of the embargo.

2.3 Oil and Gas Infrastructure Gap and the Business Potential for Closing the Gap

There is still a significant oil and gas infrastructure gap between developed and developing countries. As a result, emerging economies' oil and gas potential is underutilised, and this gap presents an opportunity for investors to profit from it. Public-private partnerships (PPPs), innovative financing, and project financing are all options for funding this imbalance.

Private investors working with various governments to finance oil and gas infrastructure is one approach to take advantage of this gap. Nonetheless, only 13 oil and gas PPP contracts have been signed in Africa, compared to 208 worldwide and 55 in Europe (IMC Worldwide, 2022). This means that the oil and gas business will continue to expand, particularly in developing countries where demand for oil and gas products increases yearly. Project financing is one of the most efficient ways to fund oil and gas infrastructure. Financing oil and gas infrastructure provides investors enormous benefits as the sector can be profitable. However, there are risks associated with financing these projects, and managing such risks improves the chances of success.

2.4 Financing Oil and Gas Strategic Reserves in Ghana

One of the major issues of concern is how SPR is financed in Ghana. As indicated, BOST is responsible for the storage and transportation of Ghana's SPR. However, the critical question that remains in the discussions is: Which entity must finance the additions to the oil and gas strategic reserves and/or how must it be financed?

BOST, despite all of its efforts, is not able to meet the required oil and gas strategic storage. This, in part, stems from its debt situation and the inadequate support from the Government of Ghana (GoG). In the U.S., the government provides budgetary support for the strategic reserve of petroleum products.

The Congressional Budget Office in 1990 argued that the two main ways of financing strategic oil and gas reserves are through outright purchase of the products or leasing.[2] However, the DOE federal register (final rule) in 2007[3] offers other options such as royalty-in-kind exchanges, SPR shares, and deferrals. These options for financing are briefly described and situated within the Ghanaian perspective.

2.4.1 Direct Purchase

This involves the acquisition of oil and gas through outright purchase whether outright or on credit on agreed terms. The direct purchases of oil and gas for strategic reserve purposes are usually contingent upon the availability of funds, and the rate of purchase must also be contingent upon trends in price volatility. This form is the easiest way to acquire petroleum products for the SPR. This is the predominant way BOST finances its purchases.

2.4.2 Royalty-in-Kind-Transfers

These involve the collection of oil and gas from leases on government-owned properties (oil fields) in lieu of cash royalties. An arrangement could be made for the transfer of oil and gas, received in kind as royalties, to be transferred to BOST for their strategic storage. The quantity of oil and gas received in kind must be equivalent to the dollar or cedi equivalent of the royalties. The oil and gas must be taken directly from the oil mining firms in Ghana by BOST and stored in any of its depots, or the suppliers may be required to deliver oil and gas of comparable value. That said, there is a need for BOST to continue its drive to expand and build new depots. This approach minimises the costs associated with acquiring oil and gas for strategic reserves.

2.4.3 Going Public with SPR or Public Capitalisation of the SPR

Private investors would be able to buy shares that correspond to a specific amount of oil in the reserve using this kind of financing. Even though the oil would actually belong to the government, the investors would still be guaranteed the market value of the oil reflected by the shares to which they had a title. A secondary market might potentially be used to exchange these shares. One of the most efficient ways of allocating risk in a market economy is to allow investors to determine whether to assume a certain risk or not. An advantage to going public with the country's SPR will afford investors the opportunity to decide whether it is worthwhile undertaking the risk. If the financing of SPR is shifted to the private sector, the risks associated with future oil prices are also transferred. Again, this form of financing will reduce the burden/deficit on the government/BOST. Insofar as reduced inflationary expectations cause lower interest rates, if these reductions help to lessen the financial and business community's inflationary expectations, interest rates may become slightly lower as a result.

2.4.4 Deferrals

Another method that could be used to finance the additions to SPR is *deferrals*. This method involves deferring scheduled deliveries to the SPR to obtain additional crude oil. In Ghana's case, the delivery of SPR to BOST could be referred to a later date in exchange for a premium, which would be paid to BOST in oil. The determination of how much premium is to be paid should be a function of the length of deferral as well as prevailing market conditions.

2.4.5 Development of an Industrial Petroleum Reserve (IPR)

This method of funding SPR encourages businesses to take the lead and cover a larger portion of the development costs. It takes the form of mandating that all oil importers and refiners keep a specific amount of their annual usage in a depot specifically created to hold emergency oil and gas supplies. The key advantage of this strategy is that the privately owned reserve might serve as a buffer when there are disruptions in the country. In other words, the SPR may not always be used by the government as a safeguard against slight, transient interruptions. The Industrial Petroleum Reserve (IPR) will serve as the first layer of defence against these interruptions and act as a supplement to the SPR.

To conclude, although all of these options (outright purchase, leasing, royalty-in-kind transfers, deferrals, etc.) are available to BOST, there is a need for the GoG to inject additional finance through budgetary allocations to BOST for the efficient storage of oil and gas reserves. Given the nature of the storage of strategic reserves in Ghana, there is a need for a broader stakeholder engagement on how the financing of oil and gas storage by BOST must be financed. However, ultimately, given the artificial nature of oil storage, more finance will be required from the government.

2.5 A Case Study of Oil and Gas Storage in Ghana

In Ghana, BOST is the company solely entrusted with the responsibility of oil storage. BOST's role is primarily to store and transmit fuels in a safe, secure, and profitable manner. BOST continues to develop a network of infrastructure required to store and aid in transporting and distributing oil throughout Ghana. This infrastructure includes but is not limited to storage tanks, transport logistics, and pipelines. It maintains Ghana's strategic oil and gas reserves. BOST has been tasked with strategically maintaining a reserve stock of at least six weeks' worth of national consumption in the short to medium term. However, it is required to have a minimum equivalent of

12 weeks of national consumption in reserve in the long term. BOST has consequently developed a strategic number of networks of oil and gas pipelines and storage facilities for petroleum across Ghana.

2.5.1 Overview of BOST

The company has six strategic depots across Ghana. They are located at *Buipe, Kumasi, Accra Plains, Akosombo, Bolgatanga,* and *Mami Water*. These depots are critical for oil storage and distribution, and some of them are linked together by a pipeline interconnection system. BOST has three levels of interconnectivity among its depots, pipelines, river barges (RBs), or bulk road vehicles (BRVs) as transportation mechanisms between depots with no pipeline linkages. BOST has a pipeline that connects the Tema Oil Refinery (TOR) to the Accra Plains depot. This pipeline is further connected to the *Mami Water* depot and finally to the *Akosombo* depot where it ends. The second pipeline connects the Buipe depot to the Bolgatanga storage point. To get petroleum products to the Northern zones of Ghana, the products are conveyed through the first pipeline network (TOR – Accra Plain Depot – Mami Water – Akosombo pipe network). At the Akosombo depot, the products are then loaded on RBs and transported to Buipe. They are then transported to Bolgatanga through the 261 km second pipeline network (Buipe – Bolgatanga pipeline). As part of the transport infrastructure, BOST has built four RBs to transport petroleum products from the Akosombo depot to the Buipe depot before the final pipeline conveyance to Bolgatanga. At the Kumasi depot, products are received for storage through BRVs from the Accra Plains Depot.

2.5.2 The Partial Dependence of the Security and Safety of Oil in Ghana on the Sustainability and Efficient Delivery of the Mandates of BOST

BOST currently has a combined storage capacity of 427,500 m^3 across all the six depots it currently runs. The distributions among the depots are shown in Figure 2.1.

BOST continues to expand its storage capacity but is confronted with several challenges, the most significant of which is a lack of adequate financial injection.

2.5.3 Crucial Features in the Optimal Management of Oil and Gas Storage and Terminals in Ghana

Advancements in technology and the need for cost-efficiency have resulted in fundamental changes in the way storage terminals around the world are managed, and the management of terminals in Ghana is no exception. Ghana's oil and gas continue to be an essential resource for the country regarding its budgetary plans. Therefore, the optimal storage of its hydrocarbons is equally

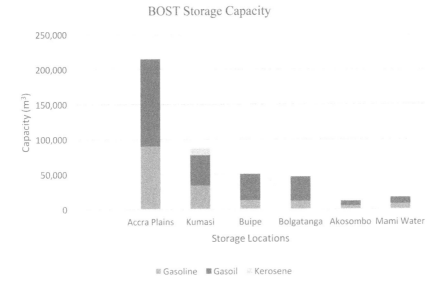

Figure 2.1 Storage capacity of Ghana's BOST

Note: Values are as of February 2022.

essential. Oil and gas are pumped from the oil fields into tank farms. The oil is stored and cleaned up before being pumped to terminals and the refinery. It is critical to emphasise that the oil is stored, refined, and pumped only after it has been desalted or the salt and water have been removed. There are also hydrocarbon dispatch terminals that receive oil from tank farms through pipelines for storage. The efficient management of these storage facilities is critical for businesses' operational efficiency.

As a result, it is critical to select an appropriate location for these types of facilities and to operate them as effectively and safely as possible. Even more important is the management of these storage facilities. While it is essential to maintain hydrocarbon storage tanks, one critical feature in Ghana's storage management is the availability of skilled and qualified personnel to provide protection and safety for the staff or workers required to improve the efficiencies of other processes. Fortunately, several parameters on storage tanks, such as pressure, viscosity, and temperature are now measured by workers using modern equipment such as flow meters, thermometers, and fluid quantity meters, rather than manually. This reduces the risks associated with staff safety.

At the heart of the operations of oil and gas terminals in Ghana are the safety and precautionary measures taken by the relevant organisations. This is usually based on regulations from the relevant authorities such as the Petroleum Commission, Energy Commission, Ministry of Energy, National Petroleum Authority (NPA), Environmental Protection Agency (EPA), and company-specific policies in line with the other regulatory and legal frameworks such as the EPA Act 1994 (Act 490). The firms that man the various oil and gas storage facilities and terminals have incorporated into their operations, health, safety, security, and environmental standards to the greatest benefit of all stakeholders. In the Ghanaian context, these firms provide adequate resources, training, proactive risk mitigation techniques, and general guidelines to be followed in the areas where terminals and other storage facilities are. These guidelines include:

- Switching off all mobile phones
- No smoking allowed in these areas
- Observance of all safety protocols
- Adherence to emergency instructions
- Wearing protective clothing and equipment.

Firms in Ghana continue to adopt internationally accepted best practices in managing oil and gas storage. The operations, administration, management, and safety of terminals in Ghana also encompass regular maintenance, emergency response mechanisms, procedural writing, etc. Another feature of optimal management includes the prevention of pollution, response to spillages, planning for contingencies, regulatory compliance, and other miscellaneous support systems for the various terminal facilities.

Managing and storing hydrocarbons is a challenging process. However, the safety of people, plants, property, equipment, and the protection of the environment must be central in every optimum management process. As much as possible, firms have prioritised the automation of critical processes to ensure minimum human contact. While there is still work to be done, it is encouraging to see Ghana continue to adopt internationally recognised best practices in this area for managing oil and gas storage.

2.5.4 Storage Tank Inspection, Audit, and Calibration in Ghana

A proper audit, inspection, and calibration ensure storage tank integrity. The risk of leakage is typical, considering the nature of petroleum products. The leakages may cause loss of revenue, environmental contamination, or, more likely, disasters. To ensure the safety of workers, the environment, and other stakeholders, it is important to periodically inspect, audit, and calibrate storage tanks following relevant standards, codes, and regulations. It is required that all inspections meet international codes and standards (such as the EN, API, BS, and DIN) and can be tailored to meet specific needs. Ghana's primary storage tank inspection, audit, and calibration services offered include magnetic flaw scanning, ultrasonic thickness measurement, non-destructive testing (NDT), safety system control, subsoil corrosion assessment, tank floor measurement and shelling, environmental impact assessment, and hydro-tests.

Tank calibration is essential for reliable quantity measurement and serves as a foundation for good business within the oil and gas industry. In Ghana, all firms rendering calibration services on petroleum storage tanks are authorised by the NPA, which, among other things, requires them to provide documents evidencing the legality of the firm and a detailed business plan. The business plan, as a requirement, must show in detail the methods of calibration adopted by the firm and the types of instrumentation and equipment to be used for the calibration service delivery by the firm. The NPA's licensing framework requires that companies show evidence that their personnel have the requisite knowledge, training, and experience in the calibration of storage tanks and BRVs. Companies are also required to show that they have the requisite infrastructure (facilities and equipment) and have been certified by way of obtaining permits from the Ghana National Fire Service and EPA before being authorised to calibrate.

Tank calibration is required for oil and gas companies, especially when they purchase new equipment, when observations appear suspect, or when there is a discrepancy between the indications on an instrument and the output of a surrogate instrument. Other reasons for which calibration services may be required include modifying or repairing an existing instrument, the passage of time, and using instruments for more than a predetermined number of operating hours. Calibration may also be needed before or following a critical measurement, as per the instrument manufacturer's recommendations. Calibration is required for any storage tank type (surface, underground, or vertical), safety valves, and BRVs for OMCs and fuel stations.

Knowing the exact size of a tank and the amount of oil or gas it can hold can reduce losses caused by inaccurate measurements. Several instruments (e.g. prover tanks, flow meters, and digital flow meters) and equipment are deployed by firms that provide calibration services. These instruments must be certified by the Ghana Standard Authority (GSA). They ensure that the calibration services are fast, precise, and efficient. Others have adopted high-level laser calibration technology to provide fast, safe, cost-efficient, and accurate calibrations. This will assist their clients (oil and gas companies) in further reducing costs and time spent managing storage tanks. Firms that perform good calibrations on their bulk storage tanks and BRVs better understand the current state and dynamics of the bulk storage tanks' dimensions. This provides data to the oil and gas company, allowing it to plan long-term maintenance of the storage facilities.

2.6 Storage and Liquefied Petroleum Gas (LPG) Programme in Ghana

Ghana is a low-middle income country located in West Africa. According to World Bank data, the population of Ghana was approximately 29.8 million in 2020 with about 50% of the population living in rural areas. The gross domestic product (GDP) of Ghana was 65.7 billion U.S. dollars in 2018 with a GDP growth rate of 6.3%. In 2010, only 23% of households in Ghana used LPG; while the Ministry of Energy's Sector Strategy and Development Plan included a target of 50% LPG access by 2015. This was to be achieved through the development of LPG infrastructure, the injection of millions of new cylinders into the market, and pricing incentives to encourage distributors to expand their operations to rural and deprived areas.

Unfortunately, by 2015, the goal of expanding LPG access to 50% of Ghana's population had not been achieved. However, a new study by Global LPG Partnership in 2017 suggests that only 40% of households will be using LPG by 2030. The shortfall in realising the set targets led to the GoG launching the Rural LPG (RLP) promotion program which was targeted at reducing the use of fuelwood. The main aim of RLP was to provide LPG access to 50% of the country's population by providing a cumulative total of 170,000 LPG cookstoves to rural households by the end of 2017. As of the end of November 2017, 149,500 rural households had received LPG cookstoves.

This led to the following measures being proposed:

- Expedite the establishment of a natural gas plant to produce LPG from the associated gas to be produced from the Jubilee Oil and Gas field. It is estimated that 10,000 barrels (1340 t) a day of LPG could be produced from the gas from the Jubilee Field.
- Re-capitalise Ghana Cylinder Manufacturing Company (GCMC) to expand production capacity. The production of cylinders would focus on relatively small size (4 and 6 kg) cylinders that will be affordable to households in rural communities.
- Construct LPG storage and supply infrastructure in all regional and district capitals in the long term. In the medium term, it is intended to develop district capital LPG infrastructure (MoE, 2010).

Even though BOST is responsible for the storage and safety of Ghana's SPRs, the company lacks appropriate storage facilities for its LPG and has begun several projects to supplement its present capacity in the six depots. These projects will mainly involve the construction of underground tanks at strategic points across the country. The construction of these tanks is aligned with both its growth strategy and its contribution to the climate action imperative as LPG has been identified as one of the transition fuels. The company has established that if enough storage facilities are available, it will be able to meet the increasing demand for LPG among its consumers as well as support the government's revenue generation. Despite the lack of suitable LPG storage facilities in Ghana, the country's history of the use of LPG is fascinating because only three decades ago, the usage of LPG for both domestic and commercial purposes was almost non-existent, necessitating an LPG promotion effort.

The consumption of LPG rose steadily from 43,500 tonnes in 1999 to 299,500 tonnes in 2019. About 50% of the LPG consumed locally is produced by the Ghana Gas Company. The rest of the supplies are from TOR and imports from various bulk-distributing companies (BDCs), with the top three importers being Fuel Trade, Eco Petroleum (Quantum), and Blue Ocean. These three BDCs currently own and operate LPG facilities in Tema and Takoradi. There are currently five (5) LPG terminals in Ghana, with a combined capacity of 26,539 MT.

2.6.1 The Ghana LPG Promotion Programme

The LPG promotion programme began in 1989 and was aimed at curbing deforestation. The programme was to switch from the use of firewood for cooking to the use of LPG, considered clean and safe. At its inception, the program's primary goal was to encourage wider adoption and use of LPG as a substitute for fuelwood and charcoal to reduce the rate of deforestation and environmental degradation (Ahunu, 2015). In the initial stages, the programme targeted people in urban areas. However, it was expanded in 2013 to bring on board the rural areas. Since the inception of this programme, the government has adopted several schemes to promote the use of LPG. To improve access, affordability, and availability, the government's primary targets were households, small and large-scale food vendors, and public institutions (UNDP 2014). The government engaged in several educational campaigns on the benefits, safety, and health regulations on the use of LPG.

The promotion programme began with the free distribution of LPG cylinders to urban households. These households were only required to bear the cost of filling the cylinder with gas (Asante et al., 2018). This free distribution campaign was later expanded to some targeted public institutions where LPG cylinders and accessories were installed. According to the Global LPG Partnership (2018), the estimated number of cylinders in circulation in Ghana by 1997 was 600,000, an increase from 80,000 cylinders in 1989 (representing a 650% increment).

From the programme's onset, the government has made efforts to make LPG more affordable. The government introduced subsidies to make LPG cheaper for domestic household usage. On the other hand, commercial vehicle drivers took advantage of this and switched from using petrol and diesel to using LPG as fuel. However, in an effort to restore fiscal stability, the government discontinued LPG subsidies in 2013 (Asante et al., 2018). Following the removal of the subsidy in 2013, the government launched a RLP promotion programme. The programme aimed to increase the use and availability of LPG in rural domestic households. As part of the RLP, the government planned to distribute 170,000 cylinders to rural households by 2017. This goal was not met, as only 150,000 cylinders were distributed in Ghana's 108 districts as of 2017 (Asante et al., 2018).

To expand the promotion programme, the government established the GCMC and Sigma Gas Ghana in the early 2000s to promote access to LPG. Also, the government established refilling stations and encouraged private sector participation in petroleum product storage and distribution as part of its efforts. As a result, many refilling stations have sprouted up across the country.

To continue the promotion campaign in recent years, the government introduced a delivery model known as the cylinder recirculation model in 2017. Like the original 1989 approach, this model was designed so that LPG customers pay for a pre-filled cylinder while the distributor keeps the cylinder. This model has not yet been operationalised. The model is expected to improve LPG safety, storage, and distribution while lowering the LPG usage cost when fully operational. LPG retailers oppose this model over fears that their role or service may be diminished or they may become extinct (Global LPG Partnership, 2018).

The LPG promotion programme has aided in the transition from firewood to LPG as a fuel source. However, much more needs to be done, particularly in rural areas. The LPG programme has benefited both the Ghanaian government and its citizens. This is manifest in increased job opportunities, the availability of quick and convenient alternative fuel, a reduction in health and environmental issues, and an increase in government revenue mobilisation. The programme's main challenges continue to be a lack of effective LPG safety education, rising LPG costs, a lack of access to LPG, and a disregard for LPG transport safety protocols (Seforall, 2020).

2.7 Conclusion

The management of oil and gas storage is critical for long-term energy security. Oil and gas storage balances out any inconsistencies in demand and supply. Oil and gas storage management necessitates strategic infrastructure that can function as storage facilities. The most common storage methods are underground and above-ground tanks. The transportation of oil and gas is also essential. The use of tankers, pipelines, barges, railroads, or tank trucks remains the main modes of transporting oil and gas. Emerging and developing countries generally have a deficit in storage infrastructure and strategic PPP arrangements and innovative financing can address this. Ghana's BOST has been tasked with safeguarding the country's strategic reserves and facilitating oil and gas transportation across the country and it is taking the required steps to ensure that its mandate is delivered to provide petroleum security to the people of Ghana.

Notes

1 The Russian-Ukraine war in March 2022 has proven otherwise.
2 Congressional Budget Office, 1990. The size and financing of the strategic petroleum reserve. Staff memorandum.
3 Procedures for the acquisition of petroleum for the strategic petroleum reserve. Federal Register/Vol. 71, No. 216/Wednesday, November 8, 2006/Rules and Regulations.

References

Ahunu, L. (2015). LPG Promotion Program. *Africa Centre for Energy Policy*. http://acep.africa/wp-content/uploads/2019/11/THELPGPROMOTIONPROGRAMME1.pdf

Asante, K. P., Afari-Asiedu, S., Abdulai, M. A., Dalaba, M. A., Carrión, D., Dickinson, K. L., & Jack, D. W. (2018). Ghana's rural liquefied petroleum gas program scale up: A case study. *Energy for Sustainable Development, 46*, 94–102.

Corbett, M. (2013). Oil shocks of 1973-74. *Federal Reserve history, 22*. https://www.federalreservehistory.org/essays/oil-shock-of-1973-74

Global LPG Partnership (2018). *National feasibility study: LPG for clean cooking in Ghana*. Global LPG Partnership, KfW and European Union.

IMC Worldwide-InfraPPP. Retrieved March 8, 2022 from https://www.infrapppworld.com/subsectors/oil-gas

Krusche, J. (2012). Third-party access in the gas sector. https://wikis.fuberlin.de/display/oncomment/Third+Party+Access+in+the+Gas+Sector

Lynch, M. C. (1997). Nature of energy security. *Breakthroughs, 4*, 4–5.

MoE. (2010). Energy sector strategy and development plan Ghana. https://ouroilmoney.s3.amazonaws.com/media/documents/2016/06/09/energy_strategy.pdf

Seforall (2020). Energy safety nets: Ghana case study. Retrieved March 5, 2022, from https://www.seforall.org/publications/esn/ghana

Stevens, R. (2014). The strategic petroleum reserve and crude oil prices, University of California, Berkeley, "Strategic Petroleum Reserve Inventory". Retrieved April 19, 2021 from shorturl.at/aGKNS

Tolley, G. S., & Wilman, J. D. (1997). The foreign dependence question. *Journal of Political Economy, 85*(2), 323–347.

UNDP (2014). *Liquefied petroleum gas (LPG) substitution for wood fuel in Ghana – Opportunities and challenges*. United Nations Development Programme in Ghana.

3 The Business of Oil Refining in Africa

George Acheampong, Ishmael Ackah, and Amin Karimu

3.1 Introduction

Many Emerging and developing countries are blessed with numerous natural resources such as oil, gas, and coal. For instance, South Africa has about 40% of the World's gold deposits and Venezuela has the largest proven oil deposits in the World. Africa as a region has an abundance of natural resources but high levels of poverty (Mahomoodally, 2013). Even though the exact financial capacity of those assets is unknown, Africa is well-endowed with minerals and fossil fuels.

New discoveries of oil and gas in Africa in places where such resources have never been thought to exist in large quantities show that the continent is still 'virgin' in many aspects of oil and gas exploration and development (AfDB, 2009). The exploration and exploitation of these resources, however, are yet to benefit the population. Shell D'Arcy led a team to discover oil in commercial quantities in Nigeria in 1956 (NNPC, 2021). This was the first oil discovery in Africa, and it was found in a small village called Oloibiri in the eastern Niger Delta region in Bayelsa State. Nigeria became an oil producer in 1958 when its first oil field began producing 5,100 barrels per day (bpd) (NNPC, 2021). Currently, Nigeria is the largest producer of oil in Africa and sixth globally. Its daily production is around 2.5 million barrels. Only high-value, low-sulphur crude oils are produced in Nigeria: Bonny Light, Antan Blend, Bonny Medium, Brass Blend, Ukpokiti, Escravos Light, Pennington Light, IMA, Odudu Blend, Qua-Iboe Light, and Forcados Blend (NNPC, 2021). The exploration and exploitation of these resources, however, have yet to benefit the population of more than 200 million.

Africa's overall crude oil production in 2017 was around 8 million bpd, with Sub-Saharan Africa accounting for about 5.5 million bpd of that total.[1] The stabilisation of crude oil prices in 2017 aided in the expansion of the region's production as well as the creation of new investment opportunities.

Surprisingly, Africa's top oil-producing countries are also big importers of refined petroleum products, despite being among the world's fastest-growing economies. While the continent's crude oil production is more than enough

DOI: 10.4324/9781003309864-5

to satisfy demand, domestic refining capacity is far below demand, forcing the region to export most of its crude and rely on refined-product imports to meet expanding internal market demands (Silva & Paixão, 2018).

This chapter analyses the business of oil refining in Africa by focusing on factors to consider in siting a refinery, the supply chain of a refinery, infrastructure requirements, the input-output of a refinery, demand for refined products, refining margins for the industry, trends in the refining business, as well as health, safety, and environmental concerns of the refining industry.

3.2 Determinants of Refinery Location

Petroleum products are by-products of the refinement of crude oil. Most of the petroleum is turned into petroleum products, which include a variety of fuels. Hydrogen, light hydrocarbons, reformate, and pyrolysis gasoline are some of the intermediate products produced by oil refineries. Rather than being shipped, they are frequently mixed or further processed on-site. As a result, chemical factories are frequently located near or integrated with oil refineries. In an ethylene factory, for example, light hydrocarbons are steam-cracked, and the ethylene produced is polymerised to make polyethylene. A minimal sulphur level is required in all but the heaviest goods to guarantee successful separation and environmental protection. The crude sulphur contamination is converted to hydrogen sulphide and removed from the product stream using catalytic hydrodesulphurisation and amine gas treatment. Hydrogen sulphide is converted to elementary sulphur and supplied to the chemical sector via the Claus method. This process liberates a significant amount of thermal energy, which is then utilised in other areas of the refinery. To absorb the surplus heat, an electrical power plant is frequently included in the refining process.

3.3 Oil and Gas Refinery Supply Chain

The oil and gas industry plays an essential role in modern economies; it is very critical to the growth and development of economies because its products are widely utilised in social and economic activities. For instance, in terms of infrastructure monetary value, the industry is currently the largest in Ghana. Ghana also experienced a sharp rise in GDP growth from 4.8% in 2009 to 14% in 2011, when it began exporting oil in commercial quantities (Hermas & Rockson, 2020). Oil and gas have also constituted 80% of Ghana's total energy consumption since 2000 (Hermas & Rockson, 2020). The industry also provides jobs and revenue to the government. These statistics highlight the significance of the oil and gas industry to the economy of Ghana.

The oil and gas industry operates through a supply-chain system that encompasses exploration, production, refining, distribution, and marketing of the products by the OMCs (Chima, 2007; Tanoh, 2017). Many operational activities take place within each stage of the supply chain processes. For instance, the exploration involves seismic, geophysical, and geological operations of identifying the sites that contain crude oil, whilst the production processes involve the extraction of crude oil, its storage, and facilities engineering (Chima, 2007; Tanoh, 2017). The oil production fields in Ghana include the Sankofa field, TEN field, Jubilee field, and Saltpond Oil field (Oxford Business Group, 2021; Tanoh, 2017). In Ghana, these operations are undertaken by institutions such as Kosmos Energy and Tullow Ghana Limited. Oil exploration and production are, however, regulated by the Ghana National Petroleum Commission (GNPC) on behalf of the Ministry of Petroleum (Tanoh, 2017).

Refining deals with the conversion of crude oil into finished products (oil and gas) required for marketing (Chima, 2007). In Ghana, Tema Oil Refinery (TOR) is currently responsible for this stage of the supply chain operations (Tanoh, 2017). At the distribution stage, the finished products are kept in reservoirs and tanks. This is done to enable the transportation of oil to be affected according to the demand of the consumers. This operation is handled by Bulk Oil Storage and Transportation (BOST) Company Limited. BOST is also responsible for the distribution of gas in the country (Tanoh, 2017).

Marketing, on the other hand, involves the retail sale of gas and oil products such as petrol and diesel (Chima, 2007) by the Oil Marketing Companies (OMCs) to the final consumers. Examples of OMCs in Ghana include Ghana Oil Limited (GOIL) and Total Ghana Limited. The National Petroleum Authority (NPA) was established by an Act of Parliament in 2005 to regulate the refining, distribution, and marketing of petroleum products. The Energy Commission, on the other hand, regulates these operations in relation to natural gas (Tanoh, 2017).

The main challenge facing the oil and gas refinery industry along the supply chain is the inability to distribute the final products to consumers at the possible minimum cost (Chima, 2007). To achieve this target, effective supply-chain management strategies are therefore required to enable the companies to coordinate their operations along the value chain. This will help the companies to remain competitive at a lower cost of production while optimising their production and higher profit efficiencies (Chima, 2007). It will also enable the industry to grow and employ more people to improve their living standards along the refinery supply chain.

3.4 Oil and Gas Infrastructure

The oil and gas industry plays an important role in the growth and development of economies. The contribution of the oil sector largely depends on the level of infrastructure and technologies used in various supply chain processes. In terms of infrastructure monetary value, the industry is currently the largest in Ghana. Statistics from Bank of Ghana also show that the value of exported crude oil increased to $4.57 billion in 2018 (Oxford Business Group, 2021). Oil and gas infrastructure includes the equipment, building facilities, and installations that aid the oil sector companies in running their operations efficiently. These infrastructures are essential to upstream, midstream, and downstream oil and gas producers in satisfying the demand of end-use consumers (Oxford Business Group, 2021).

The upstream supply chain sector, whose operations include the exploration and the production of crude oil (Tanoh, 2017), needs infrastructure in their exploration and extraction operations. The upstream sector invests in infrastructures such as exploration and production facilities, and other interventions (Amponsah & Opei, 2014). These include seismic vessels, pipe laying and dredging ships, floating drilling units and underground equipment for exploration, offshore oil and gas drills, rigs, drilling pipes, well-monitoring instruments, valves, hoisting systems, cranes, turntables, and pumps (International Trade Administration, 2017). A constant source of power is also required for the smooth operation of the exploration and extraction facilities.

The midstream sector includes all operations between the oil wellhead and the refinery. These include the transportation of crude oil from oil fields to refineries, processing, and storage of petroleum products (Amponsah & Opei, 2014; Tanoh, 2017). These producers require infrastructures to refine and process the crude oil into petroleum products to satisfy the needs of consumers. The infrastructures that aid the operations of the midstream sector include pipelines such as the West African Gas Pipeline Project (WAGP) to transport the crude oil and processed oil and gas, operating tanker ships to transport the crude oil, a refinery such as TOR to convert the crude oil into finished products, and storage facilities such as storage tanks and reservoirs (Amponsah & Opei, 2014; Oxford Business Group, 2021). Other infrastructures include a plant for electrical generation and an electrical grid for power distribution.

The downstream sector is also responsible for the refining of crude oil, purification of raw natural gas, and distribution and marketing of finished products (Amponsah & Opei, 2014). This sector, which sometimes encapsulates the mid-stream sector, deals directly with the ultimate consumers (Tanoh, 2017). Infrastructure is therefore required by this sector to aid in the delivery and sale of oil and gas to retail companies and customers. To ensure efficient service delivery, the sector employs infrastructures such as a refinery in the production of oil and gas for consumption, storage facilities, wholesale, and retail distribution facilities such as oil distribution trucks and vehicles, and fuel service stations which handle the sales of oil and gas to the final consumers (Ghaithan et al., 2017). Since energy companies use complex infrastructures that need frequent maintenance, a robust oil and gas infrastructure management system is therefore essential in the effective operation of the oil and gas supply chain to ensure a constant supply of the products to consumers at a possible minimum cost (Amponsah & Opei, 2014).

3.5 Input–Output of Oil Refinery

Based on the crude oil composition and market demands, refineries can produce varying quantities of petroleum products. The bulk of oil products is used as 'energy carriers', such as various grades of fuel oil and gasoline. Gasoline, jet fuel, diesel fuel, heating oil, and heavier fuel oils are only a few of the fuels that may be mixed to make gasoline, jet fuel, diesel fuel, heating oil, and heavier fuel oils, U.S. Energy Information Administration (EIA,2021). Heavier (less volatile) fractions can be used to make asphalt, tar, paraffin wax, lubricating oil, and other heavy oils. Chemicals used in chemical processes to generate plastics and other valuable materials are among the products of refineries. Elemental sulphur is frequently manufactured as a petroleum product since petroleum commonly includes a small percentage of sulphur-containing compounds. Petroleum products can also create carbon and hydrogen in the form of petroleum coke. Other oil refinery operations, such as hydrocracking and hydrodesulphurisation, frequently employ the hydrogen generated as an intermediate product.

The four categories of petroleum products include light distillates (LPG, gasoline, naphtha), medium distillates (kerosene, jet fuel, diesel), heavy distillates, and residuum (heavy fuel oil, lubricating oils, wax, asphalt) as shown in Figure 3.1. Different feedstocks must be blended, appropriate additives must

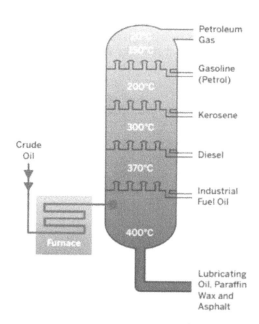

Figure 3.1 A diagram with the four categories of petroleum products in a refinery process
Source: CME Group (2022)

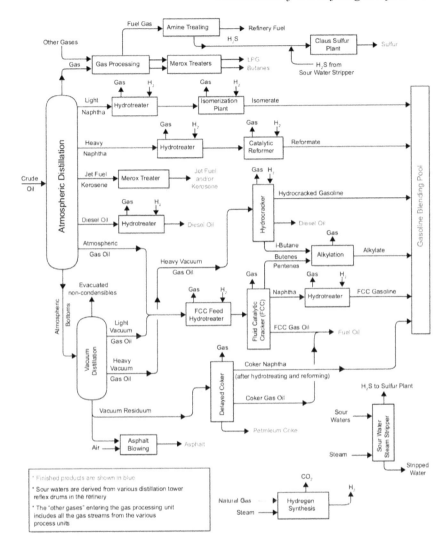

Figure 3.2 Schematic flow of oil refining
Source: Milton Beychok

be added, short-term storage must be provided, and bulk loading to trucks, barges, product ships, and railcars must all be done.

The schematic flow diagram represented in Figure 3.2 displays the numerous unit operations and the flow of intermediate product streams that occur between the intake of crude oil feedstock and the end products in a typical oil refinery. Only one of the hundreds of alternative oil refinery setups is depicted in the diagram. The diagram also excludes any refinery facilities that provide utilities like steam, cooling water, and electricity, as well as storage tanks for crude oil feedstock, intermediate products, and finished products.

3.6 Demand versus Capacity

3.6.1 Product Demand Analysis

The existence of a market for a product contributes to the functioning of any economic unit (Acheampong & Ackah, 2015). Businesses can profit from supply and demand mismatches in this way. The importation of petroleum products in Africa has shown some inconsistent growth between 2010 and 2020. This can be seen in Figure 3.3. The most significant growth was 18.4% and this was recorded in 2015. The average daily import of petroleum products from 2010 to 2020 in Africa ranged between 1.6 million barrels and 10 million barrels as shown in Figure 3.4.

A dive into the data for 2020 shows that Nigeria tops the chart with an average daily import of 4.7 million barrels. This is followed by three North African countries Morocco, Egypt, and Libya with an average daily import of 2.4 million barrels, 1.5 million, and 1.5 million barrels, respectively.

In 2020, the most demanded petroleum product in Africa was distillate. An average of 1.7 million barrels was demanded on a daily basis. This was followed by gasoline with an average demand of 1.1 million bpd. In total, the composite product demand for petroleum products was an average of 4 million bpd as shown in Figure 3.5.

3.6.2 Capacity Factor Analysis

One of the basic concerns for refinery profitability or otherwise is refinery capacity utilisation. One of the reasons for refineries' poor performance in Africa is that capacity utilisation is often less than ideal. The relevance of the aforementioned notion stems from the fact that refineries have a high capital cost and a low unit cost of production, requiring them to run at high utilisation rates in order to be viable. A significant proportion of the refineries in Africa are either under maintenance, out for an upgrade, or lack the required crude oil to operate.

Due to a lack of regular maintenance, the current refineries in Nigeria, which have a total installed capacity of 445,000 bpd, are plagued with operational issues and are far from running at full capacity (Silva & Paixão, 2018). According to official data released by the Nigerian National Petroleum Corporation (NNPC), the maximum capacity utilisation was just under 37% in 2017, and they produced at 14% capacity in 2018. Even at full capacity, the four would only be able to provide a fifth of Nigeria's gasoline requirements. As a result, the country is compelled to import the great bulk of refined products it consumes.

The Business of Oil Refining in Africa 37

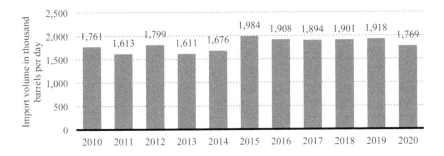

Figure 3.3 Import volumes of petroleum products from 2010 to 2020
Source: Statista (2021a)

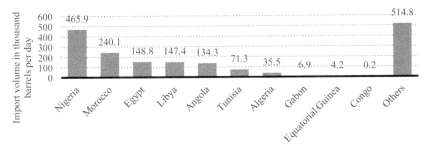

Figure 3.4 Import volumes of petroleum products in Africa, 2020
Source: Statista (2021a)

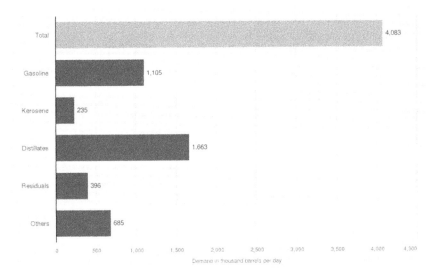

Figure 3.5 Oil demand in Africa as of 2020, by petroleum products (1,000/day)
Source: Statista (2021b)

The Ras Lanuf oil refinery in Libya is still offline, with no indication of when it will reopen since its closure in 2013 (SP Global Platts, 2020). In West Africa, TOR, Ghana's only oil refinery, was down at the time of writing and owing to a lack of crude and feedstock, the plant was unlikely to reopen for several months. Over the last several years, the facility has been plagued by a slew of problems, including periodic outages at its Crude Distillation Unit (CDU) and Fluid Catalytic Cracking (FCC) units. Because the CDU only has one furnace, the refinery's capacity is limited to roughly 30,000 bpd (SP Global Platts, 2020). Also, Engen, one of South Africa's refineries, has announced that it will proceed with the conversion of its Durban refinery into a terminal. The company suffered a fire and explosion on December 4, 2020, the refinery was closed down.

The refinery-to-terminal conversion is scheduled to start in the third quarter of 2023 (SP Global Platts, 2020). Again, the Astron Energy Cape Town refinery in South Africa is expected to reopen 'at some time' in 2022, according to the firm. The refinery was shut down after a fire occurred in July 2020. The Limbe refinery in Cameroon, which was destroyed by fire at the end of May 2019, is still not operational. The relaunch was not expected until 2021, according to local media. Table 3.1 has details of the status of some of the refineries in Africa and their capacities.

These out-of-service refineries have affected the petroleum industry in Africa greatly. If all these refineries were to be in service, the continent could have had access to over 3 million barrels of petroleum products on a daily basis. But the current story is not worth telling. With Ghana's only oil refinery being out of service, the country is expected to depend exclusively on the importation of petroleum products for its economic activities. This could mean that the government would have little control over petroleum prices. Nigeria, the largest producer of Crude oil in Africa and sixth globally, is also the largest importer of petroleum products in Africa.

It is obvious that African Nations are not efficiently utilising their investments in the refinery of oil. For the period 2014–2019, the average production from all the refineries in Africa amounted to 105 million metric tons per year. Within the period, the highest output from the refineries in Africa was a little over 109 million metric tons. This means that there was an average daily production of 298,880 metric tons, which amounts to about 1.9 million barrels. However, this figure is almost the same as the average daily import of petroleum products in 2019 (Figure 3.6). The estimated daily output from the oil refineries is 49% lower than the 3.7 million distillation capacity that is expected to be available to serve the continent.

3.6.3 Product Pricing Analysis

Profit margin is one key indicator of the financial performance of a refinery company (Segal, 2021). This is determined by the difference between the composite product price and the cost of crude oil. The process of setting

Table 3.1 Oil refineries in Africa

Country	Refinery	Owner		Status
Algeria	Adrar	CNPC/Sonatrach	13	N/A
	Algiers	Sonatrach	79	N/A
	Arzew	Sonatrach	90	N/A
	Hassi Messaoud	Sonatrach	27	N/A
146	Skikda	Sonatrach	462	N/A
Angola	Luanda	Sonangol	65	Being Upgraded
Cameroon	Cape Limbo Limbe	Societe Nationale	70	Expected in 2021
Chad	Ndajamena	CNPC	20	N/A
Congo	Pointe Noire	Coraf	25	Expected in 20222
Egypt	Alexandria (Ameriya)	EGPC	88	N/A
	Alexandria (El Mex)	EGPC	115	N/A
	Alexandria (MIDOR)	EGPC	100	Expected in 2022
	Assiut	EGPC	90	Being Upgraded
	El Suez	EGPC	68	Being Upgraded
	Mostorod	EGPC	145	N/A
	Nasr El Suez	EGPC	146	N/A
	Nasr Wadi Feran	EGPC	9	N/A
	Tanta	EGPC	54	N/A
Gabon	Port Gentil	Ste. Gabonaise	24	N/A
Ghana	Tema	Tema Oil	45	Under Maintenance
Ivory Coast	Abidjan	Societe Ivoirienne	84	N/A
Kenya	Mombasa	Government	70	Under Conversion
Liberia	Monrovia	Liberia Petroleum	15	N/A
Libya	Azzawiya & Benghazi	Libya NOC	120	N/A
	Brega	Libya NOC	10	N/A
	Ras Lanuf	Libya NOC	220	Under Maintenance
	Sarir	Libya NOC	10	N/A
	Tobruk	Libya NOC	20	N/A
Morocco	Mohammedia	SAMIR	200	N/A
Niger	Zinder, Ganaram	CNPC	20	N/A
Nigeria	Kaduna	NNPC	110	Being Upgraded
	Port Hartcourt	NNPC	210	Being Upgraded
	Warri	NNPC	125	Being Upgraded
Senegal	M'Bao (Dakar)	Ste. Africaine	24	Being Upgraded
Sierra Leone	Freetown	SLPRC	5	N/A
South Africa	Cape Town	Chevron	100	Expected in 2022
	Durban	Engen (Petronas)	150	Under Conversion
	Durban	Shell/BP	180	Online
	Sasolburg	NPRSA (Sasol/Total)	108	Suspended Operation
Sudan	Khartoum	CNPC	100	N/A
	Port Sudan	Sudan Government	47	N/A
Tunisia	Bizerte	Ste. Tunisienne	34	N/A
Zambia	Bwana Nkubwa Area	Zambia Government	24	Being Upgraded
Total			3,721	

Source: SP Global Platts (2020)

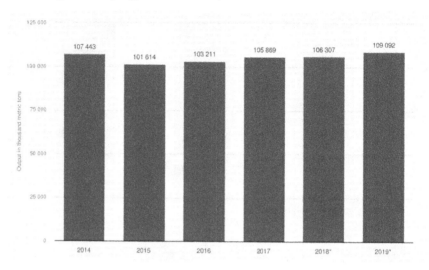

Figure 3.6 Total outputs of refineries in Africa from 2014 to 2019 (1,000 metric tons)
Source: Statista (2021c)

petroleum product pricing has certain consequences for refinery profitability. When a market is deregulated, refined product prices are set by market fundamentals, giving refineries some flexibility in terms of complete cost recovery. The downstream sector for most African countries is regulated. Ghana is one of the few countries with a deregulated downstream sector.

The price of petroleum products is in three different parts. The first one is the ex-refinery price which includes the cost, insurance, freight, and other charges which may be country-specific. The next pricing level will be the post-refinery price. The post-refinery price will be the cost of refining the crude plus taxes and levies. These taxes and levies are also country-specific. If the petroleum products are refined by the domestic refinery companies, then they can recover the cost of operation if the market is deregulated. The last pricing level will be the pump price, which will cover the transportation, commodity price (post-refinery price), the profit margin for the oil marketing company, taxes, and levies.

In the regulated downstream sector, the volatilities in the international market are not reflected in the market (Olujobi, 2021). This then leaves a revenue gap if there is an increase in the price of crude oil. Also, the refinery companies are unable to recover the cost of their operation fully. This is the case for most African countries.

In 2015, the government of Ghana deregulated the petroleum downstream sector due to rising debt in the sector (Park, 2015). The regulation of the sector led to TOR being highly indebted. To revamp the company, the government introduced a recovery levy which was added to the price build-up of petroleum products.

Subsidies are another major challenge that impedes the financial sustainability of the downstream sector. To increase accessibility to petroleum products and reduce the cost burden to consumers, many African countries subsidise the pump prices. This then adds to the cost that has already been created by the regulation of pump prices.

3.7 Refining Margins

The profitability of the refining business depends on many factors including the cost of crude oil, the type of crude, the complexity of the refinery among others. The key parameter used to guide the likely profitability of a refinery is the refining margin, which is basically the value contribution of the refinery to the inputs used by the refinery (crude oil/feedstock). In other words, it is the value of the refined product processed per barrel of crude oil by the refinery.

The gross margin is the difference between the prices of the refined products and input costs in refining the products. The semi-variable margin on the other hand is the gross margin minus all variable cost. Another indicator of refinery profitability is crack spread, which is the difference between the price of refined products and the cost of crude oil that the refined products are processed from. This indicator ignores other variables and fixed costs associated with the refinery process. A typical crack spread is the 3:2:1 crack spread, which denotes that for every three barrels of crude, the refinery can process two barrels of gasoline and one barrel of distillate (diesel or other fuel oil). The crack spread 3:2:1 is calculated as $[(3 \times \text{price of crude} - 2 \times \text{price of gasoline} - 1 \times \text{price of distillate})]/3$.

Figure 3.7 presents benchmark refining margins (semi-margins) for three main regional refining centres in the world (United States, Europe, and Singapore). It shows significant difficulties for the refining industry in the year 2020, when some negative margins or close-to-negative values were obtained for these three main regions. The margins from Singapore were the worst in 2020 relative to the other key regional oil refining centres.

In many cases in 2020, the profitability was negative, resulting in negative refined margins. The margins are influenced by transport costs, regulatory costs, storage costs, working capital, and other internal operating costs beyond the cost of the inputs. Other influencing factors on the refining margins are seasonality and demand for refined products.

3.8 Future of Refinery Projects in Africa

It may appear surprising at first that major crude oil exporters with proven reserves, such as Nigeria and Angola, as well as more industrialised nations, such as South Africa, are buying products that they should be refining and exporting, resulting in balance of payments concerns. This, ironically, illustrates a problem that has afflicted the great majority of African countries in

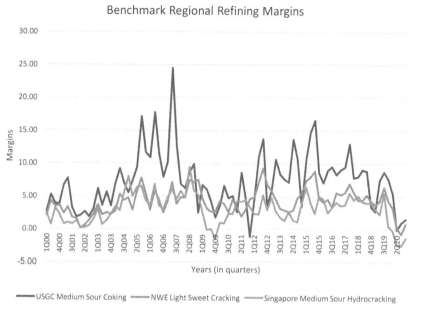

Figure 3.7 Regional refining margins (first quarter 2000 to fourth quarter 2020)

Source: Authors construction using data from BP, 2021

Note: USGC denotes US Gulf Coast and NWE is North-West Europe

recent decades. There are less than 50 refineries on the continent, many of which are outmoded and only operate at a quarter of their capacity (Silva & Paixão, 2018). In addition to being insufficient and underperforming, most of the refineries are not designed to provide the cleaner fuels required by modern engines or to comply with the most recent international environmental regulations and guidelines.

Upgrades and maintenance of existing infrastructure, as well as the construction of new refineries, are high-cost endeavours with specific financing challenges, such as the refining industry's shifting margins, which are swiftly impacted by a range of global market conditions. Furthermore, many people believe that most African countries face additional risks, such as political, civil, or economic instability, local-content requirements, corruption, currency fluctuations, or government-backed subsidies to reduce fuel prices at the pump (a significant cost to state budgets when oil prices are high), all of which could deter potential private investors. As a result, the bulk of large-scale refining projects suggested in the recent decade has either stayed on paper or been cancelled due to financial constraints. Nonetheless, an emerging revolution appears to be blowing over Africa with prospects for lessening the continent's reliance on refined-product imports. Several countries, including Nigeria, South Africa, Mozambique, and Angola, have recently announced plans to build new refineries or restore and upgrade existing ones.

According to Forbes magazine, in 2018, Aliko Dangote, the owner of the Dangote Group and Africa's richest man, decided to invest an estimated $10 billion (roughly $7 billion in bank financing and $3 billion in equity) in the construction of Nigeria's first privately owned refinery, which is expected to be completed by the end of 2022. In 2017, Angola faced a transformation in its downstream sector. The regulation of refining operations in 2017, which had been expected since the introduction of the 2013 regulatory framework on crude oil refining, sent a clear message to private companies interested in investing in the (re)organisation of the country's downstream industry (Silva & Paixão, 2018). This message was strengthened even further by the recent entry into force of a new Private Investment Law in June 2018. The new law outlines principles and standards aimed at facilitating, promoting, and expediting private investment in Angola, and it represents a significant shift in the legal framework that controls both domestic and foreign investment.

VEB, Russia's state-owned development bank, has signed investment cooperation agreements with African companies, including one to fund a Moroccan refinery (SP Global Platts, 2020). The agreements were reached during a Russian-African meeting. According to VEB, the Russian Export Group and Morocco's MYA Energy, which is part of the Marita Group, signed an agreement on an oil refinery in Morocco. The refinery would be able to process up to 5 million metric tons of oil per year. Morocco's lone refiner, Samir, was forced to cease processing at the Mohammedia facility in 2015 when crude oil deliveries were delayed due to financial concerns (Hellenic Shipping News Worldwide, 2022). Since then, attempts to resume operations or find an investor have been futile. Many more countries including Ghana, Algeria, Zambia, and Benin are on the path of revamping their oil refinery companies or constructing new ones.

3.9 Trends in Global Refining Business

The worldwide demand for oil refining is being driven largely by increased investment in refinery building, expansion, and upgrading to meet rising petroleum product demand and minimise reliance on imported refined petroleum products (Tang, 1994). Furthermore, governmental regulations relating to carbon emissions, as well as a bright outlook for the aviation and road transportation sectors, are boosting demand for refined fuels. Additionally, growing urbanisation and industrialisation, along with population growth in developing economies like China and India, have resulted in a spike in demand for passenger and commercial vehicles. The need for gasoline and diesel oil has expanded dramatically because of the expanding number of automobiles in these nations, leading to the establishment of new oil refineries to fulfil the growing demand for refined products. Also, the expanding aviation sector across the world, particularly in developing nations, has increased demand for jet fuel and kerosene (Hassan et al., 2021). Governments in developing nations have opted to expand their capacity to meet rising demand.

From 2021 to 2030, the global oil refining market is expected to develop at a CAGR of 5.3%, from $1,345.0 billion in 2020 to $3,751.5 billion in 2030.[2] The COVID-19 outbreak in the first quarter of 2020 had a moderately unfavourable influence on the worldwide oil refining industry, owing to a decrease in global demand for refined products. For example, India consumed 37.19 billion litres of gasoline in 2020, down from 42.27 billion litres in 2019.[3] In addition, the COVID-19 epidemic caused delays in several refinery upgrades. In future years, factors such as increased refining capacity in important areas such as the Asia-Pacific are likely to enhance demand for petroleum products.

3.10 Health, Safety, and Environmental Considerations in Oil and Gas Refining

Oil and gas refining is an important industry in Africa and an essential part of the national economy of countries in the continent with such industries including Algeria, Egypt, Angola, Nigeria, Libya, Morocco, and Ghana. However, potential hazards associated with refineries raise concerns especially among the workers and the communities closer to the refining sites such as the case in Ghana (Achaw & Boateng, 2012). Oil and gas refining poses a major threat to environmental safety, as well as the health and safety of the workers and members of the communities within which the companies are located (Achaw & Boateng, 2012). They serve as a major source of hazardous air, water, and soil pollutants such as carbon monoxide, particulate matter, nitrogen oxides, waste disposed of in landfills, wastewater, oil residues, and other pollutants produced from the treatment processes (Achaw & Boateng, 2012; Oppong, 2014; Sakyi et al., 2012; Toseafa, 2018).

Risks to safety and health thus exist at all levels of the industry, including production projects, plant operations, repair, building, transportation, storage, and the use of oil-derived goods. The volumes of compounds, materials, and products that are processed, handled, or used in the industry also exasperate life-threatening occurrences (Oppong, 2014; Toseafa, 2018). Workers in the industry are also susceptible to life-threatening hazards such as accidents, falls, machine-contact injuries, fires, and explosions (Achaw & Boateng, 2012; Oppong, 2014). The compounds, wastes, and hazards can lead to death, dermal, and visibility issues, cancer, respiratory diseases, and other health issues and are also detrimental to properties and the environment if not controlled or properly managed. Environmental, safety, and health management must therefore be a vital component of the industry's activities.

Despite the existence of legislation that addresses the aspects of safety in the industry, in many African countries, it is characterised by a poor regulatory environment (Sakyi et al., 2012). For instance, in Ghana due to the efficient regulatory regime, most companies adopt their own safety regulations to direct their operations, which is the case for some of the African countries with oil and gas industry. The regulatory institutions in some of the African countries are also under-resourced and this affects their mandate of effectively monitoring the oil and gas industry as is the case in Ghana (Achaw & Boateng, 2012). These shortcomings raise concerns about the ability of the regulatory bodies to discharge their responsibilities of protecting the safety and health of the citizens and the environment (Achaw & Boateng, 2012).

Due to the hazardous nature of oil and gas refining, stringent environmental, health, and safety guidelines and regulations that cover the entire supply chain process must be put in place to safeguard the ecosystem. These include the need for the government to empower the regulatory institutions to establish environmental protection guidelines and regulatory structures that are unique to the oil and gas refining sector (Sakyi et al., 2012). Such regulations must include government-prescribed environmental codes and regulations that operators must meet. They must also capture the need for oil and gas companies to implement health, safety, and environmental management systems to ensure that they operate within the industry's standards (Achaw & Boateng, 2012; Sakyi et al., 2012). Furthermore, the companies must have adequate logistics, protective and safety equipment, and measures to secure the health and safety of the workers. In addition, to enable the regulatory agencies such as FDI and EPA to effectively implement and enforce the regulations and monitor the operations of the oil and gas industry, they must be restructured and adequately empowered in terms of human capital and financial resources (Sakyi et al., 2012).

3.11 Conclusion

This chapter sought to provide a deep analysis and discussion of the business of oil refining in Africa, where there are increasing discoveries of oil in economic quantities with great revenue generation potentials for the continent, especially in oil refining. Despite the increasing discoveries and production of oil in Africa, the region is a net importer of refined products, reducing the revenue-generation potential of the industry to African economies and further increasing the vulnerability of the continent to energy security. The chapter has presented an analysis of various aspects of the refining industry such as factors to consider in determining where to locate a refinery, the supply chain of a refinery, infrastructure requirement, the input-output of a refinery, demand for refined products, refining margins for the industry, trends in the refining business, health, safety, and environmental concerns of the refining industry.

Notes

1 See https://www.mirandalawfirm.com/download/1188/5f4215a52efe2fb24ea684da6ceb7b69/petroleum_africa_september_2018.pdf
2 See https://www.alliedmarketresearch.com/oil-refining-market-A12367
3 See https://www.mordorintelligence.com/industry-reports/oil-refining-market

References

Acheampong, T., & Ackah, I. (2015). Petroleum Product Pricing, Deregulation and Subsidies in Ghana: Perspectives on Energy Security. *Deregulation and Subsidies in Ghana: Perspectives on Energy Security*. MPRA Paper 66116, University Library of Munich, Germany.

Achaw, A. W., & Boateng, E. D. (2012). Safety practices in the oil and gas industries in Ghana. *International Journal of Development and Sustainability, 1*(2), 456–465.

AfDB (2009). *Oil and gas in Africa*. Oxford University Press.

Amponsah, R., & Opei, F. K. (2014). Ghana's downstream petroleum sector: An assessment of key supply chain challenges and prospects for growth. *International Journal of Petroleum and Oil Exploration Research, 1*(1), 1–7.

Chima, M. C. (2007). Supply-chain management issues in the oil and gas industries. *Journal of Business & Economics Research, 5*(6).

CME Group. (2022). https://www.cmegroup.com/education/courses/introduction-to-energy/introduction-to-refined-products/a-look-into-the-refining-process.html

Ghaithan, A. M., Attia, A., & Duffuaa, S. O. (2017). Multi-objective optimization model for a downstream oil and gas supply chain. *Applied Mathematical Modelling, 52*, 689–708.

Hassan, T. H., Sobaih, A. E. E., & Salem, A. E. (2021). Factors affecting the rate of fuel consumption in aircrafts. *Sustainability, 13*, 8066.

Hellenic Shipping News Worldwide. (2022, January 23). https://www.hellenicshippingnews.com/upgrades-launches-in-focus-in-africa/

Hermas, A., & Rockson, S. (2020). Examining prospects and challenges of Ghana's petroleum industry: A systematic review. *Energy Reports, 6*, 841–858.

International Trade Administration (2017). *2017 top markets report: Upstream oil and gas equipment*. Department of Commerce.

Mahomoodally, M. F. (2013). Traditional medicines in Africa: An appraisal of ten potent African medicinal plants. Hindawi, 2013, 617459.

NNPC. (2021). https://nnpcgroup.com/NNPC-Business/Business-Information/Pages/Industry-History.aspx

Olujobi, J. (2021). Deregulation of the downstream petroleum industry: An overview of the legal quandaries and proposal for improvement in Nigeria. *Science Direct, 7*, e06848.

Oppong, S. (2014). Common health, safety and environmental concerns in upstream oil and gas sector: Implications for HSE management in Ghana. *Academicus International Scientific Journal*, (09), 93–106.

Oxford Business Group. (2021). Ghana's oil and gas infrastructure continues to develop as Companies explore Onshore and Offshore potential. https://oxfordbusinessgroup.com/overview/period-growth-oil-and-gas-infrastructure-continues-develop-companies-explore-onshore-and-offshore

Park, S. (2015). https://cuts-accra.org/pdf/Will_the_Deregulation_of_the_Petroleum_Sector_Result_in_Competition.pdf

Sakyi, P. A., Efavi, J. K., Atta-Peters, D., & Asare, R. (2012). Ghana's quest for oil and gas: Ecological risks and management frameworks. *West African Journal of Applied Ecology, 20*(1), 57–72.

Segal, R. (2021, March 19). https://www.investopedia.com/terms/p/profitmargin.asp

Silva, R., & Paixão, R. (2018). *Tapping into Africa's refining potential*. Miranda Law Firm. https://www.mirandalawfirm.com/download/1188/5f4215a52efe2fb24ea684da6ceb7b69/petroleum_africa_september_2018.pdf

SP Global Platts. (2020, November 5). https://www.spglobal.com/platts/en/market-insights/latest-news/oil/110520-refinery-news-roundup-some-of-libyas-refineries-resume-ras-lanuf-remains-offline

Statista. (2021a, October 4). https://www.statista.com/statistics/1209650/import-volume-of-petroleum-products-into-africa/#:~:text=As%20of%202020%2C%20the%20import,1.9%20million%20barrels%20per%20day

Statista. (2021b, October 4). https://www.statista.com/statistics/1209642/africa-oil-demand-by-petroleum-product/

Statista. (2021c, November 29). https://www.statista.com/statistics/1192530/oil-refinery-capacity-in-african-countries/

Tang, F. C. (1994). Analyzing the oil refining industry in developing countries: A comparative study of China and India. *The Journal of Energy and Development*, *19*, 159–178.

Tanoh, D. A. (2017). The supply chain of the oil and gas industry in Ghana. http://www.reportingoilandgas.org/the-supply-chain-of-the-oil-and-gas-industry-in-ghana/

Toseafa, H. K. (2018). A Study on health and safety practices at Tema Oil Refinery (TOR) in Ghana. https://dk.upce.cz/bitstream/handle/10195/71925/Annotation_Hero_Tosefa.pdf?isAllowed=y&sequence=1

U.S. Energy Information Administration. (2021, July 26). https://www.eia.gov/energyexplained/oil-and-petroleum-products/

4 Downstream Petroleum Sector in Ghana

Mapping the Key Marketing Issues

Kobby Mensah, Ernest Yaw Tweneboah-Koduah, Beatrice Boateng, and Chris Atadika

4.1 Introduction

In this chapter, we attempt to map out some key issues in the downstream petroleum sector in relation to marketing in emerging economies. This is important for us to understand issues on the consumption of petroleum products from demand, supplier, and regulator perspectives, to enable industry players to identify solutions to address them. Downstream oil marketing is both product and service-dominant, consumer-to-business and business-to-business oriented, and the market is regulated and deregulated at the same time. The petroleum industry has three key sectors, the upstream, the midstream, and the downstream subsectors that underpin the total value creation and delivery of petroleum products. This study focuses on the downstream, although Figure 4.1 demonstrates the subsectors and their roles from exploration to sales.

The downstream petroleum sector operates in a highly competitive environment characterised by low margins and high stock turnover (Sartorius et al., 2007). Consumers actively evaluate a petroleum product when they experience the forecourt through pricing, promotion, and service quality (Abah, 2020). In recent times, pricing seems to have become the dominant factor in consumers' evaluation of petroleum products. However, increasing competition and highly volatile pricing regime in the sector make it imperative for managers to identify other factors that could influence consumers' choices. The question is: What makes a customer opt for one petroleum (filling/service) station over the other? The answer to this question is found in the factors of downstream petroleum activities, as identified in Figure 4.2, which is limited in the literature (Sartorius et al., 2007). Existing studies focus on promotion and loyalty schemes to influence choice-making, as opposed to understanding factors of downstream petroleum activities that influence organic choice of petroleum products (Wahid, 2009). The liberalisation and deregulation of the oil industry in Africa as an economic reform policy has resulted in the proliferation of oil marketing companies (OMCs) in most countries on the continent. With this study's sharp focus on emerging economies, a robust deliberation to map out some key marketing-related

DOI: 10.4324/9781003309864-6

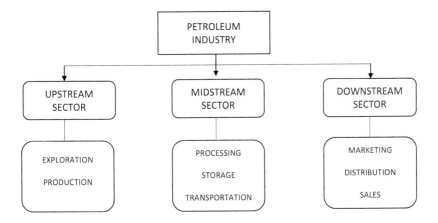

Figure 4.1 Petroleum industry value chain framework
Source: Authors' construction

issues in the downstream petroleum sector is necessary. As illustrated in Figure 4.2, a detailed online search on the petroleum downstream subsectors returned some of these core issues dominant in news items. However, we found stakeholders, policy, pricing, and incidents as the most recurring issues. We will thus look at these issues and how they affect downstream petroleum marketing.

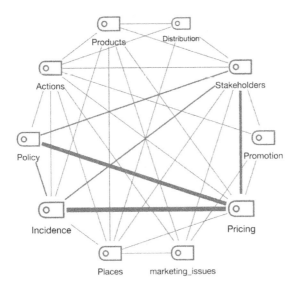

Figure 4.2 Marketing factors in the petroleum downstream sector

4.2 The Petroleum Industry in Emerging Economies

In Ghana, for example, the downstream sector currently has about 170 OMCs operating in retail with lots of service stations across the country serving both the motoring public, individual consumers, and organisations (NPA, 2021). This proliferation of OMCs and their service stations offer consumers of petroleum products a wide spectrum of choice. Consumers now have the choice of the brand of fuel from among the brands on offer at these service stations (Sartorius et al., 2007). This has intensified competition among companies in the industry. Hence, this study seeks to map out the key issues that influence both consumer and supplier behaviours in the sector.

Besides, in Ghana, the association of oil marketing companies (AOMCs) sponsor over 1,800 licensed retail outlets (NPA, 2021). The players are made up of both indigenous and global brands, offering choice in a competitive market. The intense competition is evident in the OMCs market share statistics, where the top 5 are identified as Ghana Oil Company Limited (Goil) with 16%, VIVO Energy Ghana Limited has 8%, Total Petroleum Ghana Limited has 8%, ZEN Petroleum Limited has 7%, and PUMA Energy Distribution Ghana Limited has 5% (National Petroleum Authority [NPA]2021) (Figure 4.3). The top 20 OMCs have a combined market share of 74% and the rest have 26%.

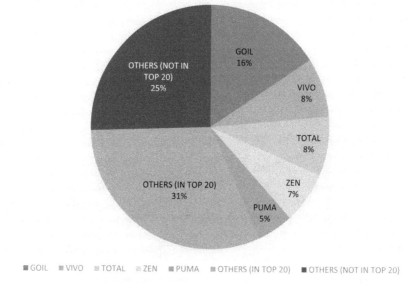

Figure 4.3 Ghana's OMC Market Share Statistics (NPA, 2021)

Source: Authors' own construction

In Nigeria, the downstream petroleum activities are dominated by distribution, pricing, policy action, and product factors. Crude oil was discovered in Nigeria some 65 years ago, making the country one of the oldest petroleum markets on the continent of Africa. In 2019, Nigeria was ranked as the 13th in the world for the production of crude oil with an average output rate of about 2 million barrels daily (KPMG, 2019). Nigeria has a robust downstream petroleum sector that remains key to the growth of the Nigerian economy. However, it is fraught with internal and external challenges. According to a KPMG report in 2019, the Nigerian downstream petroleum sector was inundated with inappropriate product pricing, pipeline vandalism, and non-functional refineries among others (KPMG, 2019).

In recent times, pricing has been one of the major public discourses in the petroleum industry in Nigeria. Discussions and debates have centred on the regulation and deregulation of petroleum product pricing. As pricing affects consumer choice, a deregulation policy was enacted to allow the market forces instead of government to determine downstream oil pricing. In the old regime when government was in control of pricing, concerns were raised about the politicisation that underpinned oil pricing as opposed to rational economic theory (KPMG, 2019). As a result, the Petroleum Products Pricing and Regulatory Agency (PPPRA) was tasked to ensure the elimination of exploitation through deregulation in order to allow a competitive market.

In distribution, the downstream sector in Nigeria has some major stakeholders, key amongst them being the Nigerian national petroleum corporation (NNPC), which is responsible for product distribution, retail services, and research and development. Issues affecting distribution, such as pipeline vandalism and non-functional refineries (KPMG, 2019), are some of the key challenges facing the sector. The passing of the petroleum industry bill (PIB) 2021 was to curb monopolistic tendencies that could create barriers to entry into the market. The daily average consumption of petroleum products has seen an increase from 2021 to 2022 with projections into 2024 indicating increasing consumption rate. Figure 4.4 shows the average daily consumption of petroleum products in Nigeria.

This rising statistic indicates increasing consumption in the Nigerian petroleum market which should then translate into increasing supply, but the growth of supply is faced with rampant leakages in the pipeline networks mainly due to poor maintenance and damage. In terms of distribution and in relation to supply of petroleum products to meet heavy demand, the Major Oil Marketers Association of Nigeria (MOMAN) has statistics indicating that close to 80% of its members transport and distribute using trucking, the most popular method, to reach consumers. The market share of petroleum product sales in the Nigerian petroleum market was dominated by independent marketers from 2016 to 2020. In 2018, the number of petroleum retail outlets (fuel stations) across the various states of Nigeria owned by independent marketers was 25,270 with 3,565 owned by major marketers and 362 owned by the government agency NNPC (DPR and FSDH & MOMAN (2021). Figure 4.5 shows the market share distribution of the key players in the retail of petroleum products in the Nigerian market.

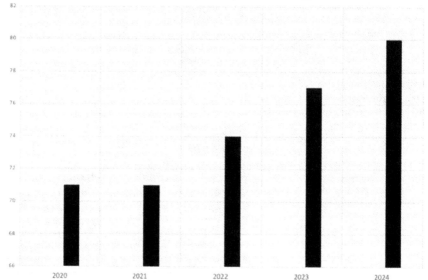

Figure 4.4 Petroleum consumption in Nigeria
Source: Petroleum Products Pricing and Regulatory Agency and FSDH & MOMAN (2021)

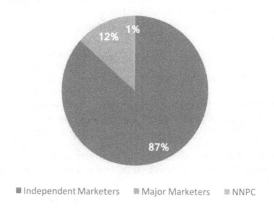

Figure 4.5 Retail outlets of key players, 2018
Source: FSDH & MOMAN (2021)

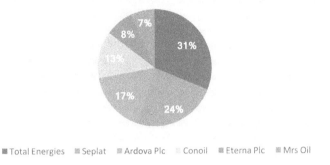

Figure 4.6 Petroleum industry revenue share among firms (2021)
Source: FSDH & MOMAN (2021)

The Nigerian petroleum downstream market is one that is amalgamated with these five major players: NDEP PLC, Midoil Refining & Petrochemicals Company Limited, National Petroleum Corporation (NNPC), Indorama Eleme Petrochemicals Limited, and KBR Inc. In 2021, Total Energy was the firm with the highest revenue share in the petroleum industry in Nigeria, while Mrs Oil was the firm with the lowest revenue share. Figure 4.6 shows the revenue share distribution among the major petroleum downstream firms in the Nigerian market.

The Nigerian petroleum market is not the only petroleum market in an emerging economy that is booming and showing competitiveness in the downstream sector. Some oil experts in Africa opine that Kenya will be the next major producer of oil in Africa. The Kenyan downstream petroleum market is led by two French firms and has other major players like National Oil Corporation of Kenya, Total Kenya, Vivo Energy, and OLA Energy. This in addition to over 1,700 service stations belonging to more than 70 OMCs indicates the availability of numerous options to consumers. Government policy intervention in the Kenyan petroleum market has resulted in the absence of price wars. Figure 4.7 indicates the market share of the top 5 major players in the Kenyan petroleum downstream market.

4.3 The Marketing Factors in the Petroleum Downstream Sector

4.3.1 *Product*

There have been no significant developments in and public discourse about petroleum products in the case countries beyond the conventional products

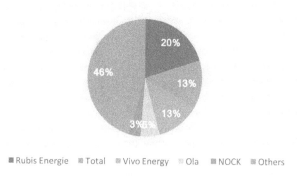

Figure 4.7 Kenyan petroleum downstream

and services that come with downstream petroleum. Petroleum products are sold mainly from service stations that are usually located within road networks. Products and services offered by service stations, especially in urban centres, are petrol (gasoline), vehicle maintenance, and convenience stores providing convenient mobile payment services. The exchange of value between OMCs and their consumers happens at the service stations. Research in the case countries shows that public discourse in relation to petroleum products and services has been mostly about fuel quality, safety, and accessibility issues at service stations, as captured in policy statements, stakeholder engagements, pricing, and incident reports, as illustrated in Figure 4.2. Reports in the industry suggest increasing upgrades to service stations in their design, construction, and operations well above industry standards. Industry safety reports observe that service stations are mostly equipped with double-wall tanks, leak detection, overfill prevention, flame arrestors, oil separators, and other key safety features while providing priority access and parking for persons with disabilities. In recent times, branding has also become a very important subject to the downstream petroleum service providers due to the increasing competition in the sector (Amoako, 2022; Keller, 2000).

4.3.2 Distribution

Distribution is the primary component of the marketing mix that makes products and services available to clients. A strong channel strategy is essential for the success of a business, and channel selection is influenced by the channel's ability to meet customers' perceptions, requirements, and expectations (Amoako, 2022; Verhoef et al., 2007). Evidence in the case countries shows that location is the most important factor for consumers when choosing a service station (Bilgin & Danis, 2016) and impacts on the long-term performance of these stations considerably (Brown, 1989). It is noted in the literature that a consumer's brand choice and purchase behaviour are positively related to distribution intensity. The term 'distribution intensity' refers to the level of availability of a certain product (Amoako, 2022). OMCs in emerging markets consider location as a priority in their distribution model, and in the case countries selected for this chapter, three types of distribution intensity are identified: intensive distribution, selective distribution, and exclusive distribution. In intensive distribution, providers of petroleum products saturate the market by appropriately using all outlets available. With the selective distribution strategy, producers make products available to a limited number of outlets in a geographical location. The extreme form of selective distribution is where only one or two major retailers or wholesalers are utilised in a specific geographical location to distribute products to customers is termed exclusive distribution (Chukwuma et al., 2018). OMCs ensure that their brand is present in as many locations as possible through intensive distribution. It should be emphasised that not all businesses can afford this strategy due to the high cost of establishing a petrol station. However, most motor vehicle users require the availability of fuel service stations for their daily journeys and so OMCs require an intensive approach to be successful.

It is evident that leading OMCs in the case countries use the intensive distribution model whereas the less competitive alternatives prefer exclusive and selective distribution. This approach in the distribution of downstream petroleum is different from conventional marketing, where providers of luxury goods use selective distribution to serve a niche market (Jain et al., 2021). In the case of downstream petroleum, however, selective distribution is rather for less competitive OMCs with a small client base. As OMCs are aware that their long-term performance can be considerably boosted by smart location decisions and secondary attractions, like convenience shops (Brown, 1989), players in the industry augment their core products with other services such as these convenience shops that attract customers who have proven to be interested in patronising a one-stop-shop rather than making several stopovers for multiple transactions (Amoako, 2022; Bilgin & Danis, 2016).

4.3.3 Pricing

Pricing is the most discussed element of the factors influencing the downstream petroleum sector in emerging markets. Pricing in the case countries is partly regulated and partly deregulated. In Kenya, government policy intervention in petroleum pricing has resulted in the absence of price wars. In Nigeria, the petroleum pricing deregulation policy was enacted to allow the market forces, rather than government, to determine downstream oil pricing – a departure from the old regime when government was in control of pricing – which raised concerns of politicisation (KPMG, 2019). As a result, the PPPRA was tasked to ensure the elimination of exploitation through deregulation to allow a competitive market.

Ghana's NPRA, for example, aims to ensure full cost recovery, government revenue generation, and price consistency through the policy of the Unified Petroleum Price Fund (UPPF). Other pricing policies such as the imports parity price (IPP) benchmark are used to determine full cost recovery along the value chain. The 'landed cost' of refined petroleum imported to Ghana, as determined by the IPP benchmark, includes the worldwide price for refined fuel, freight charges, currency rate, customs and port duties, insurance, and losses. It represents the price that the bulk-distribution companies (BDCs), who are licensed to import, would pay if a product was imported into Ghanaian ports. There is a two-week inventory window, in which a pricing reference like Platts is used by the NPA to calculate the two-week average of the FOB prices of the products. The equation is then updated with the historical average cedi-to-dollar exchange rate for the previous two weeks. The ex-refinery price is then computed in Ghana pesewas per litre after ancillary costs like port taxes are applied. The ultimate ex-pump price, which is the price at which the public buys fuel at various filling stations, is calculated using approved taxes and levies imposed by Parliament, as well as various OMC (distribution) margins.

Ex-pump fuel prices are generally 35–40% taxed and margined. The government's sole authority to interfere in the price build-up through the NPA means that the entire cost of the commodity is not always passed on to consumers through final ex-pump pricing. There are however concerns of non-transparency in downstream petroleum pricing, where it is alleged that consumers are in the dark on the pricing mechanism such as cross-subsidisation, the TOR recovery levy, indirect and direct taxes, refinery margins and profits, and subsidy margins. The source of the concerns, according to industry experts, is the automated adjustment algorithm. In the past what prevailed was a capping system in which price changes on global markets, which account for just 65 percent of the price increase, did not instantly reflect in local pricing. The local pricing considered exchange rate fluctuations and inflation to preserve parity. The controversy on pricing has been feisty, with industry players being very critical of the government's lack of transparency.

4.3.4 Stakeholders

Stakeholders are entities (institutions, organisations, groups of people, and individuals) with a 'stake' or 'interest'. The phrase also encompasses individuals who are impacted by policies, decisions, and actions that control the exploitation and consumption of natural resources. Stakeholder types and interests are extremely important to businesses because they help improve strategic and operational performances (Fritz et al., 2018; Madumere, 2021). The most important steps in stakeholder management are identification and categorisation. Direct (principal) stakeholders and indirect (secondary) stakeholders are the two types of stakeholders. Direct stakeholders are parties with direct interest in the operations of an institution (Chanya et al.,

2014; Madumere, 2021). In the downstream petroleum sector, for example, the petroleum firm, host community, government (both local and national), financial institutions, investors, and regulatory agencies are direct stakeholders in oil and gas operations. NGOs, academics, the media, and foreign governments are indirect stakeholders (Madumere, 2021). The term 'stakeholder' does not always denote mandates or functions of each participant in the policy-making process. The term 'actors' best captures policy roles. Individuals and organisations that strive to influence policy proactively are referred to as 'influential actors'. Each of the stakeholders have an impact on the success of oil and gas operations. An influential actor such as COPEC is always advocating value for consumers of fuel in Ghana. For example, it has expressed its frustrations about the increases in petroleum taxes (Joy Online, 2012). It complains about how deregulation has brought about hardships in the lives of citizens and proposes that the Price Stabilisation and Recovery Levies (PSRL) be repealed to stop the steady rise in petroleum product prices. OMCs in emerging markets have also shown interest in other stakeholder sustainability initiatives. For example, research shows that industry players collaborate with local stakeholders to rehabilitate educational institutions, donate educational materials to school children, and build hand-pump water borehole stations for the people of the communities they operate in. They also collaborate with other regulatory stakeholders, such as petroleum authorities and the driver and vehicle licensing authority to organise training and certification programmes and to create guidebooks on road safety to reduce accidents. These partnerships are to ensure that safety and compliance are emphasised in the petroleum downstream sector.

4.3.5 Policy

Research shows that downstream petroleum sectors in emerging markets are regulated by Acts of Parliament, with dedicated regulatory bodies. The role of the regulatory bodies is to guarantee that the industry is efficient, profitable, and fair, while also ensuring that consumers get good value for money (NPA, 2021). Institutions responsible for policy in most emerging markets are the ministries of energy, local commissions, and other international organisations. Stakeholders call on governments to focus policy on storage infrastructure, distribution, and usage equipment, especially towards access to petroleum products in rural areas. They also call for petroleum deregulation to eliminate inefficiencies in the industry, advocating private sector participation in oil and gas procurement, which has largely been the exclusive duty of government agencies in most emerging markets. In Ghana, for example, the private sector is now authorised to import finished petroleum products (about a third of total oil demand) into Ghana through open and competitive bidding under its deregulated framework (Amponsah & Opei, 2014). Research in the case countries shows substantial improvements in the role and participation of locals in the downstream sector. Governments in case countries have enacted local content policies to ensure the development of a locally owned petroleum downstream industry capable of attracting increasing local value-added investments and jobs. They set up local content committees to supervise, organise, manage, and monitor petroleum downstream activities (KPMG, 2019; NPA, 2021). Although deregulation in the sector was to allow operators complete control over final pump pricing, it has, however, contributed to gasoline price fluctuation in these case countries, especially with recent surge in fuel costs. In Ghana, for example, the deregulation was to allow OMCs to set prices for their products as a means to resolving the legacy debt.

4.4 Conclusion

It is noted in this chapter that the petroleum downstream sector in emerging markets offers key products and services such as gasoline, vehicle maintenance, and convenience stores. From the analysis of news items on the case countries, the most prevalent factors of public discourse were pricing, policy, stakeholder, and operational incidences in the sector. On policy, it is noted that all case countries have a mixed regulatory petroleum downstream sector that is partly regulated and partly deregulated. For example, in Ghana, the private sector is authorised to import finished petroleum products. Individual supplier brands are also allowed to set their own pump prices but based on a formula agreed upon with the regulator, which includes the UPPF policy and the IPP benchmark policy. In terms of player dominance, there is a mixed picture in the case countries. Evidence suggests that both the Ghanaian and Kenyan markets are dominated by major global suppliers, including Total Energies, Shell, and others. The Nigerian market also has a significant presence of global oil companies, such as Total Energies, which controls a significant share of the market, but there is a good mix of both global and local supplier brands. Players in the sector make claim of constantly working to serve customers with high-quality fuel and lubricants at the most competitive pricing, as well as world-class customer services such as checking for leaks, easy mobile payment methods, lube bays, a quick shopping option, and places of convenience at service stations.

References

Abah, A. J. (2020). Branding and consumer behaviour of selected petroleum products in Port Harcout, Rivers State, *International Journal of Advanced Academic Research*, 6(11), 43–69.

Amoako, G. K. (2022). Distribution intensity and purchase behavior-mediating role of brand equity in oil marketing companies (OMCs): An emerging markets perspective. *Business Perspectives and Research*, 10(1), 46–64.

Amponsah, R., & Opei, F. K. (2014). Ghana's downstream petroleum sector: An assessment of key supply chain challenges and prospects for growth. *International Journal of Petroleum and Oil Exploration Research*, 1(1), 001–007.

Bilgin, M. H., & Danis, H. (Eds.). (2016). *Entrepreneurship, business and economics-vol. 2: Proceedings of the 15th Eurasia business and economics society conference.* Springer.

Brown, S. (1989). Retailing and the importance of micro-locational linkages. *Management Decision, 27*(5). https://doi.org/10.1108/00251748910132566

Chanya, A., Prachaak, B., & Ngang, T. K. (2014). Conflict management on use of watershed resources. *Procedia-Social and Behavioral Sciences, 136,* 481–485.

Chukwuma, A. I., Ezenyilimba, E., & Aghara, V. N. (2018). An assessment on how intensive distribution by small and medium scale bakeries in South-Eastern Nigeria affects their sales volume. *Scholars Journal of Economics Business and Management, 5*(3), 864–873.

Fritz, M. M., Rauter, R., Baumgartner, R. J., & Dentchev, N. (2018). A supply chain perspective of stakeholder identification as a tool for responsible policy and decision-making. *Environmental Science & Policy, 81,* 63–76.

FSDH AND MOMAN (2021, August). Nigerian downstream petroleum industry report: A new dawn. *The 3rd Edition of the Annual Nigerian Downstream Petroleum Industry Report by MOMAN in partnership with FSDH.* Retrieved April 15, 2022 from https://moman.org/2021/09/13/a_new_dawn/

Jain, S., Mishra, S., & Mukhopadhyay, S. (2021). Critical success factors for luxury fashion brands in emerging markets: Insights from a qualitative study. *Journal of Global Fashion Marketing, 12*(1), 47–61.

Joy Online (2012). Retrieved April 8, 2022 from https://www.myjoyonline.com/government-commits-to-review-taxes-on-fuel-in-mid-year-budget-after-drivers-strike-abbas-imoro/

JoyNews. (2021). Retrieved April 15, 2022 from https://www.myjoyonline.com/petroleum-deregulation-has-rather-increased-fuel-prices-copecghana/#:~:text=Executive%20Secretary%20at%20Chamber%20of,of%20Ghanaians%20particularly%20fuel%20consumers

Keller, K. L. (2000). The brand report card. *Harvard Business Review, 78*(1), 147–158.

KPMG. (2019). Downstream oil and gas sector watch. *Newsletter.*

Madumere, N. (2021). The impact of stakeholder management on the oil and gas industry in Africa: A case study of oil companies and African host communities. *African Journal on Conflict Resolution, 21*(2), 8–32.

NPA. (2021). Petroleum downstream statistical bulletin, Fourth Quarter Publication. Retrieved April 6, 2022 from http://www.npa.gov.gh/Data/Documents/statistical-bulletin/2021/Petroleum%20Downstream%20Statistical%20Bulletin%20for%204th%20Quarter%202021.pdf

NPA. (2021). Retrieved April 19, 2022 from http://www.npa.gov.gh/

NPA. (2021). Retrieved April 7, 2022 from http://www.npa.gov.gh/our-function/pricing-planning

Sartorius, K., Eitzen, C., & Hart, J. (2007). An examination of the variables influencing the fuel retail industry. *Acta Commercii, 7*(1), 218–235.

Verhoef, P. C., Neslin, S. A., & Vroomen, B. (2007). Multichannel customer management: Understanding the research-shopper phenomenon. *International Journal of Research in Marketing, 24*(2), 129–148.

Wahid, A. Z. B. A. (2009). *Customer loyalty and petrol station's convenience* (Doctoral dissertation, Universiti Sains Malaysia).

5 Oil and Gas Operations, Transportation, and Logistics Management

Anthony Afful-Dadzie, Iddrisu Awudu, and Bright Ansah Owusu

5.1 Introduction

Oil and gas are one of the most primary and widely used forms of energy from the Stone Age to today's modernised and complex world (Sorensen, 2013). Oil and gas are energy sources for automobiles, electricity generation plants, homes and electronic appliances, and even spacecraft (Chaturvedi et al., 2022). Extracts from processed oil and gas are also useful in medicine, cosmetics, road construction, and cleaning agents.

The oil and gas industry is very important to every economy, including that of emerging and developing countries (EDCs). The industry serves as a source of employment and foster the creation of indirect jobs in the broader economy (Ologunde et al., 2020). The economies of EDCs have seen substantial economic growth in the last decade (BP Energy Outlook, 2020) leading to massive demand for oil and gas in industries such as energy, transport, and manufacturing. Data from the 2020 energy outlook by IEA (2020) predicts 30 years of continuous growth in gas demand in several EDCs.

The enormous contributions of oil and gas to the economies of EDCs have forced governments and other stakeholders to show much interest in the oil and gas industry, with the hope of reaping the huge benefits associated with this important natural resource. One area crucial to the realisation of such benefits is the oil and gas supply chain. The oil and gas supply chain is characterised by a sequence of operations (in the upstream, midstream, and downstream sections of the industry), transportation, and logistics (Chima, 2007). Of greater importance is the design, coordination, and continuous improvement of the supply chain in a manner that leads to reduction in production and delivery costs, distance covered, and delivery time.

The sustainability of the oil and gas industry is largely dependent on the performance of the operations, transportation, and logistics management (OTLM) of the supply chain. From the economic standpoint, the OTLM of the oil and gas supply chain is of greater importance as it greatly influences the cost of the final product. However, it is also the portion of the industry that requires significant financial investment to achieve the efficiency needed to drive down the cost of the final product. The OTLM also has an impact

DOI: 10.4324/9781003309864-7

on the environment, whether in operations, transportation, or the type of logistics employed. In the sections that follow, we delve into the operations, transportation, and logistics components of the oil and gas supply chain, highlighting the challenges and issues confounding EDCs, particularly those in Africa.

The rest of the chapter is arranged as follows. The first three sections focus on operations, and provide a discussion on oil and gas operations in general, the quality of oil and gas products, and the state of crude oil refineries in EDCs. This is followed by a discussion on the state of the technology in contemporary oil and gas business. The last two sections provide a discussion on oil and gas transportation and logistics, followed by the conclusion of the chapter.

5.2 Oil and Gas Operations

Oil and gas operations include exploration, production, transformation, and refining of crude oil which are fossil fuels formed by a mixture of hydrocarbons from the remains of animals and plants that lived millions of years ago in a marine environment (EIA, 2021). The exploration phase is capital intensive and takes several years before oil is found in commercial quantities. The production, transformation, and refining phases are depicted in Figure 5.1. The production phase involves the extraction of crude oil and natural gas from the ground, and these become the input for the transformation phase.

In the transformation phase, the input is first taken through a separation process where hydrocarbon molecules are separated by atmospheric distillation. After separation, the separated product is taken through a conversion process (also known as catalytic cracking) to convert the heavier hydrocarbon molecules to lighter products. This is followed by the treating phase which removes sulphur from the hydrocarbon molecules. Molecules that are corrosive or that cause air pollution are also removed at this stage. The refining phase yields several products such as petrol, diesel, heating oil, jet fuel, waxes, lubricating oil, and asphalt as shown in Table 5.1.

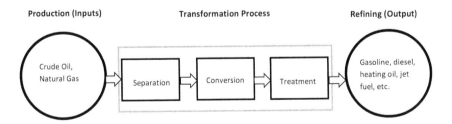

Figure 5.1 A depiction of oil and gas operations

Table 5.1 List of major final products from natural gas and crude oil and their usage

Product	Usage
Light fuel gas	Industrial fuel
	Raw material in petrochemical industries
Liquefied petroleum gas	Domestic or industrial fuel
Gasoline	Fuel for automobiles
Jet fuel	Fuel for reaction engines, gas turbines and rockets
Kerosene	For heat generation and lightening lamps
	For pest disinfectant
Diesel oil	Fuel for domestic heating facilities
	For automobile usage (cars, trucks, marine, etc.)
	Fuel for low-power industrial facilities
Light oil	Base oils in motor oil production
	Lubricant in sewing machines/bicycles
Heavy oil	Base oil with high viscosity in engine oil production
Parafins and waxes	Used in electrical insulation
	Used in preserving food materials
Heavy fuel oils	Fuel for high-power heating facilities and large diesel engines
Asphalt and tar	Used in road construction

5.3 Quality of Oil and Gas Products in Emerging Economies

The increasing demand for oil and gas products in emerging economies has led to the proliferation of substandard products on the market (Hanson, 2012). For instance, a 2016 report indicates that fuels shipped to Ghana, Nigeria, and some other African countries had 300 times more sulphur and twice as many cancer-causing hydrocarbons than the permitted levels in the European Union. This ultimately leads to poor air quality. The report cited Swiss commodity trading firms exploiting weak regulatory standards to sell unwholesome petroleum products to African consumers (Guéniat et al., 2016; UN, 2016). Factors that account for lower quality products include limited refinery capability, which leads to increases in 'black market' imports and sales, lack of regulatory standards and enforcements, and lack of infrastructure to support compliance monitoring. Many EDCs lack the capability to monitor and enforce quality because the resources and technology needed requires substantial financial commitment. For example, it is estimated that it would cost Ghana about 300 million US dollars to put in place the needed infrastructure to monitor the compliance of low-sulphur diesels (Authentix, 2017). This has led to increases in adulterated petroleum products on the market. As an example, it is widely believed that many oil marketing companies in Ghana sell adulterated fuel, with 32% of fuel stations believed to have at least one tank with diluted fuel (Authentix, 2019). Poor fuel quality has severe consequences particularly on health, and also results in equipment degradation (CBOD, 2021), and governments in EDCs must endeavour to put in place measures for monitoring despite the cost involved. To tackle the problem of substandard products, the introduction of the petroleum product marking scheme (PPMS) and the bulk road vehicle (BRV) tracking system for instance by the National Petroleum Authority of Ghana (CBOD, 2021) is highly encouraged.

5.4 Crude Oil Refineries in Emerging Economies

There is increasing demand for petroleum products in EDCs for economic activities such as power generation, transportation, and domestic use (Aguilera et al., 2016). However, most countries in EDCs are not able to meet their demand from local refineries and tend to rely on imports (Gershon et al., 2019). This problem stems from lack of investment in refining capacity and the deterioration of existing infrastructure (BP, 2017). In most EDCs, refineries operate below capacity while most new refining investments do not progress beyond their initial concept stage (Wiley, 2018). In Africa, for instance, many countries do not have refineries and depend entirely on imports from regional neighbours or outside the continent. Those that have operational refineries are unable to produce enough to meet their oil and gas demand and rely on imports to supplement demand (Wiley, 2018). For example, Nigeria, the sixth largest oil producer in the world currently does not have a national refinery capable of processing even half of its crude oil (Bala-Gbogbo, 2019). Ghana's Tema Oil Refinery (TOR) cannot process oil from Ghana's main oil field, the Jubilee Oil Field, since the oil is of a higher grade (Ghanaweb, 2014).

Figure 5.2 presents the refinery status of countries in Africa, showing the range of countries with operational refineries, non-operational refineries, or no refineries. In all, there was about 3628 thousand barrels per day refinery capacity in Africa as of 2020 (Abdoun, 2020). Meanwhile, the overall refining output in Africa is generally low due to the frequent shutdowns and intermittent operation of the few refineries available (Abdoun, 2020; Matthews, 2014). For instance, refinery output in South Africa fell by 28 percent in 2020. Refineries such as the Limbe refinery of Cameroon, TOR of Ghana, and refineries managed by the Nigeria National Petroleum Commission (NNPC) have all been shut down or operate intermittently, with output far below capacity (S&P Global, 2021). Other emerging economies, mostly in sub-Saharan Africa, have non-functional refineries due to lack of appropriate technology or use of outmoded technology. In some instances, the technology may become unused for several years, subsequently becoming obsolete due to lack of or inadequacy of human and logistical infrastructure work with the available technology.

The current state of refineries in Africa coupled with expected demand growth for petroleum products has compelled governments and private investors to improve crude oil processing and refineries in these African countries. This is being done through ongoing maintenance, upgrades, and launches of existing and or new refineries. The Dangote Group is currently building

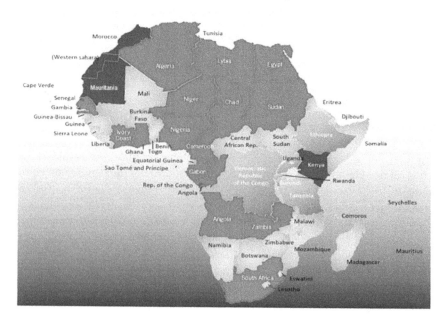

Figure 5.2 The oil refinery status of African countries

Source: Abdoun (2020)

Note: Countries in red have refineries currently in operation; countries in dark red have refineries but currently not in operation; countries in grey do not have refineries.

a 12 billion US dollar refinery in Lekki, Nigeria. This refinery, slated to be commissioned in 2022, is capable of processing 650,000 barrels per day (S&P Global, 2021). Other refineries under construction in Nigeria include the Azikel Refinery and Ogbele Refinery. Table 5.2 provides a list of refinery projects that have been launched which should increase the total oil refinery capacity in Africa. This trend in refinery investment must be continued. Nigeria, for instance, stands to benefit if it could expand its refinery to target the West African sub-region.

5.5 State of Technology in the Oil and Gas Supply Chain

The technology employed in the oil and gas supply chain is crucial. Technology can significantly improve the management level, efficiency, and data security of the oil and gas industry (Lu et al., 2019; Zeynalli et al., 2019). The technologies of social media, mobile computing, cloud computing, analytics, and the Internet of Things (IoT) – the principal drivers of digital transformation – will be invaluable for the smooth management of the oil and gas supply chain in diverse ways.

In a 2014 survey, 88 percent of companies in the oil and gas industry were reported to be undergoing digital transformation, though only 25 percent

Table 5.2 Refineries proposed or under construction in some selected African Countries

Refinery	Capacity (b/d)	Country
Dangote	650,000	Nigeria
Hassi Messaoud	100,000	Algeria
Tiaret	100,000	Algeria
Kenya	Not Available	Kenya
Tema	150,000	Ghana
Takoradi	150,000	Ghana
Lobito	200,000	Angola
Cabinda	60,000	Angola
Soyo	100,000	Angola
Albert Graben	60,000	Uganda
Condensate	200,000	Nigeria
Red Sea Coast	200,000	Sudan
Morocco	100,000	Morocco
Punta Europa	10,000	Equatorial Guinea
Cogo	10,000	Equatorial Guinea
Kamsar	12,000	Guinea
Walter Smith	5000	Nigeria
Paloch	40,000	South Sudan
Kribi	80,000	Cameroon
Pointe Noire	50,000	Congo
Akwa Ibom	200,000	Nigeria

Source: S&P Global (2021)

understood what digital transformation really is and the consequences of undergoing such a transformation (Solis et al., 2014). Digital transformation in the oil and gas industry is yet to take shape in emerging economies to the levels seen in developed countries (D'Almeida et al., 2022).

This gap is a result of numerous factors including inadequate capital to invest in new technologies and low skill levels among personnel. For example, personnel need to be able to collect and interpret data flowing in from the production process, integrate and transform the data for better insight, and share the knowledge with various experts in order to take quick collective decisions on the optimisation of the business process. This expertise is something that most EDCs lack.

Political instability in many EDCs is another factor that accounts for low digital transformation in the oil and gas industry (Petrenko et al., 2022). Due to political instability and interference in most EDCs, a company may lose its assets or shut down in the event of threats to its operations. For example, total energies has suspended its 20 billion US dollar liquefied natural gas (LNG) project in Mozambique indefinitely due to rising security threats in the area (Beaupuy, Burkhardt, & Nhamire, 2021). Events like this repel investments in the oil and gas industry in EDCs and every effort must be made to ensure lasting political stability in EDCs.

5.6 Oil and Gas Transportation

Crude oil transportation and logistics are well researched in the literature (see American Geosciences Institute, 2019; Frittelli, 2014; Green & Jackson, 2015; Perisic et al., 2018; Wang et al., 2017). Overall, the nature of the oil and gas supply chain, especially in the midstream and downstream, largely depends on the transportation mode available and the state of the product being transported. Oil and gas can be transported by sea using ships and pipelines, and on land by trucks and pipelines. The choice of a transportation mode depends on several factors including financial resources, availability of waterways, and the state of road transport infrastructure. Other equally important factors include safety, health, cost of maintenance, and ability to respond to disasters such as explosions and leakages. This chapter discusses three modes of transportation, namely pipelines, trucks, and vessels. These three transportation modes are important because of their significance for most EDCs.

5.6.1 Pipelines

Pipelines are constructed above-ground, underground, and underwater with varying sizes capable of moving vast quantities of crude oil and natural gas. Pipelines offer the safest and most economical means of transporting petroleum products (Green & Jackson, 2015). This makes pipelines a reliable transportation mode in the petroleum industry since new technology has helped to advance its safety through the use of sensors for monitoring important indicators like temperature, pressure, and tampering. Additionally, climate change concerns make pipelines a preferred mode of oil and gas transportation. Pipelines do not leave traces of carbon in the atmosphere, which affect air quality, and do not cause acid rain or ozone depletion. However, the use of pipelines in oil and gas transportation has some disadvantages, especially for EDCs. The initial investment cost is huge and discourages many EDCs from building such facilities. Thus, oil and gas companies that are not financially sound may not be able to opt for this mode of transportation despite its numerous benefits.

In addition, building a pipeline involves strategic planning which includes determining the shortest and most economical routes, the number of pumping stations, terminal storage facilities, and in the case of natural gas, compression stations as well. Additionally, since pipelines transport enormous quantities of oil and gas, whenever an accident happens, it results in huge economic losses.

While there are many pipelines operating around the world, EDCs have very few oil and gas pipelines, with most of them not functional or operating intermittently because of inadequate capital investment and technical operations of the facilities. Most of the pipelines in EDCs such as those in Africa have smaller capacities and sizes, which do not result in economies of scale

Table 5.3 Some selected oil and gas pipelines in Africa

Name	Capacity	Size (km)	Country(ies) connected	Status	Commodity
Cameroon-Chad pipeline	225,000 bpd	1070	Cameroon-Chad	Operational	Crude oil
Sudeth pipeline	Not available	1000	South Sudan-Ethopia	Ongoing	Crude oil
Transnet pipelines	4.2 million bpd	3000	South Africa	Operational	Crude oil
Tazama pipeline	1,100,000 tonnes	1710	Tanzania-Zambia	Operational	Crude oil
Nember creek trunk line	600,000 bdp	97	Nigeria	Operational	Crude oil
West Africa gas PIPELINE	13,000,000 cmpd	678	Nigeria-Benin-Togo-Ghana	Operational	Natural gas

for owners of the pipelines. Table 5.3 lists a selected number of oil and gas pipelines in Africa and their characteristics.

One of the major cross-country pipelines in Africa is the West African Gas Pipeline (WAGP) project. This pipeline became operational in 2011 and has a capacity of 474 MMscf/day and transports natural gas from Nigeria to Benin, Togo, and Ghana for electricity generation and other industrial uses (Debrah et al., 2020). Uganda, Tanzania, and the French oil company total energies, and the China national offshore oil corporation (CNOOC) have also signed a series of agreements to build a heated pipeline that will carry crude oil from Uganda to Tanzania. The 1400 km pipeline would be the longest electrically heated crude oil pipeline in the world if completed (Bradstock, 2021).

5.6.2 Trucks

Another popular mode of transporting oil and gas is through trucks, especially to fuel stations. The commonly used trucks are tankers – special cylindrical containers connected to trucks. Generally, trucks carry small quantities of oil over short distances and seldom carry crude oil. Instead, trucks typically move refined petroleum products such as gasoline, diesel, and natural gas to demand-centres.

The advantage of trucks over other modes of transportation is the ability to schedule shipment at any time and move them more freely at any place. Also, crude oil or natural gas can move in smaller quantities to limit the impact of damage in case of cracks or leaks. These advantages in using trucks have made them very popular in most EDCs, particularly those in Africa with inadequate infrastructure for the other modes of transportation. Trucks are also the main sources of oil and gas transportation for landlocked countries in Africa such as Burundi, Rwanda, and Burkina Faso. Trucks are, however, not without disadvantages. The major disadvantage of truck transportation is its limited capacity, which makes it less than ideal for transporting larger quantities of oil and gas in a short period of time. In addition, road infrastructure in most EDCs is deplorable and often lead to truck accidents in the transportation of oil and gas.

In all, it is anticipated that trucks will continue to be a major means of transporting oil and gas in EDCs for the foreseeable future, particularly in Africa, since the nature of it affords even private individuals the opportunity to own one.

5.6.3 Vessels

The use of vessels is the second cheapest mode of transporting oil and gas due to the large volumes that are transported internationally and domestically (Frittelli, 2014). Vessel shipment includes the use of barges and tankers for oil and gas transportation and is usually for importation, especially to countries with seashores. While smaller vessels typically transport refined petroleum products such as gasoline, diesel and jet fuel, large vessels transport large quantities of crude oil averaging 2 million barrels per movement (Frittelli, 2014).

The use of vessels (tankers) in natural gas transportation is risky due to high pressures and the possibility of explosions. To ensure safe transportation, natural gas is turned into LNG and transported by specially designed tankers with double hulls and additional safety features.

In general, vessel transportation has longer lead times and cannot be used when there is a given quantity to be delivered quickly. In times of canal blockage, a vessel may be stuck for several months and will lead to accumulated charges, fines, and delay in delivery of the consignment. Such crises affect crude oil transportation and can erode the great advantage that it offers.

However, the reliance on vessels for the importation of oil in EDCs is projected to increase due to increasing demand for oil and gas and the inability of EDCs to finance undersea pipeline projects like the Nord Stream gas pipeline connecting Germany and Russia.

5.7 Oil and Gas Logistics

Logistics in the oil and gas industry refers to the overall process of managing the acquisition, storage, and transportation of resources to the destination (Waters, 2019). The goal of logistics management in the oil and gas industry is to ensure that the right amount of inputs is obtained at the right time and transported to the appropriate location in good condition for the customer (Lai & Cheng, 2016). Two crucial variables that impact on oil and gas logistics are depots and locations. A depot and its effective management can lead to significant reductions in operational cost and risk (Wan et al., 2020; Yang, 2019). Oil and gas depot logistics management must be done in accordance with local, national, and international codes and standards, and legal and statutory requirements. Relevant standards to adhere to include safety guidelines, good industry practice, environmental health, safety, operation, and maintenance and inspection of terminals. The deployment of enterprise resource planning (ERP) such as system application products (SAP) is encouraged since it helps to streamline and automate business processes and functions at depots, thereby creating a leaner, more accurate and efficient operation. In addition, the use of ERP in depot management leads to effective inventory management, improved customer relationship management, and enhanced regulatory compliance (Wei et al., 2017).

In addition to ERP, the use of radio frequency identification (RFID) technology in the oil and gas industry helps to provide a quick, flexible, and reliable way to electronically track and control a diverse range of items and activities. RFID collects data such as temperature of storage tanks, and the number of trips made by a delivery truck, and stores it on tags using frequency communications. Using RFID can improve the equipment maintenance process by quickly providing critical personnel with the necessary information to manage equipment.

The location of logistics facilities in the oil and gas industry is very important and is usually decided taking into consideration availability of personnel, security threats, the impact on the natural environment, transportation infrastructure, as well as the economic environment (Lyu et al., 2019; Żak & Węgliński, 2014).

Availability of personnel with the requisite technical knowledge greatly affects the location of logistics of the midstream and downstream sectors of the oil and gas industry. In most EDCs, there is inadequate supply of personnel with the requisite skills to support the logistic operation of the oil and gas companies. Most companies in EDCs therefore rely on expatriates for technical logistics operations. To help redress this inadequacy, local content requirement laws must be enacted to force oil and gas companies to invest in local personnel to reduce the over-reliance on expatriates (Pegram et al., 2020).

Security threats to the operations of oil and gas companies, such as piracy and militant attacks on oil and gas installations are also a major consideration when locating oil and gas logistics. According to Nwachukwu et al. (2020), piracy can control, influence, and impact the economic prosperity of oil and gas companies due to attacks on their logistics.

Availability of infrastructure also affects the location of logistics in the oil and gas industry. According to Liang and Liu (2020), improvements in infrastructure such as port facilities enhances logistics performance which promotes trade and economic growth. In most EDCs, these oil and gas logistics infrastructure are limited in supply. For instance, there is only one gas pipeline operating in West Africa for transporting natural gas from Nigeria to Benin, Togo, and Ghana. There are also very few port terminals where oil and gas vessels can dock to discharge petroleum products. Storage facilities are also inadequate, which makes it impossible to stockpile petroleum products to take advantage of fuel price reductions. It is thus imperative that EDCs focus on improving the needed infrastructure to attract oil and gas businesses.

5.8 Conclusion

This chapter looked at oil and gas OTLM in EDCs, specifically within the African context. The chapter provides an overview of the oil and gas sector from a general perspective and then narrows down to the African context. It also explores challenges such as operations, refinery capacity, lack of state-of-the-art technology, transportation, and logistics. It also highlights feasible solutions that can be adopted by EDCs to make an immediate impact on the operations of oil and gas industries including capacity increase for refineries, using current emerging technologies, deployment of smart logistics tools such as active ERP and RFIDs. It concludes that the oil and gas sector is an important part of the economy of EDCs, especially in Africa, and should be given critical attention to achieve impactful economic gains. We find that increasing EDCs' capacity to refine crude oil is the crucial step needed to make significant economic gains. Also, once capacity is increased, then tools and techniques needed to boost operations, logistics, and transportation are deployed to realise efficient and productive operations which will increase profit margins for EDCs.

References

Abdoun, A. (2020). Sub-regional level cooperation in Africa take the lead to implement lower sulfur fuels. August 14, 2020. *Stratas Advisors*. https://stratasadvisors.com/Insights/2020/08142020-Africa-fuel-quality

Aguilera, M. V. C., da Fonseca, B. B., Ferris, T. K., Vidal, M. C. R., & de Carvalho, P. V. R. (2016). Modelling performance variabilities in oil spill response to improve system resilience. *Journal of Loss Prevention in the Process Industries, 41*, 18–30.

Authentix. (2017). Fuel quality is on the rise in Africa. https://authentix.com/tag/ghana/

Authentix. (2019). Fuel authentication case study: Ghana. https://authentix.com/fuel-authentication-case-study-ghana/

Bala-Gbogbo, E. (2019, October 21). Africa's biggest crude producer remains stuck on imported fuels. *WorldOil*. https://www.worldoil.com/news/2019/10/21/africa-s-biggest-crude-producer-remains-stuck-on-imported-fuels

Beaupuy, F. D., Burkhardt, P., & Nhamire, B. (2021, April 26). Total suspends $20BN LNG project in Mozambique indefinitely. *Bloomberg*.

BP. (2017). BP statistical review of world energy 2017. *Statistical review of world energy, 65*. https://www.connaissancedesenergies.org/sites/default/files/pdf-actualites/bp-statistical-review-of-world-energy-2017-full-report.pdf

BP Energy Outlook. (2020). Edition 2020. *Google Scholar*. https://www.bp.com/content/dam/bp/business-sites/en/global/corporate/pdfs/energy-economics/energy-outlook/bp-energy-outlook-2020.pdf

Bradstock, F. (2021). The story behind the world's longest electrically heated oil pipeline. *Oil Price.com*. https://oilprice.com/Energy/Energy-General/The-Story-Behind-The-Worlds-Longest-Electrically-Heated-Oil-Pipeline.html

CBOD. (2021, November 4). NPA reduces contaminated fuels from 32% to 2.5% – NPA boss. *Ghana Chamber of Bulk Oil Distributors* (CBOD). https://cbodghana.com/5285-2/

Chaturvedi, B. K., Nautiyal, A., Kandpal, T. C., & Yaqoot, M. (2022). Projected transition to electric vehicles in India and its impact on stakeholders. *Energy for Sustainable Development, 66*, 189–200.

Chima, C. M. (2007). Supply-chain management issues in the oil and gas industry. *Journal of Business & Economics Research (JBER), 5*(6), 27–36. https://www.clutejournals.com/index.php/JBER/article/view/2552/2598

IEA. (2020). World energy outlook 2020. OECD Publishing, Paris. https://doi.org/10.1787/557a761b-en

D'Almeida, A. L., Bergiante, N. C. R., de Souza Ferreira, G., Leta, F. R., de Campos Lima, C. B., & Lima, G. B. A. (2022). Digital transformation: A review on artificial intelligence techniques in drilling and production applications. *The International Journal of Advanced, 119*, 5553–5582.

Debrah, S. K., Nyasapoh, M. A., Ameyaw, F., Yamoah, S., Allotey, N. K., & Agyeman, F. (2020). Drivers for nuclear energy inclusion in Ghana's energy mix. *Journal of Energy, 2020*, 8873058.

EIA. (2021). Natural gas explained—U.S. Energy Information Administration (EIA). https://www.eia.gov/energyexplained/natural-gas/

Frittelli, J. (2014). *Shipping US crude oil by water: Vessel flag requirements and safety issues* (No. R43653). Congressional Research Service.

Gershon, O., Ezenwa, N. E., & Osabohien, R. (2019). Implications of oil price shocks on net oil-importing African countries. *Heliyon, 5*(8), e02208.

Ghanaweb. (2014, August 11). TOR will need $200million to refine Jubilee crude. *Ghanaweb Business News*. https://www.ghanaweb.com/GhanaHomePage/NewsArchive/TOR-will-need-200million-to-refine-Jubilee-crude-320693

Green, K. P., & Jackson, T. (2015). *Safety in the transportation of oil and gas: Pipelines or rail?* Fraser Institute.

Guéniat, M., Harjono, M., Missbach, A., & Viredaz, G. V. (2016). Dirty diesel. How Swiss traders flood Africa with toxic fuels. *Public Eye*. https://www.publiceye.ch/fileadmin/doc/Rohstoffe/2016_PublicEye_Dirty_Diesel_Report.pdf

Hanson, G. H. (2012). The rise of middle kingdoms: Emerging economies in global trade. *Journal of Economic Perspectives, 26*(2), 41–64.

Lai, K. H., & Cheng, T. E. (2016). *Just-in-time logistics*. Routledge.

Liang, R., & Liu, Z. (2020). Port Infrastructure connectivity, logistics performance and seaborne trade on economic growth: An empirical analysis on "21st-century maritime silk road". *Journal of Coastal Research, 106*(SI), 319–324.

Lu, H., Guo, L., Azimi, M., & Huang, K. (2019). Oil and gas 4.0 era: A systematic review and outlook. *Computers in Industry, 111*, 68–90.

Lyu, G., Chen, L., & Huo, B. (2019). The impact of logistics platforms and location on logistics resource integration and operational performance. *The International Journal of Logistics Management, 30*, 549–568.

Matthews, W. G. (2014). Opportunities and challenges for petroleum and LPG markets in Sub-Saharan Africa. *Energy Policy, 64*, 78–86.

Nwachukwu, P. I., Obasi, E., Akpuh, D., & Olaiya, S. (2020). The impact of piracy on economic prosperity in Niger delta region of Nigeria. *International Journal of Research and Innovation in Social Science (IJRISS), 4*, 325–330.

Ologunde, I. A., Kapingura, F. M., & Sibanda, K. (2020). Sustainable development and crude oil revenue: A case of selected crude oil-producing African countries. *International Journal of Environmental Research and Public Health, 17*(18), 6799.

Pegram, J., Falcone, G., & Kolios, A. (2020). Job role localisation in the oil and gas industry: A case study of Ghana. *The Extractive Industries and Society, 7*(2), 328–336.

Perisic, J., Milovanovic, M., Petrovic, I., Radovanovic, L., Ristic, M., Speight, J. G., & Perisic, V. (2018). Application of a master meter system to assure crude oil and natural gas quality during transportation. *Petroleum Science and Technology, 36*(16), 1222–1228.

Petrenko, Y., Denisov, I., & Metsik, O. (2022). Foresight management of national oil and gas industry development, *Energies, 15*(2), 491.

S&P Global. (2021). Refinery news roundup: Some refineries in Africa remain offline. https://www.spglobal.com/platts/pt/oil/refined-products/jetfuel/051821-refinery-news-roundup-some-refineries-in-africa-remain-offline

Solis, B., Li, C., & Szymanski, J. (2014). The 2014 state of digital transformation. *Altimeter Group, 1*(1), 1–33.

Sorensen, B. (2013). *A history of energy: Northern Europe from the stone age to the present day.* Routledge.

UN. (2016). West African countries ban Europe's dirty fuel imports [Online]. UN Environment Programme. Retrieved February 15, from https://www.unep.org/news-and-stories/press-release/west-african-countries-ban-europes-dirty-fuel-imports

Wan, J., Zheng, Y., Li, Y., Mei, H., Lin, L., & Kuang, L. (2020, March). Oil depot safety inspection and emergency training system based on virtual reality technology. In *IOP Conference Series: Materials Science and Engineering* (Vol. 782, No. 4, p. 042018). IOP Publishing.

Wang, T., Li, T., Xia, Y., Zhang, Z., & Jin, S. (2017). Risk assessment and online forewarning of oil & gas storage and transportation facilities based on data mining. *Procedia Computer Science, 112*, 1945–1953.

Waters, C. D. J. (2019). *Logistics: An introduction to supply chain management.* Red Globe Press.

Wei, O. C., Idrus, R., & Abdullah, N. L. (2017, July). Extended ERP for inventory management: The case of a multi-national manufacturing company. In *2017 International Conference on Research and Innovation in Information Systems (ICRIIS)* (pp. 1–5). IEEE.

Wiley, F. (2018). Africa looks to new refineries to reduce continent's product deficit. *Oil and Energy Trends, 43*, 4–7.

Yang, S. (2019, October). Optimization of oil depot operation process. In *IOP Conference Series: Earth and environmental science* (Vol. 332, No. 2, p. 022044). IOP Publishing.

Żak, J., & Węgliński, S. (2014). The selection of the logistics center location based on MCDM/A methodology. *Transportation Research Procedia, 3*, 555–564.

Zeynalli, A., Butdayev, R., & Salmanov, V. (2019, October). Digital transformation in oil and gas industry. In *SPE Annual Caspian Technical Conference.* OnePetro.

6 Procurement and Supply Chain Management in the Oil and Gas Industry

Joshua Ofori-Amanfo, Prosper Biaka Konlan, and Florence Newman

6.1 Introduction

In this chapter, we examine the growing importance of procurement and supply chain management in the oil and gas industry. We explore the opportunities by which supply chain management activities can be utilised to facilitate sustainability management in the industry. With sustainability management becoming a key concern for many sectors in all economies, we are keen on understanding the characterisation of the procurement and supply chain management function and the extent to which its strategic and operational activities can be exploited to drive sustainability initiatives in the oil and gas industry in emerging economies.

Camilleri (2017) argues that suppliers in the oil and gas industry in developing economies are frequently criticised for their social and environmental deficits due to the pressure to increase productivity levels. The deficit may be demonstrated by organisations' irresponsible behaviour towards their employees, suppliers and the environment in general, which in the long term could negatively affect the organisation's competitiveness. Firms are currently coming under pressure from national regulatory bodies to implement sustainable supply chain practices in the industry (Rentizelas et al., 2020). Such practices are expected to mitigate the overall procurement and supply chain risks and improve supply chain performance for network players.

The chapter examines the criticality of the procurement and supply function in creating value to sustain the development of the burgeoning oil and gas industry in developing economies. The chapter contributes to improving understanding of the value-creation potential of the procurement and supply chain function in the context of a sustainable oil and gas industry.

6.2 The Nature of the Oil and Gas Supply Chains

The oil and gas value chain is vast, long, and complex, with a multiplicity of stakeholders involved in the activities of production, processing, storage, and transportation of the products from the industry. A complex web of relationships involving upstream and downstream linkages of supply chain partners and stakeholders characterise the value chain. Complexity in the chain is driven by the competitive business environment, mergers and acquisitions, outsourcing, customer requirement, strategic alliances, new technologies, and dynamic markets (Manuj & Sahin, 2011; Yusuf et al., 2018). The value chain falls into two distinct but related segments: the upstream and the downstream supply chains. Shqairat and Sundarakani (2018) describe the upstream supply chain activities to include crude oil exploration and drilling, forecasting production needs, the production process, and the shipment of the crude oil to refineries. The downstream activities comprise the refining of the crude oil and processing of the natural gas, determining processing quantities, and moving processed products to strategic storage locations for access by customers (Hussain et al., 2006; Shqairat & Sundarakani, 2018).

Given the many steps and linkages involved in energy processing, oil and gas supply chains are justifiably complex in nature (Hussain et al., 2006). These linkages represent the interface between companies and materials that flow through the supply chain. It must be noted that, within each stage of the process, there are many operations. For instance, exploration includes seismic, geophysical, and geological operations, while production operations include drilling, reservoir, production, and facilities engineering. The industry is highly automated and optimised, so supply chain disruptions can rapidly escalate to become industry-wide or nationwide crisis. Oil and gas companies must be aware of these risks so they can put in the necessary effort in risk management to reinforce the integration of the supply chain. Enhancing supply chain visibility in the industry is equally of critical importance in minimising inefficiencies and disruptions (Fernandes & Barbosa-Povoa, 2009).

The oil and gas value chain has many small- and medium-sized enterprises (SMEs) providing support services to the large firms. The efficient and effective management of these SMEs is crucially important to supply chain success as they contribute significantly to competitiveness of the value chain (Shqairat & Sundarakani, 2018; Yusuf et al., 2014). The industry deals with a multiplicity of supplies which widely vary ranging from gloves to pipes, valves, cranes, chemicals, cement, steel, and drilling rigs (Christopher, 2007). The objective of supply chain management here is to deliver maximum customer service at the least cost possible. It is important to ensure that supply chain partners can respond quickly to the precise resource needs of their customers, protect themselves from supplier problems, and buffer their operations from the implied demand uncertainty. Oil and gas companies can enhance their profit margins if they manage their purchasing dollars in the entire supply-chain processes (Christopher, 2007). Capability in procurement and supply chain management is, therefore, essential for assisting stakeholder firms to optimise production and distribution costs and to meet customer demand. Figure 6.1 is a representation of the value chain in the oil and gas industry depicting the upstream and downstream segmentation as presented by Shqairat and Sundarakani (2018).

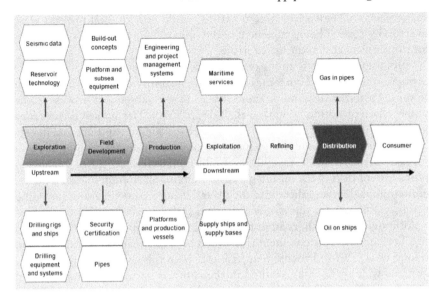

Figure 6.1 The value chain of the oil and gas industry

Source: Shqairat and Sundarakani (2018)

6.3 Procurement as a Critical Risk Factor in Oil and Gas Projects

Hong et al. (2018) described procurement as a series of coordination processes by firms to obtain the resources including, materials, skills, capabilities, and facilities to pursue their core business activities. The procurement function is responsible for the acquisition of external resources to facilitate the continuity and maintenance of the operations of a firm at the most favourable conditions including the minimisation of risk.

The oil and gas supply chain particularly stands the danger of multiple disruptions if inter-firm risks are not appropriately managed. Johnsen et al. (2019) argue that the oil and gas supply chain has complex supply networks where a very large number of both upstream and downstream actors are involved. The industry is engulfed with a high level of uncertainty and probability of the occurrence of a risk event at multiple phases of the supply chain. Thus, the identification as well as the effective management of procurement and supply chain risks is critical to the success of the industry (Van Thuyet et al., 2007).

Many developing economies have limited manufacturing activities, which limits the ability of the domestic economy in supporting the procurement needs of the oil and gas industry. Consequently, there is heavy reliance on overseas parts and component suppliers among supply chain partners. This situation potentially causes delays in project completion times and cost overruns. For instance, Ahmad et al. (2013) reveal that 47% of completed oil and gas projects in Yemen had time overruns, while 40% of total projects were overrun by costs. The management of the supply chain function is significant for minimising cost and time overruns.

"Procurement risk is the probability of variance associated with supply disruption in which its outcomes result in the inability of the purchasing firm to meet customer demand or cause threats to the subsequent process in the supply chain operation" (Hong et al., 2018, p. 1550). The authors further suggest that procurement risk can be managed by reducing exposure and uncertainty in price, lead time, and demand, in order to ensure continuous flow of supplies (material, skills, capabilities, facilities) (Hong et al., 2018). Managing procurement risks of the oil and gas firms involves an attempt to deal with the numerous challenges inherent in the overall value chain operations including design, build, service support, and disposal (Johnsen et al., 2019).

Although some authors attempt a classification of procurement risks from supply chain risks, procurement risk should be seen as part of the supply chain (Hong et al., 2018). Procurement risk relates to the risk of supply discontinuity as well as the risks entailed in the contract between the buying firm and its suppliers. Within this spectrum, there are uncertainties, which can affect the buyer-supplier relationship such as poor coordination between the internal customer and the source of supply. Implied from this understanding of procurement risk is the notion that procurement risk is part of the broader spectrum of supply chain risks.

Kassem et al. (2020) identified tendering and contract-related risks as among the most frequently mentioned risk factors affecting the oil and gas industry. This factor falls within the control of the procurement and supply chain function. Tendering is critically important in complex projects as inadequate tendering knowledge and poor tendering practices can cause an endless flow of disputes among contracting parties. The tendering process, particularly in developing economies, may also be marred by corrupt practices leading to the selection of inexperienced and incompetent contractors that put the success of projects at risk (Chen & Wang, 2009; Van Thuyet et al., 2007). Kassem et al. (2020) summarises tendering and its related factors to include inadequate tendering capacity, lack of detailed specifications, unclear contract terms and conditions, and corruption. Tendering-related inefficiencies often lead to increased cost of procurement, poor quality of procured items, disputes, litigations, and judgement debt as well as time overruns. Resource and material supply risk has been described in the literature as a key procurement risk factor often causing delays in projects (Kassem et al., 2020). Materials-supply risks include, material cost fluctuations, poor quality of construction materials, delivery delays, shortage of modern equipment, as well as shortage and low productivity of labour.

Oil and gas projects in developing economies are confronted with numerous risk factors including procurement risks which threaten the successful execution of such projects. Procurement risks, if not effectively managed, can have negative consequences which may include excessive project costs due to cost overruns, recruitment of contractors lacking capacity and experience, poor quality of procured materials, lack of trust and confidence in the industry by stakeholders, and ultimately abandoned projects and underdeveloped oil and gas resources. Developing economies should, therefore, be aware of the enormous challenges presented by the procurement and supply chain function to this industry and build capacity to implement sustainable supply chain practices that create value for the citizenry.

6.4 Managing Procurement and Supply Chain Risks in the Oil and Gas Industry

Supply chain decisions such as selecting a supply chain partner, developing a supplier, outsourcing, designing procurement terms and conditions, etc., are embedded with risks. These risks, when not considered at the decision stage, can eventually revert to bite the firm. It is important that firms develop a good understanding of the strategies which can be employed to manage risks in order to make robust procurement and supply chain decisions. It must be emphasised that robust procurement decisions contribute not only to the profitability but also the sustainability of the oil and gas supply chain. Modarress et al. (2016) argue that there is increasing pressure on oil and gas supply chains to sustain their profits due to the frequent cases of oil price crashes since 2015. With this emerging industry trend, the need for managing supply chain risks becomes even more crucial in order to sustain production.

A key strategy for managing supply chain risks in the industry is the use of supplier risk intelligence. Building intelligence on supplier risk will involve the acquisition and analysis of supplier risks to provide an understanding of all potential risks; the development of sourcing and market strategy implementation; and empowerment of business to appropriately anticipate uncertainty from the market and adjust before competitors. Supplier risk intelligence is relevant to all operations including operations in the dynamic oil and gas industry (Johnsen et al., 2019).

Supply chain market intelligence is equally significant in decisions about market selection, determination of the right price, and the benchmarks which will enable the targeted competitive edge to be achieved (Manuj & Mentzer, 2008). Supply market intelligence empowers oil and gas firms to cope strategically with challenges in the supply chain. Companies are able to employ best-in-class supply chain risk mitigation practices to minimise the impact of risks. The first step is to gain an understanding of the supply chain with reference to the major categories of spend, identify costs and sourcing options for the categories of spend and determine appropriate interventions to mitigate risks.

Mapping the supply chain is another strategy to mitigate supply chain risks, particularly, where evidence of over-reliance on a country or concentration of sourcing from a geographic location exist (Johnsen et al., 2019). Mapping the supply chain involves excellent appreciation of supplier behaviour in addition to knowing the sources of components and parts. Firms which are good at supply chain mapping are better prepared when disruptions occur (Pagell & Shevchenko, 2014). When firms can anticipate the source of disruption, they become prepared to execute avoidance and mitigation strategies such as redirecting capacity to alternate sites, stocking inventory, and identifying alternative sources of supply.

Contract and supplier relationship management are frequently found not being up to the mark in the oil and gas industry, and hence firms assume supplier risks (Manuj & Mentzer, 2008). Improving supplier relationship management requires supply chain partners to employ the concept of supplier benchmarking. Firms must measure suppliers' performance for the different spend categories and continuously engage in dialogue to bring suppliers in unison with the necessary obligations in terms of training, safety, equipment, and staffing requirements (Hong et al., 2018; Pagell & Shevchenko, 2014).

The volatile market in the oil and gas industry exposes procurement to various types of uncertainties and risks. Hong et al. (2018) have classified these uncertainties and risks into disruption risks and operational risks. Disruption risk concerns the loss from an unexpected event resulting from a natural disaster, labour unrest, political instability, or equipment malfunction. Operational risk, on the other hand, refers to the probability of loss attributable to poor coordination of supply chain activities between chain partners. Following the classification, Hong et al. (2018) developed a framework (as presented in Figure 6.2) summarising the various procurement risks

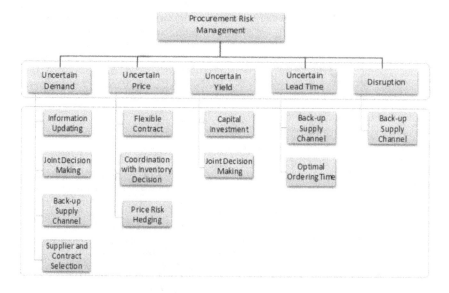

Figure 6.2 Procurement risk management framework
Source: Hong et al. (2018)

and the relevant strategies to manage them. Within the framework, the key risk factors in procurement and the accompanying strategies to deal with them have been highlighted. The framework is thus helpful in enabling supply chain managers to understand the scope of uncertainties which potentially confront the procurement and supply chain function and how managers can keep them under control.

6.5 Leveraging Supply Chain Efficiencies in the Oil and Gas Industry

Efficiency is one attractive performance objective in many industries as it contributes significantly to the profitability of the firm. Supply chain efficiency has been found to be a valuable source of competitive advantage (Anand & Grover, 2015; Salehzadeh et al., 2020). To maximise efficiency, the supply chain needs to be conceptualised as an integrated value-adding process with the objective of meeting the needs of the final customer. All supply chain partners, therefore, have a role to play in identifying and eliminating non-value-adding activities to achieve the target of improving the efficiency of the overall chain.

Organisational efficiency implies the ability of a firm to produce goods and services at a relatively low cost. By extension, for firms to be efficient, maximising resource usage and focusing on waste elimination will be essential activities towards reducing overall production cost. Organisational efficiency forms the basis of defining supply chain efficiency. Supply chain efficiency measures a firm's ability to get the right quality product to the right place at the right time at the least cost possible. Balocco et al. (2011) posit that efficiency strives for the maximisation of output using the minimum input possible. Thus, a supply chain is considered efficient when it can concurrently achieve the lowest possible cost and meet the customer's expectations on a product or service (Lam, 2018). Achieving supply chain efficiency calls for a sustained effort among supply chain partners emphasising resource and process maximisation through the elimination of all non-value-adding activities.

Oil and gas companies may exploit the value creation potential embedded in their supply chains to enhance their overall competitiveness. The value chains in the industry must not only focus on minimising the total cost of operations but also target customer responsiveness. Supply chains need to be both cost-led and service-led. Because of the risky nature of supply chains in the industry, the tendency exists for firms to focus much attention on avoiding or minimising risks rather than on using the supply chain to exploit opportunities for value generation (Anand & Grover, 2015)

Fierro Hernandez and Haddud (2018) state that it is paramount to coordinate efforts toward creating value by all stakeholders both external and internal, to achieve superior service solutions. In today's dynamic and competitive business environment, efficient supply chains are deemed to provide competitive advantage to firms. It must be emphasised, however, that efficient supply chains can increase the vulnerability of firms as the supply chain becomes highly stretched, bearing fewer buffers to mitigate potential disruptions (Lam, 2018; Modi & Mabert, 2010). Supply chain vulnerabilities could, however, be minimised with strategies that improve supply chain integration, collaboration, and visibility among network partners. Achieving efficiency in oil and gas supply chains involves attaining three major goals: strengthening supplier relationships, reducing production costs, and increasing sales (Manuj & Mentzer, 2008). Again, supply chain planning and automation as well as coordination among supply chain partners will engender efficiency both in service and quantity deliveries.

To leverage supply chain efficiency in the oil and gas industry, there must be a concerted effort to increase supply chain resilience and security with the hope of avoiding potential disruptions and price jumps due to friction between oil market players. Stability must become a primary interest for businesses. Furthermore, optimising supply chain performance provides an advantage for firms to substantially reduce cost and enhance performance (Negi, 2021). Managing the supply chain involves assuming an integrated view across a series of organisational processes. Integration should constitute a fundamental success factor in supply chain management and should happen both vertically and horizontally (Hashmi et al., 2020). Integrated processes need to be implemented in all phases of the supply chain. Quick access to information from many points of the supply chain is necessary to drive operations efficiently. Consequently, advanced IT solutions in oil and gas value chains become critically important in order to achieve integration and enhance greater supply chain visibility.

Increased cooperation and collaboration are typically demonstrated in integrated supply chains. Collaboration and cooperation happen both horizontally and vertically, as well as internally and externally. Manuj & Mentzer (2008) emphasise that cooperation must occur at all management levels involving cross-functional coordination across the supply chain. Close partner relationships are inevitable for undertaking supply chain activities in a cooperative way to improve efficiency.

In today's competitive business environment where competition has shifted from between firms to between supply chains. The performance of the supply chain has become a critical success factor for partners in the chain. It is paramount that supply chains leverage on efficiency practices to enhance the overall supply chain surplus. Negi (2021) proposes a supply chain efficiency framework (Figure 6.3) to improve the supply chain and overall business performance.

Negi's framework, made up of three components, prescribes the key metrics for achieving efficiency in supply chains. The components include defining supply chain efficiency, measures to achieve supply chain efficiency, and measures to assess results by way of improved supply chain efficiency outcomes. The integration of the three components solidifies the basis for supply chain performance improvement. The framework provides the approach

Procurement and Supply Chain Management 81

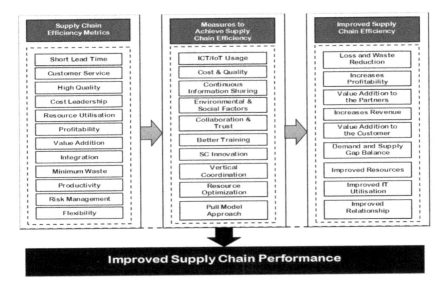

Figure 6.3 The supply chain efficiency framework
Source: Negi (2021)

which can be adopted by oil and gas firms to engineer supply chain efficiencies. The framework also forms the basis for measuring supply chain efficiency performance (Negi, 2021).

6.6 Sustainability Practices in Oil and Gas Supply Chains

Sustainability describes "the state of the global system, including environmental, social and economic aspects, in which the needs of the present generation are met without compromising the ability of future generations to meet their own needs" (ISO, 2017). The traditional parameters of supply chains are price, quality, and reliability. However, stakeholders' awareness and pressure have compelled firms to incorporate sustainability measures in their supply chain processes.

Pagell and Shevchenko (2014, p. 45) explained sustainable supply chain management as a firm's ability to "maintain economic viability while doing no harm to social or environmental systems." Sustainable supply chain management encompasses the sustainability features associated with the goods or services as well as the suppliers in the supply chain to contribute to sustainable development (Rentizelas et al., 2020). Sustainable supply chain management implies managing materials, information, and financial flow among supply chain partners in a way that the economic, environmental, and social objectives emerging from the customers' needs and demands of stakeholders are satisfied.

Sustainability is thus a notion denoting how firms can implement effective procedures and practices in their supply chains whilst exploiting the supply chain function to compel suppliers to embrace and employ sustainability processes directed at decreasing the economic, environmental, and social impacts of firms' actions. The implementation of sustainability concepts and practices guarantees the economic, environmental, and financial viability of the firm in both the short term and the long term. A firm devoted to sustainable supply chain practices will commit to producing a long-term strategy to acquire goods or services that will add value to its supply chain performance (Hashmi et al., 2020).

The characterisation of the global oil and gas supply chains provides a context for pursuing sustainable and ethical practices. The complex nature of these supply chains, coupled with the associated supply chain vulnerabilities and growing industry regulations, is putting pressure on firms in the industry to be more sustainable in their practices (Signori et al., 2015). Janus and Murphy (2013) state that firms are now required to disclose their effort and initiatives towards addressing sustainability issues in their internal and external supply chains. Naghi Beiranvand et al. (2021) argue that because oil and gas products are widely used in economic and social activities, the industry is particularly important for sustainability practices. Oil and gas is a high-risk industry where the smallest error could lead to drastic consequences on supply chain partners, their employees, society, and environment. This risk calls for firms in the industry to highly embrace sustainable supply chain practices.

Firms in the industry must develop and implement sustainability strategies taking into consideration constraints imposed by global supply chain decisions. The implementation of appropriate sustainability practices will result in "the integrated management of those specific supply chain risks that are related to the natural environment, the society and the viability of the firm" (Giannakis & Papadopoulos, 2016, p. 456). Oil and gas supply chain partners can employ mechanisms such as defining codes of conduct for suppliers' business operations, engage in collaboration with suppliers, and ensure supplier certification with ISO14001 (Agi & Nishant, 2017; Juettner et al., 2020). Ahmad et al. (2013) make the claim that oil and gas firms use supplier management and development strategy as proactive approaches aimed at equipping suppliers with managerial and technical skills with a view to improving sustainability in the supply chain.

According to Naghi Beiranvand et al. (2021), the sustainability performance of oil and gas supply chains can be measured using ten criteria, namely: financial performance, risk performance, operational performance, strategic performance, logistics performance, performance of communication and information technology, return performance, market performance, performance of internal structure, and performance of growth and innovation. Firms in the industry must, therefore, consistently ensure that their sustainability efforts are measured and improved in line with established sustainability performance dimensions.

6.7 Conclusion

This chapter has amply demonstrated the value and the practical relevance of effectively managing the procurement and supply chain function. It provides a detailed exposition of the nature of the oil and gas supply chains after and an analysis of procurement as a critical risk factor in oil and gas projects. It has also examined how procurement and supply chain risks can be managed in the oil and gas industry and further explored the avenues for leveraging supply chain efficiencies in the oil and gas industry. Finally, it discusses sustainability concerns in the oil and gas supply chains.

The insights provided were focused on how the expertise in procurement and supply chain management could be leveraged to optimise sustainable procurement and supply chain performance in the oil and gas industry. The chapter provides the theoretical foundations and best practices supporting excellence in oil and gas supply chain management. It concludes that to achieve sustainability management in the oil and gas industry within the context of emerging and developing economies, the management of the procurement and supply chain function is undeniably a fundamental success factor.

References

Agi, M. A. N., & Nishant, R. (2017). Understanding influential factors on implementing green supply chain management practices: An interpretive structural modelling analysis. *Journal of Environmental Management, 188*, 351–363.

Ahmad, S. A., Issa, U. H., Farag, M. A., & Abdelhafez, L. M. (2013). Evaluation of risk factors affecting time and cost of construction projects in Yemen. *International Journal of Management, 4*(5), 168–178.

Anand, N., & Grover, N. (2015). Measuring retail supply chain performance: Theoretical model using key performance indicators (KPIs). *Benchmarking: An International Journal, 22*(1), 135–166.

Balocco, R., Miragliotta, G., Perego, A., & Tumino, A. (2011). RFID adoption in the FMCG supply chain: An interpretative framework. *Supply Chain Management: An International Journal, 16*, 299–316.

Camilleri, M. A. (2017). The rationale for responsible supply chain management and stakeholder engagement. *Journal of Global Responsibility, 8*(1), 111–126.

Chen, P., & Wang, J. (2009). Application of a fuzzy AHP method to risk assessment of international construction projects, *Proceedings – 2009 International Conference on Electronic Commerce and Business Intelligence*, pp. 459–462.

Christopher M. C. (2007). Supply-chain management issues in the oil and gas industry. *Journal of Business & Economics Research, 5*. California State University, Dominguez Hills.

Fernandes, L. J. A. P. & Barbosa-Povoa, S. R. (2009). Risk management in petroleum supply chain. In A. P. Barbosa-Povoa, & M. I. Selana (Eds.), *Proceedings of the 14th Congress of APDIO, Vencer Novos Desafios nos Transportes e Mobilidade*, pp. 55–66.

Fierro Hernandez, D., & Haddud, A. (2018). Value creation via supply chain risk management in global fashion organizations outsourcing production to China. *Journal of Global Operations and Strategic Sourcing, 11*(2), 250–272.

Giannakis, M., & Papadopoulos, T. (2016). Supply chain sustainability: A risk management approach. *International Journal of Production Economics, 171*, 455–470.

Hashmi, M. H. A., Khan, M., & Ajmal, M. M. (2020). The impact of internal and external factors on sustainable procurement: A case study of oil and gas companies. *International Journal of Procurement Management, 13*(1), 42–62.

Hong, Z., Lee, C. K. M., & Zhang, L. (2018). Procurement risk management under uncertainty: A review. *In Industrial Management and Data Systems, 118*(7), 1547–1574.

Hussain, R., Assavapokee, T., & Khumawala, B. (2006). Supply chain management in the petroleum industry: Challenges and opportunities. *International Journal of Global Logistics & Supply Chain Management, 1*(2), 90–97.

ISO (2017). Sustainable Procurement—Guidance, ISO 20400: 2017.

Janus, B., & Murphy, H. (2013). Sustainability reporting and the oil and gas industry-challenges and emerging trends. *SPE European HSE Conference and Exhibition-Health, Safety, Environment and Social Responsibility in the Oil&Gas Exploration*, Amsterdam, 27–29 October.

Johnsen, T. E., Mikkelsen, O. S., & Wong, C. Y. (2019). Strategies for complex supply networks: Findings from the offshore wind power industry. *Supply Chain Management, 24*(6), 872–886.

Juettner, U., Windler, K., Podleisek, A., Gander, M., & Meldau, S. (2020). Implementing supplier management strategies for supply chain sustainability risks in multinational companies. *TQM Journal, 32*(5), 923–938.

Kassem, M., Khoiry, M. A., & Hamzah, N. (2020). Theoretical review on critical risk factors in oil and gas construction projects in Yemen. *Engineering, Construction and Architectural Management, 28*(4), 934–968.

Lam, H. K. S. (2018). Doing good across organizational boundaries: Sustainable supply chain practices and firms' financial risk. *International Journal of Operations and Production Management, 38*(12), 2389–2412.

Manuj, I. & Mentzer, J.T. (2008). Global supply chain risk management strategies. *International journal of Physical Distribution and Logistics Management, 38*(3), 192–233.

Manuj, I., & Sahin, F. (2011). A model of supply chain and supply chain decision-making complexity. *International Journal of Physical Distribution & Logistics Management, 41*(5), 511–549.

Modarress, B., Ansari, A., & Thies, E. (2016). Outsourcing in the Persian Gulf petroleum supply chain. *Strategic Outsourcing, 9*(1), 2–21.

Modi, S. B., & Mabert, V. A. (2010). Exploring the relationship between efficient supply chain management and firm innovation: An archival search and analysis. *Journal of Supply Chain Management, 46*(4), 81–94.

Naghi Beiranvand, D., Jamali Firouzabadi, K., & Dorniani, S. (2021). A model of service supply chain sustainability assessment using fuzzy methods and factor analysis in oil and gas industry. *Journal of Modelling in Management, 18*, 117–146. https://doi.org/10.1108/JM2-01-2021-0010

Negi, S. (2021). Supply chain efficiency framework to improve business performance in a competitive era. *Management Research Review, 44*(3), 477–508.

Pagell, M., & Shevchenko, A. (2014). Why research in sustainable supply chain management should have no future. *Journal of Supply Chain Management, 50*(1), 44–55.

Rentizelas, A., de Sousa Jabbour, A. B. L., Al Balushi, A. D., & Tuni, A. (2020). Social sustainability in the oil and gas industry: Institutional pressure and the management of sustainable supply chains. *Annals of Operations Research, 290*(1), 279–300.

Salehzadeh, R., Tabaeeian, R. A., & Esteki, F. (2020). Exploring the consequences of judgmental and quantitative forecasting on firms' competitive performance in supply chains. *Benchmarking: An International Journal, 27*(5), 1717–1737.

Shqairat, A., & Sundarakani, B. (2018). An empirical study of oil and gas value chain agility in the UAE. *Benchmarking, 25*(9), 3541–3569.

Signori, P., Flint, D. J., & Golicic, S. (2015). Toward sustainable supply chain orientation (SSCO): Mapping managerial perspectives. *International Journal of Physical Distribution and Logistics Management, 45*(6), 536–564.

Van Thuyet, N., Ogunlana, S. O., & Dey, P. K. (2007). Risk management in oil and gas construction projects in Vietnam. *International Journal of Energy Sector Management, 1*(2), 175–194.

Yusuf, Y., Gunasekaran, A., Papadopoulos, T., Auchterlounie, W., Hollomah, D., & Menhat, M. (2018). Performance measurement in the natural gas industry: A case study of Ghana's natural gas supply chain. *Benchmarking, 25*(8), 2913–2930.

Yusuf, Y. Y., Musa, A., Dauda, M., El-Berishy, N., Kovvuri, D., & Abubakar, T. (2014). A study of the diffusion of agility and cluster competitiveness in the oil and gas supply chains. *International Journal of Production Economics, 147*(Part B), 498–513.

7 Digital Technology and Innovations in the Oil and Gas Industry

Eric Afful-Dadzie, Emmanuel Awuni Kolog, John Effah, Vincent Omwenga, and Sulemana B. Egala

7.1 Introduction

Digital technologies and innovations have traversed every facet of the economy including banking and finance sectors, healthcare sector, extractive sector, and energy sector. The energy sector, in recent years, has seen tremendous improvements in its innovativeness aimed at improving business processes and operations, as well as reducing risk and uncertainties in the exploration, development, production, and sale of its products. As one of the largest global economic sectors in terms of value, the oil and gas (O&G) industry generates about $3.3 trillion in revenue.[1] However, key industry actors in the value chain, namely the upstream, midstream, and downstream, have been beset with several challenges, including increasing production costs, market fluctuations (demand and supply), and oil spillage (Abudu & Sai, 2020; Inkpen & Moffett, 2011). For instance, Forbes reports that many investors are fleeing the industry due to their inability to demonstrate deferential and cash flows.[2] The exigencies of the COVID-19 pandemic augmented this trend as a result of the disruptions in the O&G value chain with reductions in exploration and production supply. As a remedy, key stakeholders in the O&G industry continue to pursue the development and deployment of digital and other innovative technologies to mitigate the effect of uncertainties in the industry. Consequently, several cutting-edge technologies are being deployed by O&G companies in pursuit of optimising the efficiency of every aspect of the O&G supply and value chain. Artificial intelligence (AI), 3D printing, big data analytics, drone technologies, process automation, and robotics are among the technologies that are paving the way for innovation in the industry.

Oil and Gas management encompasses a series of processes and activities undertaken to plan, organise, direct, coordinate, control and to harmonise and harness physical, financial, and human resources in its value chain. O&G management processes are a collection of activities aimed at making the most efficient and most effective use of resources in order to improve the exploration, development, production, and sale of O&G. Key to management effectiveness is the deployment of digital technologies and innovations to boost

DOI: 10.4324/9781003309864-9

capital productivity. For instance, the digitalisation of routine management tasks and processes using advanced analytics and agile methodologies significantly improves productivity. It must be noted that O&G projects differ in scope and purpose and, therefore, simply digitalising O&G processes does not necessarily guarantee a desired result. Every new project presents a set of opportunities and challenges as well as a new learning curve that either affords or presents the opportunity for enhanced performance (Hamilton et al., 2019). Therefore, it is necessary to implement a vast array of management practices and technologies to enhance the capital-intensive performance of O&G projects.

This desk review, seized with the socio-ecological fabric of the O&G industry and its attendant innovations, provides an empirically grounded and realistic assessment of the sector's technological advances over the decade. It focuses on how digital technologies and innovations are constantly impelling management of the O&G industry forward, while taking cognisance of the new socio-technical, health, and environmental challenges and opportunities they present. Thus, the review explores the technological trends, including digital innovations and challenges in the O&G industry. In the following sections, it discusses existing technological trends in the O&G industry, technology convergence in the sector, policy, and innovation strategies as well as challenges and opportunities. The chapter finally offers conclusions and recommendations.

7.2 Technological Trends in the Oil and Gas Industry

Innovation has always been a driving force in the O&G industry. Given that the O&G industry is noted for its conservatism when it comes to innovation, technological trends in the industry in the last few decades have not been widespread, even though there have been significant gains in improving business processes in the value chain. In the past, oil field discoveries prompted by reflection seismography, which revolutionised petroleum exploration in the 1920s, led to high levels of daily oil production. The invention of fluid catalytic cracking to improve refining in 1937 contributed to the creation of the majority of the world's gasoline supply. Recently, horizontal drilling and hydraulic fracturing, also known as "fracking," have enabled the commercial exploitation of unconventional O&G deposits that were previously uneconomical (Evensen et al., 2020). For instance, a Price Waterhouse Coopers (PWC) innovation survey reports that wells in the Permian Basin were no longer pumping until the introduction of fracking, creating a resurgence of production over the years (Hurley & Hunter, 2013). This advanced horizontal drilling technique enabled the drilling of multiple wells from a single site, thereby increasing productivity and reducing the geographic footprint of the sector (Idachaba, 2012). In the following section, we review some existing technologies that are revolutionising or can revolutionalise the O&G industry if explored.

7.2.1 Artificial Intelligence and Robotic Process Automation

The commercialisation of AI and robotic process automation (RPA) is reported to have evolved in the 1970s (Li et al., 2021), although this adventure was long explored by researchers in the industry (Ben et al., 2019). The process brought some momentum into the O&G industry following the latter's transition into the O&G 4.0 concept using advanced digital technologies and innovations as its core focus. The paradox of recovering O&G reserves/wells, geometrical setbacks, and uncertainty in return on investment (ROI) necessitated an unconventional operational approach and business models in the O&G value chain. Consequent to this, computing and technological resources centred on risk control, sustainable development, and quality O&G are used by leveraging the capabilities of AI and RPA innovations.

AI has been utilised extensively in oilfield development, including oilfield production dynamic prediction, plan optimisation, residual oil identification, fracture identification, and improved extraction of oil (Li et al., 2021). The use of AI in the O&G industry is advancing rapidly as the concept of AI steadily permeates numerous aspects of the industry. Intelligent drilling, intelligent prediction, intelligent production, intelligent pipeline, and intelligent refinery are classic examples of its application. Using AI algorithms, developers have created a variety of useful application technologies for exploration and development. The use of techniques such as artificial neural networks (ANNs) has already demonstrated promising results in reducing exploration risks and increasing exploration well success rates (Giuliani et al., 2019).

Innovative drilling equipment, such as autonomous drilling rigs and intelligent drill pipes, has drastically improved drilling quality while simultaneously reducing costs. The primary application of AI technology in oilfield development is to optimise the development plan based on oilfield output history (Giuliani et al., 2020). Moreover, AI provides a more precise method for designing fracturing schemes and selecting operating wells and target layers. The most important goal in O&G development is to predict future development based on existing data and to create a reasonable development plan. To allow further numerical simulation prior to prediction, it is necessary to match historical data. Due to the complexity of actual oilfield development, multiple elements interact simultaneously, making it more difficult to match historical data with conventional methods. With the advancement of AI, it has been demonstrated that neural networks may be used to match oilfield development history (Giuliani et al., 2020).

Another way of transforming the O&G industry to watershed the issues of error-prone manual operations into a wholly digitised enterprise is the use of RPA. Using this technology reinforces intelligent processing automation and workflow automation. With this tool, repetitive, mundane, and high-volume tasks are performed to boost capabilities and save time and cost. RPA has the potential to make up for many of the mistakes of the past by completing unnecessarily time-consuming tasks in a cost-effective manner. Obviously, RPA is capable of increasing the consumption of infrastructure onsite or cloud-enabling seamless processes, enhancing reliability and resilience to improve business processes in the industry. RPA helps to eliminate inefficient processes, streamline those that remain, and create value in new and better ways.

7.2.2 Big Data Analytics

Big data analytics is the practice of gathering, evaluating, cleaning, manipulating, modelling, and integrating raw data to generate actionable insights for enhanced decision-making. The O&G industry generates large amounts of both structured (temperature and pressure) and unstructured (video recordings) data that is never used. With the rise of big data, all of that data can finally be put to use once it has been analysed. The increasing volume, velocity, and variety of data generated by the O&G firms makes it daunting to manually process them for operational decision-making (Kakate, 2020). A few of such industry data includes, drilling data, maintenance data, 3D seismic surveys, safety data, production control, and monitoring data. The administration and analysis of these data have created unique hurdles for businesses in the sector.

The O&G industry's key innovation push has been to analyse these massive amounts of data, with a specific focus on enhancing exploration, development, production, and safety efficiencies. Big data analytics is crucial in operational areas such as exploration, drilling, reservoir engineering, and production. Predictive maintenance, smart drilling, and smart oilfields all use analytics to increase the profitability of extracted barrels. For instance, deep learning, which is the product of ANN, has emerged and is currently advancing the O&G sector. The algorithm, when implemented, has the capability to select data from the environment and make its own decisions. With deep learning algorithms, any fault that emerges in the process of drilling and exploring oil could be automatically rather than manually addressed. This has so far been touted progressively in the maintenance practices in the O&G field.

Big data analytics enables targeted oil exploration by analysing geologic data to determine the optimal drilling locations and well configurations. An intelligent hydrate platform enables the digital transformation of the oilfield by providing intelligent, real-time management of gas hydrates (Evensen et al., 2020). The precision of this data is beneficial to operational delivery and real-time efficiencies across the industry. They also help to accelerate data-driven innovations and improve the health-and-safety environment through incident reporting to identifying high-risk situations. O&G companies make use of these insights to ensure that potentially dangerous situations do not arise again.

7.2.3 Blockchain Technology

Blockchain technology and its potential applications are gradually being deployed in the O&G industry. The blockchain is a distributed, decentralised ledger that tracks the history of digital assets. Peer-to-peer transmission and encryption are all part of the system, as is distributed data storage. One of the most significant aspects of blockchain technology is the fact that transactions are distributed rather than being recorded in a single database. As a result, blockchain data cannot be changed, making it a real disruptor in most industries like finance, cybersecurity, healthcare, and O&G (Lu et al., 2019).

In O&G management, blockchain technology is primarily used for trading, management and decision-making, supervision, and cybersecurity (Cann & Catmur, 2017). With regards to trading, the multifaceted nature of the O&G value chain (exploration, development, processing, and sale) requires several contracting and transactional processes. Specifically, smart contracting is a computer-mediated contract where records are stored in computer language instead of legal language. A typical example is Ethereum, which supports the development of the smart contract. The Ethereum virtual machine receives transaction requests and generates new transaction requests and events from outsiders. Users can access a transactional ledger, but once has been confirmed, it cannot be changed or forged. Smart contracts cut down on the number of manual steps in the contracting process. This makes the process easier, cheaper, and more efficient. Blockchaining aids in expediting cross-border payment in the sale of large quantities of O&G using cryptographic currency such as Bitcoin and Ethereum. Blockchain uses in O&G transaction processes reduce the time required for intermediaries and verification for liquidity in the sector (Lu et al., 2019).

Furthermore, before doing exploration, development, and other activity in the O&G industry, firms must obtain land use rights. Understanding the origins of the land/sea might be challenging because of the multiple records of ownership and disputes in a distinct database. Thus, land acquisitions and transactions are extremely vulnerable to fraud, and therefore land mobility, value, and ownership may all be tracked using blockchain technology. Ownership loss or mismatch and possible ownership disputes would be reduced, and tax authorities would have a real-time record of the exact transfer of value in land transactions (Liang et al., 2017).

7.2.4 Remote Sensing and Internet of Things

The term "Internet of Things" refers to physical objects that are equipped with sensors, processors, software, and other technologies that connect and exchange data with other devices and systems over the Internet or other communications networks. Remote sensing relies heavily on the physical devices that house the sensors. In the O&G industry, remote sensing has a lot to offer. Remote sensing has proven to be an essential tool for downstream and upstream O&G operations through infrastructure evaluation for well-site design and exploration through large-scale regional reconnaissance. The upstream and downstream applications of remote sensing include pipeline mapping, wellsite planning, and the detection of environmental change.

High-resolution visual data sets like WorldView or RapidEye, as well as radar and multispectral/hyperspectral data sets, have been extensively used in O&G exploration (Lord, 2017).

O&G exploration was hindered in the past by factors such as low spatial and spectral resolution of data sources. Remote spectral analysis, on the other hand, has alleviated some of these issues. The hydrocarbon system beneath the Earth's surface can be better understood through spectral analysis, which can reveal and map potential geologic structures (Yakymchuk & Korchagin, 2019). For instance, surface impediments, such as extensive forests, have historically hampered the discovery of geologic faults that might otherwise be visible. Remote sensors calculate multiple returns from an active laser scanner hundreds of times per second, resulting in a 3-D image of the ground. Scanner pulses may be reflected by a tree or other obstruction, or they may find their way to the ground, revealing previously undetected defects. The technology of remote sensing is used for high-resolution surface modelling to supplement ground surveys, temporal analysis to identify surface changes over time before they become hazards, feature identification for infrastructure mapping, and hydrologic modelling to reduce flooding around oilfields.

7.2.5 Printing Technology

In its broadest meaning, 3D printing refers to the use of additive manufacturing to build three-dimensional items. Bits of thin material are added layer by layer in additive manufacturing to construct the desired physical 3D product. Although 3D printers have existed since the 1980s, the technology has only recently demonstrated the potential to become a game-changing innovation (Amundrud, 2017). The popularity of 3D printing has risen as a result of companies that have lately made them publicly available at low pricing. Modern 3D printers come in a variety of sizes and price points, ranging from industrial to desktop. Objects can be printed in several materials, with the most common being plastics and metals (including alloys). 3D printers do not yet have the speed or cost-effectiveness to compete with traditional mass-production methods. However, for low-volume customer-specific products, its capacity to manufacture bespoke items with fewer supply chain processes is ideal (Al Tartoor et al., 2020). Because specialised components and tools are so ubiquitous in the O&G business, 3D printing comes as a huge help. Also, given that 3D printing can make parts on demand, it may be able to eliminate the requirement to stock spare parts.

7.2.6 Internet of Things and Electronic Monitoring

Electronics, software, sensors, and network connections can be embedded in practically any device, including wearable gadgets, automobiles, equipment, and buildings. With the ability to send data without human intervention, previously unimaginable amounts of data can be captured and shared with other devices or via a central platform. Smart O&G companies are increasingly focusing their Internet of Things (IoT) projects on inventing novel data management techniques, utilising IoT infrastructure, and developing new business models, as opposed to focusing solely on automation. IoT can be used to optimise upstream and downstream activities in the O&G industry (Wanasinghe et al., 2020). For instance, IoT can enable wellheads and pump stations to be signed online or remotely. Remote-controlled drilling tools do not only get the work done; they gather troves of data along the way to be sent back to the company's central system to improve decision-making. Using sensors to monitor inventory levels of onshore oil tanks, automatically dispatch trucks when the tanks need to be emptied and provide alerts to maintenance teams on the performance of above-ground pumps in order to prevent fatalities, are additional applications of IoT in the O&G industry. In addition, IoT could incorporate cloud-based digital dashboard visualisations and communicate information in a manner that facilitates proper decision-making. IoT is said to alleviate the apparent complexities in well drilling and workforce shortage by enabling automation and remote operations. Ultimately, safety is increased and time spent on operational activities on each site is reduced (Priyadarshy, 2017).

7.2.7 Drone Technology

Some of the obvious challenges in the O&G industry have mainly been environmental, safety, and security issues. Key to stemming the rising impact of these challenges is regular inspection and maintenance of oilfield infrastructure. In the past, O&G asset inspection was undertaken by humans, which came with its inherent risks (Sow, 2018). For instance, the conventional approach for performing inspection of storage tanks, cooling towers, flare stacks, and boilers was performed using scaffolds and helicopters. The challenge that faces this conventional method is that it could lead to fatalities, and in some cases, it came with some financial burdens due to plant shutdowns. Deloitte consulting reports that the global O&G industry spends about $37 billion a year on monitoring nearly 10 million kilometres of pipelines.[3] Following this, several autonomous aerial navigation technologies have been launched to help stem the cost of operations and maintenance of infrastructure. Drone technology is currently being used for the inspection, maintenance, and repair operations on oilfields with increased efficiency and less risk (Sudevan et al., 2018).

7.3 Technology Convergence, Policy, and Innovation Strategies

Technology convergence is the fusion of two or more distinct technologies to form an entirely new converged technology. Convergent technologies are characterised by: (1) performing a hybrid purpose through the performance of multiple functions, (2) gathering and processing data in a variety of formats, as well as leveraging machine learning techniques to improve the user experience, and (3) directly connecting to a network and/or integrating with other devices to provide consumers with ubiquitous access. In the O&G industry, technology convergence encompasses a wide range of technologies including AI, big data analytics, intelligent process automation, IoT, and smart home/office devices. The convergence of these technologies replaces single-function technologies or even renders them redundant. Digitisation trends and automation technologies have the potential to greatly increase process efficiency and O&G plant efficiency. This is due to their capacity to run operations seamlessly and enable informed decision-making through data analysis employing a converged system. The O&G industry has relied on conventional technologies such as fixed-wing planes and a human crew to monitor operations. However, because human inspection is prone to error, this does not provide for precise monitoring. Inspection of hazardous and crowded locations is likewise becoming more challenging. As a result, the O&G business now needs to adopt disruptive technologies.

Given the exogenous nature of the O&G value chain, technology convergence alone may not provide the necessary impetus to propel the industry to the desired status due to some infringement on firms' value proposition. This phenomenon thus requires O&G firms to adopt an innovative strategy. As O&G firms strike for innovative strategic positioning within an existing disparate technological system, it may be punctured by the emergent implications of the convergence phenomena. Understanding the convergence technologies from such a sequential and chronological standpoint may give a foundation for developing firm-specific innovative strategies and operationalising convergence-oriented activities into improved operational processes in the industry. Note that the transition from standalone to a strategic technological convergence requires the establishment of dependencies between the various segmented technologies. These dependencies are not just about developing products in the industry, but also about creating a web of processes, technologies, transportation and storage, supply chain, knowledge management, and capital project delivery across all segments. O&G firms can create a web of interlocked assets through a convergence of technology and innovative strategy that encourages collaboration. Contrary to creating and running an individual parallel infrastructure, O&G firms can form alliances, share data, and technology infrastructure through innovative strategies.

While ensuring O&G laws and regulations are complied with, there is the need to ensure compliance with the laws pertaining to the existing technologies in the O&G industries. For instance, the Data Protection Act 2012 and the Cybersecurity Act 2020 in Ghana are intended to ensure data security and privacy protection. Additionally, policies are essential to guide behaviour especially when IT technology is concerned. The sector is obliged to develop policies that pertain to their environment in order to guide behavioural use of IT.

7.4 Challenges and Opportunities of Digital Technology in Oil and Gas Industry

7.4.1 Challenges

A PwC innovation survey noted that most O&G companies found some aspects of innovation challenging. Top among these challenges were measurement, talent, and finding the right partners.

7.4.1.1 Challenges of Measuring IT Critical Success Factors

Most organisations find it challenging to identify the reasonable metrics as a benchmark to established ICT standards. Process automation and AI adoption in the O&G industry, for example, have the potential to overcome many of the challenges of the past by completing tedious tasks in an extremely cost-effective manner. Nonetheless, it has been argued that the success of innovation is better measured through the financial lens. For instance, ROI may be the basis upon which O&G firms gauge their innovation successes. However, this process may be misguided since key critical success factors are not necessarily contingent on financial gains. The absence of standardised measure of innovation success has culminated in the development of several disparate KPI's and approaches by individual firms.

7.4.1.2 Talent Acquisition and Management Challenge

In a broader sense, finding skilled innovators with novel ideas for technology convergence on board O&G projects poses a challenge. Demographics also play a major role in the talent drain in the sector due to the constant retirement of researchers and engineers without a commensurate number of graduates enrolling into the realm of petrochemical and allied O&G disciplines to fill the gaps. The spillover is a brain drain in the sector, thus hampering continuity. The value of well-documented and efficient processes will be lost in the event of a business continuity crisis, forcing business teams to rely on manual transaction processing.

7.4.1.3 Finding the Right Collaboration

In the contemporary business realm, innovation does not just depend on how smart people are, but how smart people are able to connect with other smart people. External collaborations have huge prospects, but identifying the right partner is a herculean task. This challenge hampers innovative strategies in the O&G firms. Additionally, the capabilities of convergent technologies in the industry such as analytics – which enable predictive maintenance, smart drilling, and smart oilfields to drive profitability on extracted barrels – have evolved. The shift from organisational centricity, in which O&G firms determine what to produce, to individual centricity, in which tech-savvy stakeholders expect personalised involvement, necessitates a fundamental adjustment in the inventive approach.

7.4.1.4 Regulatory, Data, and Digital Privacy Challenge

As a result of technological convergence, which allows for increased data consumption and acquisition, stakeholders may be concerned about their digital privacy. Because a single piece or aggregation of data can be used to identify, locate, track, and monitor oilfields remotely, data collection and use in the O&G business are tied to digital privacy problems. Concerns concerning digital privacy will become more apparent as convergence technologies become more widely adopted.

7.4.2 Opportunities

Amid the challenges brought forth by the innovative drive, several opportunities are also presented to O&G firms. Note that, although too much innovation can be a drain on resources in the O&G industry, the reverse may well be catastrophic because opportunities lost may not be regained especially when competition is confronted. Naturally, not all innovation processes pay off, yet taking the risk and turning them into opportunities may be a breakthrough to a radical change.

There is a compelling opportunity to reduce risk and enhance transactional values and economic pressures to reduce costs by using converged technologies. Companies in the O&G industry may be interested in a low-cost, high-speed, secure convergent innovative system that reduces costs while increasing transparency, providing an audit trail, and speeding up transactions. The phenomenon presents an opportunity to the players in the industry to develop a comprehensive and standardised instrument to measure the effectiveness of innovation successes. Following this, the continuous acquisition and utilisation of data that creates privacy issues open an avenue to formulate data protection regulations specific to data use in the sector.

Further, O&G firms stand to gain high pay-offs if executives project the culture of innovation beyond the C-suit by allowing all employees to participate in high-profile projects and recognise people's efforts. This will help retain talented employees and minimise the brain drain in the industry. In doing so, collaborations among a diverse range of partners, including strategic partners, academia, research institutions, and digital start-ups, have to be elevated. A typical opportunity is the collaboration between total and the French robotic engineering firm Cybernetix in the development of an inspection, maintenance, repair (IMR) system called SWIMMER.[4] The subsea IMR system is capable of staying underwater for three months within a range of 50 km.

7.5 Conclusion

The fourth industrial revolution, also known as 'industry 4.0'", introduces a variety of digital technologies that have the potential to transform the entire industrial and social landscape. This transformation will impact the energy sector, specifically the O&G industries. According to the International Energy Agency's (IEA) Sustainable Development agenda, the industry will continue to play a vital role in meeting the world's energy needs until 2040, accounting for nearly half of the primary energy mix. On top of this, businesses continue to make hydrocarbons more affordable, reliable, environmentally friendly, and accessible to as many individuals as possible. Yet, the prevailing challenges in the O&G industry including health, environmental, and security issues have festered, thus hampering the attainment of these goals. Nonetheless, the past decades have seen a renaissance of digital technologies and innovations (e.g., AI, IoT, big data analytics, RPA, and drones) and a convergence of technologies to mitigate the ever-growing number of constraints. The innovative trajectory has brought about some challenges to the O&G firms, particularly the drain on resources and the inability to measure the successes of these innovations. Yet, with unwavering commitment, consolidation of these weaknesses could be turned into a competitive advantage.

Notes

1 https://www.ibisworld.com/global/market-research-reports/global-oil-gas-exploration-production-industry/
2 https://www.forbes.com/sites/uhenergy/2021/03/10/challenges-and-trends-for-the-oil-and-gas-industry/?sh=2d48b948167f
3 https://www.enr.com/articles/41865-canadian-company-proposes-to-cut-pipeline-monitoring-costs-with-automated-drones
4 http://total.com/en/energies-expertise/oil-gas/exploration-production/strategic-sectors/deep-offshore/ innovation/preparing-aging-facilities

References

Abudu, H., & Sai, R. (2020). Examining prospects and challenges of Ghana's petroleum industry: A systematic review. *Energy Reports*, 6(2), 841–858.

Al Tartoor, Y., Khalaf, A., & Awadallah, M. (2020). Adaptive framework for resilient supply chain using 3D printing in oil and gas industry. *Abu Dhabi International Petroleum Exhibition & Conference*.

Amundrud, P. N. (2017). *Opportunities for automation, internet of things, big data analytics and 3D printing within oil and gas drilling, production and transport*. University of Stavanger.

Ben, M., Holmas, H., Santamarta, S., & Forbes, P. (2019). Going digital is hard for oil and gas companies—but the payoff is worth it. In *Bcg* (pp. 1–13). bcg. https://www.bcg.com/publications/2019/digital-value-oil-gas.aspx

Cann, G. & Catmur, E. (2017). Blockchain: Overview of the potential applications for the oil and gas market and the related taxation implications. *Deloitte*. https://www2.deloitte.com/content/dam/Deloitte/global/Documents/Energy-and-Resources/gx-oil-gas-blockchain-article.pdf

Evensen, O., Womack, D., & Spencer, L. (2020). Essential tactics to foster innovation in oil and gas. *Research Insights*, *1*, 1–18. https://www.ibm.com/downloads/cas/VOJ540GZ

Giuliani, M., Cadei, L., Montini, M., Bianco, A., Grimaccia, F., Mussetta, M., & Niccolai, A. (2020). Hybrid artificial intelligence techniques for automatic simulation models matching with field data and constrained production optimization. *International Petroleum Technology Conference 2020, IPTC 2020*. https://doi.org/10.2523/iptc-19621-abstract

Giuliani, M., Cadei, L., Montini, M., Bianco, A., Niccolai, A., Mussetta, M., & Grimaccia, F. (2019). Hybrid artificial intelligence techniques for automatic simulation models matching with field data. *Society of Petroleum Engineers - Abu Dhabi International Petroleum Exhibition and Conference 2018, ADIPEC 2018*. https://doi.org/10.2118/193080-ms

Hamilton, A., Koelman, J., & Vermeltfoort, K. (2019). Improving oil and gas project management | McKinsey. *McKinsey&Company*. https://www.mckinsey.com/industries/oil-and-gas/our-insights/how-the-oil-and-gas-industry-can-improve-capital-project-performance

Hurley, M., & Hunter, R. (2013). Gateway to growth: Innovation in the oil and gas industry. *PWC*, 1–18. https://www.pwc.com/gx/en/oil-gas-energy/publications/pdfs/pwc-gateway-to-growth-innovation-in-the-oil-and-gas-industry.pdf

Idachaba, F. (2012). Current trends and technologies in the oil and gas industry. *International Journal of Emerging Technology and Advanced Engineering*, *2*(7), 5–8.

Inkpen, A., & Moffett, M. H. (2011). *The global oil & gas industry: Management, strategy and finance*. PennWell Books, LLC.

Kakate, E. (2020). Information technology: A sustainable competitive advantage trend in Nigerian oil and gas industry. *International Journal of Business & Law Research*, *8*(3), 100–108.

Li, H., Yu, H., Cao, N., Tian, H., & Cheng, S. (2021). Applications of artificial intelligence in oil and gas development. *Archives of Computational Methods in Engineering*, *28*(3), 937–949. https://doi.org/10.1007/s11831-020-09402-8

Liang, X., Shetty, S., Tosh, D., Kamhoua, C., Kwiat, K., & Njilla, L. (2017). ProvChain: A blockchain-based data provenance architecture in cloud environment with enhanced privacy and availability. *Proceedings—2017 17th IEEE/ACM International Symposium on Cluster, Cloud and Grid Computing, CCGRID 2017*, 468–477. https://doi.org/10.1109/CCGRID.2017.8

Lord, B. (2017). Remote sensing techniques for onshore oil and gas exploration. *Leading Edge*, *36*(1), 24–32. https://doi.org/10.1190/tle36010024.1

Lu, H., Huang, K., Azimi, M., & Guo, L. (2019). Blockchain technology in the oil and gas industry: A review of applications, opportunities, challenges, and risks. *IEEE Access*, *7*, 41426–41444. https://doi.org/10.1109/ACCESS.2019.2907695

Priyadarshy, S. (2017). IoT revolution in oil and gas industry. In *Internet of things and data analytics handbook*, IEEE, 513–520. https://doi.org/10.1002/9781119173601.ch31

Sow, P. (2018). *The Use of Drones in the Oil and Gas Industry: A 4.0 Contract 1, 2 Penda Sow*. *VII*(Xii), 1–14.

Sudevan, V., Shukla, A., & Karki, H. (2018). Current and future research focus on inspection of vertical structures in oil and gas industry. *International Conference on Control, Automation and Systems*, *2018-October*, 144–149.

Wanasinghe, T. R., Gosine, R. G., James, L. A., Mann, G. K. I., De Silva, O., & Warrian, P. J. (2020). The internet of things in the oil and gas industry: A systematic review. *IEEE Internet of Things Journal*, 7(9), 8654–8673. https://doi.org/10.1109/JIOT.2020.2995617

Yakymchuk, N. A., & Korchagin, I. N. (2019). Technology of frequency-resonance processing of remote sensing data: Results of practical approbation during mineral searching in various regions of the globe. *Part I. Geoinformatika*, *3*, 29–51.

8 Oil and Gas Project Management

Kwasi Dartey-Baah, Saviour Ayertey Nubuor, Paul Gbahabo, and Kwesi Amponsah-Tawiah

8.1 Introduction

Projects are becoming increasingly common in various aspects of human endeavour. Project-based models of work have found their way into large and small commercial entities, non-profit organisations, and public sector organisations. Although the nature of project management may vary across sectors regardless of scope or context, project-based work involves goal setting, resource management (usually time and money), groups of people, and some level of uncertainty regarding the attainment of project goals (Barr, 2006). Projects are momentary tasks created to achieve clear objectives. Management of projects, therefore, deals with the use of various processes and techniques to carry out tasks to meet the specifications of projects and their stakeholders Project Management Institute (PMI) (2017). The management of projects as a subject entails cudgelling several vital parts in the management field like task performance, scope management, and utilisation of resources among others (Venter, 2005).

The oil and gas industry, just like other industries globally, was badly affected by the emergence of the COVID-19 pandemic, thus raising questions of uncertainty about its future. According to Barbosa et al. (2020) and Norouzi (2021), producers of oil and gas and other governmental institutions that are engaged in the crude oil and gas sectors had to shed some of their profit margins because of the unfavourable prices by which their products were sold on the world market. In an attempt to address the nervy demand, major oil-producing countries like Nigeria, Saudi Arabia, and Iraq decided to vend their petroleum products using cut rates and many organisations that trade in oil and gas reduced the levels of production and the development of new budgets for projects.

In preparation for an economic recovery, some corporations put strategic measures in place by cutting down capital expenditures and withholding the re-purchase of shares to safeguard dividends and create value in the long run. Corporate bodies called on governmental institutions globally to put strategies in place to mitigate any further adverse effects on the oil and gas industry (IEA, 2021). It is hoped that measures put in place by governments

DOI: 10.4324/9781003309864-10

will go a long way in protecting the employees and the organisations during turbulent times.

With dwindling production and other challenges within the oil and gas industry, there is a need to lengthen pay-back and break-even times and to re-examine business plans. The fall in prices and profit margins makes it necessary for all relevant stakeholders within the value chain to reduce expenditures. The most appropriate way to realise this goal with optimal performance is to increase efficiency; and the most feasible way to increase efficiency in a projectised organisation is to engage in the discipline of project management. In a turbulent business environment like that of the oil and gas industry, there is now a greater demand for increased performance through project management in any of the diverse sections (i.e., exploration, drilling, refining, sales, and marketing) (Jiang, 2014). The need for effective and efficient management of projects has, therefore, become crucial in view of the numerous examples of project failures around the world (Narayanan & Huemann, 2021). Therefore, this chapter is aimed at presenting a view of how project management can be used to ensure efficiency in projects within the oil and gas industry.

The remaining parts of this chapter are structured in the following manner. Section 8.2 gives a brief history of oil and gas projects. Section 8.3 offers an overview of project management; Section 8.4 describes the features of oil and gas projects; Section 8.5 presents an overview of project management practices of oil and gas projects; and Section 8.6 presents an overview of oil and gas project management in developing countries. Finally, Section 8.7 concludes the study.

8.2 History of Oil and Gas Projects

The earliest reference to the exploitation of oil and gas dates to 1875 BC in the government official records of the ancient Mesopotamian kingdom of Sumeria during the reign of King Hammurabi. The ancient Greek historians Herodotus and Diodorus documented evidence of primitive exploitation of oil seeps, springs, and wells off the coast of the Caspian Sea (the Caspian basin borders five countries comprising Azerbaijan, Iran, Kazakhstan, Turkmenistan, and Russia). Greek historians also recorded oil exploitation in ancient Babylon (present-day Iraq) between 450 and 50 BC (Barnes & Briggs, 2003; Eaton, 1886; Vassiliou, 2018).

The first commercial exploitation of oil and gas began in the Caspian basin, and by the end of the 19th century, the region accounted for 50% of global oil and gas output. The nature of oil and gas exploitation remained primitive and was through hand-dug wells throughout the Middle Ages between the 5th and 15th centuries (Vassiliou, 2018). It is only after the medieval era, particularly between the 15th to 19th centuries, that we see preliminary evidence of the development of the modern-day oil and gas industry. During this period, oil and gas projects reached an unprecedented scale because of the widespread use of oil and gas for illumination and lubrication and for medicinal purposes. This led to the massive exploration, extraction, and export of oil and gas off the Caspian shores to the rest of the world (Vassiliou, 2018). The United States of America and Russian Siberia were also pioneering oil and gas extraction sites in the 18th to 19th centuries (Vassiliou, 2018).

The Russian Tsar Peter I commissioned the world's first significant oil and gas exploration. In 1732, the first rudimentary oil and gas refinery was established in Baku to serve the local population. In 1806, David and Joseph Ruffner struck oil and gas while drilling for salt using a spring pole, drive pipe, casing, and tubing in Western Virginia. Further, between 1835 and 1837, Russian mining engineer, Nikolai Ivanovich Voskoboinikov, piloted an oil well development project by implementing a ventilation system in oil wells for increased efficiency of oil and gas extraction in the Baku region and as well pioneered the modern oil and gas distillation refinery in 1837 (Vassiliou, 2018). The first modern mechanical oil and gas drilling project, a well approximating 69 feet (21 metres), was established in the Bibi-Eybat area of Baku in 1846. This ushered in modern oil and gas drilling and a transition from the primitive practice of hand-dug pits, based on the ideas of Nikolai Ivanovich Voskoboinikov (Vassiliou, 2018).

The period from 1850 to 1875 saw the proliferation of modern oil and gas companies. From the year 1860 to 1879, a series of transportation and distribution innovations in the oil and gas sector was implemented in the United States and the Caspian basin by oil and gas corporations. The Nobel brothers (Robert, Ludwig, and Alfred Nobel), taking a cue from the American oil and gas distribution inventions, revolutionised the global oil and gas distribution business, particularly in 1877. Ludvig Nobel designed the world's first modern steam-driven oil-shipping tanker plying the Caspian Sea (Tolf, 1976; Vassiliou, 2018).

The Hamill brothers introduced the modern rotary oil and gas drilling technique in the Spindletop Texas oil fields in 1901. The Nobel brothers later popularised this method to the Absheron Peninsula oil fields in 1913. In 1927, oil explorers made the first oil discovery using seismic reflection technology in the Maud oil field of Oklahoma. Similarly, using gravity techniques, another set of oil explorers made the first oil discovery using a geophysical method in Nash Dome in Texas. Oil and gas exploration also made major scientific breakthroughs when the refraction seismology method was first successfully applied to oil discovery in the Orchard Dome of Texas (Carstens, 2008; Eaton, 1866; Tolf, 1976; Vassiliou, 2018).

The earliest oil and gas projects in the developing world were in Latin America. However, the first commercially significant oil discovery in an Arab country was the giant oil field of Kirkuk at Baba Gurgur, near the city of Kirkuk, Iraq, in 1927. In 1932, Standard Oil of California (Socal, later Chevron) discovered oil in Bahrain. In 1938, the first significant oil discovery in Saudi Arabia was made near the Persian Gulf, which became the world's second-largest oil field. In 1955, Petrofina made the first oil discovery in

Angola in the onshore Kwanza basin, the first in sub-Saharan Africa. In 1937, Royal Dutch Shell formed a joint venture named Shell/D'Arcy to explore oil in Nigeria, and in 1956 they discovered the Oloibiri oil field in Nigeria. The oil field was relatively small, but it was Nigeria's first commercially viable discovery. In the same year, Compagnie Française des Pétroles (later Total) discovered the Hassi Mes-saoud oil field in Algeria. In 1959, China found the Daqing oil field, while Socony Mobil (later Mobil) and Gelsenberg of Germany discovered Amal, Libya's largest oil field (Vassiliou, 2018).

8.3 Project and Programme Management

A project is a unique venture carried out within a time frame by people to meet agreed objectives or goals within agreed parameters of cost, time, quality, and customer requirements. It is also a problem scheduled for a solution (Juran & Godfrey, 1999).

Projects are temporary because they are definitive regarding their start and finish. They also function within resource and scope specifications. Projects are also unique as they involve a specific set of tasks that are planned to attain a particular goal Project Management Institute (PMI, 2017). The construction of a contemporary building, the establishment of software solutions, and expansion of a business into new markets are all examples of projects. Projects are different from operations in the sense that projects are unique and temporary endeavours, but operations are continuous and repetitive (Prabhakar, 2008).

To be successful in the execution of projects, one needs to be conversant with issues which are related to the management of scope, time, cost, quality, human resource, communication, risk, procurement, stakeholders, agility, and process integration.

Project management as a formal field of practice or discipline entails the application of skills, knowledge, and tools to project operations to satisfy project requirements Project Management Institute (PMI) (2017). Project management may also be described as the use of techniques, tools, and skills to satisfy the needs of stakeholders and exceed their expectations. Prabhakar (2008) also considers project management as an art involving the coordination and direction of both material and human resources throughout a project's lifecycle to accomplish specified goals within reasonable constraints. Turner and Müller (2003) assert that the definitions of project management are not complete as they fail to recognise projects as temporary organisations on their own. In their view (ibid.), a project performs a production function. It is also an agency which engages in responsible allocation, processes management, and uncertainty management within a functional organisation. This perspective is underpinned by the organisational theory perspective. Turner and Muller (ibid.) explain that from the organisational thinking perspective. The project manager is the chief executive of the project (temporary organisation). As a result, the roles of project managers such as goal-setting and motivation of team members may be emphasised more than the project-related roles such as planning and execution. Also, as agency managers, project managers are the agents of the project owner (principal). Therefore, a second rung of management and control must be set up purposely to monitor the performance of project managers (Turner & Müller, ibid.).

PMI has it that the project management process has five stages: initiation, planning, execution, monitoring and controlling, and closing (Wallace, 2016). Lock (2003) also notes that all projects are executed within a specific context or environment. A project's environment may be socio-cultural, physical, or international. Projects can also be executed at the intersection of two or more environments. Further, projects have participants and stakeholders. Stakeholders are people on whom the project's success depends because the former can influence the course of activities of the project. Thus, stakeholders can influence the project, and they can also be influenced by the project (Prabhakar, 2008). For this reason, meeting and exceeding stakeholder demands in project management involve balancing the demands of time, scope, and cost. These are called the triple constraints in the management of projects. However, projects that are purposed to deliver some products or services to consumers have an additional constraint, customer relations (Eskerod & Huemann, 2013).

8.4 Features of Oil and Gas Projects

The petroleum industry encompasses a variety of diverse actions and procedures. These actions and procedures add to the change of fundamental petroleum resources into utilisable end-products (Badiru & Osisanya, 2012). These actions are interconnected and occur inside or across individual companies, and within or across nationwide borders (Engen et al., 2019). The value chain of oil and gas products begins with the selection of appropriate zones to carry out the exploration for oil or gas (Tsiga et al., 2017). During exploration activities, hydrocarbon discoveries are appraised, and then successful products are developed and produced. Oil and gas projects consist of three categories, namely upstream, midstream, and downstream. Upstream oil and gas projects include oil and gas exploration, oil-well drilling, development and maintenance, oil and gas extraction, and oil-well decommissioning. The midstream oil and gas projects comprise petroleum refinery projects. Finally, the downstream oil and gas projects comprise oil and gas transportation and distribution projects, including oil pipelines, oil shipping vessels, and oil tankers (Badiru & Osisanya, 2016; Clews, 2016).

Aside from these broad categories, oil and gas projects require high investment outlays and are executed within longer durations. A distinct feature of oil and gas projects is the enormous capital investment cost and the high incidence of cost overruns (Clews, 2016). For instance, in a survey of 205 oil and gas projects across the world, Ernst and Young (2014) reported that 67% of liquified natural gas (LNG) projects, 65% of oil and gas upstream projects, 64% of oil pipeline projects (downstream), and 62% of oil refining projects (midstream) experienced cost overruns beyond the estimated project procurement cost. Oil and gas projects are often characterised by long time horizons spanning several months or years. Another notable feature of oil and gas projects is the significant incidence of schedule delay. Furthermore, Ernst and Young (2014), in a survey of oil and gas projects, reported that 79% of oil and refining projects (midstream), 78% of oil and gas upstream projects, 68% of LNG projects, and 50% oil pipeline projects (downstream) experienced schedule delay beyond the estimated project procurement schedule.

Additionally, oil and gas projects are often characterised by high risk and uncertainty. The considerable capital outlay may suffer a potential loss because of technical, economic, or political risks. Specifically, the technical risk may arise from the low viability of drilled oil wells and the economic risk may stem from a long spell of low commodity prices, and currency crises, while political risk pertains to the risk of expropriation (El-Reedy, 2016). The uncertainty stems from the distant horizon and the unpredictability associated with large complex infrastructure projects such as oil and gas (Caron, 2013; Clews, 2016).

The oil and gas sector is also a highly technical and sophisticated industry. Therefore, oil and gas projects are often characterised by a complex and codified knowledge base with a low knowledge spillover (Clews, 2016; Olaniran, 2017). Oil and gas projects, especially those in developing countries, are often dominated by highly technical expatriate knowledge throughout the lifespan of the projects. In addition, it is notable that seismic exploration, rotary percussion, offshore drilling, continuous distillation, and pipeline installations are technical activities requiring highly skilled knowledge in oil and gas project procurement (Clews, 2016).

8.5 Project Management of Oil and Gas Projects

There has been an improvement in the work procedures and tasks within the oil and gas industry (Helle et al., 2020). An extraordinary rise in global oil price from US$44 in April 2001 to US$144 in April 2008 led to an increase in tasks within the sector which culminated in substantial growth in the economic well-being of its stakeholders (The World Bank, 2020). The focus was on fast-tracked development of fields and the quickest period to find oil. This resulted in custom-made systems and an increase in expenditure. An austere recession from 2015 to 2020 has altered the view of the sector and moved the attention to efficiency and expense reduction. Experts in the oil and gas sector have now come to realise that other corporate bodies and sectors are using system engineering to deal with the complexities in the business environment (Lin et al., 2019).

Efficient requirements engineering is central to all organisation to "guide the ship and keep pace with the rising tide of complexity" (Hull et al., 2005). As regards mega projects, executing requirement management systems is a requisite for requirement handling and tracing (Hull et al., 2005). Requirement engineering involves the definition, documentation, and maintenance of requirements of a project. Requirement engineering becomes the process through which services provided by a system are gathered and defined. The process of requirement engineering involves the gaining knowledge about the project from sources such as customers and stakeholders of the project. Requirement management involves the analysis, documentation, tracking, prioritising, and agreeing on the requirement of the project. Requirement management further involves the regulation of the communication of the requirements of the project to stakeholders. Requirement management caters to the changing characteristics of requirement, thus ensuring that changes are incorporated on a timely basis as specified by stakeholders. The ability to modify the requirement of a project in a systematic and regulated manner constitutes an extremely important part of the process of requirement engineering. It culminates into the creation of a plan for requirement management (RMP). An RMP aids in explaining the way to receive, analyse, file, and administer all the required work of a project. The RMP entails all information from the initiation stage of the mega project to an in-depth requirement gathering throughout the lifespan of the project. Some of the major issues to be found in an RMP include overview of projects, the process of gathering requirements, tools, traceability, and responsibilities.

Efficient requirement engineering is necessary to deal with the complexities within the system, and it is important to execute a system for requirement management for mega projects even for oil and gas projects (Hull et al., 2005). The ultimate aim is to deal with a sizeable number of requirements and to enhance its quality (Baker et al., 2016; Zager et al., 2019). Even though requirement management systems have been in use in other industries and its benefits are well known, its application and execution within the oil and gas sector are inadequate (Helle et al., 2020). Even in circumstances where the companies have the required technical competency to make use of requirement management systems, there are issues of culture within the organisation that fight against the full implementation of the system (Helle et al., 2020). This is in line with the outcomes of research works that emphasise organisational dynamics as a challenge in the implementation of requirement engineering (Hall et al., 2002).

Moreover, many organisations within the oil and gas business environment historically make use of numerous *Microsoft Excel* sheets and *Word* files for requirement management. Most often, clients give extensive and in-depth requirement specifications making it possible for other requirements to be added where necessary (Engen et al., 2019; Wee & Muller, 2016). Since most oil and gas organisations made use of prosaic texts and specific standards, there are difficulties in fully understanding and verifying the requirements by end-users (Zager et al., 2019), thus, there is a need for the use of comprehensive software for the management of requirements. Requirements management software provides the tools for the oil and gas sector to execute project plans that will help limit expenses and enhance the quality control systems. The oil and gas sector succeeds principally in the availability of financial, human, and technical resources. Having RMP is essential to the success of a project since it permits engineering personnel to take control, manage the scope of work, and lead the project development cycle by optimising their financial, human, and technical resources.

8.6 Overview of Oil and Gas Project Management in Developing Countries

Developing countries often experience tremendous socioeconomic as well as political upheavals in their internal affairs. To mitigate these problems and improve living standards, most countries in the developing world are moving towards the exploitation of the naturally endowed resources via industrialisation drives to catch up with modern trends of development (Akintaro, 2002; Yanwen, 2012). The upsurge in the demand for oil and gas is fast becoming a reality for developing countries. Though the increasing demand for oil and gas is fast becoming a reality for developing countries, they also have most of the world's proven reserves. Consequently, multinational oil and gas organisations directly involved with oil exploration as well as those indirectly involved in oil and gas projects such as equipment suppliers, contractors amongst others are refocusing their attention from Europe and North American countries to developing countries (Campanella et al., 2018; Kwarteng & Sarfo-Mensah, 2019). The shift in focus means that a lot of business opportunities have opened up in the oil and gas sector for developing countries. Generally, oil and gas projects in the developing world are of a different scope and complexity. That notwithstanding, some developing countries have lots of medium to large-scale oil and gas projects which have the ability to contribute significantly to their development in the future. There are some of these countries that have such projects that have immediate relevance and the ability to spawn numerous new ones due to global demands.

About 8% of the oil and gas supply in the world is from Africa and the continent boasts many of the world's untapped resources (Graham & Ovadia, 2019; Obeng-Odoom, 2015). Like most places in the world, oil and gas projects in Africa entail massive investments, interfaces, and complex engineering activities. The scope and intricacy of these projects need special attention in the project management process. It is suggested that effective project management in the oil and gas industry is necessary in both the short and the long run. Large-scale projects ongoing in several countries in Africa include onshore and offshore oil field developments, oil and gas pipeline construction, LNG plant engineering and construction, gas monetisation projects (methanol, fertilizer, urea), infrastructural projects, and construction of refineries. However, the recent fall in commodity prices and the advent of COVID-19 has impacted the management of some of these projects.

8.7 Contribution

Apart from the provision of energy to meet the needs of society, oil and gas projects create opportunities for employment, drive technology and research, and boost local businesses. The need to build and design successful oil and gas products that satisfy the needs of stakeholders is a major concern for most oil and gas organisations. The exploration of oil and gas is made up of a system comprising many subsystems, from the hydrocarbon production subsystem to the external transport subsystem. Moreover, oil and gas projects are characterised by high ambiguity and an enormous volume of capital investments, which make the oil and gas system complex. One of the most effective tools that can lead to the successful execution of oil and gas projects is systems engineering. Systems engineering encourages the successful initiation and use of systems by employing scientific and technological approaches. Moreover, within the project lifecycle, many costs are incurred as a result of the failure of projects within their initiation and implementation stages. The implication of such failures is the lack of returns on investment. Consequently, it is imperative for organisations within the oil and gas sector to create project implementation programmes and develop schedules at the initial stages of conceptual design processes to have the avenue to evaluate possible risks and opportunities as well as incorporate stakeholders' needs and translate them into requirements.

8.8 Conclusion

The management of projects may be rather challenging, especially when the projects entail several stakeholders, very limited resources, shifting/unclear project requirements, and new or unproven methods of execution. Incidentally, these project-related challenges are compounded in the oil and gas sectors, often because of their large size and political characterisation. In dealing with the challenge of stakeholder management and scarce resources, requirement engineering can play an important role in attaining project success. Requirements management allows for minimal errors in the production process by tracking changes in specifications and facilitating communication with stakeholders during the implementation of oil and gas projects.

Additionally, project success is crucial in the oil and gas sector to make the necessary impact, to cope with a fast-changing world, and to satisfy the increasing demand for oil and gas products. However, in many less industrialised countries, project management in the public oil and gas sector is ineffective because project managers in these organisations lack the requisite project management competencies. While public sector organisations in less industrialised countries may appear to be practising project management, they are predominantly dependent on accidental project managers who lack the requisite qualification and experience. Therefore, the way forward to improved project management outcomes within the oil and gas sector is having skilled project managers who are dedicated and furnished with the know-how to deal with multifaceted circumstances in diverse situations. Competent project managers can foster a good understanding of project requirements and this has the tendency to improve the outcome of oil and gas projects.

References

Akintaro, J. A. (2002). Funding the oil and gas industry: Comparative perspective. *Alternative sources of funding for the oil and gas industry in Nigeria* (p. 169). Evans Brothers (Nig. Publishers) Ltd.

Badiru, & Osisanya. (2012). *Project management for the oil and gas industry, a world system approach* (1st ed.). CRC Press.

Badiru, A. B., & Osisanya, S. O. (2016). *Project management for the oil and gas industry: A world-system approach*. CRC Press.

Baker, J., Ferraioli, P., Pereira, L. R., Hudson, A., Barton, G., Bhatt, S., & Odegard, R. (2016). Requirements engineering for retrofittable subsea equipment. *Proceedings— IEEE 24th International Requirements Engineering Conference*, 226–235.

Barbosa, F., Bresciani, G., Graham, P., Nyquist, S., & Yanosek, K. (2020). Oil and gas after COVID-19: The day of reckoning or a new age of opportunity. *McKinsey & Company*, May, 15. Retrieved November 1, 2022, from https://www.mckinsey.com/industries/oil-and-gas/our-insights/oil-and-gas-after-covid-19-the-day-of-reckoning-or-a-new-age-of-opportunity

Barnes, A. J., & Briggs, N. J. (2003). The Caspian oil reserves: The political, economic, and environmental implications of Black Gold in the world market. Retrieved October 10, 2022, https://web.stanford.edu/class/e297a/Caspian%20Oil%20Reserves.pdf

Barr, S. (2006). Environmental action in the home: Investigating the 'value-action' gap. *Geography, 91*(1), 43–54. Retrieved October 12, 2022, https://www.tandfonline.com/doi/abs/10.1080/00167487.2006.12094149

Campanella, C. E., Cuccovillo, A., Campanella, C., Yurt, A., & Passaro, V. M. (2018). Fibre Bragg grating based strain sensors: Review of technology and applications. *Sensors, 18*(9), 3115.

Caron, F. (2013). *Managing the continuum: Certainty, uncertainty, unpredictability in large engineering projects*. Springer Science & Business Media.

Carstens, H. (2008). Finding Oil—Using Geochemistry. https://archives.datapages.com/data/geo-expro-magazine/005/005005/pdfs/5.htm

Clews, R. (2016). *Project finance for the international petroleum industry*. Academic Press.

Eaton, S. J. M. (1866). *Petroleum: A history of the oil region of Venango County, Pennsylvania: Its resources, mode of development, and value: Embracing a discussion of ancient oil operations*. JP Skelly. Retrieved September 10, 2022 from https://books.google.com.gh/books?hl=en&lr=&id=aQlZAAAAYAAJ&oi=fnd&pg=PA11&dq=Eaton,+S.+-J.+M.+(1866).+Petroleum:+aA+Historyhistory+of+the+Oiloil+Regionregion+of+VenangoVenango+CountyCounty,+Pennsylvania:+Its+Resourcesresources,+Modemode+of+Developmentdevelopment,+and+Valuevalue:+Embracing+aA+Discussiondiscussion+of+Ancientancient+Oi&ots=dUW1jHbl5j&sig=8qtIucUemwO3BpKq-sSjthBPalg&redir_esc=y#v=onepage&q&f=false

El-Reedy, M. A. (2016). *Project management in the oil and gas industry*. John Wiley & Sons.

Engen, S., Falk, K., & Muller, G. (2019). Architectural reasons in the conceptual phase: A case study in the oil and gas industry. *14th Annual Conference Systems of Systems Engineering*, 87–92.

Ernst & Young. (2014). Ghana. http://www.ey.com/GL/en/Services/Tax/Worldwide-Corporate-Tax-Guide---XMLQS?preview&XmlUrl=/ec1mages/taxguides/WCTG-2014/WCTG-GH.xml

Eskerod, P., & Huemann, M. (2013). Sustainable development and project stakeholder management: What standards say. *International Journal of Managing Projects in Business*, 6(1), 36–50.

Graham, E., & Ovadia, J. S. (2019). Oil exploration and production in Sub-Saharan Africa, 1990-present: Trends and developments. *The Extractive Industries and Society*, 6(2), 593–609.

Hall, T., Beecham, S., & Rainer, A. (2002). Requirements problems in twelve software companies: An empirical Analysis. *IEE Proceedings-Software*, 149(5), 153–160.

Helle, I., Mäkinen, J., Nevalainen, M., Afenyo, M., & Vanhatalo, J. (2020). Impacts of oil spills on Arctic marine ecosystems: A quantitative and probabilistic risk assessment perspective. *Environmental Science & Technology*, 54(4), 2112–2121.

Hull, E., Jackson, K., & Dick, J. (2005). *Requirements engineering in the solution domain* (pp. 109–129). Springer.

IEA. (2021). Gender diversity in energy: What we known and what we don't know. IEA, Paris. www.iea.org

Jiang, J. (2014). The study of the relationship between leadership style and project success. *American Journal of Trade and Policy*, 1(1), 51.

Juran, J. M., Godfrey, A. B. (1999). *Juran's quality handbook*. McGraw Hill. https://gmpua.com/QM/Book/quality%20handbook.pdf

Kwarteng, T. A., & Sarfo-Mensah, P. (2019). The impact of savings groups on female agency: Insights from village savings and loans associations in Northern Ghana.

Lin, L., Müller, R., Zhu, F., & Liu, H. (2019). Choosing suitable project control modes to improve the knowledge integration under different uncertainties. *International Journal of Project Management*, 37(7), 896–911. https://doi.org/10.1016/j.ijproman.2019.07.002.

Lock, D. (2003). *Project management*. Gower Publishing Limited.

Narayanan, V. K., & Huemann, M. (2021). Engaging the organizational field: The case of project practices in a construction firm to contribute to an emerging economy. *International Journal of Project Management*, 39(5), 449–462.

Norouzi, N. (2021). Post-COVID-19 and globalization of oil and natural gas trade: Challenges, opportunities, lessons, regulations, and strategies. *International Journal of Energy Research*, 45(10), 14338–14356. Retrieved October 12, 2022 from https://onlinelibrary.wiley.com/doi/full/10.1002/er.6762

Obeng-Odoom, F. (2015). Global political economy and frontier economies in Africa: Implications from the oil and gas industry in Ghana. *Energy Research & Social Science, 10*, 41–56.

Olaniran, O. J. (2017). Barriers to tacit knowledge sharing in geographically dispersed project teams in oil and gas projects. *Project Management Journal*, 48(3), 41–57.

Prabhakar, G. P. (2008). What is project success: A literature review. *International Journal of Business and Management*, 3(9), 3–10.

Project Management Institute (PMI). (2017). *A guide to the project management body of knowledge (PMBOK guide)*, 6th ed. Project Management Institute. Retrieved October 12, 2022 https://www.pmi.org/pmbok-guide-standards/foundational/pmbok

Wallace, W. (2016). Project management for the oil and gas industry. *Edinburgh Business School*, 1.

The World Bank. (2020). Development projects: Additional financing for Ghana oil and gas capacity building project—P148224. World Bank. https://projects.worldbank.org/en/projects-operations/project-detail/P148224

Tolf, R. W. (1976). *The Russian Rockefellers: The saga of the Nobel family and the Russian oil industry* (Vol. 158). Hoover Press.

Tsiga, Z., Emes, M., & Smith, A. (2017). Critical success factors for projects in the petroleum industry. *Procedia Computer Science, 121*, 224–231.

Turner, J. R., & Müller, R. (2003). On the nature of the project as a temporary organization. *International Journal of Project Management, 21*(1), 1–8.

Vassiliou, M. S. (2018). *Historical dictionary of the petroleum industry*. Rowman & Littlefield.

Venter, F. (2005). Project management in Ghana: Expectations, realities and barriers to use. *The Journal for Transdisciplinary Research in Southern Africa, 1*(1), 20.

Wee, D. K. Y., & Muller, G. (2016). Evaluating the effectiveness of applying a requirements management system for a subsea oil and gas workover system. *INCOSE International Symposium, 26*(1), 2346–2360.

Yanwen, W. (2012). The study on complex project management in developing countries. *Physics Procedia, 25*, 1547–1552.

Zager, M., McKinney, A., Reed, M., & Orr, K. (2019, April). Verifying process safety requirements: Similarities between aerospace and oil & gas industries. *Offshore Technology Conference.*

9 Human Resource Management Practices in the Oil and Gas Industry

James B. Abugre, Yvonne Lamptey, Simeon Ifere, and Richard Nyuur

9.1 Recruitment and Selection of Employees in the Oil and Gas Industry

Recent research highlights the benefits of hiring staff to be the foundation of high productivity in the oil and gas industry. For example, Opatha and Arulrajah (2014) make a strong case that oil & gas firms need a strong recruitment function to foster the ideals and cultural environment needed in the petroleum industry. The reason is that the oil and gas industry is significant in the energy market and in the global economy. It contributes about 3.8% of the total GDP ($86 trillion) of the world economy and 6–8% of the GDP of some developing countries such as Ghana and Nigeria (Hassan, 2020), and hence, is the backbone of many oil economies. The industry operates in different categories: the upstream (exploration and production), the midstream (transport and storage), and the downstream (refinery and marketing). The global oil and gas market is dynamic and evolving, and this makes it imperative for skilled staff to be identified, selected, and placed in their respective positions within the industry.

9.1.1 Distinctive Recruitment and Selection Practices in Developed and Developing Oil Countries

In the United States, firms in the oil and gas industries, due to competitive advantage, take the initial steps to engage professors and schools to obtain a list of good students who are studying subjects related to petroleum or oil and gas. They invite students to intern with them and receive on-the-job training. They also groom the interns for a more permanent or semi-permanent role in their firms (Siavelis & Morgenstern, 2008). Some of these firms in the United States also use traditional means of recruitment and selection by advertising job vacancies through online portals for computer programs to scan resumes for keywords that portray the needed skills. Then, the recruiting partners conduct phone or physical interviews with the selected applicants and invite them over for a hands-on practical session in the hiring

DOI: 10.4324/9781003309864-11

department in order to assess their fitness for the job role. Once the recruiters are convinced, they move on to salary negotiations and then to health and safety training in the industry (mandated by federal law) and then the applicant starts to work therefrom.

The situation is not different in Europe, where recruitment for the oil and gas industry in the UK, Scandinavia, and other parts of Europe is mostly vested in placement firms which have links with the central government and legal agencies (Derous & Fruyt, 2007). For most petroleum firms, the recruitment and selection processes are audited after the firms choose their candidates. Before permission or clearance is given for the chosen candidate(s) to start work, the following are checked: the procedures and the recruitment process, any instance(s) of discrimination, whether the job position was duly advertised, the background of the candidate and the necessary qualifications that fit the job role advertised (Adams et al., 2017).

In the Middle East, where the oil and gas industry has been a bane and a blessing, the public sector has the main responsibility of recruitment and selection of employees (Metcalfe, 2007). However, the public sector recruitment policy is perforated with corruption and nepotism which influence the kind and number of people recruited in the sector. Based on this, in 2006, the World Bank highlighted a strong need for transparent recruitment practices (Andersen et al., 2006) but it seems the policy in the Middle East has not achieved this intent. Another aspect of recruitment and selection worth mentioning in the region relates to gender. In some countries in the Middle East, there are no HR policies governing equality in recruitment, and the labour market is segregated by gender (Stevens, 2008). Many organisations support segregation officially, many ascribe roles in the oil and gas industry as either for males or for females, and this impacts investment towards education. Subsequently, the firms recruit men for some roles and women for other roles (Olawuyi, 2019).

In Africa, even though there are similarities in recruitment and selection with other regions discussed above, the story is more dramatic and comes with a flavour unique to its setting. In Nigeria for example, the recruitment of qualified staff cannot be divorced from local customs and nepotism (Anthony, 2015). There are grounded frameworks like the Nigerian Labour Act of 1974 which industries in the oil and gas sector are to draw on to recruit their employees. Many industries use these standards to an extent. However, personal interests and the existing organisational culture influence the recruitment process in the industry, as a result of corruption. The local industry has now, however, been characterised by an aging workforce and skills gap (Amenshiah & Analoui, 2019). To avoid these weak HR practices that are unproductive to firms, Abugre and Nasere (2020) recommend that effective management of HR practices in developing economies should embrace innovative and high-performance workplace practices that would stimulate employee job satisfaction thereby, enhancing the productivity of these firms.

9.2 Contracting and Local Content for Manpower in the Oil and Gas Industry

Over the years, many countries have enacted laws to ensure that the livelihoods of their citizen are improved by streamlining a few factors that affect their growth and development (Ablo, 2017). Specifically, this is in respect of local employment issues of contracting and labour procurement. Local content policies seek to address local challenges such as low levels of employment, high poverty levels, low levels of technical know-how (Nwapi, 2015), to address the local manpower needs of the industry. According to Senoo and Armah (2015), the issue of local content policy has become important for many countries, especially the developing countries, because of the perception that most of the resources are greatly benefiting foreign investors at the expense of the indigenes. This has rendered indigenes of most developing countries disadvantaged in terms of job creation and participation in the oil and gas sector, thus fuelling the perception that developing countries lack the manpower needs of their oil and gas industry.

Local content policy, therefore, means 'government policies which aim to promote local content' (Kolstad & Kinyondo, 2017, p. 411). In Ghana, the local content policy L.I. 2204 defines local content as 'the quantum or percentage of locally produced materials, personnel, financing, goods and services rendered in the petroleum industry value chain and which can be measured in monetary terms' (Aryeetey & Ackah, 2018, p. 112). Ghana's local content policy bears a huge responsibility to ensure considerable local content participation in the upstream industry of the petroleum sector and to help ensure transparency, accountability, and local human capital development (Ablo, 2015; Ablo, 2018; Baba, 2018). The policy ensures job creation, increasing value addition, a raise in the proportion of financing that comes from indigenous sources, as well as value retention of the oil proceeds in the country (Baba, 2018). The adoption of the L.I. 2204 in Ghana is aimed solely at creating a synergy between the petroleum sector and other sectors of the economy through the creation of the 'supportive industries' particularly in other sectors of the economy (Aryeetey & Ackah, 2018). The local content policy of Ghana's oil and gas expressly spells out how contracting and employment issues in the industry should be. Specifically, section 5.4 of the policy deals with the manpower process of the petroleum sector. Accordingly, section 5.4 of the 2010 Local Content and Local Participation policy framework, which focuses on the employment of Ghanaians in the oil industry, stipulates the following milestones:

- At least 50% of the management staff of international oil companies (IOCs) are Ghanaians from the start of petroleum activities;
- At least 80% within five years after the start of petroleum activities;
- At least 30% of the technical staff are Ghanaians from the start of petroleum activities of the licensee and the percentage shall increase to at least 80% within five years after the start of petroleum activities and 90% within ten years; and other staff are 100% Ghanaians.

According to Sumbal et al. (2017), local content recruitment provides not only jobs for the increasing population in developing countries but strengthens the manpower requirements of their oil and gas industry. Ablo (2016) argued that for the oil-producing countries to achieve success with the local content policy, governments must encourage the participation of the local companies. In his view, increasing local participation ensures that local workforce is recruited to be involved in providing goods and services in the oil and gas industry. The local recruits are also expected to receive professional and technological training and development to give the local companies competitive advantage in the oil and gas industry (Benin, 2017).

Therefore, research in this sector has emphasised local content recruitment, which some scholars have referred to as job role localisation (JRL) (Ackah & Mohammed, 2018). JRL has been explained as 'the process of training and developing nationals with the appropriate qualifications, competencies, and experience to enable oil and gas companies to replace expatriates with nationals' (Pegram et al., 2018, p. 105). According to Ablo (2018), JRL is a critical aspect of localisation strategy to safeguard the local content legislation. Accordingly, local content recruitment of indigenous personnel in oil and gas comes with many advantages in reinforcing the manpower base of the host countries. Thus, Pegram et al., ibid) argued that local content recruitment in the oil and gas industry gives local staff the needed confidence to function effectively in the industry, which also impacts positively on the overall growth and development of the country. For Darkwah (2013), it is evident from research that local content recruitment in oil and gas reduces costs incurred by oil companies. Reductions in the organisational cost of the oil and gas companies could culminate in high-profit margins and this depends on the cost of training and education of the local staff compared to the cost and training of expatriates (Acheampong et al., 2016).

9.3 Strategic Training and Development of Employees in the Oil and Gas Industry

According to Darkwah (2013), the importance of training and development of employees in the oil and gas industry cannot be underestimated. This stems from the fact that the activities in the industry require considerable knowledge and skilled employees to execute the strategies of the oil and gas companies. Additionally, the oil and gas sector needs expertise to replace the older ones who leave the organisation upon their retirement (Al-Mughairi, 2018). In this regard, succession planning has been considered as very crucial to the activities of the oil and gas companies.

Researchers have suggested that strategies that support continuous training and development of employees in the oil and gas sector are required to equip employees with the requisite knowledge and skills to enhance their performance. This is because the extractive industry, of which the oil and gas sector is an integral part, is constantly going through transformation due to environmental regulations. For example, there are numerous laws that control the upstream petroleum sector which companies and their personnel need to be abreast of. Some of these regulations are aimed at ensuring that the activities of oil firms are transparent, accountable, and ensure the safety of the environment (Adams et al., 2019). This calls for continuous strategic training of personnel in the sector, as the Petroleum (Exploration and Production) Act 919 (2016) defines parameters within which the Ministry of Energy operates (Ndi, 2018). The Ghana National Petroleum Corporation Law (GNPC), 1983 or PNDC Law 64 enables the country's commercial upstream petroleum organisation (GNPC) to carry out petroleum exploration and production and to enter into joint ventures and production-sharing agreements on behalf of the government (Abraham, 2017).

Strategic training in the oil & gas industry of developing countries is centred on getting more of the local staff to acquire the requisite knowledge and skills to replace expatriates in the future. According to Amadu-Kannike et al. (2020), oil producing countries in developing countries such as Brazil, Ghana, and Nigeria have adopted local content training strategies to enhance the capacity of their citizens. For instance, in Brazil, the strategic training adopted by the Brazilian government has been to enhance the competencies of their citizens through measures put in place to develop the technological and professional skills of the local staff so that local participation of local personnel would increase in the oil and gas industry. Also, Amenshiah and Analoui (2019), who conducted a study on 'the strategic approach to local competency gap reduction in the oil and gas industry in Ghana', stressed that the training and development programmes for employees in oil and gas companies have been strategised in line with the Petroleum Commission of Ghana's training policies that encourage indigenous staff in the oil and gas industry to be trained by the technical universities of Ghana. Based on these evaluations, the technical universities are to create a portfolio of training programs and strategies, which they would run on an internally distributed schedule. With their management's approval, oil firms could nominate or apply for spaces for their employees to enrol in these programmes at the universities. Given the high expectations of these specific and strategic training outcomes, oil and gas firms are realising the need to intensify their local recruitment policies.

9.4 Technological Transfer and Empowerment of Personnel in the Oil and Gas Industry

Currently, an important domain in organisational studies is technological innovation in the nature of the practices used to manage organisations. This has often been framed as management innovation and is a topic that has long attracted scholarly and practical attention (Abrahamson, 1991). The oil and gas industry transfer is one of the global industries at the forefront of technological development and knowledge. The African continent is said to possess about 7.5% and 7.1%, respectively, of the global oil and gas reserves which are located in countries such as Nigeria, Ghana, and Angola (Botes et al., 2019). The industry has highly skilled and capital-intensive requirements to generate employment opportunities, increase local entrepreneurship, generate economic prosperity, and reduce poverty in host countries (Pegram et al., 2019). Moreover, the oil and gas industry serves as a prime lever for developing a knowledge-based, internationally competitive economy, and in enhancing employees' competencies (Pegram et al., 2018). The industry is dominated by multinational companies such as ExxonMobil, BP, Schlumberger, Royal Dutch Shell, BHP, Chevron, Kosmos, Tullow Oil, ConocoPhillips, Halliburton, Paragon Engineering Services, Marathon Oil, and Murphy Oil (Grant, 2013). Accordingly, several studies have highlighted the critical role of the industry in technology transfer and personnel empowerment (Appiah et al., 2018; Pegram et al., 2018).

9.4.1 Technology and Knowledge Transfer in the Oil and Gas Sector in Developing Countries

Technology and knowledge transfer in the oil and gas industry involves the process of sharing or passing knowledge from companies to employees, suppliers, customers, and other users (Appiah et al., 2018). Globally, the oil and gas industry has been prominent in the development and deployment of technology and knowledge management techniques (Grant, 2013). Developments such as the depletion of established fields, demand for increased environmental responsibility, and the need to explore new locations including deep waters, have all influenced technological advancement and transfer in the sector. Companies recognise the importance of technologies in the speedy identification, appraisal, and exploitation of opportunities (ibid). Technological advances have made it possible for oil and gas companies to not only process unprecedented quantities of data but also deploy the full range of information and communication technologies (ibid). Moreover, the upstream oil sub-sector has witnessed more technological advances for tasks such as drilling, rig design, recovery techniques, seismic analysis, reservoir modelling, and others. Besides, the deep-water exploration has also influenced the development of highly sophisticated technologies for operations. Superior learning capabilities, management systems, innovation, and technology systems are considered critical to the competitiveness of companies in the industry such as Schlumberger, BP, Royal Dutch Shell, and Chevron. Management of such companies has also underscored the importance of not only buying in technology and knowledge from outside, but also sharing technology and knowledge faster with suppliers, and others in the industry.

Different strategies have been deployed by companies in the oil and gas sector in facilitating technology and knowledge transfer particularly from the developed to the developing countries. For instance, Schlumberger developed knowledge hubs, digital libraries, data dictionaries, databases, catalogues, manuals, and online training modules, all meant for sharing and transferring knowledge within the organisation and along its supply chain. Chevron, BP, and ExxonMobil also have databases which are deployed as knowledge support and transfer systems for employees and suppliers. There are also portals that provide opportunities for sharing knowledge and information among users. Groupware is another knowledge transfer system that enables the interaction and sharing of knowledge among groups and teams. It facilitates the creation of virtual communities for knowledge management, sharing, and transfer. For instance, ConocoPhillips has TechLink as a tool that links over 6,000 engineers and scientists worldwide to share and transfer knowledge. Moreover, BP has a virtual teamwork program that enables staff, key partners, and suppliers to regularly meet and transfer knowledge in a face-to-face manner. Chevron, Texaco, and Shell also have communities of practices linking professionals across retail, energy management, refining, drilling, and information technology businesses. Most of the technology and knowledge management tools within companies in the oil and gas sector serve as communities of practice for people including those separated by geography to share information, experiences, problems, insights, templates, common practices, tools, and best practices (Wenger et al., 2002). The various technologies and tools assist these firms in capturing and sharing knowledge and fostering collaboration and knowledge transfer among employees, suppliers, regulators, and customers. These, therefore, serve as good knowledge transfer vehicles for local labour, suppliers, and customers in the sub-Saharan African oil and gas industry.

However, studies have highlighted the global shortage of a wide range of industry-relevant skills, including managerial skills, soft skills, and technical talent such as petroleum and petrochemical engineers, as well as geologists (ILO, 2012). This situation is compounded by the increasing retirement of many experienced workers and the entry of fewer young skilled workers into the industry (ILO, 2012). In the context of Africa, Wood and Bischoff (2020) reveal that the combination of the brain drain of talent and chronic under-resourcing of universities has resulted in the undersupply of the right skills, experience, and talent in the local labour market for the industry. The skill set produced by the educational systems in Africa are considered to be inadequate for industry needs (Pegram et al., 2018). Furthermore, the collapse of many large African firms and industries due to the liberalisation process also resulted in many people turning to the informal sector with its precarious working conditions and limited opportunities for skills development and knowledge transfer (Nelson, 2017). Studies have further highlighted the lack of accreditation, poor and inadequate technical, and vocational education and training capacity in this context (Obeng-Odoom, 2015). The cost associated with training and transfer of knowledge to local labour can be very high and prohibitive (O'Donnell, 2000). These together have greatly impacted the availability of the right talent and experience in Africa for the oil and gas industry. Although expatriates with headquarters experience are considered indispensable for subsidiaries in host countries, the literature has highlighted the importance of technology, experience, and knowledge transfer to local labour (Adams et al., 2017). The increasing presence of MNCs in Africa has further generated questions regarding the implications for knowledge transfer, employee empowerment, and overall HR practices in the African region (Adams et al., 2017; Wood, 2015). Studies suggest that many companies use minimal adaptation (Adams et al., 2017) or aggressive strategies to instil their parent-company HRM practices to the neglect of local realities and the development of indigenous talent (Osabutey et al., 2015; Wood, 2015). Multinational enterprises (MNEs) especially in the natural resource industry are considered to lack the will for people investment and at the same time appear unconcerned about the skill gaps, resulting in the import of expatriate labour, including semi-skilled workers in the case of Chinese MNEs (Wood & Bischoff, 2020). Besides, the potential devastating environmental and human impact from disasters occurring due to the employment of underqualified and inexperienced labour tends to inform rigorous recruitment, selection, and succession planning processes within oil and gas firms (Wilson & Kuszewski, 2011).

Yet, studies have begun to emphasise the role of institutions in facilitating knowledge transfer and employee empowerment particularly in the oil and gas sector (Wood & Bischoff, 2020). One principal approach to knowledge and technology transfer and employee empowerment is localisation (Pegram et al., 2018). JRL involves companies in the oil and gas sector training and developing local labour with the requisite skills, competencies, education, and experience in line with government's local content legislations (ibid.). Another approach to fulfilling localisation would be through brain gain, which may involve targeted strategies in attracting citizens in the diaspora with the appropriate skills, competencies, and experiences to inpatriate and take up roles in the industry with skill gaps (ibid.) (Figure 9.1).

#	
1	Technology capabilities in the oil & gas sector: • Technology and Knowledge Management Techniques • Technological Advancement in Deep water exploration
2	Development of knowledge Hubs
3	Databases and Groupware for knowledge transfer mostly virtual communities
4	Understanding oil business through Techlink among oil & gas communities of practice
5	Budget availability for empowering localisation

Figure 9.1 Strategies and criteria for technology transfer

9.5 Rewarding and Compensating Personnel in the Oil and Gas Industry

In the oil and gas industry, compensation and rewards of personnel play a major role in the HR practices of oil firms. Reward and compensation are terms used interchangeably in the literature (Yeganeha & Sub, 2011). Reward is generally understood as what an employer gives in return for work done by an employee while 'compensation' is a term commonly used in the literature in America, implying reward. However, some argue that it conveys the notion of 'making amends for something that has caused injury or loss' (Torrington et al., 2008). Ultimately, however, both terms convey the same meaning because if a worker expends or loses energy, time, or skills in doing a job for an employer, there would be a need for remuneration.

9.5.1 Specific Compensation and Reward Methods in the Oil and Gas Industry

Labour laws and unions play leading roles in the determination of compensation in the oil and gas industry in Nigeria. The labour unions within each company use collective bargaining to negotiate a uniform minimum compensation on behalf of their members, which has the implication of rewarding low and high performers with equal allowances (housing, transportation, lunch, etc.) if they are in the same job category. Although this practice has been criticised over the years as setting aside labour factors in compensation determination, thus leading to ineffective allocation of wages and salaries with a consequent negative impact on productivity. The practice has subsisted for two reasons. First, there has been a feeling of unfairness over the years due to the assumption that foreigners are exploiting oil resources without adequate compensation of their local employees, along with a perceived lack of equity due to the disparity between the compensation of expatriates and indigenous workers. Second, the government regularly intervenes to pacify the labour unions in order to avoid strikes that could disrupt oil production and supply. The Nigerian economy is largely dependent on oil, which on the average, accounted for over 70% of government revenue and 90% of foreign exchange earnings up to 2018.

The components of compensation in the oil and gas sector consist of monetary and non-monetary benefits. The monetary benefits are expressed in fixed monetary compensation (basic salary, housing allowance, transportation allowance, etc.); incentives (performance-based bonus, profit sharing, and share schemes); benefits in kind (home ownership schemes, lunch and status car); and retirement benefits (expressed in gratuity and pension benefits). The non-monetary compensation policies are designed to recognise and reward employees with items of intrinsic value like plaques and certificates for outstanding accomplishments. Generally, the compensation level in the oil and gas industry is well above the market average but the actual reward amount within each of the compensation components is dependent on the in-house labour unions, market competitiveness, and headquarters policies. The local labour unions influence both minimum monetary compensation and annual increments for their members.

9.5.2 Emergent Trends of Compensation and Rewards in Developing Countries

The oil boom era in Nigeria, which began to change following economic recession in the mid-1980s and severely from 2016 as oil prices dwindled, has necessitated a new trend of emphasis on performance-based compensation. The mechanism of collective bargaining, which sometimes had earned employees above 50% uniform wage increases in a single negotiation, is discouraged in favour of individual merit increase. The profit sharing designated 'variable pay' is now commonly based on individual appraisal result and organisational performance rather than employees' job category and the outcome of union-management negotiation. Similarly, the allowances (housing, lunch, car, etc.) that were determined through union-management negotiation for the different categories of employees are now aggregated as consolidated or lump sum compensation and together with pension and gratuities and are subject to individual and company's output in order to link compensation to performance. These changes convey a clear message to employees about the benefits of individual and collective value addition to the company. Most staff in the oil and gas sectors in developing countries are recognising the tilt towards performance-based compensation by industry players. So, staff are ready to offer extra hours and offshore sacrifices for additional rewards.

Overall, the compensation policies in the industry have evolved towards providing financial incentives through structured merit pay increases to promote employees' commitment, job performance as well as retention. Hence, the oil and gas industry in developing countries provides a reward strategy that communicates to employees what companies value and is prepared to reward and recognise employees in support of the business. Figure 9.2 illustrates the total reward perspectives of the oil and gas industry.

Cash Pay	Non-Cash Rewards	Staff Benefits
• Salary	• Praises & 'Thank you'	• Pensions
• location payments	• Learning opportunities	• Paid leave
• Bonuses	• Event & Experiences	• Occupational sick pay
• Overtime	• Goods e.g., Cars, household items	• Company cars
• Sales Commission		
• Profit share		

Figure 9.2 Total reward perspective in the oil & gas sector

9.6 Conclusion

This chapter has discussed human resource management practices in the oil and gas industry in developing countries. Human resource management in the oil and gas sector is vibrant in developing countries and has become an exciting area of interest for understanding how human resource practices, concepts, and designs are utilised in the supply chain operations associated with the exploration, extraction, production, and consumption of oil and gas resources in the upstream, midstream, and downstream processes. The reason is that most of these oil companies are in their nascent state and, therefore, require capable human resources to efficiently manage these extractive and volatile business operations. The significant bundle of human resource practices required in the oil and gas industry includes recruitment and selection of employees; contracting and local content for manpower; strategic training and development; technological transfer and empowerment of personnel; and the rewarding of employees.

References

Ablo, A. D. (2015). Local content and participation in Ghana's oil and gas industry: Can enterprise development make a difference? *The Extractive Industries and Society, 2*(2), 320–327.

Ablo, A. D. (2016). *From local content to local participation? Exploring entrepreneurship in Ghana's oil and gas industry* (PhD thesis, University of Bergen, Norway).

Ablo, A. D. (2017). The micromechanisms of power in local content requirements and their constraints on Ghanaian SMEs in the oil and gas sector. *Norsk Geografisk Tidsskrift-Norwegian Journal of Geography, 71*(2), 67–78.

Ablo, A. D. (2018). Scale, local content and the challenges of Ghanaians employment in the oil and gas industry. *Geoforum, 96*, 181–189.

Abraham, K. K. A. (2017). Contractual agreements in Ghana's oil and gas industry: In whose interest? *Journal of Sustainable Development Law and Policy (The), 8*(2), 186–208.

Abrahamson, E. (1991). Managerial fads and fashions: The diffusion and rejection of innovations. *Academy of Management Review, 16*, 586–612.

Abugre, J. B., & Nasere, D. (2020). Do high-performance work systems mediate the relationship between HR practices and employee performance in multinational corporations (MNCs) in developing economies? *African Journal of Economic and Management Studies, 11*(4), 541–557.

Acheampong, T., Ashong, M., & Svanikier, V. C. (2016). An assessment of local-content policies in oil and gas producing countries. *The Journal of World Energy Law & Business, 9*(4), 282–302.

Ackah, C. G., & Mohammed, A. S. (2018). Local content law and practice: The case of Ghana. In J. Page & F. Tarp (Eds.), *Mining for change* (pp. 139–160). Oxford University Press. https://doi.org/10.1093/oso/9780198851172.003.0007

Adams, K., Nyuur, R. B., Ellis, F. Y., & Debrah, Y. A. (2017). South African MNCs' HRM systems and practices at the subsidiary level: Insights from subsidiaries in Ghana. *Journal of International Management, 23*(2), 180–193.

Adams, D., Ullah, S., Akhtar, P., Adams, K., & Saidi, S. (2019). The role of country-level institutional factors in escaping the natural resource curse: Insights from Ghana. *Resources Policy, 61*, 433–440.

Al-Mughairi, A. M. (2018). *The evaluation of training and development of employees: The case of a national oil and gas industry* (Doctoral dissertation, Brunel University London).

Amadu-Kannike, A., Abila, S., & Abila, D. (2020). Oil and gas local contents in Nigeria, Ghana and Brazil: A comparative analysis of legal and policy frameworks. *International Journal of Comparative Law and Legal Philosophy, 2*(3), 113–120.

Amenshiah, A. K., & Analoui, F. (2019). A strategic approach to local competency gap reduction: The case of the oil and gas industry in Ghana. *Physical Review, 47*, 777–780.

Andersen, T. B., Hansen, H., & Markussen, T. (2006). US politics and World Bank IDA-lending. *The Journal of Development Studies, 42*(5), 772–794.

Anthony, S. (2015). Impact of organisational culture on recruitment and selection practices in the oil and gas construction industry in Nigeria: Saipem in focus, *European Scientific Journal, 11*(16), 161–172.

Appiah, M. K., Possumah, B. T., Ahmat, N., & Sanusi, N. A. (2018). Policy environment and small and medium enterprises investment in the Ghanaian oil and gas industry. *International Journal of Energy Economics and Policy, 8*(4), 244–253.

Aryeetey, E., & Ackah, I. (2018). The boom, the bust, and the dynamics of oil resource management in Ghana. *United Nations University World Institute for Development Economics Research (UNU-WIDER)*, Working Paper 2018/89. wider.unu.edu

Baba, S. P. (2018). *An assessment of local content policy and its significance for foreign direct investment (FDI) in the oil and gas industry in Ghana* (Unpublished doctoral dissertation, University of Ghana).

Benin, P. (2017). *Human resource local content in Ghana's upstream petroleum industry* (Doctoral dissertations, Walden University).

Botes, A., Lane, A., & Edinger, H. (2019). *The new frontier: Winning in the African oil and gas industry*. Deloitte Publishers.

Darkwah, A. (2013). Keeping hope alive: An analysis of training opportunities for Ghanaian youth in the emerging oil and gas industry. *International Development Planning Review, 35*(2), 119–135.

Derous, E., & Fruyt, F. D. (2007). Developments in recruitment and selection research, *International Journal of Selection and Assessment, 24*(1), 4–6.

Grant, R. M. (2013). The development of knowledge management in the oil and gas industry. *Universia Business Review, 40*, 92–125.

Hassan, O. (2020). Artificial intelligence, Neom and Saudi Arabia's economic diversification from oil and gas. *Political Quarterly, 91*(1), 222–227.

ILO. (2012). *Current and future skills, human resources development and safety training for contractors in the oil and gas industry*. International Labour Office.

Kolstad, I., & Kinyondo, A. (2017). Alternatives to local content requirements in resource-rich countries. *Oxford Development Studies, 45*(4), 409–423.

Metcalfe, B. D. (2007). Gender and human resource management in the Middle East. *International Journal of Human Resource Management, 18*(1), 54–74.

Ndi, G. (2018). Act 919 of 2016 and its contribution to governance of the upstream petroleum industry in Ghana. *Journal of Energy & Natural Resources Law, 36*(1), 5–31.

Nelson, J. M. (2017). *Access to power: Politics and the urban poor in developing nations* (Vol. 5205). Princeton University Press.

Nwapi, C. (2015). Defining the "local" in local content requirements in the oil and gas and mining sectors in developing countries. *Law and Development Review, 8*(1), 187–216.

O'Donnell, S. W. (2000). Managing foreign subsidiaries: Agents of headquarters, or an interdependent network? *Strategic Management Journal, 21*(5), 525–548.

Obeng-Odoom, F. (2015). Oil boom, human capital and economic development: Some recent evidence. *The Economic and Labour Relations Review, 26*(1), 100–116.

Olawuyi, D. S. (2019). Local content requirements in oil and gas contracts: Regional trends in the Middle East and North Africa. *Journal of Energy and Natural Resources Law, 37*(1), 93–117.

Opatha, H. H. D. N. P., & Arulrajah, A. A. (2014). Green human Resource management: Simplified general reflections. *International Business Research, 7*(8), 101–112.

Osabutey, E. L. C., Nyuur, R. B., & Debrah, Y. A. (2015). Developing strategic international human resource capabilities in Sub-Saharan Africa. In C. Machado (Ed.), *International human resources management. Management and industrial engineering* (pp. 37–51). Springer.

Pegram, J., Falcone, G., & Kolios, A. (2018). A review of job role localization in the oil and gas industry. *Energies, 11*(10), 2779.

Pegram, J., Falcone, G., & Kolios, A. (2019). Quantitative and qualitative assessment of job role localization in the oil and gas industry: Global experiences and national differences. *Energies, 12*(6), 1154.

Senoo, J. E., & Armah, S. E. (2015). Assessing the effectiveness of Ghana's local content policy in the oil and gas industry. *Journal of Energy and Economic Development, 1*(1), 22–33.

Siavelis, P. M., & Morgenstern, S. (2008). Candidate recruitment and selection in Latin America: A framework for analysis. *Latin America Politics and Society, 50*(4), 27–58.

Stevens, P. (2008). National oil companies and international oil companies in the middle East: Under the shadow of government and the resource nationalism cycle. *The Journal of World Energy Law & Business, 1*(1), 5–30. https://doi.org/10.1093/jwelb/jwn004

Sumbal, M. S., Tsui, E. & See-to, E. W. K. (2017). Interrelationship between big data and knowledge management: an exploratory study in the oil and gas sector. *Journal of Knowledge Management, 21*(1), 180–196.

Sumbal, M. S., Tsui, E., See-to, E., & Barendrecht, A. (2017). Knowledge retention and aging workforce in the oil and gas industry: A multi perspective study. *Journal of Knowledge Management, 21*(4), 907–924.

Torrington, D., Hall, L., & Taylor, S. (2008). *Human resource management.* Pearson Educational Limited.

Wenger, E., McDermott, R. A., & Snyder, W. (2002). *Cultivating communities of practice: A guide to managing knowledge.* Harvard Business School Press.

Wilson, E. & Kuszewski J. (2011). *Shared value, shared responsibility: A new approach to managing contracting chains in the oil and gas sector.* IIED.

Wood, G. (2015). South African multinationals in Africa: Growth and controversy. In M. Demirbag, & A. Yeprak (Eds.), *Handbook of emerging market multinational corporations* (pp. 222–238). Edward Elgar.

Wood, G., & Bischoff, C. (2020). Human resource management in Africa: Current research and future directions–evidence from South Africa and across the continent. *The International Journal of Human Resource Management, 33*, 444–471.

Yeganeha, H., & Sub, Z. (2011). The effects of cultural orientations on preferred compensation policies. *The International Journal of Human Resource Management, 22*(12), 2609–2628.

10 Strategic Management in the Oil and Gas Industry

Obi Berko O. Damoah and Emmanuel Kwesi Boon

10.1 Introduction

Strategic management is increasingly becoming a viable tool employed by private, public, and non-governmental organisations to impact on their long-term sustainability through effective decision-making, strategy-formulation, and implementation (Issack & Muathe, 2017). Regarding firms in the oil and gas sector, strategic management enables them to adapt to the rapidly changing and complex trends in the operating environment (Johnsen, 2015). The relevance of prudent oil and gas management particularly in recent times cannot be understated because they drive national, regional, and global economies in an unprecedented manner. Yet, there is little academic research in general that shapes knowledge about strategic management of the oil and gas sector (Analoui & Analoui, 2015; Marcel & Mitchell, 2006). For organisations in the oil and gas sector to remain competitive, managers need to constantly monitor both the internal and external operating environments that can enable them to minimise strategic challenges and remain competitive and sustainable.

The oil and gas industry is the principal industry in energy markets worldwide. The industry contributes significantly to the economic development of the world. The concept of oil is mostly used interchangeably with petroleum, but oil is different from gas although in terms of uses there are similarities and differences. Oil is a liquid whilst gas is a vapour. Gas is used in cooking, heating, electricity generation, powering automobile engines, and many other purposes by individuals and institutions. In terms of similarities, both oil and gas are used as fuel. Oil and gas continue to be in high demand in emerging and developing economies because of the expansion of the automobile industry, which has resulted in a corresponding high demand for fuel. The structure of the oil and gas industry consists of upstream, midstream, and downstream segments. Organisations involved in the exploration and production of oil and gas are the upstream companies. Companies in the transportation and storage are called the midstream oil firms, whilst those in refining and marketing are the downstream organisations.

The chapter examines the strategic management of the oil and gas industry in emerging and developing countries. The chapter explores ways and

DOI: 10.4324/9781003309864-12

mechanisms in which a strategic management process can be applied in the oil and gas industry for developing and emerging economies to remain competitive. The rest of the chapter is structured as follows: Section 10.2 provides an overview of strategic management; Section 10.3 deals with the strategic management process; Section 10.4 focuses on a gap and SWOT analysis; Section 10.5 addresses strategic posture; Section 10.6 discusses development and selection of strategies; Section 10.7 presents an implementation process; Section 10.8 focuses on the strategy control process, whilst Section 10.9 concludes the chapter.

10.2 Overview of Strategic Management

Strategic management involves the act of aligning the influences of the internal business environment of an organisation with the changing trends from the external environment to deliver value to stakeholders (David & David, 2017; Godoy & Naidich, 2012). Managing oil and gas firms from emerging and developing countries from strategic management perspective is a key risk management tool and sustainability tool. As with every economy, the scope of strategic management covers all aspects of firms in emerging and developing countries, including multinational corporations with subsidiaries abroad. However, strategic management differs from operational management of oil and gas firms in emerging and developing countries. Whilst operational management addresses specific activities of firms in a specific area, strategic management impacts all aspects. Operational management activities are concerned with decisions which result in the day-to-day and/or short-term activities of firms, but strategic management decisions give rise to activities that impact on the long-term development of a firm. Furthermore, strategic management decisions are made by top management, whilst operational management decisions are made by lower-level managers. Compared to operational management activities, strategic management activities involve significant investment of resources, both financial and human (Sabri & Beamon, 2000).

10.3 The Strategic Management Process

The strategic management process is the conceptual framework used to manage organisations strategically. The conceptual framework is universal, although its application differs from organisation to organisation due to differences in country contexts (Johnson et al., 2013; Parker, 2008; Pollard & Hotho, 2006; Sabri & Beamon, 2000). The elements of the strategic management process consist of situational analysis, gap analysis, strategic posture, strategy selection, implementation, and strategy control. The six elements are classified into three phases namely, strategy formulation consisting of situational analysis, gap analysis, strategic posture and selection of strategies, implementation, and strategy control. The application of the strategic management process in oil and gas firms in emerging and developing markets to produce strategic management practices is discussed below.

10.3.1 Situational Analysis

Strategy formulation begins with situational analysis. Following Wheelen & Hunger (2011) and David (2009), situational analysis refers to understanding the environment where an organisation operates. Situational analysis is sub-divided into two steps: internal and external. Internal analysis seeks to understand a firm's strengths and weaknesses compared to competitors. Internal analysis is critical because it addresses the question whether, for example, oil and gas firms operating in developing economies can initiate a strategic move and sustain it based on their strengths in the light of their weaknesses. Being able to identify what a firm does better compared to its rivals assures the company that the new strategic initiative that is being embarked upon will be more likely to be a success because the identified strengths can be used as a basis for operating advantage. Another reason is that unearthing such exclusive advantages in the form of a strengths insulate a firm from negative influences from competitors.

In strategic management, what is considered a strength of a firm ought to be an exclusive advantage which is difficult for competitors to copy. Consequently, capacities and/or resources identified as strengths must offer a ripple effect on the weaknesses of the firm concerned. This implies that firms, including those in the oil and gas industry in emerging economies, dare not embark on a strategic initiative if they have not assessed their internal capacities and confirmed the availability of a significant number of strengths.

10.3.1.1 Conducting Internal Analysis

The strategic management field presents several approaches used to conduct internal analysis to establish a strength and/or a weakness (Henry, 2021; Rothaermel, 2018; Sholihah et al., 2019). Among the popular approaches are the resource audit and the value chain analysis.

According to Johnson et al. (2013) and Pearce and Robinson (2013), the resource audit ascertains a firm's exclusive resource advantage relative to competitors. In the resource audit, firms are disaggregated into three types of resources: basic resources (ones that are readily available to all players in an industry), threshold resources (resources required by regulators before the license to operate), and exclusive resources (resources above both the basic and threshold resources). Exclusive resources are the ones that put firms on top of their competitors. Large cash reserves, leading brand name, and competent senior executives are among the samples of exclusive resources. The confirmation of exclusive resources assures management of these firms that any proposed strategic move is likely to succeed.

The next approach is the value chain analysis which also identifies what a firm does best or poorly relative to its competitors by examining its activities and/or processes. The value chain approach examines the contribution of each activity a firm undertakes to create value for customers (Jaligot et al., 2016; Rosales et al., 2017). Human resource management, production, procurement, marketing, and engineering are examples of value-creation activities firms undertake. Once activities that create value are identified, the value chain analysis arrives at strengths and/or weaknesses by assessing the contributions of each activity to the total value a firm creates. By using either the value chain or the resource audit, companies operating in the oil and gas industry in emerging and developing markets will be able to identify their strengths and weaknesses in order to embark on strategic management activities.

10.3.1.2 Doing External Analysis

External analysis aims to identify external risks and opportunities; it addresses the question of whether there will be available and continuous business opportunities in, for example, an emerging market to justify any investments. Ensuring that there are business opportunities in a market before making a strategic move in terms of making investment is critical to achieving a competitive advantage. Doing external analysis will reveal to players in an industry the degree of external risks that is likely to limit a strategic move. Competitors' actions, influences from central government through regulations and/or laws, changes in exchange rate, government spending, and civil society actions are among the sources of external risks that pose potential limitation to efforts of firms (Chofreh et al., 2021; Nandond, 2019).

According to Crane et al. (2019) opportunities and risks have characteristics which include probability of occurrence, temporal immediacy, and social consensus. Probability of occurrence implies that there ought to be a certain degree of certainty that the opportunity exists in a market and will justify the investments firms make or in the case of risk, that there is the likelihood that it will occur and, therefore, needs to be managed. Temporal immediacy implies the probability of the event (risk or opportunity) happening quickly. Social consensus implies that there is more confirmation from stakeholders that such opportunity and/or risk is plausible. The output of external analysis, for example, assures the players in the oil and gas industry in emerging markets and developing countries that whilst existing risks can be managed in the light of any potential strategic investment that will be made, there is also the certainty of business opportunities to justify any strategic investments. Like, the approaches for conducting the internal analysis, the strategic management field offers alternative methods to guide firms to do external analysis. Two of the most popular methods for doing external analysis are the PESTLE framework and the Porter's competitive forces.

10.3.1.2.1 PESTLE ANALYSIS

Following researchers (e.g. David & David, 2017; Johnson et al., 2013; Pearce & Robinson, 2013), the PESTLE framework from strategic management answers the question: how for example oil and gas firms operating in emerging and developing countries could unravel external business opportunities and threats outside their control. The element in PESTLE is discussed as follows.

> **P-Political/Legal Influences**: The political and/or legal influence refers to government influences that either limit and/or enhance the strategic initiatives of firms. Most of these influences come in the form of policies, laws, and/or regulations. In every economy, government influences businesses through tax policies (e.g. corporate tax and income tax), environmental laws in relation to natural resources, including oil, gas, and mineral resources. Governments in emerging markets make regulations to ensure the quality of air, water, waste management, and chemical safety. Consequently, every oil and gas firm that aims to operate in emerging markets and developing economies will need to incorporate tax and environmental policies in their strategic initiatives. Influence from labour laws is another area every firm must address. In developing economies, samples of labour laws will cover child labour, working conditions, minimum wage, health and safety, discrimination, collective labour, and international labour laws, among others. Depending on the socio-economic development of a particular emerging market, government policies may either enhance or impede the strategic investment an oil and gas firm makes.
>
> **E-Economic Influence**: Economic influence is another potential source of external risk and opportunity which firms must consider in developing economies. Economic factors include inflation, exchange rate, interest rate, per capita income, and gross domestic income. In most developing countries, influences from inflation, exchange rate, and interest rate impact negatively on production cost and pose barriers to firms regarding survival, profitability, and sustainability. As a result, it will be impossible for an oil and gas firm operating in an emerging market to employ strategic management without first considering the risk implications of economic influences.
>
> **S-Social Cultural Influence:** As part of the situational analysis before embarking on a strategic investment, strategic management requires firms to analyse fully the components of the socio-cultural climate. The components of socio-cultural climate consist of population distribution, ethnicity, religion, and age distribution. The cluster of a population in a developing country determines the economic geography of that country and industry agglomeration. Understanding the age distribution of the population of in emerging economy, for instance, determines availability of human capital in the short, medium long-term.

Socio-cultural factors also determine taste and preferences in emerging economies. Such influences also manifest into practices such as attitude to time, work ethic, personal leadership, self-motivation of a citizenry, individualism versus collectivism, degree of power distance, masculinity, and future orientation of people in emerging economy (Hofstede, 2011). The foregone components have implications on oil and gas firms operating in emerging markets; meaning they cannot manage and operate strategically without analysing the tenets of socio-cultural influence.

T-Technology Influence: In recent times, technology is changing how goods and/or services are produced, warehoused, advertised, and distributed. In most cases, the technologies for the production process are external and outside the control of firms. Technological influence will also impact on production, storage, and distribution costs of firms. Depending on the existing technology in the oil and gas industry, for example, emerging market firms in these industries that are not able to leverage on technology due to its investment cost or other reasons are left behind other competitors. It is, therefore, a strategic requirement that emerging market firms in the oil and gas industry must not make any strategic move without first identifying the type of technology in the industry and ascertaining whether an existing technology will pose an opportunity or a risk

E-Ecological Influence: The ecological influence concerns the relationship between, for example, oil and gas firms in developing countries and life-support systems (e.g. air, weather, sun, water, climate change) in their respective environments. Often activities of firms impact negatively on life-support systems; consequently, in most developing economies, civil society groups in collaboration with various government ministries, agencies, and departments, advocate the protection of the life-support systems against unscrupulous activities of firms regarding their attitude to the systems. The importance of analysing the ecological environment cannot be overemphasised because bad media reportage from civil society organisations against firms whose activities pose damage to the life-support systems can lead to serious consequences, including limiting their survival and long-term sustainability. Therefore, firms will have to analyse the ecological impact before embarking on a strategic investment.

The PESTLE analysis is, therefore, imperative and forms one of the first two steps in conducting a situational analysis. Each of the variables in the framework must be estimated in terms of its impact to be incorporated into the strategic investment initiatives of, say, oil and gas companies in emerging and developing economies.

Porter's competitive five forces model is one of the popular frameworks in strategic management used to analyse external business opportunities and risks. Whilst the PESTLE framework looks at general external factors which impact on firms, Porter's five forces look at risk, and opportunity factors in a specific industry (e.g. the oil and gas industry in emerging markets). The framework argues that the degree of profit potential in say the oil and gas sector is associated with the impact of five forces at work (Berisha Qehaja et al., 2017). Therefore, the likelihood of a firm, for example, in the developing world to generate returns on its investment is partly dependent on the nature and strengths of the five forces at work (Bell & Rochford, 2016; Zhao et al., 2016). As a result, firms operating in the oil and gas industry in emerging markets will have to identify and estimate the impact of Porter's five forces prior to initiating a strategic investment. The five forces are as follows: threat of new entrants; threat of competition among rival firms; threat of substitution; threat of power of buyers; and threat of power of suppliers. These are discussed in the next sections.

Threat of Potential New Entrants: The assumption behind analysis of threat of potential new entrants is that new entrants entering, for example, the oil and gas industry in emerging markets pose a risk to existing players because they may poach key managers and win customers away from existing firms. Sometimes the new firms enter the industry with technological and innovation advantages and weaken existing firms. Therefore, one of the ways for oil and gas firms in developing economies to survive, become profitable, and remain sustainable is by constantly analysing the threat of potential new entrants. The risks associated with the threats of new entrants are universal across industries and so the oil and gas firms in emerging markets will have to analyse the threat of potential entrants and address its implications on their strategic investments.

Threat of Competition among Rival Firms: In an industry, the behaviour of existing firms is another source of risk to their competitors. Competitor actions in an industry include introduction of new products and/or services, strategic advertising and massive promotion, deliberate price cuts, costly after sales service, including provision of special guarantees and warranties, and the introduction of specific technologies. It is, therefore, a strategic requirement for every player in industry to constantly estimate their fellow competitors' actions and manage them. Therefore, as part of estimating threats and opportunities in emerging markets, the success of oil and gas firms depends in part on their capacity to estimate the actions of their fellow competitors and strategies to address their implication.

Threat of Customer Power: Volatile customer behaviour constitutes a major threat to competitors. The importance of customer behaviour is that the return of every investment is partly dependent on the sustainable relationship with strategic customers, especially those whose purchases constitute a significant portion of the production of a firm. The implicit assumption regarding how critical customer power is because the threat of customer power is outside the control of firms. In addition, the likelihood of customers switching to other producers makes it mandatory for every firm to constantly estimate the potential volatility of customer behaviour to remain sustainable. As a result, oil and gas firms working in emerging markets who decide to manage strategically will have no choice, but to identify, estimate, and manage customer power.

Threat of Supplier Power: Like, the power of the customer, the behaviour of suppliers of inputs and/or raw materials is equally volatile and therefore poses threats to producers and service providers. The threats of supplier power range from switching from buyers, price hikes, and supply failures, especially in cases where they are strategic or sole suppliers. Therefore, Porter's five forces model enables industry players to always envisage the potential risk posed by suppliers. So, like in every economy and industry, oil and gas firms doing business in emerging markets are admonished to critically consider supplier power, to estimate, and to hedge its impact in making a strategic investment.

Threats of Substitution: Substitution from Porter's perspective implies that there are times when the products in other industries can be used in place of what another firm offers. Substitute products offer options to customers and reduce the sales of other firms. As a result, strategic management cautions that firms making strategic initiatives must not leave out the impact of the threat of a substitute product from other firms. In the light of this, oil and gas firms operating in emerging markets are also required to estimate the power of potential substitute products as one of the requirements to employ strategic management.

10.4 Doing Gap Analysis and SWOT Matrix

After the operating environments have been analysed, and the potential risk and opportunity factors have been identified and estimated, the second phase in the strategic management process is for firms to do a gap analysis. Gap analysis is like drawing a dashboard based on the outcome of situational analysis and ascertaining where a firm stands in the light of the external risk, potential business opportunities, internal strengths, and weaknesses. Gap analysis follows from a SWOT analysis as shown in Table 10.1. The SWOT analysis (matrix) is a tabular representation of strengths, weaknesses, opportunities, and risks (Bell & Rochford, 2016). Gap analysis concerns the strategic insights that firms will deduce from their SWOT analysis. The implications of SWOT analysis and deducing gaps are that, for instance, the oil and gas firms operating in emerging markets are required to prepare a SWOT after conducting a situational analysis and to outline the gaps from the SWOT that need to be addressed. The outcome of the SWOT and gaps determines whether for example an oil and gas firm in an emerging and developing country is endowed with numerous strengths (exclusive advantages) compared to

Table 10.1 Sample SWOT matrix for an oil & gas company

Internal analysis	
Strengths	Weaknesses
• Large cash reserves • International brand name • Owned and partnered distribution channel	• Weak management • Inability to catch up with technology • Over centralisation of management

External analysis	
Opportunities	Threats
• Growing demand for oil and gas in emerging markets • Tax holiday policies for oil and gas firms in emerging markets	• High exchange rate volatility • Impact of COVID-19

Source: Designed by author

rivals, in order to make a strategic investment. Table 10.1 presents a fictitious example of a SWOT for an oil and gas firm from an emerging and developing market.

10.5 Strategic Posture of Oil & Gas Firms in Emerging and Developing Countries

Strategic management prescribes that the gaps that arise out SWOT analysis must be filled and this will then create a new strategic posture and/or direction for a firm. The new strategic posture out of the SWOT and the gaps identified will address a set of strategic questions such as the following.

1. What vision statement can be carved out of the gaps that emerged from the SWOT of an oil and gas firm in an emerging or developing market?
2. What mission statement can be carved out of the vision statement?
3. What strategic goals can be deduced following the mission statement?
4. What long-term objectives can be crafted from the strategic goals?
5. What annual objectives and/or targets can be developed from the long-term objectives?

What the process above implies is that at this level in the strategic management process, any oil and gas firm, for example, intending to employ strategic management, must take a strategic posture following gaps derived from its SWOT.

10.5.1 Components Strategic Posture

According to Johnson et al. (2013), and Pearce and Robinson (2013), the main components of the strategic posture are described as follows.

10.5.1.1 Vision Statement

This is the first component of the strategic posture. The vision depicts the ultimate future aspiration of a firm; it is its desired future state in undertaking a strategic initiative. From the perspective of oil and gas firms in emerging and developing markets, once the SWOT is arrived at, each oil and gas firm aiming at undertaking a strategic investment must craft a vision statement.

10.5.1.2 Mission Statement

The mission statement will for example explain the purpose of an oil and gas firm in a developing economy. In strategic management, a mission statement contains several components, but the three (3) most critical ones are a firm's products and/or services, identity, as well as its production and distribution approaches. So, once an oil and gas firm sets itself a vision, observing a mission statement is what achieves the vision.

10.5.1.3 Strategic Goals

Strategic goals are called the key result areas for achieving a mission. The strategic goals address the most important goals of the mission. Strategic goals clarify the output of the mission statement. In emerging markets, every oil and gas firm managing strategically is expected to extract specific strategic goals from its mission statement. For most oil and gas firms, samples of their strategic goals will include market share, sustainability, corporate social responsibility, technology and innovation, and ethics and compliance.

10.5.1.4 Long-term Objectives

Long-term objectives are strategic goals, as above, which are specific, measurable, assignable, realistic, and time-bound (SMART). They measure the strategic goals in a more specific fashion. In the light of this, oil and gas firms which decide to operate strategically in developing countries must break their strategic goals into specific long-term objectives whose attainment should be a minimum of three years.

10.5.1.5 Annual Objectives

Annual objectives are the aspects of the long-term objectives that are to be achieved annually. Whilst the long-term objectives make the strategic goals SMART, the annual objectives do the same, but deal with the aspects of the long-term objectives whose attainment is annual. So, all oil and gas firms doing strategic management must have annual objectives.

10.5.1.6 Core Values

Core values are behavioural competencies that define corporate processes and systems. They are a set of basic beliefs, creeds, mottos, mantras, and ideals that guide how members of an oil and gas firms conduct their lives to deliver their strategic posture. Implicitly, every oil and gas firm operating in an emerging market will have a set of core values to impact on their cultural practices.

10.6 Selection of Strategies

Following Pearce & Robinson (2013), strategies are defined in the context of two key issues in strategic management. The first aspect of strategy concerns which business a firm must engage in. The second issue concerns which market a firm must operate in. The second level of strategy is called business-level strategy, which concerns the basis on which a firm competes once the type of business to engage in and the market to operate are known. The type of business strategy that a firm chooses is critical because that is what determines the success in, say, the oil and gas industry. Types of business strategies in strategic management include differentiation, cost leadership, and niche market. The third level of strategy is called the functional level. A functional-level strategy deals with alignment of all business functions (e.g. accounting, finance, purchasing and supply, procurement, human resource management, marketing, information, communication technology, project management, administration, risk management) to the business-level strategy. The last level of strategy is called the operational-level strategy, which deals with what informs the day-to-day activities of a firm. Once goals are set, specific and targeted strategies are needed to achieve them. This will be applicable to all oil and gas firms operating in emerging markets which choose to manage strategically. Therefore, each of the oil and gas firms will have to make specific choices regarding each of the four levels of strategies to realise their strategic goals as contained in their strategic posture.

10.7 Strategy Implementation

Following Olson et al. (2018), once strategies are identified (i.e., corporate, business, functional and operational), the next stage is to convert these strategies into outputs. Among the strategies, the one that converts all others into outputs and activities is the functional strategy. Consequently, strategic execution is the operationalisation of the functional strategies of firms to achieve the annual objectives and/or the targets which were derived from the long-term objectives (Olson et al., 2018; Tawse & Tabesh, 2021). Overall, all functional strategies are put together as the organisation-wide implementation plan in the strategic management process. The implication of strategic implementation on oil and gas firms operating in emerging markets is that once strategies are formulated each firm must convert its business strategy to functional strategies consisting of annual measurable outputs aiming at achieving the long-term objectives. The implementation plans are what will help oil and gas firms to realise their strategic goals on a day-to-day basis and so no strategic plan can create results without the accompanying implementation plans. A typical implementation plan of an oil and gas firm will consist of the following elements:

- Activities and/or what is to be done annually
- Timing of execution
- The sequencing and dependencies of activity execution
- The co-execution of activities
- The results of activities
- Baseline of outputs
- Person responsible for activities
- Implementation tools (e.g. Gantt Chart, actions plan, budget)

10.8 Strategic Control

Following Johnson et al. (2013) and Pearce and Robinson (2013), strategy control is the last aspect of the strategic management process. This stage consists of monitoring, review, and evaluation of the strategic results. Strategic monitoring will consist of data collection by the oil and gas firms operating in emerging markets on the attainment of the annual objectives and/or targets of the strategic process on daily basis. This process takes place across all the functional plans where the annual targets are realised. Regarding strategic review, once data is collected regarding the annual objectives, they are examined periodically to ascertain positive and/or negative variances and to proffer remedial actions where possible. At this stage, the targets review could be monthly, bi-monthly, quarterly, half-yearly, or annually. The final stage, which is the evaluation stage, can either be mid-term or terminal. Within this stage, management seeks to ascertain the overall impactful results following the implementation of the long-term objectives.

10.9 Conclusion

The present chapter has discussed the implications of the strategic management approach to engaging in an oil and gas business in emerging and developing countries. The chapter starts by introducing the oil and gas industry and the oil and gas firms operating in emerging and developing countries as the context. The chapter presents the strategic management process in tandem and discusses in a step-by-step fashion, the implications of each of the strategic management process, and/or approach on oil and gas firms in emerging and developing countries.

References

Analoui, F., & Analoui, B. D. (2015). Strategic management in a national oil corporation: The case of Libya. *European Scientific Journal, 11*(16), 23–36.

Bell, G. G., & Rochford, L. (2016). Rediscovering SWOT's integrative nature: A new understanding of an old framework. *The International Journal of Management Education, 14*(3), 310–326.

Berisha Qehaja, A., Kutllovci, E., & Shiroka Pula, J. (2017). Strategic management tools and techniques usage: A qualitative review. *Acta Universitatis Agriculturae et Silviculturae Mendelianae Brunensis, 65*(2), 585–600.

Chofreh, A. G., Goni, F. A., Klemeš, J. J., Moosavi, S. M. S., Davoudi, M., & Zeinalnezhad, M. (2021). Covid-19 shock: Development of strategic management framework for global energy. *Renewable and Sustainable Energy Reviews, 139*, 110643.

Crane, A., Matten, D., Glozer, S., & Spence, L. (2019). *Business ethics: Managing corporate citizenship and sustainability in the age of globalization*. Oxford University Press.

David, F. (2009). *Strategic management: Concepts and cases* (12th ed.). Pearson Education.

David, F. P. S. P. R., & David, M. E. D. (2017). *Strategic management: Concepts and cases: A competitive advantage approach*. Pearson.

Godoy, M. C., & Naidich, D. P. (2012). Overview and strategic management of subsolid pulmonary nodules. *Journal of Thoracic Imaging, 27*(4), 240–248.

Henry, A. (2021). *Understanding strategic management*. Oxford University Press.

Hofstede, G. (2011). Dimensionalizing cultures: The Hofstede model in context. *Online Readings in Psychology and Culture, 2*(1), 2307.

Issack, I. A., & Muathe, S. M. A. (2017). Strategic management practices and performance of public health Institutions in Mandera County, Kenya. *International Journal for Innovation Education and Research, 5*(12), 155–165.

Jaligot, R., Wilson, D. C., Cheeseman, C. R., Shaker, B., & Stretz, J. (2016). Applying value chain analysis to informal sector recycling: A case study of the Zabaleen. *Resources, Conservation and Recycling, 114*, 80–91.

Johnsen, A. (2015). Strategic management thinking and practice in the public sector: A strategic planning for all seasons? *Financial Accountability & Management, 31*(3), 0267–4424.

Johnson, G., Whittington, R., Scholes, K., Angwin, D., & Regnér, P. (2013). *Exploring strategy text & cases* (Vol. 10). Pearson.

Marcel, V., & Mitchell, J. V. (2006). *Oil titans: National oil companies in the Middle East*. Chatham House Brookings Institution Press.

Nandonde, F. A. (2019). A PESTLE analysis of international retailing in the East African community. *Global Business and Organizational Excellence, 38*(4), 54–61.

Olson, E. M., Slater, S. F., Hult, G. T. M., & Olson, K. M. (2018). The application of human resource management policies within the marketing organization: The impact on business and marketing strategy implementation. *Industrial Marketing Management, 69*, 62–73.

Parker, L. D. (2008). Strategic management and accounting processes: Acknowledging gender. *Accounting, Auditing & Accountability Journal, 21*, 611–631.

Pearce, J. A., & Robinson, R. B. (2013). *Strategic management: Planning for domestic and global competition* (13th ed.). McGraw-Hill Irwin.

Pollard, D., & Hotho, S. (2006). Crises, scenarios and the strategic management process. *Management Decision, 44*, 721–736.

Rosales, R. M., Pomeroy, R., Calabio, I. J., Batong, M., Cedo, K., Escara, N., & Sobrevega, M. A. (2017). Value chain analysis and small-scale fisheries management. *Marine Policy, 83*, 11–21.

Rothaermel, F. T. (2018). *Strategic management: Concepts* (Vol. 2). McGraw-Hill Education.

Sabri, E. H., & Beamon, B. M. (2000). A multi-objective approach to simultaneous strategic and operational planning in supply chain design. *Omega, 28*(5), 581–598.

Sholihah, M. A., Maezono, T., Mitake, Y., & Shimomura, Y. (2019). Towards development a PSS business evaluation: Proposal of internal and external analysis for sevitizing manufacturers. *Procedia CIRP, 83*, 363–368.

Tawse, A., & Tabesh, P. (2021). Strategy implementation: A review and an introductory framework. *European Management Journal, 39*(1), 22–33.

Wheelen, T. L., & Hunger, J. D. (2011). *Concepts in strategic management and business policy*. Pearson Education India.

Zhao, Z. Y., Zuo, J., Wu, P. H., Yan, H., & Zillante, G. (2016). Competitiveness assessment of the biomass power generation industry in China: A five forces model study. *Renewable Energy, 89*, 144–153.

11 Corporate Governance in the Oil and Gas Sector

Daniel Ofori-Sasu, Patience Aseweh Abor, Collins Ntim, and Teerooven Soobaroyen

11.1 Introduction

It is obvious that the oil and gas (O&G) industry is extremely important for the economic transformation of many developing and emerging countries across the globe. Recently, the emerging O&G producers in emerging and developing contexts like those of Africa have accounted for about 8% of the global oil output. The African continent produces an average of nearly 330 million metric tons of oil annually and has huge potential for exploration and production (Faria, 2021). There is a considerable history of O&G resources across developing and emerging markets and it remains a primary driver for economic development across the region. More than half of the countries on the continent are currently net oil importers. It has been estimated that the region generated 7.2 million barrels of oil per day in 2021, up from approximately 6.9 million barrels per day in the previous year, the lowest production level since 2000. New oil and natural gas deposits have recently been discovered in a number of developing and emerging countries around the world and these emerging O&G producers have shown strong interest in receiving governance advice. In particular, they want to avoid the mistakes that have led to breaches of accountability by some manufacturers around the world. Among the many factors that have contributed to the decline in O&G production, including high and volatile oil prices, issues related to corporate governance practices have been a major concern in the O&G industry (Badeeb et al., 2016). Thus, while weak corporate governance systems pose a challenge for most developing and emerging economies, they represent an opportunity for O&G producing countries to seek guidance from developed economies to deal with those challenges. Considering the current uncertainties surrounding energy supply, the main drivers of future demand, as well as expected future global economic growth and technological development, there is a need to assess the position of emerging markets in terms of governance and the institutional framework for the O&G sector.

Despite the growing number of studies on sector governance and energy sector development, there are very few contributions to the corporate governance literature in the O&G sector of emerging and developing markets.

DOI: 10.4324/9781003309864-13

Not much is known about the state of the O&G governance structure in Africa. This chapter contains theoretical literature on corporate governance in the O&G sector in developing and emerging countries. Its purpose is to draw persuasive conclusions and suggest ways of developing the region's corporate governance mechanism as applied in the O&G sector, based on a systematic review of related work on corporate governance in the O&G sector. Given the growing belief that poor governance and the resource curse are linked (Van der Ploeg, 2011; Van der Ploeg & Venables, 2011), the mechanism of governance in the O&G sector in Africa is expected to attract more attention in academic research and in the political arena. However, the chapter provides a valuable starting point for future research in this direction.

This chapter attempts to make holistic and novel contributions to the literature. As far as we know, it provides a comprehensive analysis of the theoretical and conceptual understanding of corporate governance practices of the O&G industry in developing countries and emerging markets.

11.2 Corporate Governance: Concepts and Theories

The area of corporate governance has been widely researched because the issues of governance are unique to different economies (Abor, 2007; Abor & Fiador, 2013; Amran et al., 2014). According to Mayer (1997, p. 10), 'ways of aligning the interest of investors and managers and ensuring that firms operate efficiently for the benefit of investors' are referred to as corporate governance. Corporate governance is the central framework in which companies build trust with their stakeholders (i.e. shareholders, managers, governments, wider community, and public). Corporate governance is a direct control system to control the investment structures set up by managers and, therefore, the investments made by stakeholders (Clarke, 2003; Schmidt, 2003). Abid and Ahmed (2014, p. 851) state that 'corporate governance is a system by which banks are managed and controlled for long-term results'. Corporate governance is not only about protecting the interest of the owners, but also about creating long-term value for the company. Corporate governance is the combination of rules, regulations, or laws by which companies are managed, directed, or controlled. The term denotes the components that influence the interests of an organisation's partners, including investors, customers, suppliers, directors, and executives.

The challenges and theoretical perspective of corporate governance seem to explain the reasons why most sectors exist in the country. Thus, the theories underlying corporate governance about board structures are agency theory (Berle & Means, 1932); management theory (Donaldson & Davis, 1991); stakeholder theory (Freeman & Reed, 1983); resource dependency theory (Pfeffer & Salancik, 1978); and institutional theory (Jensen & Meckling, 1976). Jensen and Meckling (1976) proposed agency theory to explain the contradictory behaviour between owners and managers. Evidence in the literature shows that agency theory emerges from the separation of ownership and management (Jensen & Meckling, 1976; Panda & Leepsa, 2017; Ross 1973). Jensen and Meckling (1976, p. 320) state that 'this separation of management and ownership would definitely lead to managerial negligence; an observation consistent with Adam Smith's'. It is questionable whether managers would act in their interests to the detriment of the owners' interests (Berle & Means, 1932). This phenomenon would lead to the agency problem (Ross, 1973). The agency problem is likely to result in some agency costs, such as surveillance costs (Jensen & Meckling, 1976). Agency theory is thus associated with the agency problem and its remedies (Panda & Leepsa, 2017).

From the perspective of the stewardship theory, 'a higher value is placed on the objective of convergence between the principal and the agent, than the personal interest of the agent'. In this sense, stewards are viewed as managers and executives whose activities and actions are aimed at maximising shareholder wealth. This implies that the interests between managers and shareholders may align over time, leading to the pursuance of greater risk taking that may increase shareholders' value. Thus, 'the individual goals of the stewards are aligned with the goals of their leaders (Davis et al., 1997, p. 601)'.

Stakeholder theory does not only focus on shareholders, but mainly includes the various interest groups that can be directly or indirectly affected by the company and whose activities can also directly or indirectly affect the company (Voß & Freeman, 2016). According to Hill and Jones (1992), stakeholders have a legitimate claim on the firm because there exists an exchange relationship between the firm and these stakeholders. Stakeholder theory advocates that 'the interest of the firm lies on stakeholders and that the firm must be managed in the interest of these stakeholders (e.g. shareholders, creditors, managers, employees, suppliers, customers, local communities and the general public)'.

The resource dependency theory is one of the influential theories in corporate governance, proposed by Pfeffer and Salancik (1978), which states that 'to understand the behaviour of an organisation, you must understand the context of the behaviour'. The resource-based theory or dependency theory shows how the managers of an institution can be very influential and powerful in relation to corporate organisations with a competitive advantage (Conner & Prahalad, 1996). For example, board members can leverage resources not available internally to the company while advancing shareholder interests. Resource dependence theory suggests how firms' external resources affect firm behaviour.

The institutional theory stipulates that firms mimic each other based on what major stakeholders consider to be the best practices within the industry (Campbell, 2007; Doh & Guay, 2006). The social legitimacy principle is one principle that helps to give clarity to this theory. The state of a firm feeling accepted by society (considered as external stakeholders) and as a result refuses to act in line with social demands, and to go according to socially acceptable norms is at risk of being considered legitimate and, therefore, hampering the firm's growth (Doh et al., 2010). Based on this principle, firms need to strategically incorporate social and environmental demands in their planning and activities so as to obtain the goodwill of society and maintain legitimacy. Overall, the actions of agents that conflict with the interests of shareholders may affect the corporate governance structure.

Based on the theories reviewed above, the chapter explores the corporate governance practices as it relates to the O&G sector in developing and emerging economies.

11.3 Overview of Governance Practice in the Oil and Gas Sector

Over the decades, there has been an upsurge in the quest for good corporate governance practices among various sectors of the economy, and the extractive sector is no exception. The Resource Governance Index (RGI) measures the quality of the resource sector governance in resource-producing countries around the world. The index enables stakeholders, particularly governments, civil society actors, private companies, and citizens, to understand how their countries are behaving in terms of resource governance. The next section provides an overview of specific governance tools employed by RGI, as well as the World Bank Governance Indicators to ascertain how the O&G sectors in the world and in the developing and emerging economies of the world.

The governance system of the O&G sector shows the norms, institutions, and processes that determine how power and responsibilities over the exploitation, discovery, production, and exportation and importation, as well as the marketing of O&G, are exercised. Figure 11.1 shows the scores of O&G producing countries based on the 2021 natural resource governance index that guides the decision-makers of the sector. Higher values on the index indicate good resource governance.

In Figure 11.1, Myanmar has the highest score of resource governance based on the selected countries in the RGI lists, followed by Guyana, Mexico, etc., in that order. Colombia recorded the lowest resource governance index. The implication is that countries with a lower score of RGI should use those with the highest score as benchmark to improve their resource governance mechanism.

Figure 11.2 shows the scores of corporate governance practices of state-owned oil and gas producing countries in the world, based on the 2021 RGI estimations.

In Figure 11.3, Colombia and Azerbaijan recorded the highest score of corporate governance practices among their state-owned O&G companies. This means that these countries employ better or strong governance system to control or govern their state-owned O&G companies. However, Tunisia, Senegal, and Myanmar lack robust governance mechanisms that control their state-owned O&G sector.

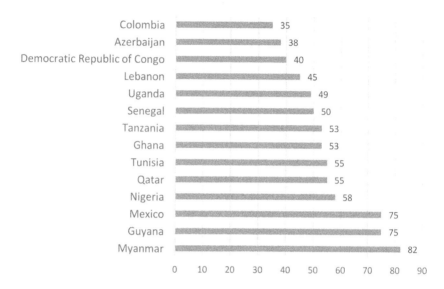

Figure 11.1 Resource governance scores of emerging oil and gas countries
Source: Authors' own construction based on data obtained from RGI index database

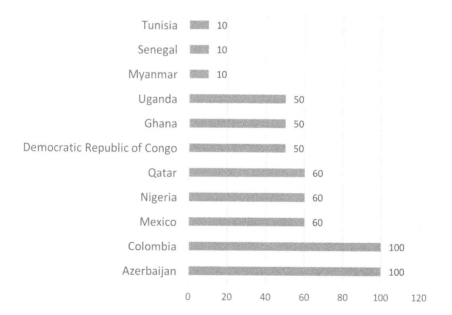

Figure 11.2 State-owned oil and gas corporate governance practice
Source: Authors' own construction based on data obtained from RGI index database

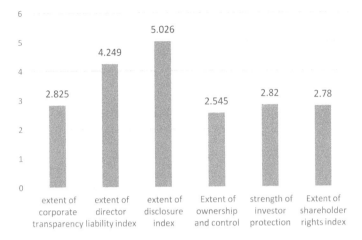

Figure 11.3 Oil and gas shareholder governance

Source: Authors' construction based on data from World Bank Development Indicators (2022)

Table 11.1 presents the ranking of countries based on the 2017 RGI. It shows the oil and gas producing countries that appear in the top 10 and the last 10.

Given a scale of >74 (good governance), '60–74 (satisfactory), 45–59 (weak), 30–44 (poor), and <30 (failing)' – the O&G sectors in Norway, UK, Canada, and the US were classified as the countries with good governance, appearing

Table 11.1 2017 RGI country ranking of the oil and gas governance

Country	Top 10 RGI 2017 Governance Index	Ranking		Country	Bottom 10 RGI 2017 Governance Index	Ranking	
Norway	86	1st	Good	Venezuela	33	43rd	Poor
UK	77	2nd	Good	South Sudan	32	44th	Poor
Canada	75	3rd	Good	Myanmar	31	45th	Poor
US	74	4th	Good	Yemen	30	46th	Poor
Brazil	71	5th	Satisfactory	Uzbekistan	29	47th	Failing
Indonesia	68	6th	Satisfactory	Democratic Republic of Congo	25	48th	Failing
Ghana	67	7th	Satisfactory	Equatorial Guinea	22	49th	Failing
Trinidad and Tobago	64	8th	Satisfactory	Sudan	21	50th	Failing
Mexico	61	9th	Satisfactory	Libya	18	51st	Failing
Argentina	57	10th	Weak	Turkmenistan	11	52nd	Failing

Note

Scale => 'Good (>74); Satisfactory (60–74); Weak (45–59); Poor (30–44); Failing (<30)'

Table 11.2 Performance shift

	2021 RGI score	Performance shift from 2017
Democratic Republic of Congo	38	+13
Ghana	78	+11
Nigeria	53	+11
Azerbaijan	56	+9
Myanmar	40	+9
Colombia	76	+5
Uganda	49	+5
Mexico	71	+3
Tanzania	55	+2
Qatar	45	+2

Source: Authors' own construction based on data obtained from RGI index database

in the four top ranking of 2017 RGI listing while Uzbekistan, Democratic Republic of Congo, Equatorial Guinea, Sudan, Libya, and Turkmenistan were classified as countries that had a failing governance system – appearing in the bottom six ranking in the same year.

On the performance shift front, Table 11.2 shows the major shift of resource governance index from 2017 to 2021. It reveals how well the governance structure of the O&G gas sector in selected countries perform over the year. A positive shift implies a good governance performance among the selected countries.

In Table 11.2, Democratic Republic of Congo recorded the highest performance shift (i.e. +13) in their governance from 2017 to 2021, followed by Ghana (+11), Nigeria (+11), Azerbaijan (+9), Myanmar (+9), Colombia (+5), Uganda (+5), Mexico (+3), Tanzania (+2), and the least recorded performance shift was found in Qatar (+2). Thus, emerging O&G countries that recorded lower scores of performance shift in their governance should put mechanisms in place by consulting their peers that have the best performance shift in governance.

Many developing and emerging countries have undertaken significant legal reforms in the O&G sector in recent decades. The RGI shows that in all but a few countries, there is an implementation gap between what the laws say and how resource management works in practice. A negative value for the compliance gap shows that in a particular O&G producing country, where legal reform has only recently occurred, the implementation of transparency and accountability provisions in that country lags behind. Table 11.3 shows the implementation gap based on the 2021 RGI estimation methodology for selected O&G countries.

As can be seen in Table 11.3, Qatar and Azerbaijan have a positive implementation gap, indicating that the governance structure of these countries focuses on implementation and enforcement of transparency and accountability rules to ensure good governance. Thus, countries with negative

Table 11.3 Implementation gap of governance in oil and gas economies

Country	2021 RGI law score	2021 RGI practice score	2021 RGI implementation gap
Azerbaijan	43	51	+8
Colombia	79	80	1
Democratic Republic of Congo	64	49	−15
Ghana	94	72	−22
Mexico	85	69	−16
Myanmar	56	41	−15
Nigeria	65	59	−6
Qatar	25	41	+16
Tanzania	67	49	−18
Tunisia	60	46	−14
Uganda	57	39	−18

Source: Authors' own construction based on data obtained from RGI index database

implementation gap should design mechanisms to monitor the capacity of government agencies, strengthen the role of auditors and parliament, and ensure solid implementation strategies.

11.4 Shareholder Governance Framework and Institutional Arrangements in the Oil and Gas Sector

To promote a sustainable governance system, policymakers have designed country-level governance frameworks that guide the governance practices of corporate organisations. These frameworks help to foster flexible control mechanisms that support an attractive governance and investment environment. On one hand, the World Bank doing business (2021) indicators[1] construct an index that captures six dimensions of protecting minority investors and shareholders' rights in corporate governance. The indicators range from 0 to 10, with higher scores indicating a higher level of governance. Figure 11.3 shows the levels of these indicators based on the 2010–2020 average for the O&G sectors in emerging and developing countries.

Given a range of 0–10, Figure 11.3 shows that the shareholder governance indicators lie between 2.5 and 5.1. 'Extent of disclosure index recorded the highest level of shareholder governance index in the oil and gas sector'. This implies that O&G companies in developing and emerging countries have a moderate rate of disclosure. In conclusion, O&G sectors in developing countries moderately review and approve requirements for related party transactions, internal disclosure requirements, as well as prompt and regular transactions with related parties. However, in the O&G sectors of developing and emerging countries, indicators of the level of corporate transparency, the level of board responsibility, the level of ownership and control, the level of investor protection, and the level of rights of shareholders are low.

On the other hand, institutional arrangements such as corruption control, government effectiveness, political stability and absence of violence/terrorism, regulatory quality, rule of law, and voice and accountability – are important for ensuring stable O&G governance. Stable governance refers to 'an end state where the state provides essential services and serves as a responsible steward of state resources; government officials are held accountable through political and legal processes; and the population can participate in governance through civil society organisations, an independent media and political parties (Milward & Provan, 2000)'. Institutional arrangement has been measured by the World Bank with the government stability index. Figure 11.4 shows government stability indicators for the O&G sector in emerging and developing countries. The data was obtained from the World Bank Governance database and these include political stability, control of corruption, regulatory quality, and government stability. The index ranges

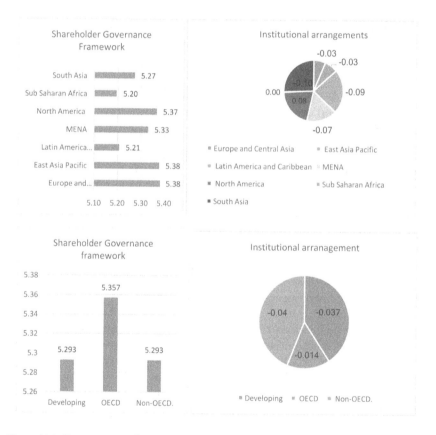

Figure 11.4 Governance and institutional framework across different oil and gas producing regions

Source: Authors' construction based on data from World Bank Development Indicators (2022)

Table 11.4 Government stability index

Control of corruption	Government effectiveness	Political stability and absence of violence	Regulatory quality	Rule of law	Voice and accountability
−0.04	−0.034	−0.005	−0.032	−0.027	−0.02

Source: Authors' construction based on data from World Bank Development Indicators (2022)

between −2.5 (weak government stability index) and 2.5 (strong government stability index). The index was computed based on the 2010–2020 average period of the O&G producing countries.

It can be seen in Table 11.4, the indicators are in negative, and this implies that institutional arrangements for the O&G sector in the region are weak.

Overall, the O&G shareholder governance framework in emerging markets and developing countries is low while institutional arrangement of oil-and-gas-producing countries in the region is weak.

In addition, the data indicates that this problem is very common in the O&G sector, but can vary from region to region. In view of that, the chapter presents an aggregate measure of the shareholder governance indicators and the institutional arrangements. The figures later highlight levels of aggregate weighted averages of shareholder governance and the institutional arrangements across different contextual settings of O&G sectors.

In relation to shareholder governance, the values of the aggregate index range from 0 (poor governance) to 10 (strong governance). From Figure 11.4, O&G producing countries in East Asia Pacific, Europe, and Central Asia have the highest average shareholder governance index compared to those in North America, MENA countries, Latin America, and Sub Saharan Africa. Similarly, OECD O&G-producing countries have the highest shareholder governance index, compared to developing countries and non-OECD countries.

In terms of institutional arrangement, the values of the index range from −2.5 (weak institution) to 2.5 (strong institutions). In Figure 11.4, it can be seen that the overall average index of institutional arrangement of oil-and-gas-producing countries, over the 2010–2020 period, is relatively stronger in North American countries and Sub-Saharan African countries compared to the average index of institutional arrangements in the other regions of the world.

Similarly, OECD oil-and-gas producing countries have the highest institutional arrangements, compared to those in developing and non-OECD regions.

Figure 11.5 shows that oil-and-gas-producing countries in lower-middle-income countries have the highest average shareholder governance index compared to those in other income brackets. Similarly, the value of the institutional arrangement is relatively stronger in lower-middle-income countries compared to the average index of institutional arrangements in the countries in other income brackets.

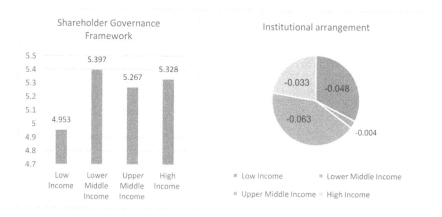

Figure 11.5 Oil and gas governance and institutional framework across different income brackets

Source: Authors' construction based on data from World Bank Development Indicators (2022)

The implication is that oil-and-gas-producing economies with low and weak shareholder governance and institutional arrangements need to adopt structural adjustment reforms to improve the governance controls.

11.5 Corporate Governance in the Oil and Gas Sector: Principles and Challenges

It is evident that new players are emerging in the O&G industry, and there is growing interest in other parts of the world to invest in emerging markets' energy sector (Alsharif et al., 2017). The O&G industry has the potential to contribute significantly to economic growth and help in the achievement of the number one goal of the sustainable development goals government. Given that poor governance and non-transparency are key issues hindering the development of the energy sector, governments, on one hand, are increasingly recognising the importance of ensuring an environment for O&G resources that boosts the development of the economy (Alsweilem et al., 2015; Collier, 2009; Extractive Industries Transparency Initiative [EITI], cited in Van Alstine, 2017, pp. 767–770). On the other hand, private institutions are looking for standards to help them manage the environmental, economic, social, and risk impacts of O&G operations. For the sustainable development of O&G resources, institutions and policymakers need to develop policies, principles, and best practices for internal governance mechanisms to support resource use in a way that does not prevent future generations from benefiting from resources (Energy Information Administration [EIA], 2017a ; Heal, 2007; Heller et al., 2014). In view of that, many international organisations have helped to design sustainable O&G development and to provide guidance on corporate governance issues for the sector. For emerging O&G countries, some are in the process of enacting a corporate governance framework to guide the practice of the industry while others have adopted a particular set of institutional arrangements designed to govern oil in an accountable manner (Heller & Marcel, 2011).

The creation of value for organisations depends on the development of strong corporate governance practices or frameworks. Basic compliance principles in governance are not enough to bridge the growing trust gap. The World Bank (2019) highlights some key principles that ensure good governance in the O&G value chain and, in consequence, promote sustainability. These include granting of contracts and licences; monitoring operations; enforcing environmental and social mitigation requirements; collection taxes; distributing income in a solid manner; and implementing sustainable development policies and projects. These principles are guided by six broad objectives that governments should target in achieving good governance practices. These objectives, according to the Natural Resource Governance Institute, are shown in Box 11.1:

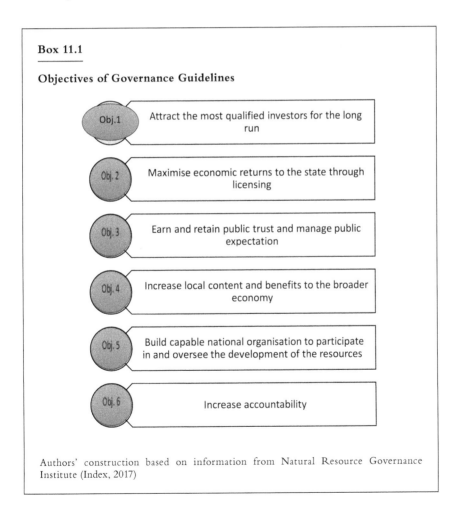

Box 11.1

Objectives of Governance Guidelines

- Obj. 1: Attract the most qualified investors for the long run
- Obj. 2: Maximise economic returns to the state through licensing
- Obj. 3: Earn and retain public trust and manage public expectation
- Obj. 4: Increase local content and benefits to the broader economy
- Obj. 5: Build capable national organisation to participate in and oversee the development of the resources
- Obj. 6: Increase accountability

Authors' construction based on information from Natural Resource Governance Institute (Index, 2017)

Good practice requires that the above objectives are focused to achieve an international standard of good governance practice and a sustainable governance system. It shows that international governance best practices may not be appropriate for emerging producers in the O&G sector (Chatham House, 2015; Marcel, 2015). However, some challenges may arise in following the principles and guidelines to achieve the goals of good governance. For example, in most emerging markets, it is difficult to attract the most qualified investors to a country with an unconfirmed resource base. There are many instances where licensing, prequalification criteria, and transparency in revenue mobilisation have become dominant challenges that confront O&G dealers in developing and emerging markets. In addition, the engagement of most governments in the petroleum sector and the participation of national organisations in resource development are weak. For most emerging O&G economies, local content budgets and capacity-building timeframes can be small and short, respectively. There is also a recurring debate about how or why inviting government action often leads to policy failure and poor governance.

The main concern about O&G governance is that developing and emerging market governments are receiving an insufficient share of the high incomes from production (The African Development Bank & African Union, 2009). This may be due, among other things, to contracts and regulations that are not designed to achieve maximum rents, and also to the oil-and-gas-related policies that are enacted to attract O&G investors have not evolved with the changing global dynamics and national mandate. Governance indicators consisting of government effectiveness, voice and accountability, political instability and violence, rule of law, regulatory quality and control of corruption, which are associated with exploration, production, and commercialisation, and the O&G investment climate in developing and emerging economies is relatively weak compared with industrialised countries. As a major source of economic prosperity and energy in developing and emerging economies, O&G resources are critical to good governance. However, they pose major governance challenges for these economies.

In response to these challenges, the new oil producers discussion group offers comprehensive recommendations for addressing the challenges faced by O&G country governance in the exploration, discovery, and early production phase. When adapting best international corporate governance practices, products from the O&G sector must take into account the national context, make practices more effective by aligning stakeholder interests for quick results, and enable incremental improvements of governance through best practices. The host government should invest in geological data, improve prequalification criteria, and create transparency to attract the most qualified O&G traders. Governments in the region, as well as national industries, must develop the capacity to engage, meaningfully participate and share information with affected communities to meet local expectations in line with the oil sector, and build trust. In this way, any form of knowledge asymmetry in oil companies is mitigated. Given the importance of licensing, the government needs to be more flexible in negotiations and tax structures to reap the early benefits associated with O&G. It is important to ensure incremental improvements in governance of the petroleum sector and build capacity to increase accountability, controls, and balances as resources are proven. Therefore, policymakers should encourage countries to adhere to good governance principles and transparency initiatives for revenue management.

While there are various facets to governance, roles and activities of governance could be categorised from two perspectives: from government and the private sector. Both have critical roles in sustainability (Zaganjor et al. 2018). From the public sector perspective, government should be responsible for providing and maintaining good governance in the O&G industry by ensuring: (1) an enabling environment to promote responsible O&G exploration and marketing which takes cognizance of the interests of other stakeholders; (2) transparency, political, social and economic stability at both macro and meso levels; (3) regulatory governance frameworks which precisely and clearly spell out the requisite requirements for all aspects of investment activities in the O&G industry, including sustainability planning, implementation, and reporting, within the governance, and the rule of law; (4) facilitation of positive multi-stakeholder interactions; and (5) general oversight, monitoring, and interfacing with regional and continental frameworks.

From the private sector perspective, it is important that the corporate governance mechanism: (1) focuses on sustainability from a business perspective, throughout the planning, implementation, and reporting chain; (2) appreciates the environment of communities in O&G exploration sites – especially the poverty in infrastructure, health, education opportunities; (3) invests in appropriate social and environmental engagement; (4) develops and adopts performance standards – measures of upliftment standards and minimisation of harm; and (5) collaborates with government to apply relevant standards in a bid to address the challenges identified.

11.6 Impact of Oil and Gas Governance

In corporate governance literature, significant differences exist in the execution of various reforms, ownership structures, institutional frameworks, and business standards and practices, between developed economies and emerging markets. From the emerging market context, the legal framework governing corporate entities is different from one economy to the other (Kyereboah-Coleman & Biekpe, 2006). Further, no single theory explains the relationship that exists between governance and wealth creation (Nicholson & Kiel, 2007). Thus, the association that connects governance structure to wealth is more 'varied and complex' than can be explained by a single theory in corporate governance, especially in the O&G sector.

It is unclear what role good governance plays and how it affects the economic performance and sustainable development of emerging O&G

economies. Although poor governance could be attributed to corporate failure, it is clear that proper governance of companies brings more good than harm (Jackling & Johl, 2009). This supports the claim that effective corporate governance helps in the attainment of high performance at both the firm and market levels (Klapper & Love, 2004). Despite its importance, the concept of O&G governance tends to be limited, especially the specific means by which this is measured. For instance, UNESCO asserts that governance – which is defined as 'structures and processes that are designed to ensure accountability, transparency, responsiveness, rule of law, political stability, equity and inclusiveness, empowerment, and broad-based participation' – can be subtle and not readily observable. On the O&G front, this is equally challenging, as many aspects are not readily observable and data is not widely available. In the literature, most studies have employed firm-specific governance characteristics for measuring governance but ignored the country-level measure of corporate governance (Appiah-Kubi et al., 2020; Agyemang et al., 2019). For instance, there is evidence that governance practices employed in developed economies may not be applicable to developing and emerging countries due to the different legal systems and institutional structures across different economies (Chakrabarti et al., 2008). Studies by Nahar et al. (2020), Prévost et al. (2002), and Young (2003) recognise the importance of corporate governance and state that good corporate governance improves company performance. However, the emergence of corporate governance was triggered by the financial crisis that hit Asian stock markets, in part due to the weak corporate governance of Southeast Asian companies (Möbius, 2002). This has triggered the development of more robust corporate governance measures that restore shareholder confidence (Dharwadkar et al., 2000). According to Monks and Minow (2004), a lot of governance reforms have been created, after the crisis, to build market investment opportunities for investors. This generated a number of studies that investigated corporate governance mechanisms in different corporate organisations.

Where the government plays a key role in the O&G sector in the developmental phases of exploration, discovery, marketing, and production of O&G, employing industry-level measures of governance may not be appropriate in ensuring that international best practices of governance are followed. It is against this backdrop that this chapter focuses on country-level measures of corporate governance since they are key indicators that capture best practices of governance as applicable in the O&G sector. Hillier et al. (2011) defined country-level governance as the 'favourable government or political structure and conditions for ecological, social and market-oriented development which is responsible for rational use of public resources and political power by the state'.

Countries that have adopted a particular set of institutional arrangements designed to govern O&G in an accountable manner can be expected to limit their exposure to the downside of declining oil wealth and to enable economic and social benefits to accrue.

In international development initiatives, good governance is anchored as a crucial goal for achieving sustainable development goals. In the UN 2030 Agenda for Sustainable Development, good governance and the rule of law, as well as an enabling environment at the national level, are important to maintain strong economic and sustainable development (The World Bank, 2019). In the O&G sector, sustainable development requires a political system that includes good governance and transparency. In light of this, some organisations such as the World Bank have developed governance structures or indicators that focus on six dimensions of institutional arrangements, namely: voice and responsibility; political stability; nonviolence; effectiveness of government; regulatory quality; rule of law; and corruption control. In addition, the World Bank has developed a shareholder governance framework for the resource sector, such as B. the Ease of Doing Business, which captures indicators such as the shareholder ease of doing business index, the level of corporate transparency, the level of director accountability, and the strength of investor protection.

Figure 11.6 shows the impact of shareholder governance on oil rent in the O&G sector of emerging markets and developing economies.

In Figure 11.6, it can be seen that shareholder governance framework is positively correlated with oil rent. The implication is that oil-and-gas-producing countries in emerging markets and developing countries are able to protect the interests of minority shareholders, reduce the risk of capital investments of shareholders, and maximise the wealth of shareholders tied to oil rents.

Figure 11.6 Impact of shareholder governance and institutional arrangements

Source: Authors' construction based on data from World Bank Development Indicators (2022)

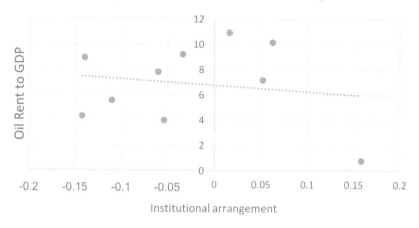

Figure 11.7 Impacts of institutional arrangements
Source: Authors' construction based on data from World Bank Development Indicators (2022)

Making informed choices and rational decisions about the O&G governance structure is critical for governance to work for less developed O&G markets. Issues of conflict, political stability, corruption, rule of law, and accountability have been a recurring feature of most developing and emerging economies throughout the pre-independence and post-independence periods. These have had far-reaching negative effects and may interfere with the governance structure and the wealth of the energy sector.

Figure 11.7 shows the impact of shareholder governance and institutional framework on oil rent in the O&G sector of emerging markets and developing economies.

In Figure 11.7, the institutional framework reduces the O&G rent in emerging markets and developing economies. This implies that countries that have less developed governance mechanisms or weak institutional arrangements are less likely to benefit from the natural resource wealth.

In general, a favourable condition of shareholder governance combined with an institutional framework contributes to a stable governance system in the O&G sector. As the experiences of developed countries have shown, the measures available to host-countries' authorities, which comprise improving the institutional frameworks, and establishing a good governance framework, are conducive to improving oil rents.

11.7 Conclusion and Policy Implications

This chapter has examined the nature and extent of governance in the O&G sectors of emerging and developing countries. The conclusion of the theoretical review and analysis in the chapter is that the potential benefits of good governance have not been fully realised by oil-and-gas-rich countries in emerging and developing economies. Several countries have demonstrated good governance in different contexts, recognising that weak or bad governance can be avoided with the right structural reforms, knowledge, institutions, regulations, and policies. So there is reason for cautious optimism that other countries in the region may have learned the hard lessons from the weak governance system in the past. With this in mind, these countries will seek strategies and policies that will enable them to reap the full benefits of applying good governance in the future.

The chapter provides a strong justification for countries with a low resource governance index to follow rich O&G countries with best governance practices as their benchmark to improve their resource governance mechanism. The state-owned O&G sectors should employ a better or stronger governance system to control their state-owned O&G companies. The study found a positive governance performance shift in developing and emerging oil-and-gas-producing countries. In addition, countries with negative implementation gaps should develop mechanisms to monitor the capacity of government agencies, strengthen the role of auditors and parliament, and ensure sound implementation strategies.

Although some emerging oil-and-gas-producing countries have a strong independent energy resource system to attract more investors, there are weak institutional arrangements that limit the positive impact of the governance framework in the O&G sector. In order to restore and improve investor confidence in oil-and-gas-producing economies, their governments must put in place appropriate institutional policies (better and more effective control of corruption, government effectiveness, political stability and absence of violence/terrorism, regulatory quality, the rule of law and voice and accountability), thereby streamlining the governance processes.

Note

1 'Extent of shareholder rights index (shareholders' rights and role in major corporate decisions); extent of ownership and control index (governance safeguards protecting shareholders from undue board control and entrenchment); extent of corporate transparency index (corporate transparency on significant owners, executive compensation, annual meetings and audits); extent of disclosure index (review and approve requirements for related-party transactions, internal, immediate and periodic disclosure requirements for related-party transactions); extent of director liability index (minority shareholders' ability to sue and hold interested directors liable for prejudicial related-party transactions); and strength of minority investor protection index (simple average of the extent of conflict of interest regulation and extent of shareholder governance indices)'.

References

Abid, G., & Ahmed, A. (2014). Failing in corporate governance and warning signs of a corporate collapse. *Pakistan Journal of Commerce and Social Sciences*, 8(3), 846–866.

Abor, J. (2007). Corporate governance and financing decisions of Ghanaian listed firms. *Corporate Governance: International Journal of Business in Society, 7*(1), 83–92.

Abor, J., & Fiador, V. (2013). Does corporate governance explain dividend policy in Sub-Saharan African countries? *International Journal of Law and Management, 55*(I3), 201–225.

Agyemang, O. S., Osei-Effah, M., Agyei, S. K., & Gatsi, J. G. (2019). Country-level corporate governance and protection of minority shareholders' rights: Evidence from Arian countries. *Accounting Research Journal, 32*(3), 532–552.

Alsharif, N., Bhattacharyya, S., & Intartaglia, M. (2017). Economic diversification in resource rich countries: History, state of knowledge and research agenda. *Resources Policy, 52*, 154–164.

Alsweilem, K. A., Cummine, A., Rietveld, M., & Tweedie, K. (2015). *Sovereign investor models: Institutions and policies for managing sovereign wealth*. John F. Kennedy School of Government. Center for Science and International Affairs and Center for International Development, Harvard Kennedy School.

Amran, A., Lee, S. P., & Devi, S. S. (2014). The influence of governance structure and strategic corporate social responsibility toward sustainability reporting quality. *Business Strategy Environment, 23*, 217–235.

Appiah-Kubi, S. N. K., Malec, K., Maitah, M., Kutin, S. B., Pánková, L., Phiri, J., & Zaganjori, O. (2020). The impact of corporate governance structures on foreign direct investment: A case study of West African countries. *Sustainability, 12*(9), 3715.

Badeeb, R. A., Lean, H. H., & Smyth, R. (2016). Oil curse and finance–growth nexus in Malaysia: The role of investment. *Energy Economics, 57*, 154–165.

Berle, A. A., & Means, G. C. (1932). *The modern corporation and private property*. The Macmillan Company. [Reprint, 1991, Transaction Publishers, New Brunswick, N. J.]

Campbell, J. (2007). Why would corporations behave in socially responsible ways? An institutional theory of corporate social responsibility. *Academy of Management Review, 32*(3), 946–967.

Chakrabarti, R., Megginson, W., & Yadav, P. K. (2008). Corporate Governance in India. *Journal of Applied Corporate Finance, 59*, 59–72.

Clarke, D. C. (2003). Corporate governance in China: An overview. *China Economic Review, 14*, 494–507.

Collier, S. J. (2009). Topologies of power: Foucault's analysis of political government beyond 'governmentality'. *Theory, Culture & Society, 26*(6), 78–108.

Conner, K. R., & Prahalad, C. K. (1996). A resource-based theory of the firm: Knowledge versus opportunism. *Organization science, 7*(5), 477–501.

Davis, J. H., Schoorman, F. D., & Donaldson, L. (1997). Davis, Schoorman, and Donaldson reply: The distinctiveness of agency theory and stewardship theory. *The Academy of Management Review, 22*(3), 611–613.

Dharwadkar, B., George, G., & Brandes, P. (2000). Privatization in emerging economies: An agency theory perspective. *Academy of Management Review, 25*(3), 650–669.

Doh, J., & Guay, T. (2006). Corporate social responsibility, public policy, and NGO activism in Europe and the United States: An institutional-stakeholder perspective. *Journal of Management Studies, 43*(1), 47–73.

Doh, J. P., Howton, S. D., Howton, S. W., & Siegel, D. S. (2010). Does the market respond to an endorsement of social responsibility? The role of institutions, information, and legitimacy. *Journal of Management, 36*(6), 1461–1485.

Donaldson, L., & Davis, J. H. (1991). Stewardship theory or agency theory: CEO governance and shareholder returns. *Australian Journal of management, 16*(1), 49–64.

Energy Information Administration (EIA). (2017a) Monthly energy review: Energy Information Administration. Retrieved June 6, 2017, from https://www.eia.gov/totalenergy/data/monthly/pdf/mer.pdf

Faria, I. (2021). The market, the regulator, and the government: Making a blockchain ecosystem in the Netherlands. *Finance and Society, 7*(1), 40–56.

Freeman, R. E., & Reed, D. L. (1983). Stockholders and stakeholders: A new perspective on corporate governance. *California Management Review, 25*(3), 88–106.

Heal, G. (2007). A celebration of environmental and resource economics. *Review of Environmental Economics and Policy, 1*(1), 7–25.

Heller, P., & Marcel, V. (2011). *Institutional design in low-capacity oil hotspots*. Revenue Watch Institute.

Heller, P., Mahdavi, P., & Schreuder, J. (2014). *Reforming national oil companies: Nine recommendations*. Natural Resource Governance Institute.

Hill, C. W., & Jones, T. M. (1992). Stakeholder-agency theory. *Journal of Management Studies, 29*(2), 131–154.

Hillier, D., Pindado, J., De Queiroz, V., & De La Torre, C. (2011). The impact of country-level corporate governance on research and development. *Journal of International Business Studies, 42*(1), 76–98.

Index, R. G. (2017). Natural Resource Governance Institute.

Jackling, B., & Johl, S. (2009). Board structure and firm performance: Evidence from India's top companies. *Corporate Governance: An International Review, 17*(4), 492–509.

Jensen, M., & Meckling, W. (1976). Theory of the firm: Managerial behaviour, agency costs and ownership structure. *Journal of Financial Economics, 3*, 305–360.

Klapper, L. F., & Love, I. (2004). Corporate governance, investor protection, and performance in emerging markets. *Journal of Corporate Finance, 10*(5), 703–728.

Kyereboah-Coleman, A., & Biekpe, N. (2006). The link between corporate governance and performance of the non-traditional export sector: Evidence from Ghana. *Corporate Governance: The International Journal of Business in Society, 6*(5), 609–623

Marcel, V. (2015). Guidelines for good governance in emerging oil and gas producers. Research Paper, Energy, Environment and Resources, Chatham House.

Mayer, C. (1997). Corporate governance, competition, and performance. *Journal of Law and Society, 24*(1), 152–176.

Milward, H. B., & Provan, K. G. (2000). Governing the hollow state. *Journal of Public Administration Research and Theory, 10*(2), 359–380.

Möbius, J. M. (2002). Issues in global corporate governance. In *Corporate Governance: An Asia-Pacific Critique*. Sweet and Maxwell Asia.

Monks, R., & Minow, N. (2004). *Corporate governance* (Vol. 3). Blackwell Publishing.

Nahar, S., Azim, M. I., & Hossain, M. M. (2020). Risk disclosure and risk governance characteristics: Evidence from a developing economy. *International Journal of Accounting & Information Management, 28*(4), 577–605.

Nicholson, G. J., & Kiel, G. C. (2007). Can directors impact performance? A case-based test of three theories of corporate governance. *Corporate Governance: An International Review, 15*(4), 585–608.

Panda, B., & Leepsa, N. M. (2017). Agency theory: Review of theory and evidence on problems and perspectives. *Indian Journal of Corporate Governance, 10*(1), 74–95.

Pfeffer, J., & Salancik, G. R. (1978). A resource dependence perspective. In *Intercorporate relations. The structural analysis of business*. Cambridge University Press.

Prévost, A. K., Rao, R. P., & Hossain, M. (2002). Determinants of board composition in New Zealand: A simultaneous equations approach. *Journal of Empirical Finance, 9*(4), 373–397.

Ross, S. A. (1973). The economic theory of agency: The principal's problem. *The American Economic Review, 63*(2), 134–139.

Schmidt, R. H. (2003). *Corporate governance in Germany: An economic perspective.* https://doi.org/10.2139/ssrn.477761

The African Development Bank, & African Union. (2009). *Oil and gas in Africa.* Oxford University Press.

The World Bank. (2019). *Governance and development.*

Van Alstine, J. (2017). Critical reflections on 15 years of the extractive industries transparency initiative (EITI). *The Extractive Industries and Society, 4*(4), 766–770.

Van der Ploeg, F. (2011). Natural resources: Curse or blessing? *Journal of Economic Literature, 49*(2), 366–420.

Van der Ploeg, F., & Venables, A. J. (2011). Harnessing windfall revenues: Optimal policies for resource-rich developing economies. *The Economic Journal, 121*(551), 1–30.

Voß, J. P., & Freeman, R. (2016). Introduction: Knowing governance. In *Knowing governance* (pp. 1–33). Palgrave Macmillan.

Young, O. R. (2003). Environmental governance: The role of Institutions in causing and confronting environmental problems. *International Environmental Agreements, 3*(4), 377–393.

12 Implementing Total Quality Management in the Oil and Gas Industry

Daniel Agyapong, Evelyn Lamisi Asuah, and Edmond Yeboah Nyamah

12.1 Introduction

Corporate survival in today's business environment has become very challenging due to the intensive nature of competition. Business orgnaisations, thus, employ a variety of techniques to enhance their commercial performance. To improve their performance, many businesses have adopted total quality management (TQM) as a key component of their business strategy. For a business to be successful, it must have an efficient quality management system (QMS) in place in order to give its products and services high quality at a low cost.

Investment in quality is one of the major strategies that makes business organisations attractive, competitive, and sustainable. Robust quality management practices help such organisations to enhance their reputation, increase profitability, attract and retain customers, and foster strong business relations with national governments and state regulators. Apart from product quality, industries in various sectors such as aviation, automobile, electrical and electronics, real estate, food processing, and oil and gas, are building quality into all aspects of their organisation to gain a competitive edge, an approach referred to as TQM. The oil and gas industries have realised the importance of quality to compete and survive in unpredictable market (Srinivas et al., 2020). The QMS is one of the key elements to the success of any oil and gas project (Prabhakar, 2017).

However, evidence of poor-quality management in industries including oil and gas points to the need for firms to improve the allocation of vital resources along their supply chains to ensure business sustainability. For instance, the slip in quality practices in oil and gas firms, such as the Shell oil spill in Nigeria, the BP oil spill, and many more around the globe due to poor quality management, have incurred negative consequences in the oil and gas industry. Hence, stakeholders in the industry strive to ensure customer-driven processes and goals for continuous improvement of their business operations to compete and survive in the unpredictable market (Srinivas et al., 2020). With such importance attached to the industry, major firms seek to integrate TQM into their organisational functions such as production, design, marketing, and customer service to focus on meeting organisational objectives and customer needs (see Prabhakar, 2017). When implemented in the oil and gas industry, total quality could: reduce operational costs; reduce defects by improving quality within the production process; and improve customer satisfaction and employee morale to reduce employee turnover and hiring and training costs for new employees. Nevertheless, there are numerous hindrances (such as inability to alter organisational culture, lack of top managers' commitment, improper planning, and absence of continuous training) to implementing total quality in developing economies' oil and gas industries.

Given the immense contribution of the oil and gas industry to income, employment, foreign direct investment (FDI), and infrastructural development of both developed and developing economies, coupled with the great risks and complexities that characterise oil and gas projects, a robust QMS is a necessary strategy to employ in the sector. Petroleum operations should establish a strict assurance system and a quality responsibility system. The role of management to ensure the quality of petroleum operations would be to establish quality objectives, build and enforce quality standards, and ensure adherence to dynamic management.

The rest of the chapter is organised as follows. The next section covers quality and TQM in the oil and gas industry, followed by emerging issues in the industry that affect quality management; the TQM implementation process; critical success factors for TQM implementation; implications of TQM for the industry; challenges of TQM implementation; and lastly, the concluding section.

12.2 Quality and TQM in the Oil and Gas Industry

12.2.1 Quality Standards

Organisations in developing economies' oil and gas industries need to operate within local, regional, and international quality standards. Local quality standards are those standards and regulations peculiar to a country that petroleum firms are expected to meet. In Ghana, for example, the Environmental Protection Agency (EPA) prescribes various environmental standards that must be adhered to by firms in the oil and gas industry, and violation of such standards attracts various degrees of sanctions. Besides the EPA, the National Petroleum Authority (NPA) and the petroleum commission regulate the downstream and upstream sectors of the industry. Additionally, other statutes control the legislative and regulatory framework for Ghana's upstream and downstream oil and gas development and marketing. In Nigeria, the Federal Ministry of Environment conducts environmental impact assessments and issues certificates to oil and gas firms. The Standards Organisation of Nigeria also provides standards to ensure safety, quality, and environmental sustainability in the Nigerian and oil and gas industry. These must be met by firms operating within the confines of the country.

Beyond local regulatory requirements are some regional regulatory standards that the industry must adhere to. The Organisation for Standardisation (ARSO) is an intergovernmental standards body formed by the African Union in 1977 with the primary mandate of enhancing standards development, harmonising standards, and implementing them to boost Africa's internal trade prospects and the competitiveness of the region's products in the global market. ARSO is certified by the International Organisation for Standardisation (ISO), the global body for standardisation. ARSO participates in and organises conferences, seminars, and training workshops to encourage and educate members on implementing international quality and environmental requirements.

The ISO is a body that sets up international standards to ensure that products and services are of high quality, safe, and dependable. ISO had 167 members as of 2021, each representing a country, with about 22% from Africa. ISO 29001 applies to all firms that would like to: (1) set up, implement, sustain, and optimise a QMS in the petroleum industry; (2) ensure conformance with the firm's policy on quality; (3) seek certification of its QMS from an authorised third-party certification body; and (4) declare its conformance with the chosen international standard. ISO 29001 establishes the standards for a QMS in the petroleum industry. Its focus is to enhance customer satisfaction through the effective implementation of the system by providing procedures for improving the system and ensuring compliance with customer and other regulatory and legislative requirements. A firm must demonstrate its capacity to consistently supply products and services that meet customer expectations and regulatory and statutory standards. With ISO 29001, petroleum quality standardisation advances to include: a stronger emphasis on target setting, performance monitoring, and metrics; clearer management expectations; and more careful planning and preparation of the needed resources to ensure quality in the oil and gas sector. ISO 29001 is projected to result in broader international adoption of time-tested industry-quality system criteria for the petroleum industry, encompassing producers of petroleum industry materials and equipment. Additionally, ISO 14001 on environmental management also sets environmental standards for all industries, including oil and gas, one of the most environmentally impacting industries.

12.2.2 Total Quality Management (TQM)

TQM is a methodology for continually improving the quality of goods, services, and processes by taking into account the expectations and requirements of customers to boost satisfaction of customers and organisational performance. With customer satisfaction as its focus, TQM is based on the participation of everyone in an organisation to improve the quality of goods, services and processes, and even the organisational culture. TQM has evolved into a strategic concept that permeates all levels and elements of an organisation's structure and staff to increase the overall quality and customer satisfaction.

Edwards Deming is generally credited for the concept of TQM. This is the management concept he developed due to his experience with Japanese people. Dr Deming began working with the Japanese in the early 1950s to help them rebuild their industries and enhance their goods. A few decades afterwards, Japan's reputation shifted from one of the producers of 'dime-store crap' to producers of high-tech, high-quality items. They had grown into formidable competitors, with significant ramifications for the steel, shipping, and automobile industries. Given their appreciation of TQM as an efficient management approach, the Japanese might have been a formidable competitor in the oil and gas business if they had the necessary resources.

TQM has proved to be an effective management philosophy in the service and manufacturing industries that leads to success, mainly when employed in the oil sector. Many firms, particularly in the oil business, use TQM as a strategy and technique to improve the quality of corporate performance.

12.3 Emerging Issues in the Oil and Gas Industry That Affect Quality Management

Several emerging issues in the industry that affect TQM include quality assurance, globalisation, technological advancement, workforce diversity, and sustainability. These are discussed in next subsections.

12.3.1 Quality Assurance

Quality is a product's capacity to meet the demands of its customers. It is claimed that customers purchase quality and not quantity, making quality essential to the survival and expansion of businesses. Hence, how to increase product quality or reassure customers about product quality has become a significant concern for managers (Ramanathan, 2020). Before procuring petroleum, a majority of the purchasers conduct a chemical analysis termed a *crude oil assay*. The testing is undertaken in specialised laboratories and provides the purchaser with an insight into the crude's specific chemical and molecular features. This thorough hydrocarbon analysis helps purchasers minimise the risk of encountering a variety of challenges, such as mechanical malfunctions, quality issues, and environmental violations (Petro-online, 2021). Managers in the oil and gas industry thus have a significant task of continually improving quality standards to thrive.

12.3.2 Globalisation

The concept of globalisation has gained popularity in recent years. The globalisation of business refers to the unimpeded flow of products, services, technology, labour, capital information, and capital beyond national borders. It implies greater economic integration between nations where managers must operate in a world with no boundaries. Globalisation encourages international competition. Thus, organisations that formerly competed against local counterparts must now compete against international firms. It is challenging for the organisation to exist and thrive in such a setting. Globalisation is a common phenomenon in the oil and gas industry. Organisations must improve product quality while lowering costs, which is difficult for executives. For the oil and gas industry specifically in developing countries, the impact of globalisation has been quite diverse. Globalisation has had both beneficial and bad effects on Ghana's oil and gas business. It has garnered revenue, aided infrastructural improvements, encouraged the creation of local content, and promoted corporate citizenship. In spite of these, there are still a few obstacles to overcome in oil production, and these obstacles include resource collateralisation, labour issues, the ecosystem, and socioeconomic life. While advanced economies consume over a half of all hydrocarbons produced, they are only responsible for a quarter of the planet's oil and gas output and hold less than 8% of the world's residual reserves. This imbalance implies that developed nations will rely heavily on developing nations for their oil and gas needs. The industry in developing nations is, therefore, faced with the challenge of meeting various international quality standards.

12.3.3 Technological Advancement

The oil and gas supply chain consists of parts such as exploration, production, refining, marketing, and finally the consumer. Technological advancement has influenced how activities in each of these parts of the chain are conducted. Some of the technological advancements in the industry are the use of automation and robotics to enable automatic drilling, which minimises employee safety issues and increases efficiency; the use of fleet management technologies such as GPS tracking systems, and Internet of Things (IoT) which provides real-time data to improve decision-making. With IoT for instance, oil firms can foretell equipment breakdown and prepare for replacements beforehand. This consequently reduces total downtime and saves the firms huge sums of money. Additionally, satellite technologies and cloud computing afford oil firms the opportunities for better communication in offshore and other remote locations, while cloud computing enables firms to make efficient decisions, practice more efficient marketing as well as ensure environmental sustainability as virtual computers can perform much more with a fragment of the energy consumed by private data servers. According to McKinsey's research, offshore operators have the potential to save operating and capital expenditures 20%–25% per barrel just by relying on connectivity to deploy digital tools and analytics. Per their estimates, the use of advanced connectivity in drilling and production among others could advance the industry's value by $250 billion dollars by 2030 (Grijpink et al., 2020).

12.3.4 Workforce Diversity and Inclusiveness

Diversification of the workforce is a defining characteristic of modern enterprises. Organisations are growing more diverse in ethnic origin, gender, national origin, and age, enabling individuals of various religions and nationalities to coexist. Oil and gas firms are increasingly relying on diverse, mixed-gender teams that integrate the skills of both men and women. They now comprise team members with distinct cultural backgrounds allowing the young and old to work together more than ever before. In the petroleum industry, diversity and inclusiveness are worthwhile business strategies that corporate leaders should consider incorporating into their firms. An inclusive work environment fosters teamwork, mutual support, and respect among all organisational members with the goal of improving the involvement and input of the company's workforce. Although managing such a diverse workforce can present a significant management challenge, typically, oil firms that promote an inclusive culture in all facets of their business fare better than their competitors. The ability to effectively manage diverse workforces could provide the necessary platform for the success of the TQM initiative.

12.3.5 Sustainability

Globally, environmental issues and technology influence nearly every industry, but none as much as it does the petroleum industry. The oil and gas business is undergoing a massive shift as a result of a tsunami of concerns over sustainability. Tagged as one of the most environmentally harmful, the oil and gas industry receives a fair share of the sustainability pressures that businesses and industries face today. Environmental regulations have become stricter with numerous environmental standards to be met by firms in the industry. Firms risk huge fines for compliance breaches never seen before. Existing sustainability plans focus on adherence to health, safety, and environmental requirements, as well as increased contributions to the communities in which oil firms operate. However, the rising momentum for a low-carbon future is putting new demands on sustainability initiatives. Oil and gas businesses are under pressure to cut emissions due to changing policies on climate, shareholder and public pressure, as well as pressure from major investors. This sustainability challenge is further complicated by the diversification initiatives of oil and gas companies. Unlike in the past, a barrel of oil seems to be no longer the primary focus of many hydrocarbon firms. Shell, for example, has set a lofty aim of generating 50% of its income from non-fuels by 2025. Nonetheless, proper quality standards could help organisations to meet most of the numerous standards imposed on oil and gas firms.

12.4 Process of Implementing TQM in the Oil and Gas Industry

A successful TQM implementation follows several laid-down steps. In this section, we discuss the implementation process of TQM in the oil and gas industry.

12.4.1 Craft the Firm's Mission, Vision, and Strategic Plan

A firm should have a clear vision, mission, and strategic plan to implement TQM properly. To strategically implement TQM, the firm has to define its goal, vision, and strategic plan in the first stage of the TQM implementation process. The firm's vision, mission, and values are part of strategic quality planning. Ishikawa (1985) believes that a company's vision and purpose must be shared among all members, including employees. This makes it easier for employees to embrace and support strategic quality plans. Strategic planning initiatives for the oil and gas industry should consider potential environmental side effects of operations and the firm's social responsibilities.

12.4.2 Develop the Firm's Total Quality Management Plan

Strategic quality planning entails the development of a specific TQM plan from the vision, mission, and strategic plan. The quality plan specifies the quality standards, regulations, criteria, and best practices for a particular product or service, ensuring that the oil and gas company meets its quality goals and customer expectations and requirements. The TQM plan should conform to local, regional and international quality standards and regulations. Before implementing TQM, the business could establish, refine, or adopt strategic planning by developing detailed directions, manuals, and modus operandi. Strategic planning could be developed, improved, or implemented by the firm by preparing clear guidelines, manuals, and standard operating procedures before TQM execution (Othman et al., 2020).

12.4.3 Establish the Firm's Total Quality Infrastructure

Successful TQM implementation necessitates a significant shift in organisational culture, as TQM may entail overhauling or altering the organisation's culture, systems, and infrastructure. The proper organisational structure must be connected to the TQM implementation project, as some structures cannot manage particular projects (Kazemi et al., 2020). Thus, the infrastructure necessary to facilitate TQM implementation should be established. Policy, institutions, service providers, and the value-adding usage of international standards and conformity assessment procedures are all covered by the Quality Infrastructure System.

12.4.4 Train the People

Employees are key players in the success of every organisation, and they must be completely aware of and committed to the firm's never-ending commitment concept. They need to be made aware of the company's objectives and to feel part of the bigger team (Kumar & Sharma, 2018). Training of employees should involve an explanation of the overall quality specifications of the products and the quality operations of the company. Improving the quality of a company is inextricably linked to increasing the efficiency of individual employees or groups within the corporation. Therefore, organisations must train and re-train their members for successful TQM implementation (Egwunatum et al., 2021).

12.4.5 Manage Process Quality

Process management is a set of behavioural and methodological techniques that emphasise the actions and activities of an organisation rather than the achievement of goals. The main focus here is on adding value to the processes involved and improving quality and productivity rates for each worker. These objectives are accomplished by advances in work methods and the deployment of operator-controlled equipment, as well as through the adoption of continuous improvement philosophies and the elimination of direct handling of materials by the operator, which aid in lowering unit costs.

12.4.6 Focus on Results

TQM executives play a critical role in attaining a company's quality improvement and increased performance goals. Hence, they must be results-oriented (Kumar & Sharma, 2017). Total quality benchmarking and measuring should be included in the company's strategy. Quality programs should focus on measuring the percentage of deviations from the benchmarked values to avert the development of similar problems in the future.

12.4.7 Publicise, Communicate, and Celebrate Successes

Successful quality programs continuously inform and engage staff and customers, discussing and applauding all initiatives and achievements. When employees are aware of progress realised, new initiatives pursued, or opportunities for continuous learning, they take greater ownership of organisational processes. Customers are satisfied by feedback opportunities because they are more aware of the level of service provided and experience a sense of belonging. When feasible, participation, acknowledgement, and communication activities should centre on group accomplishments, and resources should be utilised. Lessons learnt should be communicated transparently to enable team members to identify an evidence-based intervention, identify implementation barriers, measure baseline performance, educate stakeholders and report performance feedback to staff and senior leaders.

12.4.8 Monitor, Review, and Control

Monitoring is a continual process of assessing an organisation's quality control system, which involves engagement quality control reviews, post-issuance reviews, and periodic audits of completed activities. It is an opportunity to improve the efficiency and effectiveness of the firm's services. Monitoring, evaluation, and control of the quality control system help maintain its performance by keeping pace with evolving professional standards and the nature of a firm's operations. Managers must constantly rethink the appropriate action plans for monitoring, reviewing, and controlling quality while realising that some variation is expected.

12.5 Critical Success Factors for TQM Implementation

For TQM to succeed in any industry, certain critical factors must be ensured. The success of TQM depends on such factors as committed leadership, use of customer-based approaches, process management, efficient communication, involvement and empowerment of staff, and continuous improvement.

12.5.1 Committed Leadership

Several studies suggest that leadership is among the most critical variables influencing a company's performance. The amount of visibility and support offered by management to ensure a total quality environment is commonly seen as critical to the success of TQM (Al-Damen, 2017). Leadership is key to influencing groups of people and mobilising resources. Top management leadership and support are anticipated to play a pivotal role in promoting the procedures and habits that result in setting quality goals, allocating resources for them, evaluating their performance, and improving them (Barouch & Kleinhans, 2016). Leadership is demonstrated through top management's consistent commitment to all quality program activities, building trust and eliminating fear, providing workers with the resources they require, and training and motivation.

12.5.2 Customer-Based Approaches

With customer satisfaction as the primary focus of TQM, the way an oil and gas company interacts with its customers is crucial to the success of a TQM initiative. The company needs to listen to its customers, develop connections with them, and use customer data to improve and find new prospects for innovation. Oil firms must understand that their success is mainly dependent on their customers. Hence, they must be able to anticipate and predict consumer demands by satisfying their wants, aiming to surpass their expectations, and facilitating cost savings through rapid service and effective communication (Munizu, 2014). Continual and persistent effort must be made to develop solid contact with customers by obtaining frequent feedback through market surveys and other tools.

12.5.3 Process Management

Process management is about how a company creates, manages, and develops its work systems and processes to provide value to customers and achieve organisational success optimally (Kafetzopoulos et al., 2015). It is concerned with the optimal design, management, and improvement of processes to properly satisfy and grow the value of consumers and other stakeholders. Technology is an influential factor in process management as it provides more accessible and faster ways of getting things done. Oil and gas firms adopting and aiming to adopt TQM should consider technologies that aid in executing tasks. Effective process management could yield customer loyalty and satisfaction.

12.5.4 Efficient Communication

Information and communication are essential for a successful TQM implementation. Effective communication amongst all organisational members or stakeholders in a specific project is critical since it is inextricably tied to the quality process (Othman et al., 2020). The senior management vision of quality must be conveyed to employees. However, if the vision or plan is not communicated effectively, it may lose clarity and drive. Collecting and analysing data on competitors from customers yields helpful conclusions that may be used to improve the quality of products and services (Jayaram et al., 2014). People will be more productive and efficient if they communicate more openly and often.

12.5.5 Empowerment and Involvement of Staff

Employee participation is essential to the success of quality programs. Worker involvement is achieved by utilising work teams, delegating greater responsibility and authority to workers, seeking chances to increase staff competence, exchanging knowledge and experiences among groups and teams, and motivating employees (Al-Damen, 2017). Sahoo and Yadav (2018) explain that senior management improve their abilities and increase their engagement with the firm by empowering workers. Thus, to solve the problem of internal resistance from employees, oil companies must emphasise training and reward systems that positively impact employee participation.

12.5.6 Continuous Improvement

Continuous improvement is an integral part of TQM. It is a persistent improvement of any scale focused on waste elimination in all organisational processes and systems, with all organisational members involved (Singh & Singh, 2015). The phrase continuous implies both gradual and breakthrough progress, which may be accomplished through management's frequent evaluations (Othman et al., 2020). It enables organisations to discover innovative methods for producing superior-quality products while staying competitive and surpassing consumer expectations (Al-Damen, 2017). Continuous improvement requires proactive behaviour rather than reactive. Thus, the old axiom, 'If it is not broken, do not fix it', morphs into 'Just because it is not broken does not mean it cannot be improved'.

12.6 Implications of TQM for the Oil and Gas Industry

Studies have found that the implementation of TQM in the oil and gas industry, just like in other industries, is linked to enormous benefits for the implementing firms. This section discusses some of the gains that accrue from TQM implementation.

12.6.1 Competitive Advantage

Globally, oil and gas companies embrace quality techniques to improve operational efficiency and competitiveness (Aletaiby, 2018). Firms now need to achieve market superiority over their competitors to survive and thrive, with the increasing globalisation. As a result, a sustainable competitive advantage is needed. TQM has been widely found to improve the competitiveness of the firm. Studies from various industries, from garment-producing (Ferdousi et al., 2018) to global businesses (Ganapavarapu & Prathigadapa, 2015), indicate positive correlations between TQM and competitiveness. Empirical studies in the oil and gas industry indicate a positive relationship between TQM and competitive performance (Wibowo & Adisty, 2017).

12.6.2 Productivity

Profitability is the ultimate objective of all business enterprises. Thus, all managerial choices, including TQM adoption and execution, strive to improve the organisation's performance. Management tries to improve performance by improving productivity as firms strive to make the most out of every amount invested. Productivity is a metric that indicates a firm's efficiency by comparing the output to inputs. Empirically, studies have reported that TQM positively impacts organisational efficiency (Carmona-Marquez et al., 2019). Measurable benefits in terms of productivity and project progress have been observed through the implementation of TQM. Iyer et al. (2013) investigated the effects of QMSs and TQM on productivity and observed a high rate of productivity change (11%) due to TQM efforts. Similar efforts in the petroleum industry can help improve productivity.

12.6.3 Customer Satisfaction

TQM is a means of improving an organisation's competitiveness, effectiveness, and adaptability to improve customer satisfaction. According to Deming (1986), customer satisfaction is perhaps the most crucial metric to measure the results of TQM methods, and numerous academics have essentially confirmed this. Anil and Satish (2019) note that implementing TQM practices in Indian manufacturing firms positively impacts customer satisfaction. Additionally, Mohammed and Saturday (2019) cite increased customer satisfaction and reduced customer complaints among companies implementing TQM.

12.6.4 Profitability

Studies have shown that quality management initiatives positively affect corporate performance (O'Neill et al., 2016). Ciptono et al. (2011) assessed the sustainability of the TQM implementation model in Indonesia's oil and gas industry. They found that quality management practices had positive and significant indirect relationships with company financial performance through world-class company practice and non-financial performance. According to Handfield et al. (1998), the positive association between TQM and profitability comes from two processes. The first is efficient internal performance within the firm, which leads to reduced waste, greater efficiency, and higher return on assets. The second is higher customer satisfaction, which increases customer referrals, brand value, and loyalty. This ultimately leads to a higher market share and sales.

12.7 Challenges of Implementing TQM

There are challenges to anticipate in implementing TQM in the oil and gas industry. One of such challenges identified by researchers in TQM is implementation difficulties rather than the TQM technique and theory. Evidence suggests the major reason for TQM's poor effectiveness is its inadequate application and shallow implementation, which is the situation in many businesses (Baxter & Hirschhauser, 2004). This indicates that some businesses are unwilling to apply TQM techniques and tools thoroughly. The primary issue is a severe absence of commitment and knowledge of TQM. The TQM idea is not successfully and comprehensively executed since some companies claim to have a TQM program without fully understanding the process. Perhaps organisations are unaware of the benefits of TQM implementation. Other studies, including Egwunatum et al. (2021), Kaur et al. (2020), Sahoo and Yadav (2018), have identified additional challenges common in many industries and countries as follows:

i Absence of managerial involvement, dedication, strategy, vision, and a well-defined objective
ii Insufficient TQM knowledge and awareness
iii Inadequate physical, financial, digital, or human resources
iv Absence of critical TQM success elements knowledge or experience
v Poor strategy planning with a focus on the challenges that develop after implementation

vi Inadequate central information systems, reporting, and equipment and supplies, thus contributing to logistical challenges
vii Lack of supplier-organisation relationship

If not consciously dealt with, these challenges could hinder the success of a TQM programme.

12.8 Conclusion

We conclude by emphasising that the advantages of TQM in the oil and gas industry are endless. Any offshore project implementing a TQM system is expected to become more productive and cost-effective. With TQM, businesses could save money by eliminating waste and rejecting goods, reducing repair and rework costs, lowering warranty and customer service costs, improving the efficiency of their production processes, and practising fiscal restraint by eliminating non-essential procedures and expenses. Consequently, management time is freed up to focus on increasing production, expanding the product variety, and improving existing offerings. Therefore, to achieve a sustained competitive advantage and ensure compliance with industrial and regulatory requirements, there is a need to implement the TQM philosophy efficiently. Managers should also increase information flow and optimise reporting structures within their firms for timely decision-making. They should also allocate resources in time to implement the TQM to improve performance.

Policymakers and regulatory bodies should formulate policies that increase visibility in the oil and gas supply chain and promote environmental, social, and economic sustainability for the industry's survival. Policies towards employees' professional development in terms of quality training, involvement, and incentives should be enhanced as the success of the oil and gas organisations depends on the skills and capabilities of the employees.

References

Al-Damen, R. A. (2017). The impact of total quality management on organisational performance case of Jordan Oil Petroleum Company. *International Journal of Business and Social Science, 8*(1), 192–202.

Aletaiby, A. A. (2018). *A framework to facilitate total quality management implementation in the upstream oil industry: An Iraqi case study* (Doctoral dissertation, University of Salford).

Anil, A. P., & Satish, K. P. (2019). TQM practices and its performance effects–an integrated model. *International Journal of Quality & Reliability Management, 36*(8), 1318–1344. https://doi.org/10.1108/IJQRM-10-2018-0266

Barouch, G., & Kleinhans, S. (2016). Learning from criticisms of quality management. *International Journal of Quality and Service Sciences, 7*(2/3), 201–216.

Baxter, L. F., & Hirschhauser, C. (2004). Reification and representation in the implementation of quality improvement programmes. *International Journal of Operations & Production Management, 24*(2), 207–224.

Ciptono, W. S., Ibrahim, A. R., Sulaiman, A., & Kadir, S. L. S. A. (2011). Sustainability of TQM Implementation Model In The Indonesia's Oil and Gas Industry: An Assessment of Structural Relations Model Fit. *Gadjah Mada International Journal of Business, 13*(1).

Carmona-Márquez, F. J., Leal-Rodríguez, A. L., Leal-Millán, A. G., & Vázquez-Sánchez, A. E. (2019). Does the isomorphic implementation of the TQM philosophy effectively lead to the simultaneous attainment of legitimacy and efficiency targets? *Journal of Management & Organization, 28*(6), 1256–1279. https://doi.org/10.1017/jmo.2019.79

Deming, W. E. (1986). *Out of the crisis.* MIT Center for Advanced Engineering Study.

Egwunatum, S. I., Anumudu, A. C., Eze, E. C., & Awodele, I. A. (2021). Total quality management (TQM) implementation in the Nigerian construction industry. *Engineering, Construction and Architectural Management, 29*(1), 354–382. https://doi.org/10.1108/ECAM-08-2020-0639

Ferdousi, F., Baird, K., Munir, R., & Su, S. (2018). Associations between organisational factors, TQM and competitive advantage: Evidence from an emerging economy. *Benchmarking: An International Journal, 25*(3), 854–873. https://doi.org/10.1108/BIJ-05-2017-0110

Ganapavarapu, L. K., & Prathigadapa, S. (2015). Study on total quality management for competitive advantage in international business. *Arabian Journal of Business and Management Review, 5*(3), 3–6.

Grijpink, F., Katsap, N., Verre, F., & Ward, R., (2020/11/06). How tapping connectivity in oil and gas can fuel higher performance. https://www.mckinsey.com/industries/oil-and-gas/our-insights/how-tapping-connectivity-in-oil-and-gas-can-fuel-higher-performance

Handfield, R., Ghosh, S., & Fawcett, S. (1998). Quality-driven change and its effects on financial performance. *Quality Management Journal, 5*(3), 13–30.

Ishikawa, K. (1985). *What is quality control?: The Japanese way.* Prentice-Hall.

Iyer, A., Saranga, H., & Seshadri, S. (2013). Effect of quality management systems and total quality management on productivity before and after: Empirical evidence from the Indian auto component industry. *Production and Operations Management, 22*(2), 283–301.

Jayaram, J., Ahire, S., Nicolae, M., & Ataseven, B. O. (2014). The impact of human resources and total quality management on the enterprise. *Procedia-Social and Behavioral Sciences, 124*, 27–33.

Kafetzopoulos, D., Gotzamani, K., & Gkana, V. (2015). Relationship between quality management, innovation and competitiveness. Evidence from Greek companies. *Journal of Manufacturing Technology Management, 26*(8), 1177–1200.

Kaur, M., Singh, K., & Singh, D. (2020). Identification of barriers to synergistic implementation of TQM-SCM. *International Journal of Quality & Reliability Management, 38*(1), 363–388.

Kazemi, A., Kim, E. S., & Kazemi, M. H. (2020). Identifying and prioritising delay factors in Iran's oil construction projects. *International Journal of Energy Sector Management, 15*(3), 476–495.

Kumar, V. & Sharma, R. R. K. (2017). Relating management problem-solving styles of leaders to TQM focus: an empirical study, *The TQM Journal, 29* (2), 218–239. https://doi.org/10.1108/TQM-01-2016-0002

Kumar, V., & Sharma, R. R. K. (2018). Leadership styles and their relationship with TQM focus for Indian firms: An empirical investigation. *International Journal of Productivity and Performance Management, 67*(6), 1063–1088.

Mohammed, A. M., & Saturday, E. G. (2019). Impact of total quality management on performance of oil servicing companies in Port Harcourt. *GSJ, 7*(3).

Munizu, M. (2014). A study on relationship between TQM practices and competitive advantage: Case at basic metal industry in Indonesia. *Australian Journal of Basic and Applied Sciences*, *8*(13), 290–295.

O'Neill, P., Sohal, A., & Teng, C. W. (2016). Quality management approaches and their impact on firms' financial performance–An Australian study. *International Journal of Production Economics*, *171*, 381–393.

Othman, I., Ghani, S. N. M., & Choon, S. W. (2020). The total quality management (TQM) journey of Malaysian building contractors. *Ain Shams Engineering Journal*, *11*(3), 697–704.

Petro-Online (2021). Quality Assurance in the Oil and Gas Industry – A Guide to Crude Oil Quality Testing. https://www.petro-online.com/news/measurement-and-testing/14/breaking-news/quality-assurance-in-the-oil-and-gas-industry-a-guide-to-crude-oil-quality-testing/55006.

Prabhakar, S. (2017). Quality management system (QMS) for engineering, procurement, construction/fabrication and installation (EPCI) operations on oil and gas projects. *International Journal of Engineering and Management Research*, *7*(5), 215–218.

Ramanathan, N. (2020). Embedding sustainability concerns into quality assurance. *Total Quality Management & Business Excellence*, 1–15. https://doi.org/10.1080/14783363.2020.1858712

Sahoo, S., & Yadav, S. (2018). Total quality management in Indian manufacturing SMEs. *Procedia Manufacturing*, *21*, 541–548.

Singh, J. & Singh, H. (2015). Continuous improvement philosophy – literature review and directions. *Benchmarking: An International Journal*, *22*(1), 75–119. https://doi.org/10.1108/BIJ-06-2012-0038

Srinivas, R., Swamy, D. R., & Nanjundeswaraswamy, T. S. (2020). Quality management practices in oil and gas industry. *International Journal for Quality Research*, *14*(2), 421–438.

Wibowo, S. S. A., & Adisty, F. Y. (2017). Analysis of total quality management on competitive performance of oil and gas industry. *Journal of Applied Accounting and Taxation*, *2*(1), 22–30.

13 Performance Management in the Oil and Gas Industry

*Teddy O. Kwakye, Rita A. Bekoe,
Kingsley O. Appiah, and Robert O. Nyamori*

13.1 Introduction

Research on the petroleum industry's performance management (PM) has focused mainly on this industry's various financial performance indicators. However, the survival of companies does not depend only on their profitability and financial health. PM systems must, therefore, be designed to capture information on all aspects of the companies' value drivers. An effective PM system has the potential to highlight a more focused strategy to measure, monitor, collect, analyse, and report key performance indicators that mirror how well a firm is following its vision, mission, strategy, goals, and objectives. Such a system is required to achieve the primary objectives of the oil and gas firms, including growth, profitability, and ultimate survival.

Contemporary management within the oil and gas industry has, thus, viewed PM as a tool to monitor and evaluate the financial and non-financial performance of employees and responsibility centres within the upstream and downstream organisations. Nonetheless, the existing literature has largely overlooked the development of a comprehensive PM framework in the oil and gas industry to assist relevant stakeholders, especially in emerging and developing countries. This is not very reassuring because economic transformation through natural resource discovery and production, including oil and gas, depends on effective governance institutions, including the PM systems surrounding the upstream and downstream of the supply chain system (see Van der Ploeg, 2011). This lack of an effective governance system could explain why – unlike in developed countries – oil production in emerging countries is associated with low economic growth, high poverty levels, civil war, and authoritarian rule (Roll, 2011).[1]

This chapter reviews PM tools used in the oil and gas industry, focusing on the practical PM methods employed in less developed economies. It assesses the potential of these tools to resolve PM issues in emerging and developing countries' oil and gas industries. The rest of the chapter proceeds as follows. Section 13.2 presents the theoretical underpinnings of PM systems. The different approaches to PM based on these theories are presented in Section 13.3. Sections 13.4 and 13.5 report the PM structure and how

DOI: 10.4324/9781003309864-15

performance indicators are selected, respectively. Section 13.6 highlights lean production and benchmarking as contemporary PM tools for continuous performance improvement. Section 13.7 concludes the chapter.

13.2 Performance Management Theory and Practice

Different frameworks can be employed to make sense of PM theories and practices. However, Burrell and Morgan's (1979) social theory offers a useful framework for understanding various theoretical dimensions of PM. Burrell and Morgan (ibid.) argue that social theory is based on four fundamental paradigms informed by different assumptions about social science and society's nature. These paradigms are functionalism, interpretivism, radical humanism, and radical structuralism. While these paradigms share some commonalities, Burrell and Morgan (ibid.) argue that they are mutually exclusive: researchers operating in one paradigm approach their problems from different ontologies and epistemologies.

PM, informed by functionalist theories, assumes that performance can be defined as those efforts which improve performance. Researchers in this paradigm often focus on how defined behaviour affects performance and are keen to predict future performance to improve it. PM consists of systems to define labour's conduct and assess, rate, and evaluate it based on this system – all from the managers' perspective (McKenna et al., 2011). PM systems emphasise a search for mechanisms for management to exercise control over the labour process (ibid.) This paradigm assumes that employees and managers share the same goals, and where this is not the case, managers seek to create performance systems to achieve goal congruence (ibid.).

PM systems can be loosely characterised as input or outcome-based (results). The focus of these PM systems is often on the measurement and assessment of efficiency and profitability. The most common system used to assess performance is variance analysis, whereby established standards are measured against actual performance, with deviations that exceed a certain threshold being subjected to investigation. Studies based on these ex-ante systems have tended to be objective and predict future performance using financial surrogates of performance. This ex-post approach to PM was criticised by Johnson and Kaplan (1986). They argued that the systems had become obsolete in the face of technological change and mounting competition, were not linked with the organisation's strategy, and could not enable the organisation to respond adequately to changes in competition and the business environment.

The interpretive PM theories are not separate theories but rather a way PM is studied/researched. Interpretivism assumes a subjective ontology where there is no objective performance. Instead, performance is constructed through employees' interactions and intersubjective understanding. Within this understanding, PM depends on the context. The researcher's role is to understand this often messy and complex context and how it contributes to constructing what performance is and how performance happens (McKenna et al., 2011). Much of the research informed by interpretivism aims to understand PM implementation and practices. Two discernible approaches – atheoretical and theoretical – are mainly adopted. Atheoretical approaches are those in which the phenomenon is studied without any theoretical framework. The data is interpreted from the actors' perspective without contamination by the researcher. However, many PM studies employ pre-existing theories to make sense of phenomena – the theoretical approach.

The radical structuralist and the radical humanist paradigms are only separated by ontology: the structuralist is objective, and the humanist is subjective. Otherwise, these paradigms are common in many respects, i.e., they share a wariness of the present which they view as temporal and structured to the disadvantage of others, in this case, the workers. Even when changes that address a prior problem are enacted, these theories maintain their suspicion that the new state contains seeds for an unequal system if we are not vigilant. A common theory within these paradigms is the critical theory associated with the emergence of critical management studies (CMSs). CMS argues that PM emphasises management control over labour and the labour process. The critical theory argues that society is characterised by unequal structures, such as those based on race or gender, which skew power relations to the worker's disadvantage. Often these structures are so embedded as to seem natural and deny workers the ability to understand their situation and seek a resolution. Marxist theories emphasise the need to understand how the owners control capital to the detriment of the workers. For these theories, PM systems entrench the advantage of capital over others, including labour.

13.3 Approaches to Performance Management

Several models or approaches to PM exist. Although each PM model is unique, generally, they emphasise establishing performance objectives, monitoring the performance, assessing the performance, providing feedback, and improving performance (Eaidgah et al., 2016). Over the years, scholars and practitioners have attempted to include other new performance dimensions, such as quality, business strategy, technology, and organisational norms, to incorporate cultural and behavioural elements (Bititci et al., 2012; Melnyk et al., 2014). This has led to more balanced and improved PM systems (Bititci et al., 2011, 2012; Cocca & Alberti, 2010).

Traditionally, PM is assumed as a series of activities – performance planning, performance appraisal, and performance improvement – that an organisation engages in to examine employee and operational performance. At the beginning of the year, management develops a strategy, establishes performance objectives, and develops specific plans to achieve the objectives (Armstrong, 2009; Busi & Bititci, 2006). These plans are then implemented, and management monitors the performance against the objectives set (Busi & Bititci, 2006; Eckerson, 2010; Parthiban & Goh, 2011). Employee and operational performance are subsequently evaluated at the end of the period, and performance improvement plans are developed when performance is below expectations (Busi & Bititci, 2006; Parthiban & Goh, 2011). This conventional PM process has outlived its usefulness in a more competitive and dynamic business environment. It emphasises financial indicators that are no longer adequate to provide accurate strategic management direction and manage multiple stakeholder interests.

In recognition of these drawbacks and the widely held view that PM is crucial in strategy formulation and implementation, the strategic framework of PM evolved (Ebrahimi & Sadeghi, 2013). This approach incorporates new organisational performance facets, including quality, customer satisfaction, time, and cost, into improving organisational performance and competitive strategy by explicitly linking the principles of the dimensions with the company's key performance measures (Bititci et al., 2012; Nudurupati et al., 2011). Such systems facilitate how performance measures align with business strategy, emphasising *'what to measure and how these measures achieved strategic alignment'* (Bititci et al., 2012, p. 5). Kaplan and Norton's (1996, 2001) balanced score card (BSC) is the most widely used tool consistent with this framework (Gopal & Thakkar, 2012). The basic principles of the BSC are discussed in Box 13.1.

The visual PM (VPM) system also adds a new dimension to an organisation's performance measurement and improvement techniques by using graphic visualisation techniques to heighten its focus on sustaining competitive

---

Box 13.1

BSC in Perspective

The increased dynamic complexities resulting from technological evolution and the rising sustainability issues to prompt swift regulatory changes have necessitated a change in management systems for companies in the oil and gas industry. Oil and gas companies have adopted new PM designs based on the BSC to ensure performance excellence in pursuit of competitiveness and financial stability. BSC 'provides executives with a comprehensive framework that translates a company's strategic objectives into a coherent set of performance measures' (Kaplan & Norton, 1993, p. 4). Employing BSC allows the companies to remove inefficiencies and inconsistencies, optimise processes, supply consumers with appropriate products, minimise surplus stocks, and proactively control the demand for the products. Managers employ BSC to understand how four main performance dimensions – financial resources, internal processes, customer preferences, and operations management – interact with the overall organisational strategy to build sustainable competitive advantage. This integrated approach enables the firms to assess their business strategy performance regarding areas as their financial goals, customer choice architecture, supply chain bottleneck resolutions, and organisational learning ability and capacity-building. BSC can be applied in any of the streams, i.e., upstream and downstream, of the oil and gas industry.

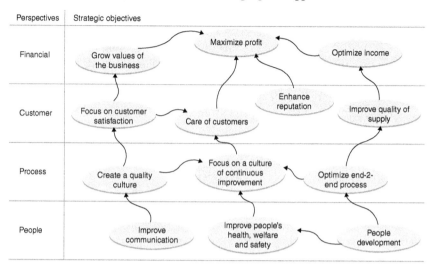

Figure 13.1 Strategy map
Source: Neely et al. (2006)

advantage (Liff & Posey, 2004). Proponents of this approach argue that representing data, information, and knowledge in a graphical format is also helpful for management to acquire deep insights into their operational performance via the clear picture created by the visual tools (Lengler & Eppler, 2007). Although existing literature recommends using visual tools at different stages in the PM process, application at the strategic development stage appears predominant (Bititci et al., 2016). Using strategy maps (Kaplan & Norton, 2000) to explain the cause-and-effect relationship between firms' actions and objectives, consistent with the performance dimensions of the BSC, is a typical application of the VPM model.

Often, the BSC is built on the organisation's strategy map that transforms corporate strategy and objectives into an interrelated set of strategic goals mapped consistently with the four BSC perspectives. Figure 13.1 demonstrates the strategy map of an energy company with the strategic aims of improving productivity, reputation, customer service, and more on using its resources.

13.4 Performance Management Structure

Better PM begins with a more focused measurement and reporting system (McCreery, 2014). Firms in the oil and gas industry require a more comprehensive PM system due to their supply chain features, manufacturing environment and nature of product as explained in Box 13.2. As illustrated in Figure 13.2, the performance of the oil and gas supply chain is primarily assessed based on: health, safety, and the environment (HSE); operational/

> Box 13.2
>
> **Why PM in the Oil and Gas Industry**
>
> A majority of the existing PM literature concentrates on discrete manufacturing with less emphasis on firms in the process industry, such as the oil and gas industry. However, the supply chain of firms within the oil and gas industry has distinct characteristics that require different PM systems. Varma et al. (2008) suggest process manufacturing environment as one of the prominent features of the oil and gas industry that distinguishes it from the discrete manufacturing firms. Moreover, the products from the oil and gas industry: (1) are highly inflammable, hence have relatively higher product handling risk; (2) can be contaminated easily, e.g., mixing kerosene with diesel (which is very common in developing countries; (3) involve bulk volumes regarding production and distribution leading to relatively high inventory carrying costs. Aside from these, the oil and gas industry faces the challenges of high transportation costs, human deficit, environmental issues, long supply chain, i.e., sourcing of crude to the finished product delivery to customers, and the price volatility of raw materials, i.e., fluctuating crude prices on the international market (Varma et al., 2008; Yusuf et al., 2018). To remain profitable and competitive in this volatile environment requires developing and implementing more comprehensive PM systems and structures in the industry.

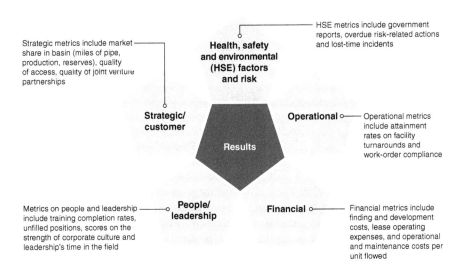

Figure 13.2 Firms' health and performance key performance indicators (KPIs)

Source: McCreery (2014)

internal business operations; financial; people/supplier management; customer/customer management; and learning and development (McCreery, 2014; Yusuf et al., 2018).[2]

The HSE provides some indicators by which employees' safety and well-being are managed in the oil and gas industry. These indicators seek to ensure that employees' general welfare is protected. The indicators used to measure HSE include recorded injury and work time lost, safety policy awareness or violations (HSE training), and incidents of non-conformance.

Determining the key performance indicators that measure the core business activities in this industry is very important. The operational indicator measures the internal business processes, such as the use of infrastructure, the rate at which natural gas (NG) flows through a pipeline, and work order compliance. It uses metrics such as reserve replacement ratio, capacity utilisation rate, operational and maintenance costs, and pipeline throughput.

The financial metrics measure the company's financial viability and health from the revenue and costs perspectives. Some indicators for this measurement include cost variance, finding cost ratio, lease operating expenses, and return on shareholders' investment.

The indicators on people and leadership measure the rate at which the company organises and completes training on the job successfully and the costs involved. In addition, it measures how employees share common beliefs and values and how such cultural values adapt to local conditions and values. Some metrics used are training completion rates, training costs, and the corporate culture's strength.

The strategic metric measures how the company is positioned in the industry to gain a competitive advantage. It considers the relationship between the company and its customers and suppliers. The indicators used include measuring the quality of the product or service provided by suppliers, the supplier's ability to meet unexpected orders, the share of the market in the basin, quality of access, customer satisfaction measures, etc.

13.5 Selecting Performance Indicator

The main aim of engaging in any business enterprise is to increase shareholders' wealth while satisfying the needs of other stakeholders by obtaining a competitive edge and providing sustainable products and services (Haji-Kazemi & Andersen, 2013). Measuring how successful firms are working to attain these goals and objectives is important to researchers and practitioners. It is without question that periodic performance evaluations and measurements are undertaken to facilitate the smooth running of organisations.

In selecting performance indicators, growth in sales, market share, and demand forecasting are all bases used. Obeidat et al. (2020) indicate that a performance measurement system should communicate expectations, provide feedback, motivate personnel through performance-based rewards, guide resource allocation, and provide better customer value.

The competitiveness of organisations is measured by the sales team's ability to equip themselves with skills and techniques to generate revenue and increase sales (Patel et al., 2019). Sales growth is determined by the yearly increase of past sales records. By providing competitive products that offer customer satisfaction, businesses can increase sales targets, thus increasing profits. Oil and gas businesses, by adopting the resource-based approach, develop the human and material resources that give them rapid expansion in sales growth, and maintain a sustainable competitive advantage (Sun et al., 2017).

Market share constitutes the firm totality of its segmented or targeted market. Market share as a determinant of organisational performance enables firms to achieve customer satisfaction and retention effectiveness. One strategy that can be implemented for an enterprise to achieve customer satisfaction and retention is to deploy marketing strategies that aim to reinforce customer loyalty by giving potential customers preferential treatment that offer them a sense of belonging (Fouché & Rolstadås, 2010). The resource-based view approach upholds the concept that oil and gas firms can gain a sustainable competitive advantage in market share if only they can create superior values that are heterogeneous and imperfectly mobile (George et al., 2016).

Industries operate in uncertainty requiring managers to think ahead and look into the future to refute specific problems that could prevent the company from achieving organisational objectives (Fouché & Rolstadås, 2010). Forecasting demand allows management to coordinate and unify plans to eliminate or minimise uncertainties. Demand forecasting involves estimating the sales of a product during a specified future period. The estimated demand could be for the entire industry or market, and the benefits of adopting a holistic approach to forecasting are enormous (Fouché & Rolstadås, 2010). The demanding nature greatly differs depending on the firm's operations and the activity for which the forecast is required (Iren et al., 2014). There are two types of demand: demand generated from many customers who buy only a small percentage of the product and the demand that comes into play when such demand is derived from a production schedule.

13.6 Performance Improvement Process

The functionalist tradition has promoted techniques that seek to improve organisational control and performance. Two of these techniques (focused on here) are lean production and benchmarking. It is not suggested that these are the only performance improvement techniques available; instead, these two are believed to provide an excellent introduction to the performance improvement concepts.

13.6.1 Lean Production

Lean production is not a technique but a particular way of seeking how a business should be managed. It is, therefore, promoted as a business improvement strategy (McEvay et al. (2013). Lean production encompasses a range of techniques, including just-in-time (JIT), total quality management (TQM), and continuous improvement strategy, to name just a few. Originally referred to as JIT, lean production philosophy is underpinned by continuous improvement and flow. Lean production distinguishes itself from traditional production, emphasising economies of scale, and fast production to full capacity (McEvay et al., 2013). Instead, lean production entrenches quality and JIT by producing to order or demand. The focus is to produce only enough to meet demand and minimise consumed resources.

The objectives of lean production are to meet customer needs, improve financial performance and capacity, reduce inventory, and ensure employee satisfaction. Introducing lean production requires cultural change throughout the organisation. While many organisations have attempted it, only a few have succeeded. Changing to lean production requires a long-term vision of achievable expectations, commitment to change from the top, disciplined measures to pursue these expectations, and an organisation-wide understanding of the need for and benefits of this change (McEvay et al., 2013). Lean production can be complemented with benchmarking – where the business can compare its strategies, processes, and performance against the best performers in its industry.

13.6.2 Benchmarking

In the oil and gas industry, lean production can be complemented with benchmarking for corporate self-assessment and comparing organisation forecasts, industry standards, regulatory requirements, and best practices in the oil and gas industry worldwide. Benchmarking involves learning from others to improve the firm's bottom line, people's profit, and plant. Following prior studies (e.g., Shvarts et al., 2018), the firm, industry, and regulatory benchmarking indicators should be modelled on three pillars: environmental management (EM), environmental impact (EI), and disclosure.

EM considers seven benchmark assessment criteria with 31 indicators. The benchmark assessment is the presence of (1) quantitative efficiency indicators, (2) the company's environmental policy, (3) energy efficiency program, (4) biodiversity conservation, (5) wildlife rescue section, and (6) voluntary insurance against environmental risks. These EM benchmark indicators have a direct association with the advancement of five United Nations Sustainable Development Goals (SDGs) – responsible consumption and production (SDG 12), life on land (SDG 15), sustainable cities and communities (SDG 11), affordable and clean energy (SDG 7), life below water (SDG 14), and climate action (SDG 13).

The EI contains 11 benchmark assessment criteria with 33 indicators. The benchmark assessment for EI includes but is not limited to the presence of (1) specific emissions of pollutants into the atmosphere, (2) specific emissions of greenhouse gases into the atmosphere, and (3) power generation from renewable energy sources (RES), including for the company's needs of an energy efficiency program. The EI benchmarks directly affect the advancement of six SDGs, specifically, clean water and sanitation (SDG 6), affordable and clean energy (SDG 7), sustainable cities and communities (SDG 11), responsible consumption and production (SDG 12), Climate Action (SDG 13), and life below water (SDG 14).

Disclosure and transparency (D&T) contains nine benchmark assessment criteria with 27 indicators. The benchmark assessment for D&T includes but is not limited to the presence of (1) nonfinancial reporting in compliance with the international requirements (e.g., global reporting initiative [GRI]), (2) public availability of information regarding seven of the EM goals for the reporting period in publicly accessible information sources, and (3) public availability of information regarding 11 EI goals for the reporting period in the publicly accessible information sources.

13.7 PM in Practice in the Oil and Gas Industry Supply Chain

Varma et al. (2008) validated the analytical hierarchy process (AHP)[3] in combination with the BSC as the primary PM system of the Indian upstream petroleum industry. The BSC perspectives are considered the first-level hierarchy, and the criteria for achieving those objectives are the second-level hierarchy. Their study provided a comprehensive PM framework that aids the determination of relative weights for the different BSC perspectives and each performance measure under the different perspectives. Varma et al. (2008) provide the following steps for PM utilising this framework based on an assumed set of performance measurement criteria and their respective weighting to illustrate the framework as provided in Table 13.1.

1. *Step 1*: Determine the values for each criterion at the second level of the hierarchy of the supply chains being compared.
2. *Step 2*: Convert the values obtained in Step 1 to a Likert scale of 1 to 9 to prepare pairwise comparison matrices for the alternative supply chains for each criterion.
3. *Step 3*: Determine the consistency ratio for each of the matrices determined in Step 2, where only consistency ratios 0, 1, or less are acceptable.
4. *Step 4*: Multiply the priority vector of each supply chain for every criterion with the criterion's weight given in Table 13.1, and add all the values obtained. This provides the performance of the supply chain at the second level of the hierarchy.
5. *Step 5*: Multiply the values obtained in Step 4 with the weights of the respective BSC perspectives. Add the values obtained to provide the composite number indicating the performance of the supply chain.

Table 13.1 Implementing the AHP and BSC PM framework in the petroleum industry

BSC perspective (1st level hierarchy)	Relative weight	Criteria under each perspective (2nd level hierarchy)	Relative weight
Customer	0.39	Purity of product	0.57
		A steady supply of finished product	0.43
Financial	0.23	Raw material prices	0.32
		Length of supply chain	0.17
		Physical risks	0.17
		Market share	0.34
Internal business process	0.19	A steady supply of raw materials	0.26
		Transportation costs	0.13
		Inventory holding costs	0.14
		Integrating with supply chain partners	0.14
		Optimisation of enterprise	0.19
		Volume flexibility	0.15
Innovation and Learning	0.19	Use of IT	0.76
		Postponement	0.24

Source: Adapted from Varma et al. (2008)

Yusuf et al. (2018) also examined the PM systems utilised in the NG industry across the Ghanaian NG supply chain, utilising upstream, midstream, and downstream companies. Premised on McCreery's (2014) performance measure categorisation, their study argued that PM in the NG industry must be based on HSE, internal business operations, financial, learning and development, and supplier and customer management. The Ghanaian NG industry supply chain generally employs a similar PM system, primarily the BSC (modified or unmodified). The BSC model is adopted to consider the interests and concerns of all the NG supply chain stakeholders. However, each stream of the supply chain has emphasised a different category. Firms in the Ghanaian upstream NG industry pay more attention to performance measures from the financial perspective, consider customer satisfaction paramount, and strive to be cost-efficient with their internal business. While the midstream emphasises HSE and financial performance measures, the downstream firms consider HSE and business performance measures paramount in their PM systems.

13.8 Conclusion

The oil and gas sector plays a strategic and social role in economies worldwide. Business in this industry is considered highly risky. It requires huge capital and technological investment to provide excellent services of discovering and exploiting new fields and converting oil reserves into production. PM systems aid oil and gas companies establish structures, systems, and processes to achieve operational excellence and competitive advantage. The primary PM theoretical underpinnings – the functionalist, interpretivist, and radical paradigms – have been explained in this chapter. It has been suggested that the functionalist theory underlies the conventional PM system of input or output (based) with a focus on financial performance indicators.

The evolution of the traditional PM framework into more balanced and strategically aligned PM models and their application in the oil and gas industry was also discussed in this chapter. The chapter has demonstrated that oil and gas companies commonly employ strategic PM frameworks, often complemented with the visual PM models, to ensure operational excellence and maintain a competitive advantage in this dynamic business environment. Notably, the chapter specified the BSC and strategy map – which transforms organisational strategy into an interrelated set of strategic objectives represented consistently with the financial, customer, internal process and learning performance perspectives – as the standard PM tool employed in the oil and gas industry.

The fundamental bases for assessing performance in the oil and gas industry – HSE, operational, financial, people, customer, and learning and development – and common KPIs for measuring these performance dimensions were also discussed in this chapter. The chapter suggested that KPIs in this industry provide a balanced view of the business to cover critical dimensions relating to business health and performance. Growth in sales, market share, and demand forecasting has also been discussed in this chapter as critical factors that oil and gas companies consider in selecting their KPIs. It is suggested that companies in the oil and gas industry choose from the many already existing standard metrics for exploration, development, and production.

Finally, the chapter discussed two primary performance improvement processes – lean accounting and benchmarking – highlighting how these processes help oil and gas companies attain operational excellence. In this chapter, lean accounting ensures improved performance through meeting customer needs, reducing inventory, and ensuring employee satisfaction. Benchmarking in the oil and gas industry involves learning from others regarding EM, EI, and D&T to improve the business. Hence, the oil and gas industry in emerging and developing countries must use EM, EI, and D&T for the environmental rating of oil and gas companies to offer the UN a more effective way of benchmarking the SDG's achievement.

Notes

1 Poor performance of supply chains has been attributed to the lack of measurement systems.
2 Some scholars argue that the upstream oil and gas industry PM systems must assess the exploration, development, and production performance, identifying performance measures under the four BSC perspectives. Others identified cost/finance indicators, task efficiency indicators, organisational indicators, learning and improvement indicators, and HSE indicators as the key performance measures in the oil and gas industry.

3 The AHP provides a framework for firms to cope with multiple criteria situations, allowing for the use of a system's hierarchical presentation to describe how changes in upper levels priority affect lower levels. This tool has been use to align BSc with organisational strategy and for benchmarking purposes (Chan, 2006; Varma et al., 2008).

References

Armstrong, M. (2009). *Armstrong's handbook of performance management: An evidence-based guide to delivering high performance.* Kogan Page Publishers.

Bititci, U. S., Ackermann, F., Ates, A., Davies, J., Garengo, P., Gibb, S., MacBryde, J., Mackay, D., Maguire, C., & Van Der Meer, R., Shafti, F., Bourne, M., and Umit Firat, S. (2011). Managerial processes: Business process that sustain performance. *International Journal of Operations & Production Management, 31*(8), 851–891.

Bititci, U., Cocca, P., & Ates, A. (2016). Impact of visual performance management systems on the performance management practices of organisations. *International Journal of Production Research, 54*(6), 1571–1593.

Bititci, U., Garengo, P., Dörfler, V., & Nudurupati, S. (2012). Performance measurement: Challenges for tomorrow. *International Journal of Management Reviews, 14*(3), 305–327.

Burrell, G., & Morgan, G. (1979). *Sociological paradigms and organisational analysis.* Ashgate Publishing Limited.

Busi, M., & Bititci, U. S. (2006). Collaborative performance management: Present gaps and future research. *International Journal of Productivity and Performance Management, 55*(1), 7–25

Chan, Y.-C. L. (2006). An analytic hierarchy framework for evaluating balanced scorecards of healthcare organisations. *Canadian Journal of Administrative Sciences, 23*(2), 85–104.

Cocca, P., & Alberti, M. (2010). A framework to assess performance measurement systems in SMEs. *International Journal of Productivity and Performance Management, 59*(2), 186–200.

Eaidgah, Y., Maki, A. A., Kurczewski, K., & Abdekhodaee, A. (2016). Visual management, performance management and continuous improvement: A lean manufacturing approach. *International Journal of Lean Six Sigma, 7*(2), 187–210.

Ebrahimi, M., & Sadeghi, M. (2013). Quality management and performance: An annotated review. *International Journal of Production Research, 51*(18), 5625–5643.

Eckerson, W. W. (2010). *Performance dashboards: Measuring, monitoring, and managing your business.* John Wiley & Sons.

Fouché, D. P., & Rolstadås, A. (2010). The use of performance measurement as a basis for project control of offshore modification oil and gas projects. *Production Planning & Control, 21*(8), 760–773.

George, R. A., Siti-Nabiha, A. K., Jalaludin, D., & Abdalla, Y. A. (2016). Barriers to and enablers of sustainability integration in the performance management systems of an oil and gas company. *Journal of Cleaner Production, 136*(1), 197–212.

Gopal, P. R. C., & Thakkar, J. (2012). A review on supply chain performance measures and metrics: 2000-2011. *International Journal of Productivity and Performance Management, 61*(5), 518.

Haji-Kazemi, S., & Andersen, B. (2013). Application of performance measurement as an early warning system: A case study in the oil and gas industry. *International Journal of Managing Projects in Business, 6*(4), 714–738.

Hyde, M., & Kellar, N. (2014). Earned value in the oil and gas industry. AACE International Transactions, 30(4), 1–29

Iren, L., Bergh, V., Hinna, S., Leka, S., & Jain, A. (2014). Developing a performance indicator for psychosocial risk in the oil and gas industry. *Safety Science, 62*(1), 98–106.

Johnson, H. T., & Kaplan, R. (1986). *The rise and fall of management accounting.* Harvard Business School Press.

Kaplan, R. S., & Norton, D. P. (1996). Linking the balanced scorecard to strategy. *California Management Review, 39*(1), 53–79.

Kaplan, R. S., & Norton, D. P. (2000). Putting the balanced scorecard to work. Focusing your organisation on strategy—With the balanced scorecard, *Harvard Business Review, 2*, 2–18.

Kaplan, R. S., & Norton, D. P. (2001). Transforming the balanced scorecard from performance measurement to strategic management: Part 1. *Accounting Horizons, 15*(1), 87–104.

Kaplan, R., & Norton, D. (1993). Building a balanced scorecard. *Harvard Business Review, 7*(5), 138–139.

Lengler, R., & Eppler, M. J. (2007). Towards a periodic table of visualisation methods for management. *IASTED Proceedings of the Conference on Graphics and Visualization in Engineering (GVE 2007)*, Clearwater, FL, USA.

Liff, S., & Posey, P. A. (2004). *Seeing is believing: How the new art of visual management can boost performance throughout your organisation.* AMACOM/American Management Association.

McCreery, J. (2014). Operational excellence: Managing performance in the oil and gas industry. *Bain & Company.* https://www.bain.com/insights/operational-excellence-managing-performance-in-the-oil-and-gas-industry/

McEvay, G., Kennedy, F., & Fullerton, R. (2013). *Accounting in the lean Enterprise.* CRC Press.

McKenna, S., Richardson, J., & Manroop, L. (2011). Alternative paradigms and the study and practice of performance management and evaluation. *Human Resource Management Review, 21*(2), 148–157.

Melnyk, S. A., Bititci, U., Platts, K., Tobias, J., & Andersen, B. (2014). Is performance measurement and management fit for the future? *Management Accounting Research, 25*(2), 173 186.

Neely, A., Micheli, P., & Martinez, V. (2006). *Acting on information: performance management for the public sector.* Cranfield School of Management.

Nudurupati, S. S., Bititci, U. S., Kumar, V., & Chan, F. T. (2011). State of the art literature review on performance measurement. *Computers & Industrial Engineering, 60*(2), 279–290.

Obeidat, S. M., Al Bakri, A. A., & Elbanna, S. (2020). Leveraging "Green" human Resource practices to enable environmental and organisational performance: Evidence from the Qatari oil and gas industry. *Journal of Business Ethics, 164*(2), 371–388.

Parthiban, P., & Goh, M. (2011). An integrated model for performance management of manufacturing units. *Benchmarking: An International Journal, 18*(2), 261–281.

Patel, H., Salehi, S., Ahmed, R., & Teodoriu, C. (2019). Review of elastomer seal assemblies in oil & gas wells: Performance evaluation, failure mechanisms, and gaps in industry standards. *Journal of Petroleum Science & Engineering, 179*, 1046–1062.

Roll, M. (2011). Introduction: Resource Governance, development and democracy in the Gulf of Guinea.In *Fuelling the world-failing the region* (pp. 8–31). German Institute of Development and Sustainability.

Sun, J., Jing, J., Jing, P., Li, Y., Chen, X., & Hu, H. (2017). Preparation and performance evaluation of stable foamy heavy oil. *Petroleum Chemistry, 57*(3), 284–292.

Shvarts, E., Pakhalov, A., Knizhnikov, A., & Ametistova, L. (2018). Environmental rating of oil and gas companies in Russia: How assessment affects environmental transparency and performance. *Business Strategy and the Environment, 27*(7), 1023–1038.

Van der Ploeg, F. (2011). Macroeconomics of sustainability transitions: Second-best climate policy, green paradox, and renewables subsidies. *Environmental Innovation and Societal Transitions, 1*(1), 130–134.

Varma, S., Wadhwa, S., & Deshmukh, S. (2008). Evaluating petroleum supply chain performance: Application of analytical hierarchy process to balanced scorecard. *Asia Pacific Journal of Marketing and Logistics, 20*(3), 343–356.

Yusuf, Y., Gunasekaran, A., Papadopoulos, T., Auchterlounie, W., Hollomah, D., & Menhat, M. (2018). Performance measurement in the natural gas industry. *Benchmarking: An International Journal, 25*(8), 2913–2930.

Part III
Sustainability Management in the Oil and Gas Industry

14 Occupational Health and Safety in the Oil and Gas Industry

Patience A. Abor, Florence Naab, Anita A. Daniels, and Aaron A. Abuosi

14.1 Introduction

One of the world's most profitable industrial sectors is oil and gas. It is an important engine of economic development and has led to the reduction of poverty and the transition of technology and competitiveness. At the same time, the sector can also be unsafe and often faces problems related to occupational health and safety (OHS) (ILO, 2017). Occupational hazards are major public health concerns (Lay et al., 2016), particularly in dangerous industries such as oil and gas (Guzman et al., 2022). Chemical, physical, biological, ergonomic, and psychological occupational hazards are common in the oil and gas industry (Chauhan, 2013).

World Health Organization (WHO, 2023) focuses on three distinct objectives related to occupational health: (1) maintenance and promotion of the health and working capacities of workers; (2) improvement of the work environment to be conducive for health and safety; and (3) development of work organisations and work culture to adhere to health and safety measures while increasing efficiency within a positive social climate. Workers in the oil and gas industry continue to be concerned about workplace safety, as they are constantly exposed to many types of occupational hazards.

A study entitled *Health and Safety of Employees* by the International Labour Organization (ILO) in 2015 recommended that industries need to make increased efforts to improve the health and safety of employees at work. More than 2.3 million workplace injuries occurred annually around the world, according to the study, and an estimated death of over 6000 workers was documented daily out of this figure (ILO, 2014). Depending on the degree of industrialisation, the incidence of work-related injuries and incidents varies across countries. In particular, emerging markets and developing countries continue to report tremendous losses in profits due to work-related accidents in developed countries (Kheni et al., 2008; Takala et al., 2014; Zheng et al., 2010).

In this chapter, we examine the context of OHS in the oil and gas industry in developing countries. We discuss international labour standards and legal frameworks on OHS, categories of occupational hazards associated with the oil and gas industry, the challenges of OHS in the oil and gas industry, and how to deal with the challenges of OHS.

14.2 The Context of Occupational Health and Safety in the Oil and Gas Industry

Enumah and Aghaji (2008) studied the Lagos Zone of Nigeria's largest and oldest indigenous oil and gas company using a descriptive cross-sectional analysis. The goal was to examine the occupational health facilities and services available in the industry's upstream and downstream operations. The study found that although there was a health and safety policy in place for employees, downstream factories lacked suitable facilities, and services. Personal protective equipment (PPE) was also in short supply and underutilised in this industry. The upstream sector, on the other hand, had appropriate occupational amenities and staff. In general, safety controls were present, but they were more effective in upstream operations than downstream operations. Only a small percentage of the workers were aware of management's safety procedures and regulations, as well as the Federal Government's workplace safety law and the company's health, safety, and environment training programs. Regular factory inspections by government regulatory authorities were recommended, as is the rectification of shortcomings in the provision of occupational safety by plant management.

Lui et al. (2020) examined the role of safety knowledge as a mediator in the causal relationship between occupational health and safety management frameworks (OHSMFs) and occupational injuries and workplace accidents in Ghana's oil and gas industry. The study focused on various aspects of OHS management systems, workplace accidents, and occupational injuries. A cross-sectional survey design was used, whereby 699 respondents were chosen from three government-owned oil and gas organisations using a convenience and purposive sampling technique. Data analysis methods included correlation, multiple regression analysis, and bootstrapping. The regression and correlation analyses revealed a moderately strong negative and significant relationship between OHSMFs and workplace accidents and injuries. The causal relationship between OHSMF and workplace accidents and injuries is significantly mediated by safety knowledge. It was revealed that safety training was a significant predictor of safety knowledge, work-related injuries, and workplace accidents. The negative relationship between OHSMF and workplace accidents and injuries indicates that current OHSMFs are either ineffective or lack acceptable safety standards for controlling hazard exposures in the industry. To improve worker safety knowledge, the study recommended to the management to invest in frequent safety training and orientations and to the government to pay close attention to the promotion and improvement of OHS management systems in Ghana.

In a related study in Nigeria, Benson et al. (2021) determined the risks associated with health hazards by identifying the various health hazards and their sources across the oil and gas industry in Nigeria. Ergonomic risks were found to be the most prevalent among the dangers studied in the industry, accounting, for 30% of risks. Other risks included physical. (26%); chemical (23%); psychological (18%); and biological (3%). Some health problems such as headaches, skin burns, eye and skin irritation, and rashes were found to have short-term health consequences on employees in the oil and gas industry. However, musculoskeletal problems, respiratory disease, leukaemia, asphyxiates, and hypertension are consequences caused by other hazards in the long term.

Also, Quaigrain et al. (2022) examined the impact of employees' knowledge of health and safety on overall compliance in the oil and gas industry in Ghana, which is characterised by high rates of injury. To quantitatively analyse both primary and secondary data sources, a positivist and deductive research strategy was used. Multiple linear regression was used to determine the effects of employees' knowledge and attitude toward occupational health hazards on overall health and safety compliance with data from a structured survey administered to the employees. According to the findings, most employees had a high level of knowledge as well as a positive attitude toward mitigating occupational health hazards. Furthermore, the study found that the majority of employees followed OHS practices. However, the study showed that the effect of employees' knowledge and attitude toward occupational health hazards does not translate into the implementation of comprehensive safety practices. Female employees, on the other hand, were found to be more knowledgeable and compliant with OHS practices than their male counterparts. The study recommends the implementation of relevant education, training programmes, and governance initiatives that enforce strict adherence to correct safety procedures.

14.3 Categories of Occupational Hazards Associated with the Oil and Gas Industry

Traditionally, occupational hazards have been classified into physical and psychosocial. The physical hazards have been further categorised under physical, chemical, biological, and mechanical/ergonomic hazards. However, in recent times, the WHO recommends two additional hazards, including personal health hazards related to personal lifestyles of workers and hazards related to the interactions between the enterprise and the community within which it is located. There is, however, a paucity of literature on the last two categories, especially with respect to the oil and gas industry. Personal health resources and enterprise-community interactions are discussed under challenges of OHS in the oil and gas sector.

14.3.1 Physical Health Hazards Associated with the Oil and Gas Industry

These hazards may cause physical changes to the bodies of workers and should not be underrated. There are quite a number of these hazards but the main ones often reported in the physical environment are noise, illumination, vibration, fire, explosion, ionising radiation, slips, and microclimatic conditions (Benson et al., 2021; Kumar et al., 2017). These hazards may cause hearing loss as a result of too much noise, laryngeal disorders because they have to shout in order to hear each other, and heat or cold strokes if the enclosed temperatures are extreme. It is important that workers are informed of their imminent exposure to physical hazards in the employee handbook, with periodic reminders through monitoring and supervision. This is important because evidence suggests that physical health hazards are 26% more prevalent in the oil and gas industry and the health risks are enormous (Benson et al., 2021).

14.3.2 Chemical Health Hazard

High exposure to heavy and dangerous chemicals is more prevalent in the oil and gas industry, posing severe chemical health hazards to the workforce in about 23% of the chance (Benson et al., 2021). Workers of such companies are at risk of chemical poisoning, damage to the central nervous system, respiratory allergies and disorders, dermatoses, cancers (such as lung, skin, bladder, and liver), reproductive disorders (such as infertility), cardiovascular disorders, and general health problems (Benson et al., 2021; Kumar et al., 2017). The best way to prevent this category of hazards is to avoid exposure to the chemicals entirely. However, this may not be a feasible preventative measure in view of the enormous economic benefits in the oil and gas industry. For this reason, effective measures must be implemented to prevent chemical hazards or manage them well if they should occur. Such measures must be fairly accessible to all workers.

14.3.3 Biological Health Hazards

These hazards include biological agents such as viruses, bacteria, fungi, and moulds (Benson et al., 2021; Kumar et al., 2017). Exposure to these agents may predispose workers to many health conditions such as asthma, pneumonia, and tuberculosis. Unfortunately, biological hazards are usually recognized late during medical treatment due to the failure of companies to implement preventive measures to minimise exposure to these hazards. Although biological hazards constitute only 3% of all the hazards in the oil and gas industry (Benson et al., 2021), there is still a need for keen attention to be paid to them.

14.3.4 Mechanical/ergonomic Health Hazards

These are hazards from the use of machinery and dangerous tools, operating in unsafe structures, and operating in an unsafe working environment. These can collectively be referred to as hazards associated with poor working conditions, which may lead to many physical health problems as already discussed. Furthermore, certain repetitive tasks and static muscular loads can expose the workers to many musculoskeletal disorders (Benson et al., 2021; Kumar et al., 2017) which often manifest themselves later in life. Such workers may only realise these problems in their retirement, a stage in life when they are more vulnerable. The literature reports permanent disability as the worst outcome for ergonomic health hazard (ibid.) In fact, ergonomic hazards are reported to be the highest (30%) of all the hazards in the oil and gas industry (Benson et al., 2021).

14.3.5 Psychosocial Health Hazards

Workers in the oil and gas industry tend to work under pressure and for long hours, which are both a recipe for psychosocial health hazards. Work pressure and poor interpersonal relationships at work are some of the known influential factors of psychosocial health hazards in the oil and gas industry. For instance, an autocratic leader or a leader who enjoys controlling personnel instead of tasks will be a source of stress to workers in this industry. Absenteeism, 'presenteeism', anxiety, and aggression at work are some of the signs of psychosocial health hazards that may occur among workers of such industries. Individual workers may exhibit signs of psychosocial exhaustion such as sleep disturbances, burnout syndrome, and depression (Benson et al., 2021), which invariably will affect productivity. A recent report indicated that psychosocial health hazards constitute 18% of all the hazards in the industry (ibid). Because psychosocial hazards are inevitable in almost every organisation, the need for an onsite psychologist to provide therapy for these issues has become relevant for many organisations.

In summary, the oil and gas industry is associated with many health hazards that need the attention of industry players. The quality of life of workers of these industries is affected by too many health risks, warranting effective, and efficient safety measures to enhance the health of these workers. It is important that potential workers of this industry are fully informed about these hazards before they are recruited.

14.4 International Labour Standards and Legal Frameworks

The ILO has developed a system of international labour standards that are aimed at promoting decent and productive work opportunities for all. The standards on occupational safety and health serve as a global framework and provide essential tools for governments, employers, and employees to establish safe practices and promote a safe working environment for all. They are conventions which are legally binding when member states ratify them. There are also recommendations which serve as non-binding guidelines. While there are over 40 standards and codes of practice adopted by the ILO to specifically deal with OHS issues, the agency also has almost half of its instruments directly or indirectly dealing with safety at the workplace.

Three key instruments on OHS are Promotional Framework for Occupational Safety and Health Convention, 2006 (No. 187), Occupational Safety and Health Convention, 1981 (No. 155) and its Protocol of 2002, and Occupational Health Services Convention, 1985 (No. 161) (ILO, 2014). Convention 187 sets out a promotional framework for recognition of existing conventions on OHS. It calls for the engagement of governments, employers, and employees to continuously promote a preventative safety and health culture at the national level through the establishment and implementation of a national policy, system, and programme on OHS in light of the conditions and practices in a country. This convention upholds the principle of prevention in relation to occupational injuries, diseases, and death. Convention 155 enjoins members to implement and periodically review a coherent national policy on occupational safety and health and the working environment. It covers the enforcement of laws and regulations concerning occupational safety through appropriate inspection systems and the provision of a working environment which prevents the exposure of workers to workplace hazards as well as to their associated risks. The protocol to this convention calls for systems to be put in place to record and report accidents, dangerous occurrences, occupational diseases, as well suspected occupational diseases. Members are expected to publish this information on an annual basis. The Convention on Occupational Health Services (No. 161) calls for the organisation of services which are essentially preventive in nature and seeks to advice employers and workers on how to maintain a safe and healthy work environment to boost the health of workers. There are other conventions like Prevention of Major Industrial accidents Convention, 1993 (No. 174) and those that focus on particular branches of economic activity and those for the protection of workers against specific risks.

However, the ratification and effective implementation of these international labour standards on OHS in most developing countries has been problematic. There are few ratifications of these key instruments by some top oil-and-gas-producing developing countries (Table 14.1). In a tripartite workshop organised by the ILO on Occupational Safety and Health in the oil and gas industry in Sub-Saharan Africa (SSA), it was reiterated that ratifying and effectively implementing the ILO standards were very vital in addressing health and safety management issues in the industry (ILO, 2017).

Though there is low ratification of ILO key instruments on OHS, it is worth noting that some of the countries have a defined regulatory framework governing the oil and gas industry. For example, in Ghana, even though there is no comprehensive national policy on OHS, there are enactments like the Factories, Offices and Shops Act 1970 (Act 328), Workmen's Compensation Act, 1987 (PNDCL 187), Ghana Health Service and Teaching Hospitals Act, 1999 (Act 526), and the Ghana Labour Act, 2003 (Act 651) among others, which guide the implementation of OHS (Anku-Tsede, 2016;

Table 14.1 Ratification of ILO convention by country and date

Country	C187	C155	P155	C161	C174
China	No	Yes [25/1/2007]	No	No	No
Brazil	No	Yes [18/5/1992]	No	Yes [18/5/1990]	Yes [02/8/2001]
India	No	No	No	No	Yes [06/6/2008]
Nigeria	No	Yes [3/5/1994]	No	No	No
Libya	No	No	No	No	No
Angola	No	No	No	No	No
Algeria	No	Yes	No	No	No
Egypt	No	No	No	No	No
Congo	No	No	No	No	No
Gabon	No	Yes [28/7/2022]	No	Yes	No
Ghana	No	No	No	No	No
Equatorial Guinea	No	No	No	No	No
Chad	No	No	No	No	No
Sierra Leone	Coming into force [25/8/2022]	Coming into force [25/8/2022]	No	No	No
Sudan	No	No	No	No	No

Source: ILO (2022)

Annan et al., 2015). However, these existing legal requirements are seen as fragmented and limited in scope. They also operate under different jurisdictions without clearly defined responsibilities and accountabilities (ibid). There are, however, some specific acts guiding the operations of the oil and gas industry in Ghana. These include the Ghana National Petroleum Corporation Act, 1983 (PNDCL.64), Petroleum Commission Act, 2011 (Act 821), 1992 Constitution of Ghana, and the Environmental Protection Agency, 1994 (Act 490). Likewise, in Nigeria, legislation on OHS includes the Constitution of the Federal Republic of Nigeria, 1999, Factories Act (CAP 1 LFN 2004, Employee's Compensation Act, 2010, Petroleum Regulations, 1969, and Mineral Oils Regulation, 1962. Though Nigeria has ratified the Occupational Safety and Health Convention, 1981, the enforcement of OHS laws and regulations has been ineffective. Odion-Obomhense and Ejikeme (2022) describe the regulatory system as dysfunctional and unenforceable. Similarly, Yang (2019) reported on the regulatory regime for offshore operations in the petroleum industry in China. Legislation in the industry was described as not only fragmented but also had absent or overlapping functions of ministries and local governments. These situations confirm the assertion by Tadesse et al. (2016) that many OHS regulations in the developing world are neither comprehensive nor properly implemented. These challenges predispose workers to several health and safety risks and also affect the safe operations of work in the environment.

In most developing countries, policy frameworks on OHS remain a big challenge, based on the assumption that policies do not work (Clarke, 2005).

14.5 Challenges of Occupational Health and Safety in the Oil and Gas Industry

OHS concerns in the oil and gas sector are highlighted according to general and specific concerns. Based on the WHO healthy workplace framework, the main problems are covered under the categories of the physical and psychosocial work environment and the resources that employees have for their own personal health and the enterprise-community involvement (WHO, 2010) (see Figure 14.1).

The furniture, equipment, air quality, materials, chemicals, and production procedures all fall under the category of the physical work environment. The physical work environment has an impact on employees' well-being, including their physical and mental health (WHO, 2010). On the other side, the psychosocial work environment pertains to organisational culture, including the behaviours, values, views, and practices in the company that may have a positive or negative impact on employees' psychological and physical health (WHO, 2010). Occupational 'stressors' are situations that have a history of elevating psychological stress.

Programs on OHS typically place minor emphasis on the psychosocial work setting and major emphasis on the physical work setting. A growing body of research has reported problems related to the physical and psychosocial occupational settings in the oil and gas industry. In Nigeria's oil and

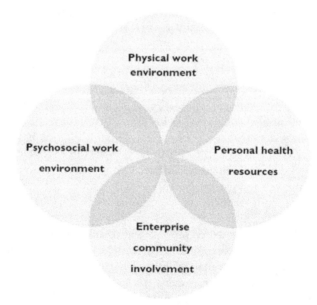

Figure 14.1 WHO healthy workplace model
Source: World Health Organization (2010)

gas business, Benson et al. (2021) evaluated the typical occupational risks and their potential health effects among oil and gas employees. They discovered that ergonomic risks accounted for 30% of all OHS hazards, while physical, chemical, psychosocial, and biological risks constituted 26%, 23%, 18%, and 3% of all risks, respectively. The authors also found some of the health risks that affect workers immediately, such as headaches, skin burns, eye and skin discomfort, and dermatitis, as well as those that affect them over the long term, such as respiratory illnesses, musculoskeletal problems, and other non-contagious conditions like leukaemia, high blood pressure, and other heart conditions.

Individual health resources are those that an organisation offers employees to help or encourage their efforts to develop or promote healthy individual lifestyle choices and to support and guide their physical and mental health. These resources include medical services, information, opportunities, and other resources (WHO, 2010). Societies in which businesses operate both have an effect and are affected by those businesses. The physical and social environment of the larger community has a significant impact on the health of the workforce. Thus, enterprise-community involvement refers to actions in which a business may participate or offer the knowledge and resources to assist the social and physical wellness of the society in which it operates, particularly the physical and mental health, safety, and well-being of employees and their relatives (WHO, 2010).

The literature on these aspects of workplace safety was reviewed due to the dearth of research on personal health resources and enterprise-community interaction in the oil and gas industry. Physical inactivity can be caused by long shifts, the absence of fitness centres or devices, and a lack of flexibility in how and when long rests can be taken when it comes to personal health resources (Stoewen, 2016). According to reports, the major public health issue of the 21st century is a lack of physical activity (Blair, 2009). According to studies, there is a significant global burden of disease related to inactivity.

Physical inactivity is responsible for 7.6% and 7.2%, of all-cause cardiovascular disease and mortality worldwide, respectively (Sooriyaarachchi et al., 2021). Given the size of their populations, developing nations have the highest proportion of persons impacted by physical inactivity, although the relative impact is highest in developed nations (Sooriyaarachchi et al., 2021). According to a study of the Nigerian petroleum industry, general BMI and the proportion of diabetes were higher than national averages. Poor workout behaviours and nutritional issues were mentioned as possible causes. The researchers suggested that policymakers should intervene through actions that promote health (Nyenwe et al., 2003). The efficacy of a regimen among overweight and obese workers of a petroleum company in Malaysia was the focus of a study conducted by Rusali et al (2016). They discovered that a planned weight management program significantly reduced both women's and men's BMI and waist circumference (WC). It also seemed to be helpful in lowering cholesterol levels in women who had been receiving individualised diet advice from nutritionists. In a research on corporate social responsibility in the petroleum sector in Nigeria, Ndu and Agbonifoh (2014) revealed that the Niger Delta is underdeveloped due to the government's unwillingness to forgo the anticipated high profits from petroleum exploration for the region's growth. They advocated creating a coordinated action strategy and developing it with the help of all Niger Delta stakeholders, as well as encouraging multinational corporations to follow the principles of Corporate Social Responsibility.

Living near petroleum establishments was linked to an increased risk of childhood leukaemia, while working in the petroleum industry was linked with a greater risk of mesothelioma, multiple myeloma, skin melanoma, cancers of the urinary bladder and prostate. However, it reduced the risk of oesophageal cancers (Onyije et al., 2021). To determine the predictors of the identified cancer risks, the authors recommended conducting additional research on better exposure assessment (ibid.). Land-use issues, acid rain, air pollution, climate change, habitat disruption, ecological pollution, and oil spills and leaks were found to be some of the environmental effects of upstream oil production in Ghana (Oppong, 2014). Frank (2011) asserts that in the 19th century, the growth that oil was expected to bring was to be measured not only in material wealth but also in the accomplishment of social stability and the attenuation of political unrest in the petroleum industry in Austrian Galicia. These findings highlight the necessity for businesses and communities to collaborate in order to ensure the health and safety of both staff and residents. The ILO lists many issues that oil and gas industry workers must deal with in relation to the special OHS problems in the sector (ILO, 2017). Offshore worker difficulties, newly emerging threats, work schedules, female employees, personal protection equipment, and corruption are a few of them.

14.5.1 Off-Shore Workers

The most significant occupational health risks related to off-shore oil exploration and production include injuries and illnesses brought on by exposure to environmental factors like climatic factors, stress from long distances travelled on water, and personal accidents. Physical separation at exploratory sites, long workdays on offshore drilling installations, and their distance from base camps can all lead to psychological issues. Therefore, some employees are unable to bear the stress of working offshore. The signs and symptoms of workplace stress might range from unusual irritability to excessive drinking, smoking, or drug use. Numerous factors can contribute to drilling and production-related injuries, including slips and falls, and accidents in machine lifting, pipe handling, improper tool use, and mishandling of explosives. Drowning, exposure to harsh weather, and seasickness are some major risks associated with offshore labour. Skin injuries from crude oil and chemical exposure are possible, as are burns from fire, steam, acid, or soil containing chemicals like sodium hydroxide (Parkes, 2010; Valentić, 2005).

14.5.2 New and Emerging Risks

The necessity to recognise new and developing dangers at work is underlined by international labour standards such as Recommendation No. 197 (ILO, 2017). The oil and gas sector makes use of cutting-edge technology. New working models have emerged as a result of the rising trend toward digitisation, which is also accompanied by new OHS concerns, a lack of a social work environment, sub-par work design, and the spread of information and communication technologies (ICTs). It is necessary to handle these brand-new employment realities and the risks they entail.

14.5.3 Work Schedule Arrangements

The unpredictable work schedules are another factor that oil and gas employees and their families may find concerning. The oil and gas business has a variety of work schedules, including fly-in, fly-out rosters (FIFO). For example, two weeks on and two weeks off, or two weeks on and three weeks off. In certain remote or foreign regions, the schedule could be two weeks on/four weeks off or even four weeks on/four weeks off. Offshore specialists typically do not have a defined work/leave cycle because they frequently switch between installations. Employees using FIFO schedules are frequently required to work long shifts, typically a 12-hour shift. Long work hours consistently have a negative impact on workers' health, attentiveness, and performance, according to the ILO (2017).

14.5.4 Women Workers

Although it is difficult to ascertain the exact percentage, women appear to have a low representation in the oil and gas sector in SSA. In the extractive sectors, which include the oil and gas business, barely 10% of professionals and 1% of board members or CEOs are women worldwide. According to one survey, women make up only 13% of the oil and gas industry's board members in Africa (ILO, 2013). However, several businesses are now employing more women. For instance, one Nigerian national oil and gas corporation has attained 30% female representation on its Board of Directors (Fraser-Moleketi et al., 2015). Depending on how well the risks are controlled, the high level of workplace hazards in the oil and gas business raises questions about the health of women working in this field. Pregnancy-related dangers for women include being exposed to potentially harmful biological agents, which can harm the foetus and increase the chance of mortality or congenital abnormalities (Iunes, 2002). However, there are enormous opportunities for women in the value chains for minerals, gas, and oil (ILO, 2013).

14.5.5 Personal Protective Equipment and Clothing

In the oil and gas sector, safety precautions are crucial for controlling accidents that result in death or serious health problems The supply of appropriate PPE and clothing is essential when dangers cannot be appropriately handled by efforts to remove or limit them. Several legal initiatives have been introduced by some SSA countries to ensure that employees receive PPE. Angola, Cameroon, Côte d'Ivoire, Mozambique, and South Africa are examples of such countries. In Mozambique, for example, it is illegal for an employer to deduct any money from a worker's salary for any services or supplies that must be provided for the worker's health and safety. In reality, all employees, including those in non-traditional employment arrangements and those employed by small and medium-sized businesses (SMEs), such as contractors and subcontractors, must be subject to these obligations (ILO, 2013).

14.5.6 Corruption

Both national development and improvements in OHS are hampered by corruption. Corruption among government employees or corporations makes it impossible to implement legislation and rules. Finding from a study by Leonard (2005) indicates that businesses frequently pay labour inspectors bribes in order to hide OHS compliance problems. This frequently leads to incomplete or inaccurate reporting. Circumstances like these originate from a lack of law or its complexity rather than the lack of dedication on the side of both inspectors and business authorities.

14.6 Dealing with the Challenges of OHS

Under the WHO framework for developing a safe working environment, steps to deal with OHS concerns are examined by looking at the physical and psychosocial work environment, individual health resources, and business-community involvement. These measures are summarised in Table 14.2.

14.7 Conclusion

OHS is a big problem in the oil and gas industry because of the prominent physical and psychosocial concerns and the threats to human health and enterprise-community involvement. Despite the diverse legislation and policies that are directly or indirectly relevant to the OHS of employees in the oil and gas industry, there is a dearth of evidence of OHS strategies to adequately address the OHS concerns described in this chapter. Given the importance of the oil and gas sector and its contribution to the economic progress of many developing nations, urgent attention must be paid to and action need to be taken to solve the OHS issues that face a teeming number of workers in this industry. To meet international requirements and standards on OHS, there should be major modifications of the legal provisions, while ensuring strict enforcement of health and safety regulations in the industry.

Table 14.2 Measures of dealing with the challenges of OHS

	Measures to deal with the challenges of the physical work place
Removal or replacement	A less hazardous chemical can be used in place of harmful one that may have detrimental effects on health, such a potent carcinogen. Meetings can also be conducted by teleconferencing rather than moving in hazardous conditions.
Engineering controls:	Stamping equipment may be equipped with noise buffers, machine protectors, and ventilation systems, among others, to expel harmful gases.
Personal protective equipment can include	Depending on the type of work, workers should be given respirators, masks, gloves, hard headgear, and safety shoes.
Administrative controls	Managers can undertake routine maintenance on mechanical equipment, promote excellent housekeeping, and educate employees on safe working techniques.
Employees returning to work	To reduce the risk of re-injury, whether or not attributable to the workplace, changes to the workplace may be necessary for employees returning to work following an illness or accident. Secondary prevention is the term used to describe this type of intervention. Examples include improving eye protection or adjusting the height of a work surface.
	Measures to deal with the challenges of the psychosocial work environment
Removal or alteration at the source	These include reassigning tasks to lessen workload, removing or retraining managers and supervisors in communication and leadership techniques, enforcing a zero-tolerance policy for workplace harassment, bullying, or discrimination, and applying all applicable legal standards and laws regarding working conditions or putting policies in place to supplement the laws.
Reduce the effect on the worker	There should be flexibility in how work-life conflicts are handled, in how much workers can pick their shift schedules, in how supervisors and co-workers can support this flexibility, in where and when they work, and in how they communicate about upcoming organisational changes.
Protect the employee	Employees should receive training in stress relief strategies, such as cognitive techniques. For instance, employees should receive education and training on how to avoid disputes or harassing incidents.
Employees returning to work	The psychosocial work environment may need to be modified for someone going back to work after an illness or accident in order to avoid re-injury or a subsequent resurgence of an ailment. For instance, the manner work is performed might be modified, the workload might be lessened, the times might change, or greater flexibility might be permitted.

(Continued)

Table 14.2 Measures of dealing with the challenges of OHS (Continued)

	Measures to deal with the challenges of personal health resources in the workplace
Provision of supportive environment	To enable and encourage employees to adopt and maintain healthy living choices, the business may offer a supportive environment and resources in the form of medical services, information, training, financial support, facilities, policy support, flexibility, or promotional programs. Providing workers with access to fitness facilities or providing financial support for fitness classes or equipment are a few examples. Other examples include encouraging employees to use active transportation such as walking and cycling—instead of passive transportation whenever possible, providing and subsidising healthy food options, and allowing flexibility in the timing and length of work breaks to accommodate exercise.
	Measures to deal with the challenges of enterprise-community involvement
Offer of assistance in the community	The business may decide to offer assistance and resources, such as starting initiatives to reduce pollution emissions and clean up production processes, or to address contaminated air or water sources in the community at large. Health screening and treatment for conditions including HIV infection, TB, hepatitis, and other common ailments should be provided to the population. Workers and their families should be given access to free or heavily discounted basic healthcare, and community-based primary healthcare institutions should be supported. The establishment of gender equality policies in the workplace to support and protect women or protective policies for other vulnerable groups, even when these are not legally required, can help groups that would not otherwise have access. These can also go beyond legally mandated standards for minimising the enterprise's carbon footprint by collaborating with local planners to build bicycle paths and pavements, among other things.

References

Anku-Tsede, O. (2016). *Occupational health and safety practices and the regulatory regime: Evidence from the infantile oil fields of Ghana, in advances in safety management and human factors* (pp. 75–88). Springer.

Annan, J.-S., Addai, E. K., & Tulashie, S. K. (2015). A call for action to improve occupational health and safety in Ghana and a critical look at the existing legal requirement and legislation. *Safety and Health at Work, 6*(2), 146–150.

Benson, C., Dimopoulos, C., Argyropoulos, C. D., Mikellidou, C. V., & Boustras, G. (2021). Assessing the common occupational health hazards and their health risks among oil and gas workers. *Safety Science, 140*, 105284.

Blair, S. N. (2009). Physical inactivity: The biggest public health problem of the 21st century. *British Journal of Sports Medicine, 43*(1), 1–2.

Chauhan, N. (2013). *Safety and health management system in oil and gas industry.* Wipro Technologies.

Clarke, E. (2005). Do occupational health services really exist in Ghana? A special focus on the agricultural and informal sectors. Accra Ghana. *Ghana Health Services, 8*(2), 23–35.

Enumah, J., & Aghaji, M. (2008). Assessment of occupational health services in a petroleum industry in Lagos, Nigeria. *Nigerian Medical Journal, 49*(1), 12–16.

Frank, A. (2011). Environmental, economic, and moral dimensions of sustainability in the petroleum industry in Austrian Galicia. *Modern Intellectual History, 8*(1), 171–191.

Fraser-Moleketi, G. J., Mizrahi, S., & Bank, A. D. (2015). *Where are the women: Inclusive boardrooms in Africa's top listed companies.* African Development Bank.

Guzman, J., Recoco, G. A., Pandi, A. W., Padrones, J. M., & Ignacio, J. J. (2022). Evaluating workplace safety in the oil and gas industry during the COVID-19 pandemic using occupational health and safety vulnerability measure and partial least square structural equation modelling. *Cleaner Engineering and Technology, 6*, 100378. https://doi.org/10.1016/j.clet.2021.100378

International Labour Organization (ILO). (2013). *10 Keys for gender sensitive OSH practice: Guidelines for gender mainstreaming in occupational safety and health.* Geneva.

ILO. (2014). Safety and health at work: A vision for sustainable prevention. In report to XX world congress on safety and health at work. International Labor Organization.

ILO. (2017). Occupational safety and health in the oil and gas industry in selected sub-Saharan African countries. Sectoral Policies Department.

ILO. (2022). Normlex: Information system on international labour standards. Retrieved April 30, 2022, from https://www.ilo.org/dyn/normlex/en/f?p=NORMLEXPUB:1:0::NO:::

Iunes, R. F. (2002). *Occupational safety and health in Latin America and the Caribbean: Overview, issues and policy recommendations.* Inter-American Development Bank.

Kheni, N. A., Dainty, A. R., & Gibb, A. (2008). Health and safety management in developing countries: A study of construction SMEs in Ghana. *Construction Management and Economics, 26*(11), 1159–1169.

Kumar, R. M., Karthick, R. B., Bhuvaneswari, V., & Nandhini, N. (2017). Study on occupational health and diseases in oil industry. *International Research Journal of Engineering and Technology, 4*(12), 954–958.

Lay, A. M., Saunders, R., Lifshen, M., Breslin, C., LaMontagne, A., Tompa, E., & Smith, P. (2016). Individual, occupational, and workplace correlates of occupational health and safety vulnerability in a sample of Canadian workers. *American Journal of Industrial Medicine, 59*(2), 119–128.

Leonard, D. K. (2005). *Africa Unchained: The blueprint for Africa's future.* Springer.

Lui, S., Nkrumah, E. N., Akoto, L. S., Gyabeng, E., & Nkrumah, E. (2020). The state of occupational health and safety management frameworks (OHSMF) and occupational injuries and accidents in the Ghanaian oil and gas industry: Assessing the mediating role of safety knowledge. *BioMed Research International, 2020,* 6354895. https://doi.org/0.1155/2020/6354895

Ndu, O. A., & Agbonifoh, B. (2014). Corporate social responsibility in Nigeria: A study of the petroleum industry and the Niger delta area. *International Review of Social Sciences and Humanities, 6*(2), 214–238.

Nyenwe, E. A., Odia, O. J., Ihekwaba, A. E., Ojule, A., & Babatunde, S. (2003). Type 2 diabetes in adult Nigerians: A study of its prevalence and risk factors in Port Harcourt, Nigeria. *Diabetes Research and Clinical Practice, 62*(3), 177–185.

Odion-Obomhense, A. A., & Ejikeme, U. (2022). Occupational health and safety legislations and management in selected oil and gas companies in Nigeria. *International Journal of Legal Developments and Allied Issues, 8*(1), 282–333.

Onyije, F. M., Hosseini, B., Togawa, K., Schüz, J., & Olsson, A. (2021). Cancer incidence and mortality among petroleum industry workers and residents living in oil producing communities: A systematic review and meta-analysis. *International Journal of Environmental Research and Public Health, 18*(8), 4343.

Oppong, S., (2014). Common health, safety and environmental concerns in upstream oil and gas sector: Implications for HSE management in Ghana. *Academicus International Scientific Journal, 9,* 93–106.

Parkes, K. R. (2010). *Offshore working time in relation to performance, health and safety: A review of current practice and evidence.* Health and Safety Executive.

Quaigrain, R. A., Owusu-Manu, D.-G., Edwards, D. J., Hammond, M., Hammond, M., & Martek, I. (2022). Occupational health and safety orientation in the oil and gas industry of Ghana: analysis of knowledge and attitudinal influences on compliance. *Journal of Engineering, Design and Technology.* https://doi.org/10.1108/JEDT-11-2021-0664

Rusali, R., Shahar, S., Wen, L. X., & Manaf, Z. A. (2016). Effectiveness of a structured weight management programme at workplace among employees of a petroleum industry in Malaysia. *Malaysian Journal of Health Sciences/Jurnal Sains Kesihatan Malaysia, 14*(2), 49–56.

Sooriyaarachchi, P., Francis, T. V., King, N., & Jayawardena, R. (2021). Increased physical inactivity and weight gain during the COVID-19 pandemic in Sri Lanka: An online cross-sectional survey. *Diabetes & Metabolic Syndrome: Clinical Research & Reviews, 15*(4), 102185.

Stoewen, D. L. (2016). Wellness at work: Building healthy workplaces. *The Canadian Veterinary Journal, 57*(11), 1188.

Tadesse, S., Kelaye, T., & Assefa, Y. (2016). Utilization of personal protective equipment and associated factors among textile factory workers at Hawassa town, Southern Ethiopia. *Journal of Occupational Medicine and Toxicology, 11*(1), 1–6.

Takala, J., Hämäläinen, P., Saarela, K. L., Yun, L. Y., Manickam, K., Jin, T. W., Heng, P., Tjong, C., Kheng, L.G., Lim, S., & Lin, G. S. (2014). Global estimates of the burden of injury and illness at work in 2012. *Journal of Occupational and Environmental Hygiene, 11*(5), 326–337.

Valentić, D., Stojanović, D., Mićović, V., & Vukelić, M. (2005). Work-related diseases and injuries on an oil rig. *International Maritime Health, 56*(1–4), 56–66.

World Health Organization (WHO). (2010). *Healthy workplaces: A model for action: For employers, workers, policy-makers and practitioners.* World Health Organization.

World Health Organization (WHO). (2023). Occupational health. Retrieved February 13, 2023, from https://www.who.int/health-topics/occupational-health

Yang, Y. (2019). Reforming health, safety, and environmental regulation for offshore operations in China: Risk and resilience approaches? *Sustainability*, *11*(9), 2608.

Zheng, L., Xiang, H., Song, X., & Wang, Z. (2010). Nonfatal unintentional injuries and related factors among male construction workers in central China. *American Journal of Industrial Medicine*, *53*(6), 588–595.

15 Corporate Social Responsibility of Multinational Corporations in the Oil and Gas Sector

Evidence from Sub-Saharan Africa

Lwanga Elizabeth Nanziri and Gifty Abban

15.1 Introduction

Africa[1] is well-resourced with oil and gas but often lacks the necessary financial capital/domestic investment and technological expertise to exploit its vast natural resource endowment, hence its need to attract foreign direct investment into the oil sector. The expected 'rents' and positive externalities, including industrialisation, technology, and knowledge transfer from oil exploitation, mostly sought after for socio-economic growth, are often elusive due to corruption and other forms of mismanagement. Multinational corporations (MNCs) employ strategies, such as transfer pricing, shell companies, offshore companies, and tax havens, to siphon off rents to their home countries (Le Billon, 2011; Sigam & Garcia, 2012; Watkins, 2013). Meanwhile, poor political governance practices by host countries and CSR failure by MNCs lead to aggravated negative externalities in these countries, with the tendency to erode the benefits that countries derive from the sector, often leading countries into the 'resource-curse' and its repercussions such as exchange rate/other economic volatilities, environmental degradation, political power contestation, and civil conflicts in some cases (Frynas et al., 2017; Hayat et al., 2013; Vicente, 2010). This is based on evidence that MNCs engage in opportunistic behaviour by setting up factories in countries with questionable human rights and those with weak regulation, which enables them to exploit the natural resources of the most disadvantaged countries, thus aggravating domestic conflict (Aguilera-Caracuel et al., 2017; Daouda, 2014).

In view of these impediments, the growth and development often experienced by oil-rich countries are not properly experienced in Africa and this raises concerns about efforts of MNCs towards societal welfare and advancement in their quest for economic gains. CSR requires an integration of social, environmental, ethical, human rights, and consumer concerns into the core strategy and business operations of firms based on stakeholder consultations for the maximisation of shared value (Plan, 2011). However, this shared value is hardly realised by oil states in Africa.

The chapter provides theoretical and empirical evidence that corporations operate through the corporate social responsibility (CSR) platform

DOI: 10.4324/9781003309864-18

to contribute to societal well-being. We also highlight societal outcry over the shortcomings of corporations in the oil and gas sector in improving the well-being of their host communities.

15.1.1 Linking MNC Activities in the Oil & Gas Sector to ESG Outcomes

The European Commission defines CSR as 'the responsibility of enterprises for their impacts on society'. To fully meet their CSR, enterprises should have in place a process to integrate social, environmental, ethical, human rights, and consumer concerns into their business operations and core strategy. This is done in close collaboration with the enterprise stakeholders, to maximise the creation of shared value not only for their owners or shareholders, but also for other stakeholders like society at large (Plan, 2011, p. 6).

The activities of oil & gas MNCs can be linked to host societal outcomes in several ways:

- Environmental outcomes: These include environmental degradation that is associated with poor management of gas flaring and oil spillages
- Socio-economic outcomes: Employment opportunities for host communities can emerge, as well as backward and forward linkages through the use of local suppliers, contractors, distributors, etc.
- Governance outcomes: These are related to corporate corruption and state capture. Here, MNCs are associated with understatement of profits, transfer pricing, under-remitting of rents and royalties, as well as bribing public officials to cut corners and cheat host communities.

Thus, given the limited resources and development challenges faced by many developing economies, policymakers in Africa regard MNC as strategic partners beyond their statutory obligations, expecting them to take on additional social responsibilities such as providing basic amenities such as water, sanitation, medical facilities, and schools, especially to host communities. This has prompted MNCs to integrate CSR into their business models, to take responsibility for their actions in society, and to play a role in redressing socio-economic and environmental challenges in their jurisdiction without being pushed by the government and civil society (Ofori & Debrah, 2014, p. 94).

However, the developmental role of CSR in Africa is still in its infancy, and the CSR of MNCs are dominantly philanthropic with no connection with key business activities of the organisation. In other words, CSR focal projects in Africa are predominantly on education, health, environment, poverty alleviation, agriculture, sport, technology, and culture (Ofori & Debrah, 2014, p. 104). Critics such as Daouda (2014, p. 144) argue that although CSR's focus on social activities is important, many CSR practices in Africa remain ambiguous sometimes, and often MNC commitment in Africa can be ascribed to *'the tree that hides the forest'*. Daouda (2014) echoes this claim to the effect that CSR activities in Africa are more of an advertising tool to anchor the aspirations of the community rather than a critical tool to foster compliance with environmental standards, poverty alleviation, compliance with labour laws, and inclusive social dialogue.

15.1.2 The Importance of CSR Behaviour for MNCs in the Oil & Gas Sector

There is a subtle link between the behaviour of MNCs, reputation enhancement, and local market legitimacy or moral obligation to the society from which wealth is generated. Investors and customers do not want to be associated with firms that have a bad reputation. Thus, socially responsible firms build a reputation which, in turn, attracts investors and loyal customers. This behaviour suggests that compliance with the expectations of society is critical to the building of a firm's reputation and the legitimisation of its activities. More recently, modern business practices have actively used CSR activities as a measure of sustainable business, and therefore, CSR activities of firms significantly influence investors' decisions whether to invest or not, in a particular firm. For example, Chakamera (2020) found that for both African and non-African MNCs, CSR practices can boost the financial performance of companies through customer satisfaction and customer retention. Similarly, Anstätt and Volkert (2016) argue that carbon disclosure projects (CDP) of firms can be understood as a useful strategic tool of CSR that is intended to build a reputation in the capital markets, to reduce financial costs for potential investors. In Ghana, Abugre and Anlesinya (2019) found that CSR improves the reputational value of MNCs. Basically, when CSR improves, firms gain reputational stake from stakeholders and the community at large. Furthermore, MNCs committing to socially responsible action can benefit from various employee outcomes such as a greater ability to attract and retain skills, development of sustainable workforce morale, and access to a wide pool of talents of individuals who are interested in associating with the firm through employment.

15.2 Theoretical Underpinnings of CSR and the Socio-Economic Well-Being of Local Communities

There are three frequently used theoretical frameworks within the CSR discourse. These are the institutional theory, the stakeholder theory, and the capability approach. However, we are not suggesting that these are the only theories.

15.2.1 Institutional Theory

The institutional framework refers to regulatory structures, governmental agencies, laws, courts, and professions which influence the operations of private sector businesses (Bruton et al., 2010). The institutional framework determines the rules and the norms of the game within a society. Firms and non-governmental organisations operate within institutional frameworks. Scholars argue that the institutional environment exerts certain direct and indirect pressures on corporations, and this affects the values, norms, organisational structures, and actions of companies (Kühn et al., 2018; Lau et al., 2018). Thus, fully functioning and efficient institutions reduce transaction costs, uncertainty, and the risk of doing business with the private sector. On the other hand, a weak institutional environment is likely to be associated with high transaction costs as an exchange of gifts before services are rendered will be the norm.

Bruton et al. (2010) and Kühn et al. (2018) have used institutional theory to examine the content and determinants of CSR reporting in Sub-Saharan Africa and entrepreneurship. MNCs operating in Africa are likely to take advantage of the weak institutional environment to indulge in rent-seeking behaviour, thus compromising the implementation of CSR. For example, Kolk and Lenfant (2010) examine MNC reporting on CSR and conflict in Central Africa. The analysis of company information suggests that CSR reporting is fairly generic, and the specific context seems to bear little influence on the type of CSR activities. Furthermore, CSR reporting on the conflict dimension receives little attention, although some MNCs show awareness, particularly about the risks.

15.2.2 Stakeholder Theory

Stakeholder theory asserts that organisations that pay attention to a broad spectrum of stakeholders such as employees, suppliers, customers, local communities, and environmental groups, will function more effectively and create more value (Phillips et al., 2019). It further states that firms are involved in numerous CSR activities to satisfy the diverse needs of different stakeholders beyond the shareholders (Chakamera, 2020). This process creates business value that is used to sustain and grow the organisation as well as give back to the stakeholders who helped to create the business value. Thus, the stakeholder theory is considered to be both managerial and prescriptive because it deals with managers' behaviour and the associations with firms and their constituencies (Harrison et al., 2010). This theory emphasises the need for MNCs to manage and satisfy the competing interests of diverse stakeholders to create business value for the organisation, rather than focusing on a sole mandate of profit maximisation.

15.2.3 Capability Approach

The capability theoretical framework, articulated by Amartya Sen, is people-centred. Given that the ultimate goal of CSR is to create value for corporations and society, a people-centred approach is a suitable theoretical framework. The capability approach provides deeper insights into how corporate activities influence the well-being of internal stakeholders such as employees and external stakeholders (the local communities). The capability approach encompasses natural resources and man-made systems which, as a result of sustainable human development governance, impact individual resources and conversion factors (Anstätt & Volkert, 2016, p. 19). The core characteristic of the capability approach is to move away from the income-led evaluation methods and focus on people's ability to achieve the things that they value. Well-being can thus be measured by assessing people's freedom and choices, rather than their income or consumption (Frediani, 2010). Sen (1997) iterates that the capability approach recognises that individuals differ in their capability to convert goods into valuable achievements due to personal and locational factors and social arrangements. Thus, the capability approach acknowledges the multidimensional nature of human beings. The core concepts of the capability approach are functionings and capabilities. Functionings describe the achievement of a person; what he or she manages to do or to be and capabilities are the freedoms that people have to achieve the lifestyle that they have reason to value (Frediani, 2010, p. 176). The capability approach can, therefore, be a suitable theoretical framework for evaluating the impact of CSR on the local community.

15.2.4 Socio-Economic Well-being

Although well-being is a common term, there is not yet a universally accepted definition of this concept. It has sometimes been used interchangeably with quality of life, happiness, and life satisfaction (OECD, 2013). Despite the absence of an agreed definition, well-being can be conceived as meeting various human needs such as being in good health, and equally, the ability to pursue one's goal, to succeed, and feel contented with life (OECD, 2013). The OECD views well-being as a complex phenomenon that is strongly correlated with its determinants, and as such requires a comprehensive framework that accounts for the large number of components that will ideally permit gauging the interrelations that shape people's lives. Against this background, the OECD has identified three pillars for understanding and measuring people's well-being:

- *Material living conditions or economic well-being* – determines people's consumption options and their control over resources;
- *Quality of life* – defined as a set of non-monetary attributes of individuals that shapes their opportunities and life chances and has an intrinsic value in different cultures and contexts;
- The *sustainability of the socio-economic and natural systems* where people live and work is important for well-being to last over time. Sustainability depends on how current human activities impact the stocks of different types of capital (natural, economic, human, and social) that underpin well-being.

Thus, the CSR of MNCs should exert a positive influence on these dimensions of well-being particularly, to ensure the sustainability of the stocks of capital. Strotmann et al. (2019) adopted the capacity approach to evaluate the effect of the CSR strategy on the reported well-being of poor rural villagers in India. The researchers' aim was to examine whether the participation of villagers in the different activities of Bayer Crop Science Model Village Project from 2011 to 2014 contributed to reported well-being. Preliminary evidence from participants revealed an improvement in subjective well-being. This was re-enforced by granular empirical analysis which showed that the 78% share of villagers who reported positive changes in well-being in the two villages were statistically higher than the corresponding 62% in the control villages. Furthermore, the test of equality of the shares confirmed that the difference of 16% points was indeed significant.

15.3 Empirical Evidence

15.3.1 Contextual Overview

Over the years and more intensely in recent times, extant literature shows that CSR has become a prominent medium through which firms support society and the business environment with the sole aim of advancing business gains while improving the socio-economic growth of host communities (Brower & Mahajan, 2013; Chun et al., 2013; Rodgers et al., 2013). Despite growth in the CSR literature in developed countries (Babikr, 2013; Kirat, 2015;), the literature on CSR initiatives is not as much documented in most developing countries (Blowfield & Frynas, 2005) and this makes it difficult to appreciate the extent of work being done and the level of activities that need to be done to enhance both performance and reporting of CSR in developing countries, especially in Africa.

Unlike advanced economies, developing countries have large portions of marginalised citizens who often need support that government resources are unable to satisfy due to under-development and low levels of economic growth, coupled with poor leadership that often tends to be exploitative. These economies, however, tend to have abundant natural resources (predominantly oil and gas) that are often exploited with the assistance of large corporations (Adams et al., 2019; Ross, 2015) that are led by the elite in these societies. Africa is a developing context characterised by fragile institutions and market systems which often influence the level of implementation and impact of CSR activities. We highlight the interplay between the attributes of Africa's political economy, societal well-being, and firm operations in the oil and gas sector.

15.3.2 Comparing CSR Initiatives from MNCs Globally and across Sub-Saharan Africa

CSR activities in advanced economies differ significantly from developing economies, particularly in Sub-Saharan Africa where there are huge socio-economic and developmental challenges. In developed economies, given the advanced industrial and manufacturing sectors, CSR initiatives are focused on reducing the carbon footprint, environmental protection/preservation, building reputation, investing in businesses that are environmentally friendly, and building brand names (Aguilera-Caracuel et al., 2017; Liu et al., 2014). For example, Aguilera-Caracuel et al. (2017) investigated the influence of internationalisation and social performance on a firm's reputation using 113 US-based MNCs operating in the chemical, energy, and industrial machinery sectors, during the period 2005–2010, using a fixed effect estimator. The results revealed that a high degree of geographic international diversification empowers MNCs to improve their social performance, which, in turn, exerts a positive influence on reputation. The findings further showed that the internationalisation of MNCs positively influences MNCs' reputation through the mediating role of social performance.

In Sub-Saharan Africa, a region plagued by a high level of unemployment, inequality, and extreme poverty, CSR initiatives mainly focus on social issues such as education, training and skill development, building and development local communities, healthcare, and wellness (Makka & Nieuwenhuizen, 2018). In other words, the CSR efforts of MNCs in Africa focus largely on local philanthropy. Kühn et al. (2018) examine the degree to which MNCs in Sub-Saharan Africa undertake CSR reporting and the content they included in their disclosure. The empirical results of 211 MNCs operating in seven Sub-Saharan African countries, using logistic regression, reveal that approximately 88% of the MNCs across all seven countries focus their CSR activities on local communities. The evidence further showed a lack of systematic implementation of CSR activities across the sample of countries. This is corroborated by Aguilera-Caracuel et al. (2017, p. 339) who argue that MNCs set up factories in countries with questionable human rights and weak regulations. However, MNCs operating in South Africa complain about the lack of a national CSR framework and the increasing number of CSR issues that firms are expected to address. The priority issues for these MNCs are education, training and skill development, building and developing local communities, and health care and wellness (Makka & Nieuwenhuizen, 2018).

15.3.3 Factors Affecting CSR of Oil-Based MNCs in Africa

CSR performance is driven by internal firm-level factors of MNCs and their subsidiaries as well as external factors in the host countries and the broader regulatory environment. The primary internal factors and external factors are discussed below.

Corporate governance and *level of operation* within the host country often influence the level of CSR engagement since these inform the extent of collaboration between stakeholders. When MNC subsidiaries are locally owned or serve local markets and use their labour or social capital, for instance, the MNC might be more committed to the host country than if these factors were non-existent (Laursen et al., 2012). The extent of this 'embeddedness' (Forsgren et al., 2007) influences the collaboration with stakeholders depending on the strength of networking with key stakeholders (Bouquet & Birkinshaw, 2008) which may enhance collaborative efforts towards impactful CSR planning and activities. As alluded to by Bondy and Starky (2014), without any form of collaboration with stakeholders, 37 sampled MNCs embarked on CSR activities that did not address the primary issue of poverty in their host countries since they were not highly engaged with local stakeholders in their operations.

Autonomy and *managerial discretion* of MNC subsidiaries are other determinant factors advanced by Morgenroth and Luiz (2016). The authors argue that the ability of MNC subsidiaries to negotiate and obtain approval from the parent company to invest in CSR depends on their long-standing history of capabilities in successful implementations and contributions to the group. This often determines the level of autonomy that allows MNC subsidiaries to confidently exercise managerial discretions that make it possible to collaborate with local stakeholders to embark on beneficial projects. Studies often employ company age and size as proxies for measuring the autonomy of subsidiaries (Husted & Allen, 2006; Luo, 2006)

Government and *local culture* set the stage for the institutional framework which issues policies and directives as well as regulates the business activities in every host country (Mehic et al., 2013). Therefore, the set of directives and regulations determines the level of CSR activities that MNCs will be required to perform to enable the governments of host countries to generate the best economic and social gains for citizens (Detomasi, 2008). Moreover, the attitude of local communities towards MNCs may influence the acceptance of their activities as well as their support to the community without prejudice or suspicions of ulterior motives by MNCs (Park & Choi, 2015; Russo & Perrini, 2010).

Pressure groups such as the media and NGOs often play a critical role in ensuring responsible actions from MNCs. Negative reports have the potential to ruin the reputation of MNCs and, therefore, firms endeavour to pursue responsible CSR activities such as protecting the well-being of employees, reducing pollution, supporting infrastructure projects, and extending philanthropic support to the needy in society (Guay et al., 2004).

MNCs mostly aim to legitimise their presence in host countries by engaging in CSR activities to build a *corporate reputation* that supports their brand image for firm value enhancement (Bouquet et al., 2009; Mittal et al., 2008; O'Shaughnessy et al., 2007). Stakeholders usually prefer to be associated with and to trade with MNCs that support the local communities' development priorities; hence, in pursuit of good citizenship, MNCs engage in CSR activities.

15.3.4 Impediments to CSR in the Oil Industry in Africa

The extant literature identifies two major factors that impede CSR performance in Africa. In oil-rich countries like Angola, Equatorial Guinea, and

Nigeria, Frynas (2005) highlights the following issues. The first is that the parochial gains of MNCs (Ottaway, 2001) often lead to undertaking short-term CSR activities that ensure business gains rather than activities that are aligned with the long-term development plan of host communities. The second is that poor political governance and corruption slow down economic growth and inhibit the success of CSR activities since firms cannot deal with the macro-level governance problems (Litvin, 2003). In the light of these macro-level concerns, Muchlinski (2001) explains that the perceived human rights offences and poor CSR performance levelled against, say Chinese MNCs, may be exaggerated since governments ought to extend more of these responsibilities to the citizens to make it possible for MNCs to follow in a more directed manner, to make CSR activities beneficial to the society. This is pertinent because MNEs are firms that cannot take on the primary duties of governments. Thus, the mere fact that Western oil companies are engaged in CSR reporting and are signatories to the Universal Declaration of Human Rights, the Extractive Industries Transparency Initiative (EITI), and the UN Global Compact, does not put them in the position to lead development as such (Pegg, 2012). It is, therefore, argued that oil-rich African states can obtain adequate benefits and growth from MNCs' CSR if they tackle the institutional weaknesses and fragilities that allow MNCs to take advantage of them (Adams et al., 2022; Contractor, 2016; George et al., 2016; Idemudia, 2011).

15.3.5 The Impact and Socio-Economic Performance of the CSR Activities of Oil Sector MNEs

Several studies have examined the impact of CSR activities of MNCs on the development of their host communities. The activities have been broadly categorised into environmental, social, governance, and ethical issues. In terms of environmental performance, there is evidence of commitment to international standards, e.g., environmental management system (EMS) (ISO 14001:2004) on sustainable business practices including safe management of emissions and waste, employee environmental training, and others (García-Rodríguez et al., 2013; Uduji & Okolo-Obasi, 2020; see Box 15.1)

The social benefits identified within the local communities of MNCs include education, small-scale business developments, infrastructure, social welfare schemes, as well as regulatory commitments in the form of taxes and royalties (Eweje, 2006). This notwithstanding, there is a backlash against unethical business practices and negative CSR practices that enhance the value of MNCs to the detriment of the communities. Besides contaminating the environment, MNC activities often spark public anger or aggravate conflict in these communities, which lead to legal actions against MNCs in the oil and gas sector (see Box 15.2).

Box 15.1

The Adoption of an ISO 14001-Based Environmental Management System (EMS) by the Luanda Oil Refinery

García-Rodríguez et al. (2013) examined how the implementation of the ISO 14001-based EMS by the Luanda oil refinery (63% owned by French MNC Total Fina and 37% owned by Sonangol, Angola's national oil company) affected the company's environmental performance. The implementation of the EMS began in 2005 and was completed in 2007. Scholars note that prior to the EMS implementation, the company's environmental efforts were in fact conducted in compliance with the regulatory authority demands. However, the actions were not formally structured. There was no documentation of processes, and the environmental department was ineffective and lacked proper planning. The end result was significant negative impacts of the firm's operations on the environment: waste production, soil contamination, wastewater generation, excessive water loss, and atmospheric and noise pollution. A third-party company had been contracted to deal with the waste generated, but the company lacked the technology to treat most of this waste, and there had been suspicions that the waste was simply being dumped without treatment. Serious pollution had been detected in Luanda Bay due to the operations of the refinery and that of other companies. The researchers found that the environmental situation of the firm had improved considerably following the implementation of the EMS. The consequences of the EMS extended beyond the company and its direct competitors and became a standard used by the government of Angola to request all companies to sign up to an environmental contract.

Source: García-Rodríguez et al. (2013); Uduji and Okolo-Obasi (2020)

Box 15.2

Effect of Oil Companies' Activity on Environment, Health, and Development in Sub-Saharan Africa

The European Parliament authorised a study in 2011 that documents the environmental, health, and developmental impact of the activities of oil companies in Sub-Saharan Africa. The study reports that the negative consequences of oil extraction in Sub-Saharan Africa are a major concern that has threatened the health, development, and livelihoods of host communities. The study's main focus is on Nigeria and Angola. Oil spills and gas flares are identified as two key environmental and health hazards in SSA. Though there are no official figures on oil spills in Nigeria, it is estimated that a quantity between 93.9 and 712 barrels are spilled daily on average whilst there are no estimates available for Angola. Oil spills have resulted in land and water pollution that have affected the livelihood of host communities that used to be farmers and fishermen. Gas flaring contributes to greenhouse emissions and has a negative impact on human health. The flaring emits such gases as carbon dioxide, methane, sulphur dioxide, nitrogen dioxide, carcinogenic substances such as benzopyrene and dioxin, and unburned fuel components including benzene, toluene, xylene, and hydrogen sulphide. The report shows that incidents of illness associated with the pollution, including gastrointestinal problems, skin diseases, cancers, and respiratory ailments, have been reported in communities along the Niger Delta. Poverty is widespread in the host communities and the CSR of oil companies have not made much of an impact, even though many researchers believe these companies are capable of doing so. Oil companies have been accused of ignoring the underlying development challenges and only addressing some symptoms of poverty. Community dissent on the operations of oil companies exists in both Nigeria and Angola.

Source: OBE et al. (2011)

Case Study: Nigerian Farmers vs Shell Petroleum Company Court Case

In January 2021, an appeals court in The Hague (Netherlands) found the Nigerian subsidiary of Royal Dutch Shell Plc liable for oil spills in two villages in the Niger Delta of Nigeria between 2004 and 2005. The oil spill occurred in the villages of Oruma and Goi. Official reports indicate that the spills were a result of damage to pipelines, although the Shell Petroleum Development Company (SPDC) claims they were acts of sabotage. The suit was filed by four farmers: Barizaa Dooh, Elder Friday Alfred Akpan, Chief Fidelis A. Oguru, and Alali Efanga with support from Friends of the Earth Netherlands, an NGO group. The plaintiffs claimed that the leak from the underground oil pipelines contaminated their land and waterways, costing them their livelihoods. The court case began in 2008, and the final ruling was obtained in January 2021. The Hague Court of Appeals ruled that Shell Nigeria (SPDC) was liable for damages from pipeline leaks in the villages of Oruma and Goi. Shell argued that it could not be held responsible for the action of a foreign subsidiary. The court held that Shell had not proven that there was sabotage in the leakages and that the company had not fit leak-detection systems (LDS) on their pipes prior to the incidents. The court ordered Shell to install leak-detection systems, clean up the oil spill, and pay compensation, the amount of which is yet to be determined.

Sources: www.ft.com/content/663c6261-338e-4f6a-8ae4-11416607db71; www.bloomberg.com/news/articles/2021-01-29/dutch-court-orders-shell-nigeria-to-compensate-for-oil-spills; www.dw.com/en/uk-court-nigerian-farmers-can-sue-shell-over-pollution/a-56551330

15.4 Conclusion

This chapter has examined the CSR strategy and implementation towards the socio-economic growth and development of oil-producing countries in Africa. It has presented an overview of the prominent activities of MNCs in Africa and identified the positive and negative externalities of their activities with the aim of identifying the net gains of FDI for the host countries. The chapter has further highlighted the predominant theories employed in the CSR literature to capture the determinants of CSR in the extractive sector including the institutional theory, the stakeholder theory, and the capability approach. It has also examined the empirical literature to reveal the contrast between CSR in advanced countries and Africa and identified the factors affecting the CSR of MNCs in Africa. Subsequently, we have presented case studies of CSR activities in Africa with the aim of examining the impact on the environment, socio-economic well-being, and governance in host countries. Prominent among socially irresponsible activities are the various forms of pollution, and short-term social impact activities. The required legal and policy interventions in the few cases identified as irresponsible activities have been proposed to contain the situation. The chapter highlights the importance of effective regulations and legal frameworks for the operations of MNCs to be mutually beneficial to all stakeholders. The sample case studies also provide insights into how host countries can fight inefficiencies that impede the implementation of policies and regulations in the oil and gas sector.

Note

1 African countries within the top 50 oil producing countries as at 2021 include Nigeria, Libya, Algeria, Angola, Egypt, Republic of the Congo, Ghana, Gabon, South Sudan, Equatorial Guinea, Chad, Sudan, and Cameroon.

References

Abugre, J. B., & Anlesinya, A. (2019). Corporate social responsibility and business value of multinational companies: Lessons from a Sub-Saharan African environment. *Journal of African Business*, 20(4), 435–454.

Adams, D., Adams, K., Attah-Boakye, R., Ullah, S., Rodgers, W., & Kimani, D. (2022). Social and environmental practices and corporate financial performance of multinational corporations in emerging markets: Evidence from 20 oil-rich African countries. *Resources Policy*, 78, 102756.

Adams, D., Adams, K., Ullah, S., & Ullah, F. (2019). Globalisation, governance, accountability and the natural resource 'curse': Implications for socio-economic growth of oil-rich developing countries. *Resources Policy*, 61, 128–140.

Aguilera-Caracuel, J., Guerrero-Villegas, J., & García-Sánchez, E. (2017). Reputation of multinational companies: Corporate social responsibility and internationalization. *European Journal of Management and Business Economics*, 26(3), 329–346.

Anstätt, K., & Volkert, J. (2016). Corporate social responsibility impacts on sustainable human development. *Ekonomski vjesnik/Econviews – Review of Contemporary Business, Entrepreneurship and Economic Issues*, 29(1), 193–210.

Babikr, O. (2013). *The white book: Practices of social responsibility in Qatar institutions and companies*. Dar Al-Sharq (In Arabic).

Blowfield, M., & Frynas, J. G. (2005). Editorial setting new agendas: Critical perspectives on corporate social responsibility in the developing world. *International Affairs*, 81(3), 499–513.

Bondy, K., & Starkey, K. (2014). The dilemmas of internationalization: Corporate social responsibility in the multinational corporation. *British Journal of Management*, 25(1), 4–22.

Bouquet, C., & Birkinshaw, J. (2008). Managing power in the multinational corporation: How low-power actors gain influence. *Journal of Management, 34*(3), 477–508.

Bouquet, C., Crane, A., & Deutsch, Y. (2009). The trouble with being average. *MIT Sloan Management Review, 50*(3), 79.

Brower, J., & Mahajan, V. (2013). Driven to be good: A stakeholder theory perspective on the drivers of corporate social performance. *Journal of Business Ethics, 117*(2), 313–331.

Bruton, G. D., Ahlstrom, D., & Li, H. L. (2010). Institutional theory and entrepreneurship: Where are we now and where do we need to move in the future? *Entrepreneurship Theory and Practice, 34*(3), 421–440.

Chakamera, C. (2020). Analysis of corporate social responsibility of the African 'internationalisers' versus non-African founded MNCs. *International Review of Philanthropy and Social Investment, 1*(1), 57–72.

Chun, J. S., Shin, Y., Choi, J. N., & Kim, M. S. (2013). How does corporate ethics contribute to firm financial performance? The mediating role of collective organizational commitment and organizational citizenship behavior. *Journal of Management, 39*(4), 853–877.

Contractor, F. J. (2016). Tax avoidance by multinational companies: Methods, policies, and ethics. *Rutgers Business Review, 1*(1), 2016.

Daouda, Y. H. (2014). CSR and sustainable development: Multinationals are they socially responsible in Sub-Saharan Africa? The case of Areva in Niger. *Cadernos de Estudos Africanos*, (28), 141–162.

Detomasi, D. A. (2008). The political roots of corporate social responsibility. *Journal of Business Ethics, 82*(4), 807–819.

Eweje, G. (2006). The role of MNEs in community development initiatives in developing countries: Corporate social responsibility at work in Nigeria and South Africa. *Business & Society, 45*(2), 93–129.

Forsgren, M., Holm, U., & Johanson, J. (2007). *Managing the embedded multinational: A business network view*. Edward Elgar Publishing.

Frediani, A. A. (2010). Sen's capability approach as a framework to the practice of development. *Development in Practice, 10*, 173–187.

Frynas, J. G. (2005). The false developmental promise of corporate social responsibility: Evidence from multinational oil companies. *International Affairs, 81*(3), 581–598.

Frynas, J. G., Wood, G., & Hinks, T. (2017). The resource curse without natural resources: Expectations of resource booms and their impact. *African Affairs, 116*(463), 233–260.

García-Rodríguez, F. J., García-Rodríguez, J. L., Castilla-Gutiérrez, C., & Major, S. A. (2013). Corporate social responsibility of oil companies in developing countries: From altruism to business strategy. *Corporate Social Responsibility and Environmental Management, 20*(6), 371–384.

George, G., Corbishley, C., Khayesi, J. N., Haas, M. R., & Tihanyi, L. (2016). Bringing Africa in: Promising directions for management research. *Academy of Management Journal, 59*(2), 377–393.

Guay, T., Doh, J. P., & Sinclair, G. (2004). Non-governmental organizations, shareholder activism, and socially responsible investments: Ethical, strategic, and governance implications. *Journal of Business Ethics, 52*(1), 125–139.

Harrison, J. S., Bosse, D. A., & Phillips, R. A. (2010). Managing for stakeholders, stakeholder utility functions, and competitive advantage. *Strategic Management Journal, 31*(1), 58–74.

Hayat, A., Ganiev, B., & Tang, X. (2013). Expectations of future income and real exchange rate movements. *Journal of Banking & Finance, 37*(4), 1274–1285.

Husted, B. W., & Allen, D. B. (2006). Corporate social responsibility in the multinational enterprise: Strategic and institutional approaches. *Journal of International Business Studies, 37*(6), 838–849.

Idemudia, U. (2011). Corporate social responsibility and developing countries: Moving the critical CSR research agenda in Africa forward. *Progress in Development Studies, 11*(1), 1–18.

Kirat, M. (2015). Corporate social responsibility in the oil and gas industry in Qatar perceptions and practices. *Public Relations Review, 41*(4), 438–446.

Kolk, A., & Lenfant, F. (2010). MNC reporting on CSR and conflict in Central Africa. *Journal of Business Ethics, 93*(2), 241–255.

Kühn, A. L., Stiglbauer, M., & Fifka, M. S. (2018). Contents and determinants of corporate social responsibility website reporting in Sub-Saharan Africa: A seven-country study. *Business & Society, 57*(3), 437–480.

Lau, A. K. W., Lee, S. H. N., & Jung, S. (2018). The role of the institutional environment in the relationship between CSR and operational performance: An empirical study in Korean manufacturing industries. *Sustainability*, 10, 834. https://doi.org/10.3390/su10030834

Laursen, K., Masciarelli, F., & Prencipe, A. (2012). Trapped or spurred by the home region? The effects of potential social capital on involvement in foreign markets for goods and technology. *Journal of International Business Studies, 43*(9), 783–807.

Le Billon, P. (2011). Extractive sectors and illicit financial flows: What role for revenue governance initiatives? U4 Issue No 13. https://www.cmi.no/publications/4248-extractive-sectors-and-illicit-financial-flows

Litvin, D. (2003). *Empires of profit: Commerce, conquest and corporate responsibility*. Texere.

Liu, M. T., Wong, I. A., Shi, G., Chu, R., & Brock, J. L. (2014). The impact of corporate social responsibility (CSR) performance and perceived brand quality on customer-based brand preference. *Journal of Services Marketing, 28*(3), 181–194.

Luo, Y. (2006). Political behavior, social responsibility, and perceived corruption: A structuration perspective. *Journal of International Business Studies, 37*(6), 747–766.

Makka, A., & Nieuwenhuizen, C. (2018). Multinational enterprises perceptions of the national corporate social responsibility priority issues in South Africa. *Social Responsibility Journal, 14*(4), 828–842.

Mehic, E., Silajdzic, S., & Babic-Hodovic, V. (2013). The impact of FDI on economic growth: Some evidence from Southeast Europe. *Emerging Markets Finance and Trade, 49*(1), 5–20.

Mittal, R. K., Sinha, N., & Singh, A. (2008). An analysis of linkage between economic value added and corporate social responsibility. *Management Decision, 46*(9), 1437–1443.

Morgenroth, A., & Luiz, J. M. (2016). Corporate social responsibility mandates within German multinational enterprises in Sub-Saharan Africa. *European Journal of International Management, 10*(6), 624–646.

Muchlinski, P. T. (2001). Human rights and multinationals: Is there a problem? *International Affairs, 77*(1), 31–47.

O'shaughnessy, K. C., Gedajlovic, E., & Reinmoeller, P. (2007). The influence of firm, industry and network on the corporate social performance of Japanese firms. *Asia Pacific Journal of Management, 24*(3), 283–303.

Obe, A. V., Donnelly, E., Baumüller, H., & Weimer, M. (2011). The effects of oil companies' activities on the environment, health and development in Sub-Saharan Africa Chatham House. Retrieved Nov 11, 2022, from https://policycommons.net/artifacts/613254/the-effects-of-oil-companies-activities-on-the-environment-health-and-development-in-sub-saharan-africa/1592858/. CID: 20.500.12592/wh8n9x.

Ofori, D. F., & Debrah, Y. (2014). Corporate social responsibility in Sub-Saharan Africa: Hindering and supporting factors. *African Journal of Economic and Management Studies*, 5(1), 93–113.

Organisation for Economic Co-operation and Development (2013). *OECD framework for statistics on the distribution of household income, consumption and wealth*. Author.

Ottaway, M., 2001. Reluctant missionaries. *Foreign Policy* (July/August), pp. 44–54.

Park, B. I., & Choi, J. (2015). Stakeholder influence on local corporate social responsibility activities of Korean multinational enterprise subsidiaries. *Emerging Markets Finance and Trade*, 51(2), 335–350.

Pegg, S. (2012). Social responsibility and resource extraction: Are Chinese oil companies different? *Resources Policy*, 37(2), 160–167.

Phillips, R. A., Barney, J. B., Freeman, R. E., & Harrison, J. S. (2019). Stakeholder theory. In Harrison, J. S., Barney, J. B., Freeman, R. E. & Phillips, R. A. (Eds.), *The Cambridge handbook of stakeholder theory*. Cambridge University Press.

Plan, A. (2011). Communication from the commission to the European Parliament, the council, the European economic and social committee and the committee of the Regions. *European Commission*.

Rodgers, W., Choy, H. L., & Guiral, A. (2013). Do investors value a firm's commitment to social activities? *Journal of Business Ethics*, 114(4), 607–623.

Ross, M. L. (2015). What have we learned about the resource curse? *Annual Review of Political Science*, 18, 239–259.

Russo, A., & Perrini, F. (2010). Investigating stakeholder theory and social capital: CSR in large firms and SMEs. *Journal of Business Ethics*, 91(2), 207–221.

Sen, A. (1993). Capability and well-being. In M. Nussbaum, & A. Sen (Eds.), *Quality of life* (pp. 30–53). Clarendon Press.

Sen, A. (1997). *On Economic Inequality*. Clarendon Press.

Sigam, C., & Garcia, L. (2012). *Extractive industries: Optimizing value retention in host countries* (p. 171). UNCTAD.

Strotmann, H., Volkert, J., & Schmidt, M. (2019). Multinational companies: Can they foster well-being in the eyes of the poor? Results from an empirical case study. *International Journal of Corporate Social Responsibility*, 4(1), 1–14.

Uduji, J. I., & Okolo-Obasi, E. N. (2020). Does corporate social responsibility (CSR) impact on development of women in small-scale fisheries of Sub-Saharan Africa? Evidence from coastal communities of Niger Delta in Nigeria. AGDI Working Paper, No. WP/18/059, 118.

Vicente, P. C. (2010). Does oil corrupt? Evidence from a natural experiment in West Africa. *Journal of Development Economics*, 92(1), 28–38.

Watkins, K. (2013). Equity in extractives: Stewarding Africa's natural resources for all: Africa progress report 2013.

16 Environmental and Sustainability Management in the Oil and Gas Industry

Albert Ahenkan, Mawuena A. Cudjoe, Amin Karimu, and Gordon Abekah-Nkrumah

16.1 Introduction

Issues of environment and sustainability management in the oil and gas industry in emerging and developing countries have moved to centre stage in the sustainable development agenda. This is due to the growing concern regarding the compatibility of the oil and gas industry to a sustainable future (Cherepovitsyn et al., 2021; Okeke, 2021). Sustainable development was defined by WCED, 1987 as *'a development that meets the demand of the present generation without compromising the ability of the future generations to meet their own needs'*. This provides a broad view of the concept of environmental sustainability within this paper. Savitz and Weber (2006, p. 6) defined sustainability as 'any process that enables a company to create profit for its shareholders while protecting the environment and improving the lives of those with whom it interacts'.

This chapter is divided into four sections. Section 16.1 presents the introduction and overview of the oil and gas industry in Africa. Section 16.2 presents sustainability challenges in the oil and gas industry, while Section 16.3 examines environmental governance within the oil and gas sector. Section 16.4 discusses how environmental impacts in the oil and gas industry are being managed, the international regulatory framework, and mechanisms for pollution prevention in the sector. The section also highlights corporate environmentalism (CE) in industry, the efforts to reduce pollution and resource use, and greening of the oil and gas industry. Section 16.5 concludes the chapter.

16.1.1 Overview of Oil and Gas Industry in Africa

Globally, Africa's oil production accounted for nearly 8% of oil production in 2020 with about 330 million metric tons of oil production on the continent that same year (Julia Faria, 2021). Natural gas production amounted to 231 billion cubic meters in the same year (Sönnichsen, 2021). Generally, two main parts are distinguished in the oil and gas industry in Africa: (1) upstream, which covers the exploration and production, and (2) downstream, which

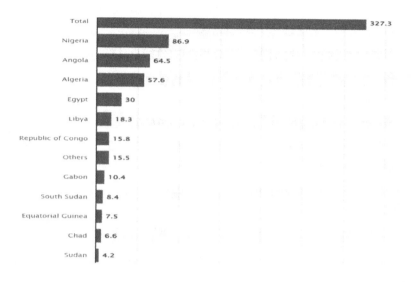

Figure 16.1 Oil production in million metric tons in Africa by country 2020

Source: Statista (2022) https://www.statista.com/chart/26878/african-countries-with-the-highest-oil-production-volume/

caters to the refining and processing of crude oil and gas products as well as distribution and marketing. Figure 16.1 shows oil production in Africa in 2020 by country.

16.2 Sustainability Challenges in the Oil and Gas Industry in Developing Countries

Although the oil and gas sector has improved the economies of most developing countries over the years, its activities such as exploration and production have significant environmental impacts on air quality, soils, surface and groundwater, marine environment, and biological diversity and sustainability of life support systems. The exploration and production of oil and gas have never been without negative environmental impacts, posing sustainability challenges for the sector, especially in developing countries (Baptiste & Nordenstam, 2009). Globally, oil and gas production is associated with many environmental impacts (Baptiste & Nordenstam, 2009) and Africa is no exception. In the context of Africa, the sustainability challenges often arise as a result of operational discharges, air emissions, waste management, oil spills, cumulative and transboundary impacts, and long-term chronic exposures to many chemicals and pollution associated with hydrocarbon production activities.

One of the fundamental problems facing the oil industry in Africa is environmental degradation. Potential environmental impacts usually refer to the likely effects of the quality and quantity of ecosystem and biodiversity. Increasingly, the oil and gas industry has become a major source of oil spills, damage to land, water contamination, air pollution, and water pollution. Some sustainability concerns include pollution of water bodies, emission of greenhouse gases, negative effects on wildlife, and seismic shifts. Besides environmental concerns, there are health and safety concerns. Ghisel (1997) noted that the extraction of fossil fuels from offshore has increased dramatically over the past five decades, emerging as one of the most exploitative activities that deplete natural resources and ecosystems. In addition to the environmental challenge, oil and gas exploitation tends to have a negative impact on the livelihoods of host communities both in the short and long-term (Iwayemi, 2006; Obi, 2010; UNEP, 2011). Despite several decades of frequent spills and associated damage to the environment, governments in oil resource-rich countries have failed to address the environmental challenge by corporations who have remained accountable for the destruction of the natural resources. For instance, Babatunde (2014) and Imobighe (2004) revealed that oil-induced environmental degradation in the Niger Delta has not only affected the traditional livelihoods but also led to conflicts within communities, among communities and between the communities and the oil companies.

16.3 Environmental Governance and Ethics in the Oil and Gas Industry

16.3.1 Environmental Governance

Environmental governance is key even in firms with very little environmental impact. Evidence from Tingbani et al. (2020) and Berrone and Gomez-Mejia (2009) suggests that aside from the widely known corporate governance mechanisms, firms in recent times would like to appoint directors with knowledge in environmental governance and ethics. Environmental governance discusses how the environment is managed. Thus, it refers to all the processes, procedures, and mechanisms put in place by governments and other stakeholders to ensure that actors in an environment in no way harm it (Lemos & Agrawal, 2006). Environmental governance can, therefore, be linked to trends involving politics and development across diverse contexts and scales in protecting the environment (Bridge & Perreault, 2009).

Environmental governance, like most governance concepts, has been defined by researchers in several ways. Whereas some studies define environmental governance in line with ethics (Rossouw, 2005; Solomon, 2007) arguing that environmental governance is aimed at enhancing and managing environmental activities within firms. Others (Merkl-Davies & Brennan, 2007; Neu et al., 1998) suggest that environmental governance is a tool for impression management. Another widely known definition of environmental governance is that it is the set of regulatory processes, mechanisms, and organisations through which political actors influence environmental actions and outcomes (Lemos & Agrawal, 2006). In this chapter, we will use the term environmental governance synonymously with interventions aimed at changes in environment-related incentives, knowledge, institutions, decision-making, and behaviours.

The environmental governance of the oil and gas industry is important because it defines whether the natural resource will be a blessing or a curse to the nation mining it. There is evidence in the literature to suggest that context-specific environmental challenges coupled with bad environmental governance have often accounted for the lack of development in the countries exploiting oil and gas resources (Badeeb et al., 2017; Frynas, 2010). This occurrence called the oil curse (a situation where countries that are rich in petroleum, have less democracy, less economic stability, and therefore do not benefit from their oil find – Ross, 2013) is attributable to the lack of proper structures and strict environmental governance, which, therefore, leads to the exploitation of such economies by multinational companies (Aaron, 2012). It stands to reason then that the quality of institutions and, by extension, the environmental governance policies and guidelines put in place to guide oil and gas exploitation, will to a large extent determine whether the oil and gas become a blessing or a curse (Mehlum et al., 2006).

The existing literature suggests a developed-developing country divide on the governance of natural resources exploitation (Comyns & Figge, 2015; Cudjoe et al., 2019; Hilson, 2012; Lemos & Agrawal, 2006; Sethi et al., 2017). Developed countries tend to have strict governance structures (Comyns & Figge, 2015) with positive outcomes for the exploitation of such resources (Lemos & Agrawal, 2006). In Japan, South Korea, the EU, Austria, Estonia, France, Finland, Germany, the UK, Hungary, Poland, Portugal, Romania, and Slovenia, policies have been formulated to ensure the efficient use of material resources (Zhongming et al., 2016). An example of a policy that ensures the sustainable use of natural resources is the raw material initiative of the European Union (European Commission, 2008). The initiative is categorised into two main policies. The resource security and the resource efficiency policy (European Commission, 2011). Whereas resource security encourages an increase in the extraction of natural resources, resource efficiency diminishes its consumption. Specific goals have been set by these countries in a bid to reduce natural resource utilisation. The Austrian government, for example, implemented a programme which aimed to cut domestic material consumption by 20% by 2020 based on 2008 levels. Using a comprehensive measure of natural material resource use, the Italian government established a goal of reducing natural resource requirements by 90% by 2050 (Bahn-Walkowiak & Steger, 2015).

On the contrary, available evidence suggests that developing countries have weak environmental governance structures and guidelines (Hilson, 2012; Sethi et al., 2017). In Africa, for example, the sources of fuel and other materials used in the construction industry come from natural sources (Fabricius et al., 2006). Over the past 50 years, the use of resources has increased exponentially (Steffen et al., 2015), resulting in biodiversity loss on the continent

(Archer et al., 2018). Available evidence suggests that community-based natural resource management or governance initiatives in Botswana, Namibia, Zambia, and Zimbabwe are faced with challenges such as multi-actor participation, weak public accountability, lack of political will, and lack of income distribution plans (Stone et al., 2020). These challenges result in negative feedback cycles, affect the system's function integrity (O'higgins et al., 2014) and consequently hinder the ability of natural resource systems to produce socially and environmentally sustainable outcomes (Pahl-Wostl, 2009).

16.3.2 Environmental Ethics

Studies that link the environment to ethics date as far back as the 1960s and 1970s when people became conscious of the effects of technology on the environment (Palmer et al., 2014). Issues of environmental ethics have become popular among researchers mainly due to the impact of economic activities of firms on the environment. Recent evidence suggests that the managers of firms have become even more careful and strict on measures put in place to secure the environment while pursuing their mandate. This is so because the larger populace has embraced the idea of taking care of the environment and has in some instances boycotted firms whose activities seem to distort the environment (Longoni et al., 2018; Yu et al., 2017). Although so much can be achieved by enacting laws and standardising ethical issues, environmental ethics transcend what is legally binding and amounts to communal awareness and consciousness of the effects of the activities of humans on the environment (Okonkwo & Etemire, 2017). Yang (2006) defines environmental ethics as the intrinsic values or beliefs (i.e., what is right or wrong) on how the environment is protected (Abedi-Sarvestani & Shahvali, 2008). It is the justification and moral motivation needed to solve ecological problems. According to Palmer et al. (2014), environmental ethics places on humans a moral obligation or duty towards the environment, including why it must be fulfilled and how it can be fulfilled.

Environmental ethics has often gained the attention of firms mainly through pressure from stakeholders. Longoni et al. (2018) indicate that there are several factors that account for the reduction of the impact of firms (especially those in the oil and gas industry) on the environment. The most prominent reason is pressure from its stakeholders. As a result, firms are not only supposed to ensure compliance with environmental values to secure sustainable economic success (Tate & Bals, 2018) but are also supposed to view environmental management as a measure of their 'social performance' (Short et al., 2016). Beyond the conventional ethics approaches emanating from stakeholder pressure, environmental ethics has a religious connotation. Beyond religion, a number of theories have looked at the link between ethics and the environment, the most prominent among them being the intra-generational equity, inter-generational equity, and the transnational effect theories.

The concept of intra-generational equity as it pertains to sustainable development requires fairness within the same generation (Shrader-Frechette, 2000). In the context of oil and gas exploitation, the concept will require that there should be no discrimination against anyone who wishes to be involved in oil and gas activities and that there should be fairness in the distribution of benefits, risk, and environmental impact arising from the mining of oil and gas. The requirement for equity is not just a matter of national-level consideration but also at the community or local levels. Many communities that host the mining of oil and gas in Africa (e.g., the Niger Delta of Nigeria) are discriminated against and are made to suffer the environmental effects of the mining of oil and gas in their communities, while they live in abject poverty. Unfortunately, existing laws have done very little to mitigate the situation. More importantly, when punitive measures such as fines have been introduced, they have been very small and insignificant, especially when compared to the revenues of the oil and gas companies. In many of these instances, firms prefer to pay the fine rather than incur costs in minimising the negative effects of their activities. In managing the environmental impacts in such a situation, best practices in the industry should be keenly followed, i.e., developing economies should learn from the developed and already standardised ones. The oil and gas industry in Nigeria has done its best in mimicking its counterparts in UK and other developed economies but for lack of capacity and resources, it still fails to meet the full expectations (Environmental Guidelines and Standards for the Petroleum Industry in Nigeria, 2018).

Inter-generational ethics suggests that there is always a link between generations and that each generation should develop its oil and gas and other natural resources in a way that ensures continuity and avoid passing on harm to the next generation. Thus, each preceding generation should ensure that it either leaves the environment in the same way it received it, or even better. Each generation should certainly not leave the environment worse than it received it to ensure the subsistence of the environment. Inter-generational ethics is akin to sustainable development. If the environment is left worse off than it was inherited through pollution, degradation, oil spills, and other unacceptable behaviours, the effects can also be passed on from generation to generation. For instance, Etemire and Worika (2018) observed that although oil production had ceased in a part of Nigeria for almost a decade, the people in that region were, by 2018, still suffering the effects of the activities in the form of uncultivatable lands, ill-health, death (higher mortality rate in children), and sinking lands.

According to Ekong et al. (2013), in Nigeria, (just like other developing economies that produce oil and gas), the effects of the oil and gas industry are usually one that passes on from generation to generation due to weak laws and regulations. Apart from these, there are no laws to guard what belongs to the future generation. Put in clear terms, the future generation has no environmental rights. Thus, once you have not been born, you are not regarded as important. While the findings of this study may not amount to the recognition of an environmental right for future generations, it demonstrates the need for actors in the oil industry to take their generational responsibilities more seriously and be ethical in their interaction with the environment.

The effects of the activities of the oil and gas industry can be borderless (Okonkwo & Etemire, 2017; Palmer et al., 2014). Here, when one generation fails to manage the oil and gas industry, it does not only affect the generation after it, but it also affects people even in different continents and the world at large, even though they might not share in the benefits the oil and gas bring. Globally, all stakeholders must ensure that they act in environmentally responsible ways. For instance, the more than 5000 oil spills recorded in Nigeria between 2000 and 2015 were seen to have led numerous cases of international arbitration and payments of fines as they had adverse effects on Cameroon (Alemagi, 2007) and led to tension between the two nations (Darkwah, 2010).

16.4 Managing Environmental Impacts in the Oil and Gas Industry

From the previous subsection, it is obvious that countries may not necessarily benefit from the oil and gas industry before they are affected by its negative impact on their immediate environment. Also, we have learned that laws have not successfully protected the public from the negative effects of the activities of this industry on the environment. The use of enforceable laws is seen as one of the ways of managing the effects the oil and gas industry has on the environment, especially in developed economies. The rules and best practices are equally existent in developing economies; it is the enforcement that fails to meet expectations. For instance, in Nigeria, a court ruled that gas flaring was to be halted with immediate effect as per Article 24 of the 1999 Constitution. After the ruling, political interference such as victimisation and the transfer of the judge thwarted the implementation of the ruling (Etemire, 2014). The law in such instances tends to be reactive rather than proactive in nature.

Most countries with developed economies are now enshrining in their laws an enforceable rule on the current generation, the duty to protect and preserve the environment for future generations (Etemire & Worika, 2018). Apart from the rules that seem to have faced challenges in mitigating the effects of the oil and gas industries on the environment, recent theories and studies suggest that the deontology approach (where humans act in a way that shows they have a duty towards others and the environment at large) can manage the effects of the activities of this industry. Managing the environmental effects of the activities of the oil and gas industry is necessary as their activities affect more areas now than they used to in years past (1–3 km to even a wider coverage (Gray et al., 1999). It is important to manage this industry because there is a huge consumption of its products, which affects a huge proportion of the world's population. For instance, Martins et al. (2019)

concluded that about 60% or 24 out of 29 European countries are heavily reliant on fossil fuel energy. In managing the impact of the activities of the oil and gas industry, there are some challenges that need to be surmounted. The most obvious is the availability of infrastructure in disposing of the wastewater produced. Even though this is a problem, Gregory and Mohan (2015) believe that players in the industry should see this as an opportunity to acquire more knowledge to bring about innovation, research, development, and growth so that findings in one locality can be a guide to the others.

The activities of the oil and gas industry and the subsequent use of their products as a source of energy result in several environmental problems. These include pollution, global warming, and delayed health problems such as breathing and lung diseases or even death (Lott et al., 2017). Stringent rules must be put in place to ensure that the effects of these activities are significantly reduced because the negative effects are experienced beyond places where the oil is extracted. Globally, efforts are being made through international agreements and the enactment of guidelines and policies, with many countries adopting the global guidelines. The activities of the oil and gas industry need to be managed for several reasons. Apart from the pressing need to reduce its environmental effects, this natural resource is unevenly distributed, non-renewable, and easily depleted. In any case, complete depletion should not be encouraged, and it can only be fair to ensure, that for sake of energy security, the current generations alone do not benefit from it at the expense of future generations (Martins et al., 2019).

New policies and strategies have been introduced to ensure that the activities of the oil and gas industry are regulated. In recent times, policies and strategies for the environment on maintaining a clean and sustainable oil and gas industry have received international attention and support. Examples of these policies include feed-in-tariffs, demand-side measures, and smart grids (Hossain et al., 2016; Saffari et al., 2018). Beyond the policies, rules, and enactments in guiding the energy sector, Lott et al. (2017) also argue that advancements in technology that lead to less environmental impacts should be encouraged. They assert that if the U.K., for instance, applies adequate technology, especially for its residential heating, it will meet its target of decarbonisation by the year 2050.

In ensuring that international policies and strategies are effective in achieving what they are enacted for, these policies and strategies need to be measured for their effectiveness or otherwise. There are energy indicators that help in this regard. These indicators border on energy efficiency, energy availability, and renewable energy. They are effective in comparing progress annually (Sheinbaum-Pardo et al., 2012; Urpelainen, 2018). Although a lot has been done through legislation, policies, and regulations on both the international and local front, there is still a lot of work to be done to bring a high level of sanity into the industry. Having a clean and sustainable energy regime remains a headache for the governments of many nations (Hossain et al., 2016; Saffari et al., 2018).

16.4.1 Pollution Prevention in the Oil and Gas Industry

There are governmental structures for pollution prevention. The review is focused on international and national legal frameworks.

16.4.2 International Framework

Concerning the international frameworks, the 1996 Ottawa declaration formed the Arctic Council, where membership ensures the environmental protection and sustainability of the Arctic region (Arctic Council, 2016). The council has recently increased its governance role in the region through international research on areas relating to environmental protection, climate change, and biodiversity (Arctic Council, 2016). In 2011, the council members negotiated and signed the search and rescue agreement, which assigns areas and responsibilities to each Arctic state to respond to emergencies (Knol & Arbo, 2014). They signed a second agreement on Cooperation on Marine Oil Pollution Preparedness and Response, which prompted countries to respond to oil spills.

The Arctic Council is made up of working groups that ensure the abatement of pollution in the oil and gas industry. One is the Protection of the Arctic Marine Environment (PAME) Working Group. The PAME is responsible for providing the industry standard for pollution prevention and safety protocols that serves as a guide to regulating the Arctic offshore oil and gas drilling and exploration (Arctic Council, 2009). The OSPAR commission, which is made up of 15 European governments (Except Russia) is focused on pollution abatement and elimination of offshore sources in the Northeast Atlantic region (Knol & Arbo, 2014). The 1971 Copenhagen Agreement between five European countries (including Denmark and Norway) also ensures the sharing of information safeguarding marine environments from oil pollution. The 1994 bilateral agreement on oil spill response between Norway and Russia includes a joint contingency plan and joint training exercises (ibid.).

16.5 Corporate Environmentalism in the Oil and Gas Industry

According to the International Energy Agency (IEA), the oil and gas industry accounts for 45% of human-induced greenhouse gas emissions globally. This significant environmental pollution has increased pressure on oil and gas firms to mitigate the pollution. Given that most oil and gas operations harm the environment, the question has always been what oil and gas corporations are doing to limit or mitigate that impact. The oil and gas industry is a major industry that must constantly engage in corporate social responsibility practices, particularly in the areas of environmental issues.

Corporate environmentalism pertains to firm-level efforts to reduce pollution and resource use along with protecting natural habitats. More importantly, firms pledge to undertake these actions beyond the requirements of the law (Chrun et al., 2016). Although historically CE efforts focused on resource conservation, their contemporary focus is on pollution reduction to reduce direct harm to humans and their communities and on the protection of environmental sinks. Globally, oil and gas companies are paying greater attention to the environmental impact of their business activities. Policymakers, citizens, stakeholders, and customers are increasingly demanding improved environmental performance from business firms. External pressures such as legislation, public concerns, and market opportunities arising from environmental concerns have compelled oil companies to integrate environmental issues into their strategic planning processes.

The operations of oil and gas companies involve activities such as land clearance, oil spills, and natural gas emissions that have potential detrimental environmental consequences, especially during exploration and production (Clark, 1982; Estrada et al., 1997). Because oil and gas reserves are commonly found in developing countries near places with significant biological variety and ecological vulnerability, such as rainforests, mangroves, and protected national parks, the environmental dangers of oil and gas activities are increased (Austin & Sauer, 2002). Investing in biodiversity and turning green, as well as adopting long-lasting materials for pipelines, are some of the steps that must be addressed.

Okeke (2021) found that oil and gas companies in Europe prioritised cutting emissions and adding value for long-term growth, strategic flexibility, and sustainable operations as the most ingrained sustainability strategy. American oil and gas companies place emphasis on strategic flexibility and value addition as their most dominant sustainability strategy in comparison to long-term growth, lowering emissions, and sustainable operations. On the contrary, oil and gas businesses in Asia emphasised emissions reduction and strategic flexibility over value creation, sustainable operations, and long-term growth (Okeke, 2021).

European and Asian firms appear to be more devoted to pursuing a low-carbon future than their American counterparts, as they aspire to substantially reduce carbon in their operations and build contemporary, lower-carbon enterprises (Okeke, 2021). Additional regulation monitoring in Europe, as well as a stronger focus in many jurisdictions on lowering methane emissions, may be the reason for this shift in focus, which has seen European and Asian oil and gas corporations prioritise reducing emissions over their American counterparts (Levy & Kolk, 2002). In comparison to the oil and gas companies in China and America, European oil and gas companies placed prominence on their impacts on the environment (Okeke, 2021). Wu et al. (2019) also observed a rise in pollution pricing schemes in Europe and China in a bid to mitigate carbon emissions and greenhouse gas emissions.

As reported by BP 2020 in response to pollution mitigation, 'we enter a new decade with a new company purpose: to reimagine energy for people and our planet. We have also set a new ambition: to become a net-zero company by 2050 or sooner, and to help the world get to net-zero' (Okeke, 2021). Likewise, CNOOC asserts that 'the Company undertakes to adjust the industrial structure and develop low-carbon energies, emphasise international cooperation and meet regulatory requirements to optimise the allocation of resources and practice energy-saving and emission reduction' (ibid.) By and large, the data examined by Okeke (2021) suggests that the oil and gas companies are adding renewable energy to their portfolios with a focus on renewable fuels and products, wind and solar energy, and biopower. Of the three continents, oil and gas companies in Europe seem to be at the forefront of sustainability effort with the highest number of items regarding the introduction of renewable energy. It is followed by Asian companies and then American oil and gas companies who seem to give less attention.

16.5.1 Greening the Oil and Gas Sector in Emerging and Developing Countries

As the oil and gas industry produces a great deal of pollution, strict regulations have been put in place to mitigate its environmental impact. Success comes to those who can meet the stringent environmental requirements in oil and gas production while also increasing profits by turning their attention to a more sustainable renewable energy. Almost every country in the world has now set renewable energy targets aimed at achieving a specific renewable energy share, output, or capacity. At the end of 2016, 124 developing and emerging nations had renewable energy targets at the national level.

According to data from the REN21 Renewable Energy Policy Database, most of the policy attention is focused on the power sector, while sectors like heating, cooling, and transportation receive far less. The most common form of regulatory policy support for renewable energy is feed-in tariffs. In 2016, Indonesia raised its solar feed-in tariffs by more than 70% and established geothermal feed-in tariff rates (Hsu et al., 2017). Ghana also has announced plans to extend the terms of its solar PV feed-in tariffs to 20 years. Existing processes in Pakistan and the Philippines were also discontinued, while Egypt imposed domestic content standards for solar PV and wind projects eligible for feed-in tariff subsidies (ibid.)

Renewable energy heating and cooling policies are commonly established in tandem with building efficiency policies and regulations, with a focus on the usage of renewable energy technology in the building sector (IEA, 2016a). The technologies are mainly promoted through a combination of regulations and financial support. Several countries advanced energy efficiency in 2016 by enacting new or modified building regulations, with 139 in place at the national and subnational levels worldwide, including at least 9 developing and emerging countries (IEA, 2016b). Indonesia's efforts to formulate a Green Building Code, as well as members of the Economic Community of West African States (ECOWAS) applying building rules in accordance with a regional directive, are examples of this. The pace of adoption of renewable cooling and heating technologies is well below the adoption rate in the transport sector.

Policies on renewable energy, which are focused on transport, have been used to achieve a variety of sector goals, including electric vehicles or fuel switching to renewable fuels or fuel economy. In developing countries, most of the policy adoption of renewable energy is focused on energy use in the road transportation sector. Concrete policy attention has been focused on energy use in a few locations in the maritime, rail, or aviation transportation sectors. Fuel economy requirements are among the most important ways to improve the energy efficiency of passenger cars in the transportation industry. At least eight nations, including Brazil, China, India, and Mexico, have adopted fuel economy standards for passenger and light commercial cars, as well as light trucks (International Council on Clean Transportation, 2014).

Directives or mandates often promote the quantity or share of renewable energy used in the transportation sector. Directives about biofuel mix are in place in 36 nations at the national or state level at the end of 2016. Of the total 36 nations, 26 are developing or emerging. Mexico's mandate was increased to cover all fuel types in 2016, while Argentina, Malaysia, India, Panama, Vietnam, and Zimbabwe also added or enhanced biofuel and/or bioethanol blend regulations. In Southeast Asia, Thailand happens to have a more comprehensive policy for biofuel which leads to a rapid increase in its production compared to other countries (Chanthawong & Dhakal, 2016). Concerning the greening of the oil and gas sector in Thailand, Bangchak is the only company that has set a goal to restructure its business portfolio by generating 50% of its revenue from refinery with the remaining 50% coming from clean energy by 2020 (Chaiyapa et al., 2018). To achieve this green investment goal, the company subdivided its strategies into two periods. The first period is from 2003 to 2009, which entails investment into only biofuels, whereas the second period from 2010 to 2020 started with the addition of the Sunny Bangchak solar power plant project to the existing biofuels investment. A rising number of municipalities in developing and emerging economies, such as Cape Town (South Africa), Chandigarh (India), and Oaxaca (Mexico), have adopted aggressive renewable energy or electricity goals.

16.6 Conclusion

This chapter has been dedicated to environmental and sustainability management in the oil and gas industry in emerging and developing countries. It started with an overview of the oil and gas industry in Africa and then went on to discuss environmental governance within the oil and gas sector where it explicitly discussed environmental governance, ethics, and the management of environmental impacts in the oil and gas industry. The chapter then went on to the various international and country-wide frameworks in place to tackle pollution. It determined that developed economies have well-spelled-out regulations on environmental governance, unlike their developing counterparts. Also, a good percentage of oil and gas comes from the developing economies, resulting in a myriad of sustainability challenges that oil and gas firms face, including the degradation of the environment. On environmental governance, the chapter observes that several pressures force firms to behave ethically with the most pressure coming from regulators and individuals who are now aware that any effects of the activities of the firm on the environment also affect them. Finally, the chapter concludes that although rules and regulations lead the pack in ensuring that the effects of the activities of these extractive firms are brought under control, these laws have not done much in the developing economies because they are almost nonexistent. What has helped to mitigate the effect of the activities of the oil and gas industry is the sense of duty towards the environment.

References

Aaron, K. K. (2012). New corporate social responsibility models for oil companies in Nigeria's delta region: What challenges for sustainability? *Progress in Development Studies, 12*(4), 259–273.

Abedi-Sarvestani, A., & Shahvali, M. (2008). Environmental ethics: Toward an Islamic perspective. *American-Eurasian Journal of Agricultural and Environmental Sciences, 3*(4), 609–617.

Alemagi, D. (2007). The oil industry along the Atlantic coast of Cameroon: Assessing impacts and possible solutions. *Resources Policy, 32*(3), 135–145.

Kotchen, M. J., & Burger, N. E. (2007). Should we drill in the Arctic National Wildlife Refuge? An economic perspective. *Energy Policy, 35*, 4720–4729.

Archer, E., Dziba, L., Mulongoy, K. J., Maoela, M. A., Walters, M. A., Biggs, R., Cormier-Salem, M. C., DeClerck, F. A., Diaw, M. C., Dunham, A. E. & Failler, P. (2018). Summary for policymakers of the regional assessment report on biodiversity and ecosystem services for Africa of the Intergovernmental Science-Policy Platform on Biodiversity and Ecosystem Services. https://cgspace.cgiar.org/handle/10568/102080

Arctic Council. (2009). *Protection of the arctic marine environmental working group: Arctic offshore oil and gas guidelines.*

Arctic Council. (2016). The Arctic Council: A background. http://www.arctic-council.org/index.php/en/about-us

Austin, D., & Sauer, A. (2002). *Changing oil: Emerging environmental risks and shareholder value in the oil and gas industry.* World Resource Institute.

Babatunde, A. O. (2014). Oil, environmental conflict and the challenges of sustainable development in the Niger Delta. *Journal of Peacebuilding & Development, 9*(2), 77–82.

Badeeb, R. A., Lean, H. H., & Clark, J. (2017). The evolution of the natural resource curse thesis: A critical literature survey. *Resources Policy, 51*, 123–134.

Bahn-Walkowiak, B., & Steger, S. (2015). Resource targets in Europe and worldwide: An overview. *Resources, 4*(3), 597–620.

Baptiste, A. K., & Nordenstam, B. J. (2009). Impact of oil and gas drilling in Trinidad: Factors influencing environmental attitudes and behaviours within three rural wetland communities. In Environmental conservation (pp. 1–8). Cambridge University Press.

Berrone, P., & Gomez-Mejia, L. R. (2009). Environmental performance and executive compensation: An integrated agency institutional perspective. *Academy of Management Journal, 52*(1), 103–126.

Bridge, G., & Perreault, T. (2009). *Environmental governance* (pp. 475–497). Wiley-Blackwell.

Chaiyapa, W., Esteban, M., & Kameyama, Y. (2018). Why go green? Discourse analysis of motivations for Thailand's oil and gas companies to invest in renewable energy. *Energy Policy, 120*, 448–459.

Chanthawong, A., & Dhakal, S. (2016). Liquid biofuels development in southeast Asian countries: An analysis of market, policies and challenges. *Waste and Biomass Valorization, 7*(1), 157–173.

Cherepovitsyn, A., Rutenko, E., & Solovyova, V. (2021). Sustainable development of oil and gas resources: A system of environmental, socio-economic, and innovation indicators. *Journal of Marine Science and Engineering, 9*(11), 1307.

Chrun, E., Dolšak, N., & Prakash, A. (2016). Corporate environmentalism: Motivations and mechanisms. *Annual Review of Environment and Resources, 41*(1), 341–362.

Clark, R. B. (1982). The long-term effect of oil pollution on marine populations, communities and ecosystems: Some questions. *Philosophical Transactions of the Royal Society of London. B, Biological Sciences, 297*(1087), 185–192.

Comyns, B., & Figge, F. (2015). Greenhouse gas reporting quality in the oil and gas industry: A longitudinal study using the typology of "search", "experience" and "credence" information. *Accounting, Auditing & Accountability Journal, 28*(3), 403–433.

Cudjoe, M. A., Abdul Latiff, A. R., Abu Kasim, N. A., & Hisham Bin Osman, M. N. (2019). Socially responsible investment (SRI) initiatives in developing economies: Challenges faced by oil and gas firms in Ghana. *Cogent Business & Management, 6*(1), 1666640.

Darkwah, A. K. (2010). *The impact of oil and gas discovery and exploration on communities with emphasis on women*. Department of Sociology, University of Ghana.

Ekong, C. N., Essien, E. B., & Onye, K. U. (2013). *The economics of youth restiveness in the Niger Delta*. Strategic Book Publishing.

Environmental Guidelines and Standards for the Petroleum Industry in Nigeria. (2018). Department of petroleum resources. *Lagos*, 315. https://www.nuprc.gov.ng/document-release-egaspin-2018/

Estrada, J., Estrada, J. H., Tangen, K., & Bergesen, H. O. (1997). *Environmental challenges confronting the oil industry* (Vol. 2). John Wiley & Sons.

Etemire, U. (2014). The 2014 Nigerian national conference and the development of environmental law and governance. *Verfassung und Recht in Übersee/Law and Politics in Africa, Asia and Latin America, 47*(4), 482–490.

Etemire, U., & Worika, I. L. (2018). Environmental ethics and the Nigerian oil and gas industry: Rumpus and Resolution. *University of Botswana Law Journal, 26*, 58.

European Commission (EC). (2008). *The raw materials initiative—Meeting our critical needs for growth and jobs in Europe, COM (2008)699*.

European Commission (EC). (2011). *A resource-efficient Europe—Flagship initiative under the Europe 2020 strategy*.

Fabricius, C., Scholes, B., & Cundill, G. (2006). Mobilizing knowledge for integrated ecosystem assessments. In *Bridging scales and knowledge systems: Concepts and applications in ecosystem assessment* (pp. 165–182). Island Press.

Faria, J. (2021) Main oil producing countries in Africa 2021. *Statista*, June 28, 2022. https://www.statista.com/statistics/1178514/main-oil-producing-countries-in-africa/#:~:text=Africa's%20crude%20oil%20reserves%20remained,amounted%20to%2036.97%20billion%20barrels

Frynas, J. G. (2010). Corporate social responsibility and societal governance: Lessons from transparency in the oil and gas sector. *Journal of Business Ethics, 93*(2), 163–179.

Ghisel, R. G. (1997). *Fifty years of offshore oil, gas development*. Hart Publications.
Gray, J. S., Bakke, T., Beck, H. J., & Nilssen, I. (1999). Managing the environmental effects of the Norwegian oil and gas industry: From conflict to consensus. *Marine Pollution Bulletin, 38*(7), 525–530.
Gregory, K., & Mohan, A. M. (2015). Current perspective on produced water management challenges during hydraulic fracturing for oil and gas recovery. *Environmental Chemistry, 12*(3), 261–266.
Hilson, G. (2012). Corporate social responsibility in the extractive industries: Experiences from developing countries. *Resources Policy, 37*(2), 131–137.
Hossain, M. S., Madlool, N. A., Rahim, N. A., Selvaraj, J., Pandey, A. K., & Khan, A. F. (2016). Role of smart grid in renewable energy: An overview. *Renewable and Sustainable Energy Reviews, 60*, 1168–1184.
Hsu, A., Rosengarten, C., Weinfurter, A., Xie, Y., Musolino, E., & Murdock, H. E. (2017). *Renewable energy and energy efficiency in developing countries: Contributions to reducing global emissions*. Third report. https://www.unep.org/resources/report/renewable-energy-and-energy-efficiency-developing-countries-contributions-0
IEA. (2016a). *IEA building energy efficiency policies database*. www.iea.org/
IEA. (2016b). *Medium-term renewable energy market report 2016*. https://www.iea.org/newsroom/news/2016/october/medium-termrenewable-energy-market-report-2016.html
Imobighe, T. A. (2004). Conflict in the Niger Delta. A unique case or a model for future conflicts in other oil-producing countries? *Oil Policy in the Gulf of Guinea: Security and Conflict, Economic Growth, Social Development*. Washington: Fredrich Ebert Stifting.
International Council on Clean Transportation. (2014). Eight countries plus EU as of 2014, per International Council on Clean Transportation. Global Passenger Vehicle Standards. www.theicct.org/info-tools/global-passenger-vehicle-standards
Iwayemi, A. (2006). Nigeria's oil wealth: The challenges of sustainable development in a non-renewable natural resources dependent economy. The Postgraduate School University of Ibadan, 31st Interdisciplinary Research Discourse.
Jackson, R. E., Gorody, A. W., Mayer, B., Roy, J. W., Ryan, M. C., & Van Stempvoort, D. R. (2013). Groundwater protection and unconventional gas extraction: The critical need for field-based hydrogeological research. *Groundwater, 51*(4), 488–510.
Knol, M., & Arbo, P. (2014). Oil spill response in the Arctic: Norwegian Experiences and future perspectives. *Marine Policy, 50*, 171–177.
Lemos, M. C., & Agrawal, A. (2006). Environmental governance. *Annual Review of Environment and Resources, 31*, 297–325.
Levy, D. L., & Kolk, A. (2002). Strategic responses to global climate change: Conflicting pressures on multinationals in the oil industry. *Business and Politics, 4*(3), 275–300.
Longoni, A., Luzzini, D., & Guerci, M. (2018). Deploying environmental management across functions: The relationship between green human Resource management and green supply chain management. *Journal of Business Ethics, 151*(4), 1081–1095.
Lott, M. C., Pye, S., & Dodds, P. E. (2017). Quantifying the co-impacts of energy sector decarbonisation on outdoor air pollution in the United Kingdom. *Energy Policy, 101*, 42–51.
Martins, F., Felgueiras, C., Smitkova, M., & Caetano, N. (2019). Analysis of fossil fuel energy consumption and environmental impacts in European countries. *Energies, 12*(6), 964.
Mehlum, H., Moene, K., & Torvik, R. (2006). Institutions and the resource curse. *The Economic Journal, 116*(508), 1–20.

Merkl-Davies, D. M., & Brennan, N. M. (2007). Discretionary disclosure strategies in corporate narratives: Incremental information or impression management. *Journal of Accounting Literature, 26,* 116–194.

Neu, D., Warsame, H., & Pedwell, K. (1998). Managing public impressions: Environmental disclosures in annual reports. *Accounting, Organizations and Society, 23*(3), 265–282.

Obi, C. I. (2010). Oil extraction, dispossession, resistance, and conflict in Nigeria's oil-rich Niger Delta. *Canadian Journal of Development Studies, 30*(1–2), 219–236.

O'higgins, T., Farmer, A., Daskalov, G., Knudsen, S., & Mee, L. (2014). Achieving good environmental status in the Black sea: Scale mismatches in environmental management. *Ecology and Society, 19*(3).

Okeke, A. (2021). Towards sustainability in the global oil and gas industry: Identifying where the emphasis lies. *Environmental and Sustainability Indicators, 12,* 100145.

Okonkwo, T., & Etemire, U. (2017). "Oil injustice" in Nigeria's Niger delta region: A call for responsive governance. *Journal of Environmental Protection, 8*(1), 42–60.

Pahl-Wostl, C. (2009). A conceptual framework for analysing adaptive capacity and multi-level learning processes in resource governance regimes. *Global Environmental Change, 19*(3), 354–365.

Palmer, C., McShane, K., & Sandler, R. (2014). Environmental ethics. *Annual Review of Environment and Resources, 39,* 419–442.

Ross, M. L. (2013). *The oil curse: How petroleum wealth shapes the development of nations.* Princeton University Press.

Rossouw, G. J. (2005). Business ethics and corporate governance: A global survey. *Business and Society, 44*(1), 32–39.

Saffari, M., de Gracia, A., Fernández, C., Belusko, M., Boer, D., & Cabeza, L. F. (2018). Optimized demand side management (DSM) of peak electricity demand by coupling low temperature thermal energy storage (TES) and solar PV. *Applied Energy, 211,* 604–616.

Savitz, A. (2013). *The triple bottom line: how today's best-run companies are achieving economic, social and environmental success-and how you can too.* John Wiley & Sons.

Savitz, A. W., & Weber, K. (2006). *The triple bottom line: How today's best-run companies are achieving economic, social, and environmental success-and how you can too.* San Francisco: Jossey-Bass.

Sethi, S. P., Martell, T. F., & Demir, M. (2017). Enhancing the role and effectiveness of corporate social responsibility (CSR) reports: The missing element of content verification and integrity assurance. *Journal of Business Ethics, 144*(1), 59–82.

Sheinbaum-Pardo, C., Ruiz-Mendoza, B. J., & Rodríguez-Padilla, V. (2012). Mexican energy policy and sustainability indicators. *Energy Policy, 46,* 278–283.

Short, J. C., McKenny, A. F., Ketchen, D. J., Snow, C. C., & Hult, G. T. M. (2016). An empirical examination of firm, industry, and temporal effects on corporate social performance. *Business & Society, 55*(8), 1122–1156.

Shrader-Frechette, K. (2000). Duties to future generations, proxy consent, intra-and intergenerational equity: The case of nuclear waste. *Risk Analysis, 20*(6), 771–778.

Solomon, J. F. (2007). *Corporate governance and accountability.* Wiley.

Sönnichsen, N. (2021). *Coronavirus: impact on the global energy industry – Statistics & Facts.* Retrieved June 16, 2021, from https://www.statista.com/topics/6254/coronavirus-covid-19-impact-on-the-energy-industry/

Statista. (2022). https://www.statista.com/chart/26878/african-countries-with-the-highest-oil-production-volume/

Steffen, W., Broadgate, W., Deutsch, L., Gaffney, O., & Ludwig, C. (2015). The trajectory of the anthropocene: The great acceleration. *The Anthropocene Review, 2*(1), 81–98.

Tate, W. L., & Bals, L. (2018). Achieving shared triple bottom line (TBL) value creation: Toward a social resource-based view (SRBV) of the firm. *Journal of Business Ethics, 152*(3), 803–826.

Tingbani, I., Chithambo, L., Tauringana, V., & Papanikolaou, N. (2020). Board gender diversity, environmental committee and greenhouse gas voluntary disclosures. *Business Strategy and the Environment, 29*(6), 2194–2210.

United Nations Environment Programme (UNEP). (2011). *Environmental assessment of Ogoniland*. Nairobi. Retrieved October 4, 2015, from http://postconflict.unep.ch/publications/OEA/UNEP_OEA.pdf

Urpelainen, J. (2018). RISE to the occasion? A critique of the World Bank's regulatory indicators for sustainable energy. *Energy Research & Social Science, 39*, 69–73.

Wu, X., Xia, J., Guan, B., Liu, P., Ning, L., Yi, X., Yang, L., & Hu, S. (2019). Water scarcity assessment based on estimated ultimate energy recovery and water footprint framework during shale gas production in the Changning play. *Journal of Cleaner Production, 241*, 118312.

Yang, T. (2006). Towards an egalitarian global environmental ethics. *Environmental Ethics and International Policy, 8*, 23–45.

Yu, W., Ramanathan, R., & Nath, P. (2017). Environmental pressures and performance: An analysis of the roles of environmental innovation strategy and marketing capability. *Technological Forecasting and Social Change, 117*, 160–169.

Zhongming, Z., Linong, L., Xiaona, Y., Wangqiang, Z., & Wei, L. (2016). *More from less—Material resource efficiency in Europe*. European Environment Agency.

17 Natural Gas and Liquefied Natural Gas Resource Management

Amin Karimu, John Bosco Dramani, and Ishmael Ackah

17.1 Introduction

Energy from fossil fuels accounts for about 80% of global energy consumption (IEA, 2021) and about 89% of global carbon emission. Most of the top-producing countries of oil and gas resources are emerging and developing countries (EDCs) with a significant reliance on these resources for revenue generation, economic growth, and jobs through trade in these fuels. Data from the World Bank for the period 2000–2019 suggest that the top five countries in the world with significant dependence on oil and gas exports expressed as a share of fossil fuels in total merchandise exports are Iraq (98.5%), followed by Algeria (97.7%), Angola (96.2%), Libya (94.2%), and Brunei Darussalam (94.1%).

Despite the significant reliance on oil and gas resources by EDCs for revenue, growth, and development, increasing environmental concerns on these fuels are bringing some focus onto natural gas due to its low carbon emission, efficiency in power generation, easy adaptability to support industrial activity, and the existence of significant reserves that are widely distributed across regions. In this chapter, the key objective is to present a comprehensive analysis of the natural gas sector in EDCs as a fuel of choice, discuss the prospects of the sector on the economy of these countries, discuss the fiscal regime of the sector, and examine the governance issues related to managing these resources, sustainability perspective via Sovereign Wealth Funds (SWF).

The chapter critically examines the status of the natural gas sector in developing and emerging economies in terms of market dynamics and trade. Furthermore, issues related to the contribution of natural gas to the economies of developing and emerging countries in terms of export earnings, GDP, and employment are presented and analysed. The policies on natural gas resources and the management thereof are also discussed, as well as the intergeneration aspects and sustainable management of these resources via SWF with a case study of Ghana.

DOI: 10.4324/9781003309864-20

17.2 Status of Emerging Economies' Natural Gas and Liquefied Natural Gas Sector in the World Economy

Africa is heavily endowed with natural resources such as natural gas and crude oil. In 1956, Africa found its first commercial quantities of natural gas in Nigeria. For the rest of the 20th century, a significant number of discoveries were made, and practically all key discoveries on the continent in recent times have been natural gas. From the *Zohr* fields in Egypt along the Mediterranean, these discoveries span the massive reserves found offshore in Tanzania and Mozambique and lately the discoveries in commercial quantities in Mauritania, Ghana, and Senegal in West Africa. This section discusses the status of the natural gas sector in emerging economies with respect to the proven reserves, market dynamics, trade, and natural gas for LNG.

17.2.1 Proven Reserves of Natural Gas (NG) and Liquefied Natural Gas (LNG), Demand, and Supply

Africa was endowed with 14.0 trillion cubic metres of proven natural gas as of 2008 and this rose to 14.4 trillion cubic metres, representing 7.3% of total global reserves in 2018 (British Petroleum [BP], 2019). Out of this, Nigeria contributes 2.7%, Algeria is endowed with 2.2%, Egypt with 1.1%, Libya with 0.7%, and the rest of Africa contributes 0.6%. This increase in total proven reserves can be attributed to an increased investment of $75 billion in the exploration and discovery of huge natural gas reserves in countries such as Mozambique, Tanzania, Senegal, and Mauritania totalling 5.7 trillion cubic metres (Africa's Energy Outlook, 2019). Figure 17.1 displays global total of proven reserves of natural gas for 2008 and 2018. In both years, the Middle East leads in the share of total proven reserves, the CIS takes the second spot, Asia Pacific third, and Africa fourth.

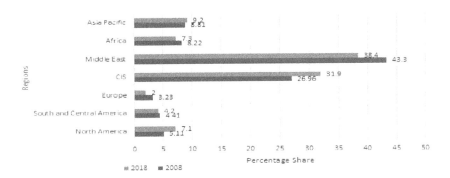

Figure 17.1 Global proven reserves of natural gas
Source: British Petroleum (BP, 2019)

In terms of production, the regional and global levels have been increasing monotonically except for Europe and Africa. Europe experienced a monotonically decreasing levels from 2008 to 2018 and is currently reporting negative growth figures. On the other hand, Africa is experiencing instability in production, as production initially fell from 203.8 to 192.1 billion cubic metres in 2008 to 2009 and thereafter soared to 206.8 billion cubic metres in 2012. In 2013, production again fell but rose marginally in 2014 before rising significantly to 235.6 billion cubic metres in 2018. Based on this trajectory, overall growth in production from 2007 to 2017 was 1.4% and this rose to 4.8% in 2018. The share of regional production in the global output stood at 27.2% by North America, 4.6% by South and Central America, 6.5% by Europe, 21.5% by CIS, 17.8% by Middle East, 6.1% by Africa, and 16.3% by Asia Pacific (see Table 17.1). This reveals that Africa is the least contributor to global production of natural gas, although the continent possesses the third highest proven reserves.

17.2.2 Natural Gas Market Dynamics in Emerging Economies

There is currently no regional market for NG in Africa, and this leads to many countries purchasing their NG outside of the continent. This can be attributed to the relatively small market size of NG and the long distances connecting the producers and consumers leading to investment insecurity (IEA, 2022). This has affected producing nations, as they grapple with supply challenges. In Sub-Saharan Africa, Nigeria, the leader in natural gas production, has been designing and developing plans to establish a regional market for the sale of its gas. Currently, a gas pipeline has been constructed covering about 600 km from Nigeria to Ghana through Togo and Benin, which is known as the West Africa Gas Pipeline (WAGP) to transport gas to the three countries. Infrastructure of this nature requires huge investments in modern storage facilities. After the construction of WAGP, Ghana developed offshore oil and gas fields that are now supplying gas to power plants in the Aboadze Power Enclave near Takoradi using the pipeline. In addition, the Ghana Gas Company uses the WAGP to transport gas from the western part of the country to Tema, an industrial hub in Ghana, thus expanding supply while reducing transportation cost.

Based on this, consumption of NG is relatively low in Africa compared with other regions of the world. Table 17.2 displays the consumption of NG in the world. The consumption in Africa has monotonically increased from the period 2008 to 2018. Compared with NG production in Table 17.1, the consumption values, though increasing, are relatively low, suggesting a wide gap between production and consumption of NG. For instance, the share of Africa's consumption in the global total consumption is about 3.9% compared with other regions such as North America (26.6%), North and Central America (4.4%), Europe (14.4%), CIS (15.1%), and Asia Pacific (21.4%). The wide difference between production and consumption of NG in Africa confirms the supply

Table 17.1 Production of natural gas in billion cubic metres

Region	2008	2009	2010	2011	2012	2013	2014	2015	2016	2017	2018	Growth rate per annum 2018	2007–2017	Share 2018
North America	759.8	765.2	775.9	820.5	850.3	860.1	915.0	949.0	942.8	961.6	1053.9	9.6%	2.6%	27.2%
S. and Cent. America	157.9	152.3	160.4	164.1	170.6	173.8	176.0	178.0	176.7	180.3	176.7	−2.0%	1.4%	4.6%
Europe	321.0	304.1	310.7	285.5	288.1	280.6	267.5	261.7	260.5	263.2	250.7	−4.8%	−1.5%	6.5%
CIS	768.6	663.2	732.7	766.2	754.3	768.5	751.4	745.0	747.2	789.1	831.1	5.3%	0.5%	21.5%
Middle East	392.3	413.8	474.7	520.0	545.5	562.9	582.7	600.3	624.1	650.4	687.3	5.7%	6.0%	17.8%
Africa	203.8	192.1	202.3	201.7	206.8	198.3	198.6	203.6	208.8	225.7	236.6	4.8%	1.4%	6.1%
Asia Pacific	426.3	447.9	494.3	499.1	508.4	518.9	539.8	564.1	581.6	607.5	631.7	4.0%	4.1%	16.3%
World	3029.8	2938.6	3151.0	3257.0	3323.8	3363.1	3431.1	3501.7	3541.7	3677.7	3867.9	5.2%	2.3%	100.0%

Source: British Petroleum (BP, 2019)

Table 17.2 Consumption of natural gas in cubic million metres

Region/Year	2008	2009	2010	2011	2012	2013	2014	2015	2016	2017	2018	Growth rate per annum 2018	2007–2017	Share 2018
North America	778.2	769.4	802.5	826.6	859.0	889.1	910.7	934.1	938.0	935.5	1022.3	9.3%	1.9%	26.6%
S. and Cent. America	138.1	132.9	143.7	148.7	157.7	163.5	168.5	174.7	171.6	172.6	168.4	-2.5%	2.3%	4.4%
Europe	625.6	577.1	622.6	580.1	565.4	554.4	500.0	508.8	537.6	560.4	549.0	-2.1%	-1.0%	14.3%
CIS	521.3	499.9	531.3	549.5	545.2	537.3	539.9	530.0	537.7	549.3	580.8	5.7%	0.3%	15.1%
Middle East	337.1	347.3	380.1	398.1	410.8	423.3	447.5	478.3	500.9	527.0	553.1	4.9%	5.6%	14.4%
Africa	94.8	95.6	98.9	107.2	115.1	116.6	119.9	128.1	135.0	140.8	150.0	6.6%	4.5%	3.9%
Asia Pacific	503.7	515.6	577.6	623.1	664.3	685.5	706.2	712.5	729.3	768.3	825.3	7.4%	5.0%	21.4%
World	2998.8	2937.8	3156.7	3233.3	3317.5	3369.8	3392.6	3466.5	3550.2	3654.0	3848.9	5.3%	2.2%	100.0%

Source: British Petroleum (BP, 2019)

challenges that producer nations encounter which impede financing of NG projects. Nonetheless, growth in consumption is currently about 4.5% which is relatively higher than production of 1.4% in the same period (see Table 17.1). In addition to supply challenges, demand is low due to high cost of gas and lack of competition among suppliers (Fulwood, 2019). The author indicates that for gas to perform the role of a transition fuel, its cost should be below $8/MMbtu and $6/MMbtu in high and low-income countries, respectively.

17.2.3 Natural Gas Trade

The dynamics of natural gas markets are basically different from those of crude oil, because the latter is highly sensitive to geopolitical issues. Natural gas is traded using an integrated and continental scale market with several pricing hubs. One of these hubs is the TransCanada Albert System which is the focal pricing hub for Canada. The Henry Hub in Louisiana represents the main pricing hub for natural gas bought and sold in the New York Mercantile Exchange. The prices of natural gas in these trading points are openly posted for bidders to bid.

In terms of exports, the global estimate between 2007 and 2019 is 9332.2 billion cubic metres with an average growth of about 2.1% per annum. Russian and the other CIS counties constitute the largest exporter of NG, with an average export of about 291.77 billion cubic metres within the period 2008–2018, representing about 34.9% of total global exports. America and the rest of North America are the second largest exporter of NG with an average of 131.7 between 2007 and 2019, with a global share of 18.4% in 2018. China and other Asian countries constitute the third exporter with a share of 8.6% and average exports of about 129.05 billion cubic metres from 2007 to 2019.The Middle East is the fourth exporter of NG with an average export of about 122.89 billion cubic metres within the period 2008–2018 and a share of 14.8% in 2018. Africa is the fifth exporter of NG, exporting about 92.2 billion cubic metres and a total global share of about 9.8% in 2018. Algeria and Nigeria have been the dominant exporters of NG in Africa for over a decade. In 2019, both countries exported about 42.5 billion and 36 billion cubic metres, respectively. Other countries such as Libya, Egypt, Equatorial Guinea, Mozambique, and Angola also contribute a significant share to the total exports of Africa. Mozambique exports all its NG through pipeline to South Africa; Equatorial Guinea exports its NG to Asia, Latin America, and Europe; Nigeria exports a greater percentage of its NG in the form of LNG with a small amount exported to neighbouring countries such as Ghana, Benin, and Togo through the WAGP (U.S. Energy Information Administration, 2013). Europe is the sixth exporter of NG, with about 8.05 billion cubic metres on the average from 2007 to 2019 and had a global share of 1.2% of exports in 2018.

With regard to imports, Europe dominates with an average of 299.45 billion cubic meters within the period 2008–2018. North American countries constitute the second largest importers of NG, with an average import of 139.16 billion cubic meters from 2008 to 2018. China, India, and other Asia countries are the third dominant importers of NG, with an average of 94.36 billion cubic meters within the years 2008–2018 and received 20.9% of global total imports in 2018. The CIS countries and Russia represent the fourth largest importers of NG with an average importation of 62.14 billion cubic meters for the period 2008–2018 and contributed to global imports by 5.8% in 2018. OECD Asia with 24.7 billion cubic meters imports from the years 2008 to 2018 is the fifth largest importer of NG and imported 19% of global imports in 2018. South America and Africa with an average import of 22.4 and 6.2 billion cubic meters are the sixth and seventh importers of NG and contributed to 2.3% and 0.3% shares of global imports. Africa's low trade in NG can be attributed to several factors such as the nonexistence of transportation infrastructure such as gas pipelines with the exception of the coastal part of Nigeria and a few tiny sub-regional projects and the WAGP that supply gas to a few West African countries.

17.2.4 Liquefied Natural Gas Trade

The conversion of natural gas (NG) into liquefied natural gas (LNG) is of increasing importance. This involves cooling the NG to −260 F (−162°C) and thus converting it from gas into liquid form which reduces it to 1/600th of the initial volume. This significant reduction in the volume permits easy transportation of the gas by tanks and vessels for domestic and regional markets. Globally, trade in LNG averaged 329.17 billion cubic meters from 2007 to 2019 with about 4.5% growth within the same period. Again, global trade in LNG rose by 9.4% to constitute about 45.7% of the total share of NG trade in 2018. In Africa, total trade in LNG averaged 50.03 billion cubic meters from 2007 to 2019, with a growth of −1.2% within the same period but contributed 7% to total global trade in LNG in 2018.

Since intra-regional trade in NG is limited in Africa, most resource-poor countries have embarked on massive importation of LNG to meet their energy needs. By 2016, the list of potential LNG importers included Morocco, Senegal, Côte d'Ivoire, Benin, Ghana, Kenya, Namibia, Sudan, and South Africa. For instance, Egypt built its regasification plant and started the importation of LNG in 2015. Recently Ghana has started the construction of a floating storage regasification unit to improve its NLG importation. Other countries such as Mozambique and Tanzania have the potential of exporting LNG within Africa. In addition, the only two trans-national gas pipelines, i.e. the WAGP permits Ghana, Benin, and Togo to import LNG from Nigeria while the one from Mozambique to South Africa allows trade in LNG within the Southern African region to thrive. The relatively short period of shipping between producers and importing countries within Africa has the potential of making these markets very attractive.

Though it is essential for African countries to develop the relevant infrastructure to explore and harness their natural gas resources, the recent interest in transitioning to low-carbon fuel footprints is likely to depress responsiveness to the needed investment in the gas sector. In addition, gas infrastructure that has already been developed due to their asset-specificity is likely to become stranded due to the transition to renewable energy. The transition to renewable energy could dampen the capacity factors of natural-gas-fired power plants with the potential to raise their financial risks. The problem of stranded assets will become significant in emerging countries with gas-fired power plants that are currently not close to their designed lifetime. Thus, many of the countries with significant gas reserves may be unable to exploit them, which could have a negative impact on GDP and employment generation in the sector.

17.3 Contributions of the NG and LNG Sector to the Economies of Producing Emerging Countries

The production and use of coal and oil are considered a major contributor to global greenhouse gas emissions. In recent years, due to increasing environmental concerns, countries and industries are exploring efficient and reliable energy sources that have a lower carbon footprint, and natural gas and LNG satisfy these requirements. In the wake of increasing interest in low-carbon transition and given some of the immediate constraints associated with renewable energy sources, demand for natural gas and its liquefied version will be high globally, and so will demand for growth and development in the EDCs. This section discusses the contribution of natural gas and LNG to the exports, employment, and the GDP of developing and emerging economies with significant endowments of natural gas.

17.3.1 Exports and Foreign Currency

Natural gas is a major revenue generator for EDCs that have significant endowments of these resources, which could bring in the needed revenue for investment in critical sectors of these countries. For instance, in 2020, the trade value of the top 20 countries in the world amounted to 97.8 billion US dollars out of the total world trade value of 99.8 billion dollars. This suggests that the top 20 exporting countries account for about 98% of the global trade value of natural gas exports in 2020. Sixteen of the top 20 countries are EDCs as shown in Table 17.3. Qatar is the topmost exporter of natural gas in the EDCs with an export value of $18.21 billion in 2020, which is about 10% of its total export value in that year. The least exporting country of natural gas among the top 20 countries is Mozambique ($0.24 billion), which is about 4.4% of its total export value in that year.

This suggests a significant foreign exchange earnings potential from these resources for EDCs, irrespective of the fact that a significant amount of the

Table 17.3 Export trade value for natural gas for the top 20 exporting countries

Country	Trade value in billion US dollars (2020)	Rank
Australia	25.71	1
Qatar	18.21	2
United States	13.16	3
Malaysia	7.30	4
Russia	6.80	5
Nigeria	5.02	6
Indonesia	3.69	7
Oman	3.26	8
Papua New Guinea	2.95	9
Brunei	2.08	10
Trinidad and Tobago	2.06	11
Algeria	1.90	12
Peru	1.40	13
United Arab Emirates	1.40	14
Angola	0.90	15
Egypt	0.52	16
Norway	0.52	17
Equatorial Guinea	0.45	18
France	0.25	19
Mozambique	0.24	20

Source: Observatory of Economic Complexity (OEC, 2022)

gas is flared in some of the EDCs in connection with crude oil production. Therefore, if all the natural gas is utilised and monetised rather than flared, the revenue generation potential is enormous since a significant number of the world population that depends on wood fuel for cooking are being motivated through various policies to uptake gas for cooking. Industrial development and the power sector are significantly moving towards gas as a key energy source, due to its low carbon dioxide emission qualities (about 50% less than what is emitted from coal), efficiency in power production, and wide geographical distribution of reserves relative to other fossil fuels. Though gas possesses great potential to be used as a transition fuel, the recent trends in energy transition rather focus on the use of renewable energy, thus diminishing the overall benefits of gas.

17.3.2 Employment and GDP Contribution

In theory, the development of the natural gas sector in countries with significant endowments of these resources will promote growth and development through the creation of additional jobs in the economy both in the upstream segment through the exploration and production of these resources as suggested by various studies (Agerton et al., 2017; Weber, 2012) and along the value chain activities such as in the petrochemical industry, refining

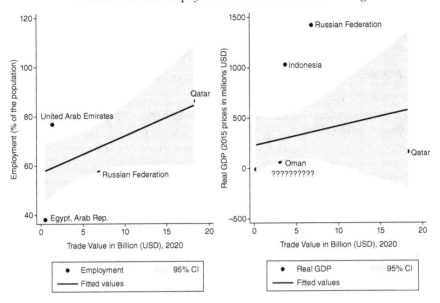

Figure 17.2 Relationship between natural gas export value, real GDP, and employment for top gas-exporting countries in the developing and emerging economies

Source: Authors' construction

and gas plants, and the transportation of these fuels to the final consumer. Figure 17.2 presents the relationship between natural gas (liquefied) export value, employment, and real GDP values for EDCs that were among the top 20 natural gas exporters in 2020. There is a clear positive relationship between gas exports and the two macroeconomic variables (employment and real GDP).

Countries with large natural gas export values are also associated with large real GDP levels. And countries with large natural gas trade values are likewise, associated with higher levels of employment. Despite this evidence regarding the association of gas exports and the two key macroeconomic variables, it is important to note that the employment and GDP benefits from the natural gas sector can only materialise when there are strong backward and forward linkages between the gas industry, agriculture, services, and manufacturing sectors.

17.4 NG and LNG Resource Management in Emerging Economies

This section deliberates on some important policy measures initiated by emerging economies for the efficient management of NG and LNG intended to foster economic growth. It also discusses some of the setbacks in an attempt to produce natural gas for domestic consumption and export to other countries. Finally, the distribution of NG and LNG revenue in Ghana is examined.

17.4.1 Natural Gas and Liquefied Natural Gas Policy

Most natural-gas-producing countries in Africa have a policy to use natural gas for economic diversification and industrialisation. In Mozambique, the natural gas masterplan requires that the gas is used for large industries, small and medium enterprises, and for power generation. According to Ledesma (2013), to overcome the resource curse, natural gas policies in countries such as Mozambique, Nigeria, Ghana, Tanzania, and other natural-gas-producing countries in the sub-region have focused on transparency by joining the extractive industries transparency initiative and the creation of economic development linkages through the implementation of local content laws.

In Tanzania, the government encourages international oil companies to invest and raise funds domestically. Indeed, the government has made changes to require companies in the extractive sector with at least $100,000 in subscribed capital to put 30% of their shares on the Tanzanian stock exchange. In addition, the country is creating a Natural Gas Revenue Fund, similar to the Norwegian SWF. It is hoped that the effective management of this fund will promote transparency, accountability, and development. Investors are also required to explicitly state corporate social responsibility plans in their proposals.

Natural gas policies in Nigeria, Mozambique, and Angola, which hitherto were export-oriented, have been changed to domestication. For example, Nigeria is working on reducing flaring to maximise its supply of gas whilst Mozambique is expanding the use of gas for electricity generation.

17.4.2 Fiscal and Institutional Framework

Fiscal regimes are key drivers of investments in natural resources including natural gas. Since all natural gas resources in Africa are state-owned, the states could design appropriate regimes that meet both economic and political goals. Often, the objectives of the host government are to maximise revenues and create employment whilst the oil company seeks to maximise profit (Kankam & Ackah, 2015). In designing the fiscal regime, Nakhle (2010) proposes that factors such as the geological promise and national laws governing contracting to be considered. Other factors include the experience of the country in natural gas production (Amoako-Tuffour & Owusu-Ayim, 2010).

According to Amoako-Tuffour and Owusu-Ayim (2010), most natural-gas-producing countries adopt one of the following strategies. The first group adopts a 'go-it-alone strategy' in which the state undertakes production by itself through a national oil company, as in Saudi Arabia. In the second group, the state grants entire private ownership, and the oil companies have full control over the operations, mainly in developed economies. Finally, the third group combines the first two in the form of partnerships of sorts between the state and the private oil companies to undertake exploration and production. This is common in African countries. Often, the Ministries of Finance and Energy manage the regime and the negotiation. The legislative arm approves any natural gas license before it becomes effective. In Ghana's first licensing regime, accountability actors were allowed to monitor and report on the process.

According to Nakhle (2010), there are two broad categories of the fiscal regime: the concessionary and the contractual. In using any of these types, countries use administrative processes or the open and competitive bidding process. Ghana, which has used the administrative process since the beginning of petroleum exploration in 1896, had its first open and competitive bidding process in October 2018 in line with the Petroleum Exploration and Production Law (Act 919). According to Rodriguez and Suslick (2009), the competitive bidding process promotes increased participation, enhances transparency, and ensures that the host country maximises revenues. The administrative process (direct negotiation) on the other hand, if not properly managed, can create opportunities for rent-seeking, secrecy, and badly-negotiated contracts. Though there is an increase in the use of open and competitive bidding processes in Côte D'Ivoire, Egypt, Equatorial Guinea, Gabon, Nigeria, Senegal, Sierra Leone, Uganda among others, administrative processes are still prevalent.

17.4.3 Fiscal and Governance Challenges

Natural gas pricing could either be a market-based price or a regulated price. Ackah et al. (2019) identify three market-based approaches prevalent in both developed and developing countries. These are *oil or product indexation* in which gas prices are linked to the prices of oil, coal, or other refined fuel. The second is the *gas-to-gas competition*, reflecting the demand and supply of a natural gas spot market. The final pricing scheme is the *netback from final product*, which is usually used in natural gas contracts where the price of gas is linked to the price of ammonia. In Africa, however, the regulated natural gas price is widely used and this is not cost-reflective. In Nigeria, for instance, Amanam (2017) recounts that due to lower-than-cost reflective natural gas tariffs, potential companies are disincentivised to invest in domestic distribution infrastructure.

There are governance challenges too. Figure 17.3 shows that the transparency and accountability index for SSA has been declining since 2011. Indeed, Arbatli and Escolano (2012) confirm this by indicating that since 2006, transparency and accountability have either deteriorated or remained stagnant. The transparency and accountability challenges stem from the secrecy around the issuing of natural gas licences, misappropriation of natural gas revenues, and corruption.

The Natural Resource Governance Institute (NRGI) ranks petroleum and mineral-producing countries in its Resource Governance Index. Among

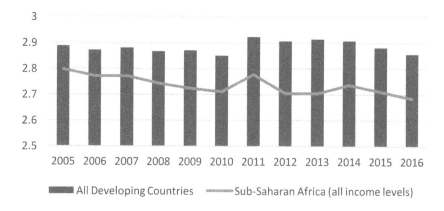

Figure 17.3 Transparency and accountability index
Source: World Development Indicators (2021)

the indicators ranked is the 'Voice and Accountability'. In the 2017 edition, Ghana ranked first in Africa for Voice and Accountability, followed by Tunisia and Tanzania. The bottom three positions were occupied by Equatorial Guinea, Sudan, and South Sudan. Indeed, mature producers like Angola scored below 50%. Other initiatives such as 'Publish What You Pay', Transparency International, and conditions of development partners have been contributing to Africa's good governance agenda.

17.4.4 Distribution of Natural Gas and Natural Liquefied Revenue – Ghana's Case

Ghana's Petroleum Revenue Management Act is perhaps one of the best petroleum revenue management laws according to international standards of ensuring transparency and accountability in the oil and natural gas sector. Act (PRMA), 2011 (Act 815), was enacted 'to provide the framework for the collection, allocation and management of petroleum revenue in a responsible, transparent, accountable and sustainable manner for the benefit of the citizens of Ghana'. The Act established a holding fund into which all proceeds from petroleum due to the government are deposited (Figure 17.4). Deposits into the holding fund are the net of the national oil company's entitlements for its share of equity participation, as it is mandated to participate in development and production of petroleum revenues on behalf of the government. Under the PRMA, the national oil company (GNPC) receives a percentage of the oil revenues, with allocations to the budget, the Ghana Stabilisation Fund (GSF), and the Ghana Heritage Fund (GHF). Not more than 70% of net revenues in the PHF, after deduction of the share of the National Oil Company (NOC), is transferred into a Dollar Account of the Annual Budget Funding Amount (ABFA), from whence it is subsequently transferred into a

Natural Gas and Liquefied Natural Gas Resource Management 253

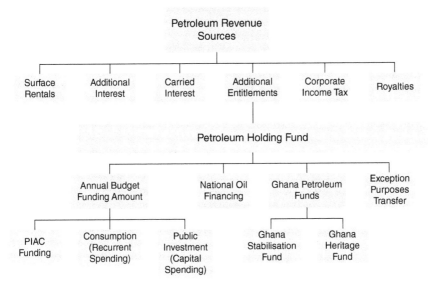

Figure 17.4 Distribution of Natural Gas and Liquefied Petroleum Revenue in Ghana
Source: Act (PRMA) (2011)

Ghana Cedi Account for spending. The share of the National Oil Company should not be more than 50% of the carried and participating interest and is approved by parliament. The ABFA is spent in accordance with, but not limited to, four priority areas selected by the Minister of Finance and approved by Parliament every three years in the absence of a long-term national development plan. Twelve priority areas have been specified in the PRMA for selection.

One of the innovations in the PRMA is the creation of the Public Interest and Accountability Committee, which provides an independent oversight of the management of oil and natural gas revenues (Graham et al., 2019). Specifically, PIAC seeks to monitor and evaluate compliance with this Act by government and other relevant institutions in the discharge of their duties in relation to the use and management of oil and natural gas revenues as required by law: to provide space and the platform for the public to debate on whether spending prospects and management of revenues adhere to development priorities, provide independent assessments on the use and management of oil and natural gas resources, and assist Parliament and the executive in the oversight and performance of related functions.

17.5 Conclusion

The key objective of the chapter is to provide a comprehensive analysis and discussion of the natural gas sub-sector, with a focus on EDCs on issues of market dynamics, the contribution of the natural gas sector to the economies, the management of the resources in EDCs, and intergenerational management of funds from natural gas resources. Utilising various reports, data, and published journal articles, the following key findings were established. First, there are significant proven natural gas reserves in several EDCs, suggesting the potential of these countries to monetise key activities within the sector to foster growth and development and to take advantage of the increasing global demand for this fuel due to its good environmental qualities. Second, despite gas flaring in a number oil producing countries in EDCs, the sector still contributes significantly to generating revenue through exports and supporting economic activity and creating jobs by providing an efficient source for power generation, which ultimately will benefit the industrial sectors of EDCs. Third, policies in the gas sector are progressively creating backward and forward linkages with the economy with the goal of utilising the resource for domestic electricity generation and industrialisation before exporting the remainder. Further, EDC countries endowed with natural gas resources, especially those in Africa, are progressively adopting the partnership fiscal regime, with increasing open-competitive tendering. In the case of intergenerational management of the resource, several EDC countries are adopting the SWF approach for sustainable management of these resources.

References

Ackah, I., Opoku, F., & Anang, S. (2019). Switching on an environmentally friendly and affordable light in Africa: Evaluation of the role of natural gas. *Insight on Africa, 11*(1), 60–77.

Africa's Energy Outlook. (2019). World energy outlook special report, IEA.

Agerton, M., Hartley, P. R., Medlock, K. B. III, & Temzelides, T. (2017). Employment impacts of upstream oil and gas investment in the United States. *Energy Economics, 62*, 171–180.

Amanam, U. U. (2017). Natural gas in East Africa: Domestic and regional use. Presymposium White Paper on Reducing Energy Poverty with Natural Gas: Changing Political, Business, and Technology Paradigms, Stanford University, CA, 9–10 May. http://www.ghanaoilpages.com/admin/documents/Natural%20Gas%20in%20East%20Africa%20Domestic%20and%20Regional%20Use_The%20Stanford%20Natural%20Gas%20Initiative_2017.pdf

Amoako-Tuffour, J., & Owusu-Ayim, J. (2010). An evaluation of Ghana's petroleum fiscal regime. An evaluation of Ghana's petroleum fiscal regime. africaportal.org

Arbatli, E., & Escolano, J. (2012). Fiscal transparency. *Fiscal Performance and Credit Rating*. Washington: International Monetary Fund.

British Petroleum (BP). (2019). Statistical review of world energy, 68th edition.

Fulwood, M. (2019). *Opportunities for gas in Sub-Saharan Africa*. Oxford Institute for Energy Studies, Oxford Energy Insight.

Graham, E., Gyampo, R. E. V., Ackah, I., & Andrews, N. (2019). An institutional assessment of the public interest and accountability committee (PIAC) in Ghana's oil and gas sector. *Journal of Contemporary African Studies, 37*(4), 316–334.

International Energy Agency (IEA). (2019). *Africa Energy Outlook 2019*, Paris. https://www.iea.org/reports/africa-energy-outlook-2019

International Energy Agency (IEA). (2021), *World Energy Outlook*, Paris. https://www.iea.org/reports/world-energy-outlook-2021

International Energy Agency (IEA). (2022). *Africa Energy Outlook 2022*, Paris. https://www.iea.org/reports/africa-energy-outlook-2022

Kankam, D., & Ackah, I. (2014). The optimal petroleum fiscal regime for Ghana: An analysis of available alternatives. *International Journal of Energy Economics and Policy, 4*(3), 400–410.

Ledesma, D. (2013). *East Africa gas–the potential for export*. Oxford Institute for Energy Studies. https://ora.ox.ac.uk/objects/uuid:5d1edf3-b67f-4c36-ad8f-7fabb2abe9ec/download_file?safe_filename=NG-74.pdf&file_format=application%2Fpdf&type_of_work=Working+paper

Nakhle, C. (2010). 4 Petroleum fiscal regimes: evolution and challenges. In *The taxation of petroleum and minerals* (pp. 105–137). Routledge.

Observatory of Economic Complexity (OEC). (2022). Trade data. https://oec.world

Rodriguez, M. R., & Suslick, S. B. (2009). An overview of Brazilian petroleum exploration lease auctions. *Terrae, 6*(1), 6–20.

U.S. Energy Information Administration. (2013). Oil and natural gas in Sub-Saharan Africa, Independent Statistics & Analysis. https://www.eia.gov/pressroom/presentations/howard_08012013.pdf

Weber, J. G. (2012). The effects of a natural gas boom on employment and income in Colorado, Texas, and Wyoming. *Energy Economics, 34*(5), 1580–1588.

World Development Indicators. (2021). World Bank. http://databank.worldbank.org/data/reports.aspx?source=world-development-indicators

18 Petrochemical Resource Management

Stephen M. Braimah and Justice T. Mensah

18.1 Introduction

Petrochemicals comprise all chemical products derived from refining petroleum. They can also be obtained from fossil fuels such as coal or natural gas. Petrochemicals essentially represent a collection of chemical compounds that fuel spectra of products across the globe. The basic units of petrochemicals are hydrocarbons which undergo separation and extraction from crude oil and natural gas (Joshi et al., 2021). They form the core of several industries, including cosmetics, electronics, packaging, textiles, and toiletries.

One characteristic common to all the industries mentioned above is their use of hydrocarbons in making a variety of plastics and polymers. The widespread use of petrochemicals in industry drives the continued increase in their global demand. Though most petrochemicals are abstracted from fossil fuels, the vestigial originates from coal or biomass. Essentially, the 'petrochemical plant' plays a crucial role in almost all extraction stages. The petrochemical plant is a powerhouse that converts natural resources into petrochemicals before they are utilised as the building blocks in other processes and products. Due to the increase in demand for, growth, and discovery of new by-products, petrochemical plants have become complex and impressive in size and engineering (Liu et al., 2022). To ensure these extraction processes are carried out expediently, vast amounts of energy are required to pass through a distillation phase to separate the hydrocarbons from the fossil fuel. From that stage, the hydrocarbons are moved into 'crackers' (certain facilities). They are converted in these crackers into beneficial chemicals called 'feedstock' (Kianfar & Salimi, 2020). The basic vocabulary of chemical feedstock includes *olefins*, *aromatics*, and *methanol*.

A chemical feedstock is any unprocessed material used as a base to change into other end products. The primary forms of petrochemicals are the base of final products such as plastic, paper, fibres, adhesives, and detergents. They are also used in the same manner to produce petrochemical intermediaries. The petrochemical intermediaries are intricate versions of the basic petrochemicals used in making several products (Gonçalves et al., 2021). They include vinyl acetate (for making paints) and ethylene glycol (for making polyester textile fibres).

DOI: 10.4324/9781003309864-21

Owing to the complexities and diversity of the components of petrochemical products, the chapter begins with the fundamentals of petrochemical products. It then describe the petrochemical products and market in emerging/developing economies, refinery and petrochemical synergy benefits, risk management in the petrochemical industry in the emerging/developing economies, and finally offers a conclusion.

18.2 Fundamentals of the Petrochemical Industry

The petrochemical industry can be described as the downstream segment of the oil and gas sector and involves the conversion of crude oil and natural gas into the production of final and intermediate products such as synthetic rubber, yarn, polymers, plastics, and detergents. These petrochemical products have become essential in almost every sphere of modern life, including their role in food, water supply, healthcare, social and physical structures, automobiles, electronics, communication, and agriculture.

The petrochemical industry relies heavily on crude oil and natural gas as raw materials. Oil and gas products such as methane and naphtha are critical raw materials in the petrochemical industry and are often referred to as feedstocks. Figure 18.1 describes the value chain of the petrochemical industry. The feedstocks are fed through a steam cracker, producing several basic petrochemicals such as propylene, butadiene, ethylene, ammonia, xylene, etc. These products are sold to other petrochemical firms or used as inputs in producing plastics and resins through polymerisation. Finally, plastics are converted into finished products used by consumers (Panella et al., 2021)

Despite the importance of crude oil and natural gas in the petrochemical value chain, advancements in transportation support the development of petrochemical industries even in countries without a buoyant oil and gas sector. The ease with which crude oil and gas can be transported via oil tankers and pipelines has led to significant growth in the petrochemical industry (Cetinkaya et al., 2018).

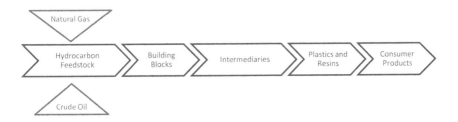

Figure 18.1 Value chain of the petrochemical industry

Source: https://www.walkwatertalent.com/wp-content/uploads/2020/01/Industry-Paper-Petrochemicals-Industry.pdf

Petrochemicals are products of global interest. Their main developments can be sourced to the emergence of raw materials from vast oil reserves, though there are other sectors from which they originate. Naturally, the petrochemical industry describes the nomenclature of chemicals obtained from petroleum and natural gas (Saygin & Gielen, 2021).

Thus, the petrochemical industry can be construed as an industry that has evolved out of oil and gas processing by adding value to the feedstock from oil and gas processing. This industry manufactures plastics, synthetic rubber, solvents, fertilisers, pharmaceuticals, additives, explosives, and adhesives. These products are contemporarily vital throughout society. They are utilised in cars, packaging, medical equipment, paints, clothing, and construction, to mention a few (Selvasembian et al., 2021).

18.3 Petrochemical Products and Market in Emerging and Developing Economies

Despite the monumental surge in recycling and efforts to limit single-use plastics, especially in Europe, Japan, and Korea, these strides are expected to be outweighed by the sharp increase in plastic consumption and disposal from the developing economies. Similarly, the difficulty in discovering alternatives to petrochemical products for numerous applications is another reason behind the massive overall increase in plastic demand. Thus, the growth in demand in developing countries outstrips curbs and recycling efforts. The incessant need for more plastics and petrochemical products in emerging economies is the leading driver of oil demand, outpacing planes, trains, and automobiles (Hundertmark et al., 2018). This demand emanates from several streams of refinery processes, mostly naphtha, ethane, and liquid petroleum gases, used as feedstock to make plastics and other chemicals. The demand for plastics is clearly the primary driver for petrochemicals. In the developing economies, perhaps as a replica of the advanced world, packaging from bottles to food wrappers represents the largest plastic market sector, accounting for close to 36% of the global demand. Essentially, recycling and efforts to curb plastic use, such as banning drinking straws, will be subsumed by the more significant increment in consumption in emerging economies (Thunman et al., 2019).

Synthetic rubber is an artificial polymer abstracted from petroleum products and by-products. It is an alternative to natural rubber. Its production process is less complicated than the natural rubber that originates from tropical climates. Several emerging economies, such as India and the United Arab Emirates, are taking a cue from countries like China, Russia, and the US. They have developed a strong appetite for synthetic rubber as variant of rubber products. It has been observed that manufacturing companies have made strides in the synthetic rubber market as a vital ingredient (Buna Rubbers) for manufacturing tires and accessories. The range of applications of synthetic rubber is very broad. For instance, there is growing penetration in the use of synthetic rubber in the automotive industry in emerging economies, which

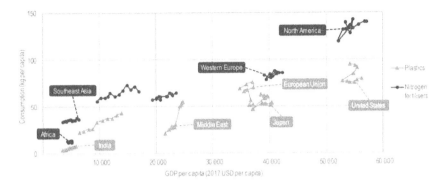

Figure 18.2 Value chain of the petrochemical industry
Source: OECD/IEA (2018). https://iea.blob.core.windows.net/assets/bee4ef3a-8876-4566-98cf-7a130c013805/The_Future_of_Petrochemicals.pdf

has been projected to provide a fillip to the demand for the synthetic rubber market. Industrialisation, growth in personal income, and growth in manufacturing output are envisaged to impact the demand for synthetic rubber in developing economies.

Petrochemical fertilisers are manufactured from large quantities of petroleum and other fossil fuels. These constitute the commonest and cheapest fertilisers, such as ammonium nitrate, superphosphate, and potassium sulphate. A cheaper cost of fertilisers is tantamount to a lower cost of production and an increase in income in an emerging economy. However, these fertilisers are unsustainable because of the finite supply of petroleum worldwide (Behera & Das, 2019). Figure 18.2, for instance, shows the correlation between plastics, nitrogen fertiliser use, and income levels across regions. Fertiliser use positively correlates with income across the various regions, suggesting that richer countries have a high per capita fertiliser consumption relative to low-income countries. Fertiliser usage in high-income countries is about ten times that in low-income countries (OECD/IEA, 2018). A similar pattern is observed in the demand for plastics: per capita, plastic consumption in high-income countries is 20 times higher than in low-income countries.

Fuelled by the rising demand, the world has experienced a sharp rise in the production of petrochemical products, with predictions still inclined towards a continuous increase to more than one-third of the current oil demand by 2030 (Cetinkaya et al., 2018). This increment is envisaged to overshadow the growth in the energy sector for trucks, aviation, and shipping. The US had experienced a bi-decade decline and stagnation in petrochemicals before the shale gas revolution promised to return a low-cost production (Cetinkaya et al., 2018). However, the Middle East remains the champion region for low-cost petrochemical products. Petrochemical products are ubiquitous and form an integral part of modern society. Apart from plastics, fertilisers, packaging, clothing, digital devices, medical equipment, detergents, tyres, and others, petrochemical products can also be found in many parts of fledgling energy systems, such as solar panels, wind turbine blades, thermal insulation for buildings and electric vehicle batteries and parts (Farias et al., 2021; Selvasembian et al., 2021). Despite the enormous benefits derived, including applications in various cutting-edge clean technologies utilised in sustainable energy systems (Bauer and Fontenit (2021), they pose sustainable challenges which need to be addressed alongside production (Thurber, 2021). Envisaging the future of petrochemical products from emerging economies, a closer look must be taken at the demand for these products to detect what we can offer to ensure a clean energy transition for the petrochemical industry in these areas.

Hitherto, the relevance of petrochemical products to developing economies was infinitesimal. The fact is that the rate of development of downstream gas and oil companies was slower, and importation was at its peak. Emerging countries have not been oblivious to this problem and have adopted important strategies to develop downstream oil sectors by discovering oil reserves and taking advantage of worldwide trends. The petrochemical and chemical products market is taking shape, growing, and modernising, with unknown oil extraction companies rubbing shoulders with many giant petrochemical-producing companies in countries such as the US, China, Iran, and Russia (Biswas et al., 2021; Boonhat et al., 2021). New production volumes, new capacities, and new technologies appear all the time. Though it may be too early to judge, the problems of modernising refineries, refinery fixed assets unavailability, and poor-quality finished products are yet to be resolved in these new economies. One significant hurdle which has led to these drawbacks is the proliferation of what some scholars refer to as nuisance taxes in the oil and gas sector, as in the case of Ghana and Nigeria. This has become challenging, especially in relation to promoting investment opportunities in the petrochemical sector to investors (Boonhat et al., 2021).

The emerging markets are faced with the pressures of constantly updating their refinery capacities to improve the technological processes and the products produced, including the depth of oil refinery and the light oil product yields. Coupled with this backdrop, there are several challenges to surmount when developing robust strategies to ensure the petrochemical industry's efficiency. They are the performance indicators, which are the growing essence of the petrochemical industry to the world, the development of related sectors and industries, the rise in consumption of petrochemical and chemical products to the levels of an industrialised economy, the emergence of high-production jobs, transitioning from the current state to innovative models, and embracing new investments into the depth of processing (Cetinkaya et al., 2018). The proliferation of new facilities, the building of refineries, the upgrading of existing refineries, and the introduction of high-efficiency installations (such as in the case of Ghana), if sustained, will demonstrate that emerging economies are witnessing positive trends in the petrochemical industry (Shinkevich et al., 2021).

The emerging markets still lag behind the world leaders in producing and consuming petrochemical products. It is hardly surprising as more raw materials from their oil and gas sectors are readily sold to these advanced economies with limited forms of processing. The US, for instance, processes over 70% of its raw materials from the petrochemical industry. Another example is Germany, which processes and consumes over nine times more of its petrochemical products than Russia (Syah et al., 2021).

Human survival is highly dependent on energy. Individuals demand energy for different uses. Energy demand has been the primary driver in the growth of the petrochemical industry. Energy consumption reflects consumer behaviour due to a worldwide need for energy-generating products. Current developments in emerging economies have led to increased demand for oil and gas products. They have created an increasing demand for information about oil and gas planning in countries such as the United Arab Emirates and the Kingdom of Saudi Arabia (Shinkevich et al., 2021). This is because the discovery of oil reserves in these new economies has restructured the national economic planning in those countries. Though fluctuations in global prices may influence and alter some economic decisions, some developing economies utilise projections and pegging costs as the basis of policies and programmes. However, any sharp decline in global oil and gas prices may lead to the inability of these emerging economies to meet extra domestic revenue expenditure, where the petrochemical sector is the mainstay of the economy. The capacity to produce petrochemical products on a large scale may also hinder and have a long-term effect on economic planning in developing countries. However, in instances where the government can refine its oil and gas (Syah et al., 2021), proceeds from sales can easily be deployed in economic planning and policies.

One effect of heavy dependence on the exploitation of vast resources of crude oil and gas by emerging economies is that their economic policies and programmes may delay when raw crude oil must be exported for foreign exchange (Thurber, 2021). Crude oil and natural gas accumulate greater value when processed before being sold on the domestic market or exported. Demand in the energy or petrochemical sector could be direct or indirect, with its economic or technological determinants. The economic determinants may emanate from the price of energy products, money income, prices of related products, consumer tastes and preferences, the population size, the extent to which the country is industrialised, and the culture of the economy. Technology determinants are highly dependent on energy utilisation efficiency as the major factor (Biswas et al., 2021). Importantly, energy demand relies on the various uses the different forms of energy can be put to satisfy different needs and wants of society. These include commercial usage, industrial usage, agricultural usage, residential usage, transportation usage, and the use of utilities. The prices of petrochemical and chemical products in these emerging markets are set by their central government and are frequently altered in, say, Ghana and Nigeria and infrequently changed in most Middle Eastern countries, e.g. Saudi Arabia and the United Arab Emirates (Saygin & Gielen, 2021; Syah et al., 2021). It also means the distribution of these products lies solely with the government to meet all forms of domestic demands. This has often led to an inconsistent price administration of petrochemical products in nations with unpredictable fuel prices and liquefied petroleum gas. The bottom line is finding a negotiation platform for government officials and economists to meet to peg prices at benchmarks they may not be sold over or below. However, the challenge is when most government policies and programmes depend on proceeds from the petrochemical sector and have limited control over the retailing market for oil and gas products (Panella et al., 2021).

Oil and gas reserves are great fortunes for any country. However, these resources are non-renewable. The discovery of oil and gas has shifted attention from the shared reliance on other individual resources to oil and gas. It is important to note that these emerging economies with crude oil and natural gas reserves depend largely on foreign exchange earnings from the sale of the two products. However, overreliance on one sector may make the development efforts of the economy. Should that sector fail, the economy may experience shocks (Panella et al., 2021). International reserves will suffer without export earnings from petrochemical products, and balance of payment deficits will accumulate. Diversification is imperative in such emerging economies, yet greater recognition must be given to more viable sectors than others. Evidently, these developing nations cannot depend on oil and gas forever (Farias et al., 2021).

Noticeable among the characteristics of these emerging economies is their tendency to be viewed as rapidly developing countries. These countries are characterised by a high supply of energy products from the petrochemical industries. They are experiencing an increasing population, becoming more urban than usual and cosmopolitan. It makes their mean real income rise, leading to a higher standard of living. The increment in foreign exchange from the oil sector, for instance, in countries such as Ghana and Saudi Arabia, makes the government launch many developmental projects (Farias et al., 2021). All these developments also have an indirect incremental effect on the literacy rate in those countries. For these reasons, tastes and preferences have undergone numerous alterations, thus increasing demands for energy and petrochemical products.

18.4 Refinery and Petrochemical Synergy Benefits

There are abundant light oil and natural gas in the US, especially natural gas liquids (NGLs) such as ethane, which make up 90% of the petrochemical manufacturing enclave. On the other hand, naphtha makes up 70% of the petroleum-based feedstock in Europe and Asia (Jacoby, 2018). According to Osundina (2016), because the US petrochemical manufacturers utilise ethane and related NGL feedstock concurrently with natural gas as their primary feedstock, the cost of ethane has a significant relationship with the price of natural gas. The two main ethane uses are as feedstock in the petrochemical production process and as a fuel. In contrast, European and Asian petrochemical producers use the refinery by-product naphtha as their fundamental feedstock, making their prices closely related to oil prices (Thunman et al., 2019).

Consequently, because oil is globally traded, every country is subjected to quite the same price, with just some discrepancies tied to quality and access to infrastructure. Interestingly, the cost of natural gas is largely determined on a regional basis. For instance, the natural gas price in North America influences North American producers. Hence, US petrochemical industries enjoy a competitive advantage should natural gas prices decline relative to oil prices. Besides the surge in supply, prices of petrochemical feedstock are greatly affected by refinery activities, which portray the correlations in the global energy value chain. Notably, finding out that US steam-cracking ethane competes with LPG (liquefied petroleum gas) or propane in the domestic market shows competition between feedstock that influences competitiveness. Similarly, naphtha competes with LPG in Europe and Asia in their regional ethylene plants (Thunman et al., 2019).

Assessing the relative price of natural gas manifests the competitiveness of US petrochemical companies, and the wider the promulgation, the more benefits the world should realise from ethane. When oil prices decrease, heavier feedstock, including naphtha and Liquefied Petroleum Gas, becomes more competitive than lighter feedstock like ethane.

In any case, the Gulf Cooperation Council (GCC) possesses a more significant relative cost advantage over the US and Europe. The GCC petrochemical industries use ethane to produce ethylene, the most produced and consumed feedstock in petrochemicals globally. The sweeping decline in ethane cost worldwide compared to crude oil has led to a historically favourable cost advantage for the GCC, particularly when oil prices increase. The availability of cheaper feedstock to the GCC earns GCC petrochemical industries more significant margins than other global players. However, the GCC seems to have hit rock bottom as the depletion of resources rich in cheap feedstock is declining, while there is a higher demand from other industries (Shabaneh & Wu, 2018).

In addition to this challenge faced by the GCC are the discovery of shale gas in the US and the capacity expansion and adjustment of the petrochemical industries in China and Iran, respectively. For this reason, there has been a shift in the balance of power among regional players in the feedstock. In a way, the discovery of these new feedstock origins in the US, China, and Iran eventually endangers the profitability of the GCC industries. Meanwhile, there is a greater probability that these new sources will lead to an excess feedstock supply, pushing the conservative feedstock sources out of the market. To deal with a global ethane supply crunch in the petrochemical industry, there is a need to pave the way for other feedstock, such as naphtha. Naphtha, though an expensive feedstock, when cracked, produces olefins and aromatics, which yield more refined chemical products (Al-Maamary et al., 2017).

18.5 Risk Management in Petrochemical Industries in the Emerging/Developing Economies

Petrochemical feedstock accounts for over 12% of the global oil demand. This percentage is expected to increase with time due to the need for plastics, fertilisers, and other products, especially in developing economies. Meanwhile, it is puzzling how the growth in demand for petrochemicals and its ramifications on the environment and security has received minor consideration (Shinkevich et al., 2021).

Though increased recycling and attempts to control single-use plastics have been in the pipeline in Europe, Japan, and Korea, the combined plastics and disposables consumption in the developing economies outweigh the efforts of the three advanced countries (Thurber, 2021). Finding alternatives to petrochemical products for many applications has become the major obstacle leading to divergent motives behind the control measures as demand keeps rising.

However, the problems experienced in the production and refining of petrochemical products are complex. The process must undergo selective chemical reactions. It is worthy of note that during the process, the desired end-product is not always obtained at the first stage; other products emerge alongside. In such cases, obtaining the intended products will lead to the higher cost of coming out with other by-products, after factoring in the latter's overhead (Bauer & Fontenit, 2021). Likewise, the difficulty in installing petrochemical machinery makes it highly capital-intensive for investments classified as the integrated complex and the minimum economic size. Installing any petrochemical plant depends on the capacity to sell or the selling price of envisaged petrochemical products generated in the future (Boonhat et al., 2021).

With regard to the petrochemical industry, the main problems with developing economies are that they suffer from a narrow market size, which leads to limited-sized installations. Production cost becomes marginally competitive and sometimes very high if no government intervention exists. For these reasons, governments' continuous initiation of moves to export petrochemicals to highly industrialised countries of America and Europe, though questionable, is inevitable. These emerging economies have always stalled in their processes of industrialisation in their bid to boost the economy and make their production and refining cheaper. In other cases, countries that form a strong bond in their regions respond to intense domestic demands to install advanced refinery facilities that will be more beneficial to their citizens (Biswas et al., 2021).

An emerging risk facing the development of the oil and gas sector, and by extension, the petrochemical industry, relates to the concept of 'stranded assets'. The quest for a decarbonised global energy sector and the transition to cleaner energy have implications for the financing of energy projects. Today, development finance institutions and some leading financial institutions are transitioning their funding away from fossil fuels towards renewable energy financing. Thus, for many resource-rich developing countries that still have vast deposits of oil and gas yet untapped, access to the needed investments to build the oil and gas industry is becoming constrained, and this will eventually limit the ability of these countries to harness these resources.

18.6 Conclusion

Petrochemical products present a variety of benefits to the worldwide. Their usefulness ranges from transportation and medicine to even domestic purposes. Countries such as the US and European nations that have discovered oil and natural gas reserves previously have tested and tried to trade-off between their petroleum sector and other industries within the economy to strengthen economic planning policies. It can be adduced that the petrochemical products and refineries integrate to provide synergy benefits that can never be played down. Emerging and developing economies are novices in the field, and their incapacity has basically turned them into petroleum-extract-and-export countries.

References

Al-Maamary, H. M., Kazem, H. A., & Chaichan, M. T. (2017). The impact of oil price fluctuations on common renewable energies in GCC countries. *Renewable and Sustainable Energy Reviews*, 75, 989–1007.

Bauer, F., & Fontenit, G. (2021). Plastic dinosaurs–Digging deep into the accelerating carbon lock-in of plastics. *Energy Policy*, 156, 112418.

Behera, B., & Das, A. (2019). Management efficiency and profitability: A case study of petrochemical industry. *Splint International Journal of Professionals*, 6(3), 7–15.

Biswas, S. K., Mathur, U., & Hazra, S. K. (2021). *Fundamentals of process safety engineering*. CRC Press.

Boonhat, H., Lin, R. T., & Lin, J. T. (2021). Association between residential exposure to petrochemical industrial complexes and pancreatic cancer: A systematic review and meta-analysis. *International Journal of Environmental Health Research*, 33(1), 116–127.

Cetinkaya, E., Liu, N., Simons, T. J., & Wallach, J. (2018). Petrochemicals 2030: Reinventing the way to win in a changing industry. Chemicals: Our Insights. *McKinsey & Company*. Retrieved February 08, 2023 from https://www.mckinsey.com/industries/chemicals/our-insights/petrochemicals-2030-reinventing-the-way-to-win-in-a-changing-industry

Farias, C. B. B., Almeida, F. C., Silva, I. A., Souza, T. C., Meira, H. M., Rita de Cássia, F., Luna, J. M., Santos, V. A., Converti, A., Banat, I. M., & Sarubbo, L. A. (2021). Production of green surfactants: Market prospects. *Electronic Journal of Biotechnology*, 51, 28–39.

Gonçalves, D., Bordado, J. M., Marques, A. C., & Galhano dos Santos, R. (2021). Non-formaldehyde, bio-based adhesives for use in wood-based panel manufacturing industry—A review. *Polymers*, 13(23), 4086.

Hundertmark, T., Mayer, M., McNally, C., Simons, T. J., & Witte, C. (2018). How plastics waste recycling could transform the chemical industry. *McKinsey & Company*, 12, 1–1.

Jacoby, D. (2018). *From Bogotá to Beijing: Development and life after globalization*. Rowman & Littlefield.

Joshi, A., Shah, V., Mohapatra, P., Kumar, S., Joshi, R. K., Kathe, M., & Fan, L. S. (2021). Chemical looping-a perspective on the next-gen technology for efficient fossil fuel utilization. *Advances in Applied Energy, 3*, 100044.

Kianfar, E., & Salimi, M. (2020). A review on the production of light olefins from hydrocarbons cracking and methanol conversion. *Advances in Chemistry Research, 59*, 1–81.

Liu, X., Zhai, Y., Li, S., Niu, Q., Liu, X., Wang, Z., & Xu, M. (2022). Hydrothermal carbonization of petrochemical sludge: The fate of hydrochar and oil components. *Journal of Environmental Chemical Engineering, 10*(5), 108234.

OECD/IEA 2018. The future of petrochemicals towards more sustainable plastics and fertilisers. https://iea.blob.core.windows.net/assets/bee4ef3a-8876-4566-98cf-7a130c013805/The_Future_of_Petrochemicals.pdf

Osundina, O. (2016). *The story of Nigeria's petroleum industry*. Novum Pro Verlag.

Panella, K., Serafeim, G., & Trinh, K. (2021). Accounting for product impact in the oil and gas industry. Harvard Business School Research Paper Series 21-140.

Saygin, D., & Gielen, D. (2021). Zero-emission pathway for the global chemical and petrochemical sector. *Energies, 14*(13), 3772.

Selvasembian, R., Mal, J., Rani, R., Sinha, R., Agrahari, R., Joshua, I., Santhiagu, A., & Pradhan, N. (2021). Recent progress in microbial fuel cells for industrial effluent treatment and energy generation: Fundamentals to scale-up application and challenges. *Bioresource Technology, 346*, 126462.

Shabaneh, R., & Wu, K. (2018). Assessing the impact of natural gas on natural gas liquids: Policy challenges and imperatives (No. ks-2018-dp42).

Shinkevich, A., Barsegyan, N., Petrov, V., & Klimenko, T. (2021). Transformation of the management model of a petrochemical enterprise in the context of industry 4.0 challenges. In *E3S Web of Conferences* (Vol. 296, p. 06008). EDP Sciences.

Syah, R., Davarpanah, A., Elveny, M., Ghasemi, A., & Ramdan, D. (2021). The economic evaluation of methanol and propylene production from natural gas at petrochemical industries in Iran. *Sustainability, 13*(17), 9990.

Thunman, H., Vilches, T. B., Seemann, M., Maric, J., Vela, I. C., Pissot, S., & Nguyen, H. N. (2019). Circular use of plastics-transformation of existing petrochemical clusters into thermochemical recycling plants with 100% plastics recovery. *Sustainable Materials and Technologies, 22*, e00124.

Thurber, M. (2021). Gas markets usually start with industrial applications. Energy for growth, Stanford University. Retrieved February 06, 2023, from https://www.energyforgrowth.org/wp-content/uploads/2021/02/Gas-and-Development.pdf

19 The Role of Oil and Gas in Sustainable Development in the Global South

Asaah Sumaila Mohammed and Joshua Yindenaba Abor

19.1 Introduction

Theoretical arguments, particularly in the 1960s, asserted that the presence of natural resources in any country would result in rapid development (Karl, 2007; Rostow, 1990). This fuelled a frenzy for the exploration of various natural resources, particularly those with high economic value at the time, such as gold, diamonds, oil and gas, and timber (Rostow, 1990). The growth and development dynamics of countries such as Russia, Norway, Saudi Arabia, and the United Arab Emirates are clear examples supporting the liberal economists' arguments of how oil and related resources contribute to accelerated development (Wen, 2011). Oil and gas exploration and production presumably open up domestic markets for foreign direct investment (FDI) which invariably contributes to GDP, local infrastructural development, and employment (Gelb et al., 2014; Henstridge et al., 2012; Oleka et al., 2014). Some studies have found a positive correlation between growth in the oil and gas sector and corresponding growth in gross domestic product (GDP), improvements in social services and infrastructure, and to local employment among others in some African oil and gas-producing countries such as Algeria, Angola, Nigeria, and Libya (Africa Development Bank, 2009; KPMG, 2013).

An increasing number of resource-rich developing countries have formed sovereign wealth funds (SWF)[1] to address these particular oil dependency issues. SWFs aid budget stability in the face of global oil market volatility and promote responsible present and future oil windfall investments (Gelb et al., 2014; Idemudia, 2009; International Monetary Fund, 2010; Oleka et al., 2014). Many countries that depend on oil, including Kuwait, Norway, Qatar, Saudi Arabia, and Venezuela, have established SWFs in order to secure extra oil income during periods of high oil prices and access those reserves during periods of low oil prices (Oleka et al., 2014). Due to significant trade surpluses, many of these governments have built up sizable foreign reserves, some of which have invested in a wider variety of financial products than is customary for foreign reserves in an effort to increase the yield on their foreign asset position. Many nations have found success using SWFs as powerful tools to address both micro and macroeconomic issues. For instance, they have contributed to reducing the

DOI: 10.4324/9781003309864-22

tax burden on citizens and funded governmental or private research and development initiatives in many economies (Oleka et al., 2014). Due to their ability to stabilise economies by funding infrastructure projects, as well as act as tools for the global asset market and turn scarce raw materials and commodities into long-term capital-growing entities through innovative asset management and profit reinvestment projects, SWFs have the potential to strengthen the economies of developing countries (Idemudia, 2009; International Monetary Fund, 2010). Studies have suggested that SWFs have aided in the development of a number of nations, including Libya, Singapore, Kuwait, and Norway, to name a few (Gelb et al., 2014; Oleka et al., 2014). However, there has been much criticism of SWFs both locally and internationally. The internal challenges against SWFs are primarily political, as well as the legality and transparency of such funds (Oleka et al., 2014).

Despite the potential for national development that oil, gas, and other natural resources provide, this promise is sometimes viewed with some scepticism, mostly because of the underwhelming contribution that resource endowments have made to sustained social and economic development. After years of oil and gold mining, African nations like Nigeria, Ghana, and Angola, to name a few, have seen a number of unsustainable development consequences including conflicts, rising youth unemployment, rent-seeking, and erratic economic growth (Idemudia, 2009; International Monetary Fund, 2020; Karl, 1997; Mohammed et al., 2022). These revelations are counterintuitive in the context of sustainable development theory, and they paint a bleak future for these nations and many others in the global south. Even now, these nations continue to engage in resource extraction, and they have also endorsed the UN Sustainable Development Goals (UN SDGs). Therefore, the issue is: what has changed in their existing system and plans for using the money they make from oil and gas extraction to help the UN SDGs to be achieved?

This chapter, therefore, provides an overview of the concept of sustainable development and the UN SDGs, as well as an examination of how some countries in the global south are leveraging oil and gas resources to support SDG achievement despite financial constraints. The first section provided an overview of the SDGs and how their implementation is progressing despite obstacles. The second section looks at how global financial challenges impede implementation progress in general. The third section looks at how specific countries in the global south are using oil and gas resources to achieve the SDGs in specific areas. The chapter concludes with policy recommendations for effective utilisation of oil and gas resources for sustainable development in the global south.

19.2 Overview of the Sustainable Development Goals of the United Nations

The United Nations (UN) Conference on sustainable development (SD) in Rio de Janeiro in 2012, 20 years after the 1992 'Earth Summit' at the same location, began discussions on a new agenda and the process of setting post-2015 goals.

The SD declaration, 'The Future We Want', was unanimously adopted, paving the way for the UN SD summit. The vision 'Transforming Our World: 2030 Agenda for Sustainable Development' was adopted in September 2015. In July 2015, the Addis Ababa Action Agenda of the Third International Conference on Financing for Development, one of the foundation stones of the 2030 Agenda, was adopted following negotiations and agreements on development finance practices, partnerships, and investments, as well as measures to achieve the new agenda (United Nations, 2015a).

The SDGs aim to end poverty, ensure shared prosperity, and protect the environment for future generations. The goals sought to build on their predecessors, addressing some of the criticisms levelled at the MDGs while also taking into account emerging development challenges. Seventeen SDGs and 169 targets for 2030 were adopted, and 232 indicators were chosen to track global, regional, and national progress, providing an evidence-based framework for monitoring progress over the next 15 years (Table 19.1).

The global and regional implementation of the newly adopted 2030 SDGs began in 2016. Countries were encouraged to take ownership of the SDGs and align national development plans with the global agenda to ensure effective implementation and synergy among the various goals. Governments were also encouraged to mobilise private and public actors at the local, national, and international levels to ensure policy coherence and inclusivity (Allen et al., 2018; United Nations, 2015b). From 2016 to 2021, 176 countries conducted at least one voluntary national review (VNR) through collaborative efforts involving all relevant stakeholders (UNDESA, 2016). The VNRs were presented to the high-level political forum on sustainable development (HLPF) and aided in identifying country-specific challenges and gaps for better support and cooperation (UN, 2015b). Early assessments of SDG implementation show that many countries made significant progress in aligning the global framework with national policy frameworks by establishing institutional mechanisms for coordinating actions and embarking on several multi-stakeholder consultations (UNDESA, 2016). Few, however, were successful in prioritising, engaging in effective planning to ensure synergy between national and international goals, and conducting policy monitoring and evaluation (Allen et al., 2018).

Prior to the Covid-19 pandemic, global progress on the SDGs was dismal. Many countries were falling short of their targets for 2030. Key indicator improvements were slow and uneven, both across and within countries. Progress on poverty alleviation has been slow. Poverty fell at a slower rate in the developing world, by 2% points from 2015 to 2019, compared to a 6-point decrease from 2010 to 2015. (United Nations, 2020; World Bank, 2021). Food insecurity increased, economic growth slowed, and manufacturing growth slowed, the proportion of the urban population living in slums increased, consumption, production, and resource use remained unsustainable, actions to limit climate change, ocean acidification, and biodiversity losses were woefully inadequate, and conflicts and terrorism persisted in

Table 19.1 The list of the millennium development goals (MDGs) and the sustainable development goals (SDGs)

MDGs	SDGs
1. Eradicate extreme poverty and hunger	1. End poverty in all its forms everywhere
2. Achieve universal primary education	2. End hunger, achieve food security and improve nutrition and promote sustainable agriculture
3. Promote gender equality and empower women	3. Ensure healthy lives and promote well-being for all at all ages
4. Reduce child mortality	4. Ensure inclusive and equitable quality education and promote lifelong learning opportunities for all
5. Improve maternal mortality	
6. Combat HIV/AIDS, malaria, and other diseases	
7. Ensure environmental Sustainability	5. Achieve gender equality and empower all women and girls
8. Develop a global partnership for development	6. Ensure availability and sustainable management of water and sanitation for all
	7. Ensure access to affordable, reliable, sustainable, and modern energy for all
	8. Promote sustained, inclusive, and sustainable economic growth, full and productive employment, and decent work for all
	9. Build resilient infrastructure, promote inclusive and sustainable industrialisation, and foster innovation
	10. Reduce inequality within and among countries
	11. Make cities and human settlements inclusive, safe, resilient, and sustainable
	12. Ensure sustainable consumption and production patterns
	13. Take urgent action to combat climate change and its impacts
	14. Conserve and sustainably use the oceans, seas, and marine resources for sustainable development
	15. Protect, restore, and promote sustainable use of terrestrial ecosystems, sustainably manage forest, combat desertification, and halt and reverse land degradation and halt biodiversity loss
	16. Promote peaceful and inclusive societies for sustainable development, provide access to justice for all, and build effective, accountable, and inclusive institutions at all levels
	17. Strengthen the means of implementation and revitalise the global partnership for sustainable development

Source: United Nations (2021)

many parts of the world (United Nations, 2020). Although there were modest increases in maternal and child health indicators, educational achievements for boys and girls, women empowerment, access to water and sanitation services, sustainable and modern energy, and inequality reductions, these gains were insufficient to meet the 2030 targets (United Nations, 2020).

The global pandemic, which has cost over 4 million lives worldwide and is still having a negative impact on countries' execution of the 2030 agenda, has made the situation even worse. The upward tendencies of recent years or decades have either halted or are being reversed (United Nations, 2021). The global situation is concerning, as many nations in the global south are experiencing economic and debt problems, as well as shrinking fiscal resources and rising food prices (International Monetary Fund, 2021). As a result, countries are witnessing increased poverty – at least 119 million people were expected to descend into extreme poverty by 2020 – hunger, and disruptions in critical health and education services (United Nations, 2021).

19.3 Sustainable Development and Financing Challenges

The debate over sustainable development centres on how a sustainable world must strive to meet the basic requirements of current generations ('intragenerational equity') without jeopardising future generations' ability to meet their own needs ('intergenerational equity'). To accomplish this, strict procedures for financing sustainable development that meet the demands of present and future generations would be required. Sustainable development finance is a type of financing that uses a combination of clean and innovative sources to address the demands of current and future generations. The funding method could come from both local and foreign sources, including public and commercial funds like environmental finance, private sector finance, and innovative finance for sustainable development (Abekah-Nkrumah et al., 2021).

Financing for development projects has traditionally been obtained from foreign aid, including debt relief. However, many development partners have pulled back on their contributions and even if they all meet their pledges, funding from this source would still be inadequate to fund the more expansive and sustainable development, especially the Global Development Goals (GDGs) (GDGs) (Gaspar et al., 2019). Significant investment is required to be able to finance sustainable development in developing countries (Schmidt-Traub, 2015). Developing countries tend to experience a huge difference between the required financing for sustainable development and the current levels of funding to create a sustainable development financing gap. The financing gap is also prevalent within sectors of the economy and infrastructure tends to have a very huge financing gap. For instance, power infrastructure represents the greatest financing need of about US$950 billion, whereas education and health together need US$390 billion, which is less than half of the amount power infrastructure requires. However, investments in these sectors still fell short (Doumbia & Lauridsen, 2019).

There is a general recommendation for substantial investment and financing from private and public sources to be able to address these financing gaps. In 2015, during the third International Conference on Financing for Development in Addis Ababa, financing was categorised into private and public sources. It was further categorised into domestic and foreign sources. Domestic financing sources comprised tax revenue and private savings, whereas foreign sources were made up of private and public sources. Private sources were comprised of FDI, portfolio investments, and international remittances, whereas public sources included Official Development Assistance (ODA), debt, and other official flows (Doumbia & Lauridsen, 2019; Eze, 2021).

The challenge with respect to financing sustainable development is that it is the responsibility of government, and the lack of resources needed to address the development needs is common in developing countries that are already confronted with many economic difficulties. In order to attain the infrastructure-related SDGs as well as limit climate change to 2°C in line with the 2015 Paris Climate Accord, lower- and middle-income countries need to spend around 4.5% of their GDP (Fay, & Rozenberg, 2019). However, the lowest-income countries rather experience the largest financing gap. Though developing countries are the ones requiring more financing for sustainable development, the financing has mostly been directed to the developed countries (Eze, 2021). For instance, the Green Climate Fund, which is a partner for developing countries and would have helped to meet the climate action, is being underfunded (Morris, 2018). It is suggested that growth in SDG spending in future is likely to take place in more developed countries than the developing ones (Kharas Homi, 2019).

Domestic revenue mobilisation (DRM) was deemed a potential alternative by the International Monetary Fund (IMF) prior to the economic crisis caused by the advent of the COVID-19 pandemic. The epidemic has had a significant economic impact on countries, particularly in the developing world. Given the link between GDP and tax revenue, this has had a substantial impact on numerous sectors, resulting in a considerable drop in GDP and, therefore, a reduction in tax income. The International Monetary Fund (2020) indicates that world's real GDP growth is about −4.4%, with −3.3% for emerging economies and −4.4% for advanced economies. It is expected that with countries experiencing dwindling GDP output, the percentage of their GDP spent on financing the SDGs will increase in order to maintain the needed investment. However, this may be difficult for countries to achieve under the prevailing economic conditions (Eze, 2021).

Although emerging and developing countries witnessed some increase in tax revenue before the pandemic, this was far lower than that of developed countries. For instance, tax revenue increased from 11% to 15% of GDP from 2000 to 2017, but this was 11% lower than that of developed economies (Gaspar et al., 2019). DRM is also related to the size of the economy, which tends to favour lower and upper-middle-income countries more than their low-income counterparts. As suggested by the IMF, developing countries can mobilise 3%–5% of GDP by intensifying efforts at DRM. However, this will only amount to US$5 billion for low-income countries, US$95 billion for lower-middle-income countries, and US$60 billion for upper middle-income-countries. This situation clearly shows a disparity in resources and development needs (Kharas Homi, 2019). Cross-border flow is also an important source of finance that the public sector can attract to increase investments. However, in spite of the increase in cross-border flow to developing countries like Africa, net cross-border flow has not been so great due to outflow of FDI during shocks such as a fall in prices of commodities (Kharas Homi, 2019).

These developments seem to suggest the difficulties countries will have in meeting all the SDGs by 2030. Therefore, a cooperative initiative is required (Runde et al., 2020). Developing countries also need to leverage their oil and gas resources in order to raise the needed financing to drive sustainable development. This need is discussed in the next section.

19.4 Leveraging Oil and Gas Resources for Sustainable Development: Experiences from the Global South

19.4.1 The Case of Ghana

Ghana's Petroleum Revenue Management Act, 2011 (PRMA) provides a framework for a sustainable, ethical, accountable, and responsible management of petroleum revenue for the benefit of Ghanaians (Oshionebo, 2018). The PRMA specifies particular regulations for the acquisition, use, reinvestment, and saving of petroleum income. It is anticipated that these regulations will encourage careful and accountable administration of Ghana's petroleum income. The PRMA establishes the Petroleum Holding Fund (PHF) and the Ghana Petroleum Funds (GPF) to ensure efficient management and investment of petroleum earnings. The Ghana Heritage Fund and the Ghana Stabilisation Fund make up the GPF. The Ghana Stabilisation Fund is designed to mitigate the effects of unexpected decreases in petroleum revenue and/or maintain public expenditure capacity. When petroleum supplies run out, the Ghana Heritage Fund will act as an endowment to support the growth of future generations.

The importance of petroleum money to Ghana's economic growth cannot be overstated. For the past five years, there has been a progressive commitment from the government to achieving sustainable development through the allocation of oil and gas revenues to priority areas (Acquah-Andoh et al., 2018). The steady increase of allocation to the ABFA from 2017 to 2019 was due to the increase in revenue from the PHF. Education had the largest share of ABFA in 2017 and 2018 where much of the amount was invested in the free senior high school (SHS) policy aimed at ensuring equal access to education at the SHS level (SDG 4). The period of 2019 to 2021 recorded a decrease in revenue from the PHF and saw much of the investment shifted to the development of road, rail, and other critical infrastructural development. This included the spot improvement, upgrading, rehabilitation, asphaltic overlays, and rails development, whilst the other critical infrastructural development was in the form of installation of new streetlights; drainage, water, and sanitation projects; construction of medical facilities; drilling of boreholes, and construction and small dams. Regardless, in the last five years, all major areas of the economy, particularly industrial development, were prioritised in order to achieve socio-economic growth and reduce poverty among the population. These are expected to eliminate poverty and raise citizens' overall living standards, resulting in the achievement of the SDGs by 2030. The contribution of oil and gas revenue to the priority areas of the economy for the period of 2017–2021 is summarised in Box 19.1.

Box 19.1

Oil and Gas Contribution to Sectoral Development in Ghana: 2017–2021

In the 2017 financial year, petroleum revenue was GH736.03 million, which was used to fund the ABFA. At the end of 2017, GH 332.29 million had been used, while GH 203.74 million remained unutilised. Education received GH 202.38 million (61%) while agriculture received GH 49.07 (3%) and road, rail, and other vital infrastructure received GH 41.62 million (12%). Health received GH 8.66 million (3%) while GIIF received GH 29.22 million (9%) and PIAC received GH 1.35 million.

In the 2018 financial year, a total allocation for the ABFA was GH₵ 827.25 million. From this amount, the agriculture priority area received GH₵ 126.21 million (1757.16% increase over the figure in 2017), road, rail and other critical infrastructure development had GH₵ 255.69 million a 513.559% increase). The physical infrastructure and service delivery in health and education received GH₵ 22.91 million (a 162.12% increase from 2017) and GH₵ 419.44 million (an increase of 107.47%), respectively.

In 2019, ABFA available for spending was GH₵ 3.72 billion, out of which GH₵ 1.86 billion was utilised, leaving a balance of GH₵ 1.86 billion. The agriculture sector received an amount of GH₵ 71.14 million (a decrease of 43.28% from 2018). Road, rail, and other critical infrastructure development received GH₵ 579.44 million (an increase of 126.84%). Also, the physical infrastructure and service delivery in health and education received GH₵ 46.70 million (a 104.1% increase from 2018) and GH₵ 570.58 million (an increase of 35.96% from 2018), respectively.

The total amount of disbursement for the priority areas in the 2020 financial year was GH₵ 2.72 billion. Out of that amount, agriculture received GH₵ 79.455 million (2.85%), road, rail, and other critical infrastructure development had GH₵ 1.23 billion (70%), and health and education both received GH₵ 698.04 million (25.20%) whilst industrialisation received 31 million (1.15%).

In the 2021 financial year, disbursement of ABFA to priority areas was GH₵ 914.98. Out of this amount, agriculture received GH₵ 2.70 million (0.31%), physical infrastructure and service delivery in education and health both received GH₵ 408 million (43.81%), road, rail, and other critical infrastructure received GH₵ 503.78 million or (54.06%) whilst industrialisation had GH₵ 188.50 thousand.

19.4.2 The Case of Nigeria

Following several years of oil production, Nigeria decided in October 2009 to establish the Nigeria SWF, which was followed by the establishment of the Nigerian Sovereign Investment Authority (NSIA) in May 2011. This initiative aims to leverage oil resources to reduce poverty and inequalities while also protecting future generations. The establishment of the Nigerian Sovereign Wealth Fund (NSWF) with a $1 billion seed capital is by far one of the most significant economic policy decisions made in the country in recent times (Idemudia, 2009; Oleka et al., 2014). The NSIA subsequently established the future generations' fund (FGF) with the goal of investing in a diversified portfolio of appropriate growth investments in order to provide future generations of Nigerians with a solid savings base when Nigeria's hydrocarbon reserves are depleted. The Nigeria Infrastructure Fund (NIF) is another NSIA initiative that aims to invest in infrastructure projects in Nigeria that meet targeted financial returns while also contributing to the development of critical infrastructure in Nigeria. Transportation, energy and power, water resources, and agriculture are all potential areas for investment in order to stimulate growth and diversification of the Nigerian economy, attract foreign investment, and create jobs for Nigerians (Migap, 2014; Oleka et al., 2014).

In establishing the connection between the oil and gas industry and sustainable development, consideration is given to the year-by-year allocation of revenues from the budget to the priority areas of development. Even though much is expected from the government to leverage oil and gas revenue to eradicate poverty in the country, there is a steady allotment of funds from yearly budgets to tackle the issue of poverty (Ejiogu et al., 2019). This is accomplished by investments in physical infrastructure and service delivery in areas such as education, health, agriculture, transportation, and industrial development, all of which represent a deliberate attempt to attain overall development. Box 19.2 summarises the instances of oil and gas extraction contribution to reducing poverty vis-à-vis the socio-economic development of Nigeria.

19.5 Conclusion and Recommendations

Oil and gas resources, without a doubt, offer opportunities for socio-economic growth and invariably contribute to the United Nations' SDGs. There is ample evidence that progress in achieving the UN SDGs is hampered, particularly in the global south, by weak domestic financial and technical capacities. As a result, the extraction of oil and gas presents enormous prospects for Ghana and Nigeria, both of which have achieved only little progress toward reaching the SDGs. Ghana's recent discovery and commercial production of oil and gas have contributed a great deal to the country's economic growth and prosperity. The present global economic crisis triggered by COVID-19 and the Russia-Ukraine conflict has exacerbated the financial obstacles to achieving the SDGs.

> **Box 19.2**
>
> **Oil and Gas Contribution to Development in Nigeria**
>
> Structurally, Nigeria's economy depends on the revenue from oil and gas, contributing to 80% of government revenues and around 40% of GDP. The oil sector is the government's greatest revenue-generating unit. And the government is always concerned about the volatility of oil prices and their influence on oil revenue, which will undoubtedly have an impact on fiscal factors.
>
> Invariably, the proceeds from the sector also assist government to cater for expenditure on public goods and render essential services to the public, thus concentrating on the priority areas of the economy that can trigger socioeconomic growth. This contributes to the achievement of the SDGs. Specifically, these priority areas of the economy are infrastructural development, construction of roads, provision of health services, security, and the building of schools, among others.
>
> The dedication of the Nigerian governments to education cannot be overstated. For example, the education sector received N369.6 billion of the overall budget in 2016, followed by N550.5 billion in 2017, N605.8 billion in 2018, N620.5 billion in 2019, and N671.07 billion in 2020. This promise of funding for education is just one of many areas of development sponsored by the 80% contribution of oil and gas revenue to the state for development.

It has been observed that Ghana and Nigeria have clear frameworks for applying revenue from oil and gas for their national development. Budgetary allocations from oil and gas funds have been prioritised for critical areas such as education, health, agriculture, and general infrastructure. These sectors which are intricately linked to most of the SDGs have received financial support from the national budget progressively and consistently. Although insufficient to meet the financial demands of those sectors in their respective countries, the quantities are significant in comparison to past years without oil and gas, especially in Ghana.

It has, however, been observed that though these countries have developed frameworks for utilising oil and gas revenue for priority national development sectors, a specific outline for targeting the SDGs is missing. Limited evidence exists to suggest how the two countries have consciously planned to achieve the SDGs with injections from oil and gas revenue. It appears oil and gas revenues are sparingly spread within the priority sectors without concentration on specific targets of the SDGs. This has also been observed in related studies on local content and application of oil and gas revenues in Ghana (Ackah & Mohammed, 2018). This would make any assessment of the contribution of oil and gas to achieving the SDGs in the global south problematic. This appears to be the case in a number of other developing countries.

In conclusion, the widely held belief that oil and gas resources can help poor countries improve their fortunes is dubious in the context of long-term development. The governance arrangement and institutional capacity to follow strict basic principles of financial prudence and discipline are uncertain.

The culture of rent seeking and corruption, although in the spotlight in many developing countries, continues to hinder progressive and effective utilisation of extractive resources for sustainable development.

Some recommendations are necessary to avert this:

- The establishment of SWFs is highly recommended to ensure intergenerational transfers of resources and to ensure that the current generation does not jeopardise the growth of future generations. The World Bank has identified SWFs as the backbone of finance for Africa's extractive developing countries (Gelb et al., 2014). SWFs could invest some of their assets in banks across the continent to supplement their long-term deposits. Given SWFs' long-term investment horizons, this should help address the continent's scarcity of long-term resources.
- Strict regulatory policies on financial discipline and applications to targeted areas for achieving the SDGs are paramount.
- A robust monitoring and evaluation system and plan for tracking specific indicators for targeted SDGs are required for effective utilisation of oil and gas revenue for sustainable development.

Note

1 Financial reform instrument owned by a sovereign state, where a nation's savings are accumulated for foreign direct investment and development purposes (Oleka et al., 2014).

References

Abekah-Nkrumah, G., Assuming, P. O., Abor, P. A., & Mohammed, J. I. (2021). Financing *sustainable development*: New *insights for the present and the future*. Routledge.

Ackah, C. G., & Mohammed, A. S. (2018). Local content law and practice: The case of Ghana. In J. Page & F. Tarp (Eds.), Mining for change: *Natural* resources and industry in Africa (pp. 139–160). United Nations University World Institute for Development Economics Research (UNU-WIDER). Oxford University Press. https://doi.org/10.1093/oso/9780198851172.003.0001

Acquah-andoh, E., Gyeyir, D. M., Aanye, D. M., & Ifelebuegu, A. (2018). Oil and gas production and the growth of Ghana's s economy: An initial assessment. *International Journal of Economics and Financial Research*, 4(10), 303–312.

Africa Development Bank. (2009). *Oil and gas in Africa*. Oxford University Press.

Africa, K. P. M. G. (2013). Oil and gas in Africa: Africa's reserves, potential and prospects. *Retrieved*, 12, 14.

Allen, C., Metternicht, G., & Wiedmann, T. (2018). Initial progress in implementing the sustainable development goals (SDGs): A review of evidence from countries. *Sustainability Science*, 13(5), 1453–1467.

Doumbia, D., & Lauridsen, M. L. (2019). Closing the SDG financing gap: Trends and data. *EMCompass*, 73, 1–8.

Ejiogu, A., Ejiogu, C., & Ambituuni, A. (2019). The dark side of transparency: Does the Nigeria extractive industries transparency initiative help or hinder accountability and corruption control? *The British Accounting Review*, 51(5), 100811.

Eze, K. (2021). *Principal challenges to financing the sustainable development goals*. The Pub, MPPGA Student Media. https://www.pubpoli.com/posts/2021/1/26/7cpgb7sulm6vcq7l4r0j9g1flkslu4

Fay, M., & Rozenberg, J. (2019). Beyond the gap: How countries can afford the infrastructure they need while protecting the planet. World Bank Group.

Gaspar, V., Amaglobeli, D., Garcia-Escribano, M., Prady, D., & Soto, M. (2019). *Fiscal policy and development: Human, social, and physical investments for the SDGs*. International Monetary Fund.

Gelb, A., Tordo, S., Halland, H., Arfaa, N., & Smith, G. (2014). *Sovereign wealth funds and long-term development finance: Risks and opportunities*. World Bank Policy Research Working Paper (6776).

Henstridge, M., Cabello, M., Haglund, D., Lipschutz, K., Jakobsen, M., & Williams, R. (2012). *Enhancing the integrity of the oil for development programme: Assessing vulnerabilities to corruption and identifying prevention measures—Case Studies of Bolivia, Mozambique and Uganda*. NORAD Report, 7, 12.

Idemudia, U. (2009). The quest for the effective use of natural resource revenue in Africa: Beyond transparency and the need for compatible cultural democracy in Nigeria. *Africa Today, 56*(2), 2–24.

International Monetary Fund. (2010). *Investment objectives of sovereign wealth funds—A shifting paradigm*. IMF Working Paper, WP/11/19, Washington D.C, pp. 1–17

International Monetary Fund. (2021). *Macroeconomic developments and prospects in low-income countries 2021*. International Monetary Fund.

International Monetary Fund. (2020). *World economic outlook: A long and difficult ascent*. International Monetary Fund.

Karl, T. L. (1997). *The paradox of plenty: Oil booms and petro-states*. University of California Press.

Karl, T. L. (2007). *Oil-led development: Social, political, and economic consequences*. Center on Democracy, Development, and the Rule of Law, Freeman Spogli Institute for International Studies.

Kharas Homi, M. J. (2019). *How much does the world spend on the sustainable development goals?* Brookings. https://www.brookings.edu/blog/future-development/2019/07/29/how-much-does-the-world-spend-on-the-sustainable-development-goals/

Migap, J. P. (2014). Enhancing infrastructural growth in Nigeria: The sovereign wealth fund strategy. *International Journal of Economic Development Research and Investment, 5*(2), 61–74.

Mohammed, A. S., Graham, E., & Dary, S. K. (2022). Rising expectations and dying hopes: Local perceptions of oil and gas extraction in Ghana. *Energy Research & Social Science, 88*, 102529.

Oleka, D. C., Ugwuanyi, B. U., & Ewah, E. B. (2014). Sovereign wealth fund and economic growth in Nigeria: An empirical analysis. *IOSR Journal of Economics and Finance (IOSR-JEF), 4*(5), 1–20.

Oshionebo, E. (2018). Sovereign wealth funds in developing countries: A case study of the Ghana petroleum funds. *Journal of Energy & Natural Resources Law, 36*(1), 33–59.

Rostow, W. W. (1990). *The stages of economic growth: A non-communist manifesto*. Cambridge University Press.

Runde, B. D. F., Metzger, C., & Abdullah, H. F. (2020). Covid-19 demands innovative ideas for financing the SDGs. Center for Strategic & International Studies, CSIS Briefs.

Schmidt-Traub, G. (2015). *Investment needs to achieve the sustainable development goals understanding the billions and trillions.* SDSN Working Paper, Version 2 (Sustainable Development Solutions Network), pp. 1–137. http://unsdsn.org/resources/publications/sdg-investment-needs/

United Nations. (2015a). *Addis Ababa action agenda of the third international conference on financing for development (Addis Ababa action agenda).*

United Nations. (2015b). *Transforming our world: 2030 agenda for sustainable development.*

United Nations. (2020). *The sustainable development goals report 2020.*

United Nations. (2021). *The sustainable development goals report 2021.*

United Nations Department of Economic and Social Affairs (UNDESA). (2016). Synthesis of voluntary national reviews 2016. Division of Sustainable Development, United Nations.

Wen, Z. (2011). An empirical study of the linkage between resources development and economic development-taken Shanxi province as an example. *Energy Procedia, 5*(70873079), 1394–1398. https://doi.org/10.1016/j.egypro.2011.03.241

World Bank. (2021). *PovcalNet database.*

20 The Future of the Oil and Gas Industry in Emerging and Developing Countries

Joshua Yindenaba Abor, James Atambilla Abugre, George Nana Agyekum Donkor, and Amin Karimu

20.1 Introduction

The enormous economic influence the oil and gas sector has on numerous economies makes the future of this sector vital for the entire world. Despite the fact that oil and gas will remain important sources of energy for decades to come, authorities and the public in general are already re-evaluating their significance. The oil and gas industry has faced numerous challenges in recent times. Among these are increasing shifts towards renewable energy sources, the impact of climate change, rising cost of developing oil and gas projects, insecurity and governance challenges, and weakening relationships between communities and oil-extraction firms. Therefore, the sector can survive in this increasingly complex global context only if it acknowledges the true scope of these persistent challenges and confronts their implications by taking the lead on solutions that are comprehensive and balancing.

Since the Industrial Revolution, oil and natural gas have been essential to the expansion and development of the global economy. Because oil has been so crucial to the development of modern economies in both the industrialised and developing worlds, the 20th century is commonly referred to as the 'Age of Oil'. The majority of the world's energy system and demands depend on oil and natural gas today. Around 31% of the primary energy used globally comes from fuels based on oil, while another 21% comes from natural gas (World Economic Forum, 2016). This instrumental role of oil and gas has become a driving force for global economic transformation to the extent that the discovery of oil and gas in emerging and developing countries in commercial quantities in recent times becomes linked to expectations of enhanced well-being and economic transformation, especially in the developing world of Africa and Asia.

However, scholars remain split over the extent to which oil and gas have met the expectations of the citizenry by enhancing their economic well-being. Mcclay (2022) posits that nearly two-thirds of revenues of oil-producing countries come from the sale of oil and gas. He further argues that 40%–50% of the national budgets of oil-producing nations is funded directly from the revenues of oil and gas, or that oil and gas are used as collateral to secure loans to finance critical social infrastructure. This observation is consistent with other empirical

DOI: 10.4324/9781003309864-23

findings that oil and gas are important natural resources and have propelled economic growth and increased the global competitiveness of producing nations in global trade and its associated advantages to the domestic economies.

Findings by other researchers such as Scott and Picard (2020) suggest that the extraction of oil and gas in most developing countries of Africa has become a tool of economic distortion and the deprivation of a majority of the citizens. Corruption, neglect of other critical sectors of the economy such as agriculture, oil spillages, and their effects on human and aquatic life, and worsening climatic conditions, among others, have characterised the discovery of oil and gas in most developing nations. These do not work to the benefit of the ordinary citizen, and hence oil and gas discoveries have become more of a 'curse than a blessing'.

In recent times, however, despite the immeasurable contributions of oil and gas to the development of the global economy, there have been systemic shifts in their demand. According to the International Energy Agency (IEA, 2021), the global use of renewable energy will increase by over 60% to 4,800 GW in 2026 – equivalent to the current total use of global power capacity of fossil fuels and nuclear combined. Renewables are set to account for almost 95% of the increase in global power capacity through 2026, with solar PV alone providing more than half. The amount of renewable capacity added over the period of 2021–2026 is expected to be 50% higher than from 2015 to 2020 for all regional blocs across the globe, with China, the United States, India, and Europe leading the pace.

This chapter, therefore, discusses the future of oil and gas in emerging economies in contemporary global dynamics. Market conditions and key players of oil and gas are also analysed as well as the systematic shifts that have emerged and the gradual transition to the use and impact of renewable energy on market participants. The effect of environmental considerations in the choice of a global energy mix is examined as temperatures rise incessantly within the progressive industrialised world of today.

The rest of the chapter is structured as follows. Section 20.2 discusses the exploration of oil and gas and how the environment is being impacted by the activities. The effect on the environment and how food and water quality is affected is examined. Market players along the value chain of the oil and gas sector are analysed in Section 20.3, with each stakeholder and the role it plays in getting the final products of petroleum ready for consumption. Section 20.4 examines how the world is transitioning to renewable energy use through the analysis of demand trends and challenges confronting the oil and gas industry, while Section 20.5 concludes the chapter.

20.2 The Drivers of the Future of Oil and Gas

20.2.1 The Environment

In 2017, the oil and gas sector was directly and indirectly accountable for more than 40% of the world's greenhouse gas emissions (Scott and Picard,

2020). As a result, the activities of oil and gas constitute major primary drivers of global warming and climate change issues.

The majority of greenhouse gas emissions from the burning of oil and gas occur when they are used to power transportation, provide electricity, or produce heat. Additionally, as oil and gas are extracted and processed, greenhouse gases are emitted as pollutants into the environment, and these have contributed significantly to the global impact of climate change over the years. Scott and Picard (2020) further estimate that to get a barrel of oil processed for the final user, on the average 95kg of CO_2 equivalent is emitted into the atmosphere. However, because different extraction procedures are used, these emissions vary depending on the density of the oil produced. The emissions intensity is less than 45 kg CO_2e per equivalent barrel of oil on average at the lower end of the scale with the highest being four times more than 200 kg CO_2e/boe. In the same vein, the production of natural gas results in emissions of roughly 100 kg CO_2e/boe. Similar to oil, there are significant differences between various gas sources and supply lines. For the generation of natural gas, the maximum emissions intensity is roughly four times more than the lowest.

Collectively, the total amount of emissions from the extraction of oil and gas was 5,227 million tons of CO_2 equivalent (Mt CO_2e). This equates to about 15% of all combustion-related emissions from the energy industry. Methane venting and avoidable fugitive emissions account for more than half (57%) of the emissions produced during the extraction of oil and gas. About one-third of all worldwide greenhouse gas emissions in 2017 came from the combustion of oil and gas, which resulted in total emissions of about 18 billion tons CO_2e (11.4 billion tons from oil and 6.7 billion tons from gas) (International Energy Agency, 2019).

The recent climatic changes and conditions have several impacts on the activities that are carried out in the environment and on the inhabitants that depend on it for existence. The consequences have become more devastating in countries including emerging ones that use less sophisticated technologies in the production of oil and gas. The intergovernmental panel on climate change in 2020 concluded for instance that climate change effects emanating from oil and gas activities could worsen the plight of the poor and other vulnerable groups and communities of oil-and gas-producing countries through the deepening of poverty levels and widening inequalities. A majority of these affected people and communities in Africa and Asia are more prone to drought, water scarcity, and flooding. Natural ecosystems as well as water, food, and livelihood security are expected to be affected by the impacts of oil and gas activities on the climate. The impacts are also expected to further affect poorer communities more, with the poorest 20% having to experience severe job losses in the next decade.

Rozenberg and Hallegatt (2015) estimate that without concrete and practical interventions to mitigate the suffering of the poor from the impacts of oil and gas activities on the climate, more than 100 million additional people could be living in extreme global poverty by 2030. Thus, the gains made in eradicating the extreme poverty of more than 720 million people could be reversed. The effect would be to plunge the vulnerable into a cycle of harsh economic hardships, thereby undermining the Sustainable Development goals of ending hunger and eradicating extreme poverty on the global scale by 2030.

Additionally, it is predicted that the poor will experience an increase in illnesses as a result of climate change. One hundred and fifty million more people could be exposed to malaria if global warming increases by 2°C to 3°C. In addition to reducing hygiene and sanitation, rising temperatures and a lack of water will promote the growth of other infections. Schistosomiasis and cholera outbreaks could happen more frequently, and the incidence of diarrhoea could rise by 10%, with children being the most susceptible. Each year, more than 100 million individuals fall into poverty as a result of health-care costs, of which climate-change-related activities contribute nearly half. Climate change is probably going to cause this number to rise further (Scott & Picard, 2020).

Crops and dwellings of vulnerable families can also be destroyed by other climate-related shocks, such as floods, droughts, storms, heatwaves, and pests, plunging them into extreme poverty. Climate change is predicted to cause these shocks to become more severe and frequent. Poorer families experience a larger loss of income and assets during disasters than affluent families. Additionally, poor people sometimes lack safety nets like insurance, savings, or assistance from government programs, and their dwellings are typically of lower quality and are less resilient to natural disasters and environmental hazards. Droughts by themselves could push 100 to 150 million people into poverty every ten years.

20.2.2 Food Security and Safety

In the United States, conventional and unconventional oil and gas production produces 2.5 billion cubic meters of wastewater annually (Scott & Picard, 2020). Usually, hazardous compounds and heavy metals are included in this. It is frequently disposed of in storage pits, which are sometimes required to have linings. These pits have the potential to release volatile organic compounds that are detrimental to nearby ecosystems and cardiovascular health. They also have potential to release benzene, a known carcinogen, and hydrogen sulphide. Additionally, wastewater is disposed of in injection wells dug into porous rock (such as sandstone or limestone), which must be kept apart from water sources. In certain places, drilling companies purify wastewater before applying it to fields, spreading it on roads, or reusing it. Deep-water drilling waste is often released into the ocean. Discharges can travel more than 2 km from the well, though their volume and composition vary depending on the site. The ocean floor's marine life is impacted by these releases.

Oil and gas extraction, storage, and transportation also contaminate water resources through spills and leaks in addition to wastewater discharge. Drilling sites, both onshore and offshore, as well as wastewater storage facilities, experience accidental leaks. When oil is transported by land (pipeline, rail, and road) and sea, oil spills happen. Twelve percent of the oil that enters the water comes from oil spills (with the rest coming from shipping, drains, and deliberate dumping) (World Bank, 2018). However, due to the concentration of oil in one location, spills from tankers harm local marine and coastal habitats significantly and permanently. The consequences result from the suffocation of species, toxicity of chemicals, alteration of the ecosystem, and unintended consequences of operations and chemicals used to clean up spills (International Energy Agency, 2006).

Drilling activities, processing facilities, and transportation (roads and pipelines) for oil and gas affect the land, and the ensuing soil, plant, and water contamination harms resources utilised for food production. Oil and gas waste and spills may contain hydrocarbons, toxic substances, nuclear waste, acids, and chemical contaminants that could impact soils, vegetation, and eventually groundwater. Resources used in agriculture can potentially be harmed by air pollution and fires caused by spills. Crop yield, land productivity, and agricultural income are negatively impacted by oil spills. Loss of organic matter and topsoil, nutrient leaching, pH changes, salinisation, and other types of soil deterioration are all caused by oil contamination of soils. Spills on a regular basis might render soil utterly useless.

These environmental and social impacts over the years have raised serious concerns regarding the dignity of the affected people and communities due to the adverse grave impacts on their basic human rights. The right to food, a safe environment, life, and property can be greatly affected by the extraction of oil and gas, especially in the developing countries. Pollution from oil spills is harmful to the ecosystem, aquatic life, and farmlands, and thus affects the right to improved standard of living.

20.2.3 Emerging Technologies

It is becoming increasingly important to drastically reduce emissions and maintain the increase in global temperature to less than 2°C by the middle of the century. The transportation industry, which is a primary focus of efforts to meet these objectives because it is a large contributor to global greenhouse gas (GHG) emissions, is rising. Transportation emissions climbed by 32% between 1990 and 2016, and in 2016 the industry was responsible for 24% of all greenhouse gas emissions worldwide. Most of these emissions (74.5%) come from light, medium, and heavy-duty on-road vehicles, with freight transportation accounting for more than half of this total (IEA, 2018a). In contrast to the developing countries, the OECD countries' proportion of global transportation emissions has decreased from 70% in 1971 to 42% in 2016. The transport sector emissions are predicted to increase by 1.5 times between 2010 and 2050, substantially tripling in non-OECD countries while hardly rising in OECD nations.

Fuel consumption reduction and fuel substitution are the two main ways to cut GHG emissions. Raising fuel efficiency is one strategy to combat rising oil use, while replacing oil with natural gas, hydrogen, biofuels, and electricity is another. Since hydrogen and methanol have not yet achieved widespread commercialisation and natural gas's relative benefits in terms of reducing greenhouse gas emissions compared to oil are limited, it is imperative to concentrate on the prospects for alternative fuels for transportation, specifically biofuels and electricity. Because they come from renewable sources and may be utilised with both existing on-road and non-road transportation, biofuels have been an especially enticing alternative as a transport fuel.

Since 2005, consumer interest in battery electric and plug-in electric vehicles (EVs) has been rising, and their sales have increased significantly in recent years. The stock of EVs increased to over 2 million by 2018, with the majority of them being sold in China, the US, and the EU. More than one million EVs were sold globally in 2017 (IEA, 2018b). However, only 2.2% of all vehicles on the road today are EVs. Adoption has been constrained by a lack of infrastructure for charging, expensive batteries, and range-related problems. According to the IEA, in order to maintain the increase in global temperature below 2°C, the global passenger car stock should include at least a 14% share of electric cars by 2030; this requires an annual growth rate of about 40% between 2017 and 2030. This may be feasible if aggressive national policies are followed to incentivise their purchase (IEA, 2018b).

20.3 Market Players in Oil and Gas Industry

Oil and natural gas, the two primary fuel sources in the world, are important providers of energy and has an influence and effect on the international economy. For such an extremely complex and capital-intensive industry, processes and mechanisms usually employed to produce and distribute oil and gas require modern technology. The oil and gas sector constitutes one of the biggest in terms of value, generating an estimated revenue of $5 trillion in 2022, contributing nearly a quarter to global gross domestic product (Mcclay, 2022). This huge influence and the contribution of the industry make it the single most important sector that determines global and domestic trade dynamics in terms of production of goods and services, inflationary pressures, economic growth, and general macroeconomic stability, especially in emerging and developing economies during times of shocks.

The market of oil and gas is segmented into three main areas and or players. These include the upstream, midstream, and downstream segments. These three streams are discussed separately below.

20.3.1 Upstream Segment of Oil and Gas Market: Exploration and Production

The methods and techniques used to locate possible sites for drilling and extracting oil and gas are known as oil and gas exploration. Geological surveys are carried out using a variety of techniques, including seismic imaging for offshore exploration and soil testing for onshore exploration. Energy companies enter into production-sharing agreements, where the state keeps equity and participation rights, in order to gain access to mineral rights granted by authorities or a concession deal, which grants ownership of any oil and gas discovered to the producers.

Upstream enterprises are those engaged in the discovery and production of oil and gas. Before drilling to extract the minerals, these businesses scan the planet for raw material deposits. These companies are commonly referred to as 'exploration and production' or 'E&P' firms. The upstream market is associated with high risks, large investment capitalisation, prolonged duration, and technologically advanced intensity because it takes time to identify and drill for oil. The cash flow and operating income of an E&P company almost always include a line item related to the production of oil and gas.

One of the capital-intensive industries is oil and gas production, which involves expensive machinery and the use of qualified skilled labour. Once a corporation identifies the location of the oil or gas, drilling plans are made. The length of the drilling process can be influenced by the drilling depth, rock hardness, weather, and distance from the site. By providing up-to-date and timely information and trends, data tracking employing advanced technologies can aid in exploration efficiency and quality assurance. Although all drilling rigs have the same fundamental parts, the drilling techniques differ from the type of crude and or gas and the location's geology.

E&P firms typically do not own their own drilling machinery or staff. Instead, they contract out the drilling of wells to corporations, and these companies typically bill E&P companies based on the length of time they spend working for them. Unlike exploration and production firms, drillers do not accrue revenue directly related to the production of oil and gas. A well's production is generated and maintained throughout time through a variety of actions after it has been drilled. These processes – which are collectively referred to as well servicing – include logging, cementing, casing, perforating, fracturing, and upkeep. Thus, within the oil and gas industry, oil drilling and oil servicing constitute two distinct commercial operations.

The exploration and production of oil and gas is a complex environment that requires a huge investment of resources in terms of machinery, capital, infrastructure, and human expertise. Prospecting and discovery of oil involve the use of high-technology equipment. The costs of all these resources have in recent times, increased, which makes the discovery and drilling of oil and gas expensive to the host nations. This phenomenon has compelled most emerging countries to rely on foreign firms with the needed capital to invest with unfavourable terms to the detriment of the local citizens. These dynamics in the oil and gas production are facilitating the shifts and transitioning into renewable energy sources, which are cheaper to explore and environmentally friendly.

20.3.2 Midstream Segment of Oil and Gas Market

Transportation, storage, and marketing of petroleum products, natural gas, and refined goods are all classified under the midstream industry. Unrefined crude oil is moved via two main modes: pipelines, which move the majority of the oil through for at least a portion of the route, and tankers, which cross inter-regional waterways. Pipelines move the goods to another carrier or directly to a refinery after the oil has been extracted and separated from the gas. Then, petroleum products are transported via tanker, truck, rail, or additional pipelines from the refinery to the market.

High regulation, particularly regarding pipeline transmission, and low capital risk are further characteristics of the midstream sector. Naturally, the segment is also reliant on the performance of upstream businesses. The business of upstream production is frequently integrated with the transportation and storage of oil. In their yearly financial statements, major oil firms like Shell and BP typically combine production and transportation costs. In addition, the governments of the countries whose territories oil pipelines pass through own these pipelines. Because of this state ownership, midstream is frequently absent from the oil production value chain as a distinct component.

20.3.3 Downstream Segment of Oil and Gas Market

Downstream activities are the processes used to convert crude oil and natural gas into finished goods for consumption. These involve converting crude oil into various forms of energy, such as gasoline, diesel, and liquefied natural gas. The closer a company is to the process of feeding consumers with petroleum products, the more downstream it is considered to be. The industry players that have the closest connection to common consumers are those in the downstream sector. The midstream process involves shipping and moving crude oil after it has been found and extracted (the upstream phase). The downstream process occurs when the oil is refined, marketed, distributed, and sold. However, midstream operations may be used to refine crude oil into petroleum products in some cases, especially with the operations of integrated oil companies.

The downstream industry also plays a significant role in other economic sectors and industries, including the medical sector. Some of the supplies and tools used and required by medical professionals are significantly influenced by the downstream process. Similar to this, the downstream process is crucial to the agricultural industry because of its connection to insecticides, fertilisers, and the fuel required for farming machinery.

The activities of the midstream sector account for nearly half of the environmental challenges that come from the oil and gas industry. The refinery process leads to the emission of various carbons and other gases that are inimical to the biosphere and well-being of mankind. Also, the refinery and distribution processes require the use of huge machinery that is so highly sophisticated that substantial capital investment and specialised skills are needed for their execution. These are required to ensure that minimum environmental standards are followed and safety measures guaranteed to reduce the impact of the excesses that are associated with the midstream activities in the oil and gas sector. Consumption of petroleum products has, therefore, been hinged on the midstream sector. The cost and quality of the midstream operations determine the affordability of the products by consumers. This has a direct impact on the future demand for petroleum products which must compete with less expensive substitutes of renewable energy sources, thereby causing shifts to the cheaper substitutes.

20.4 Energy Transition and the Prospects of the Oil and Gas Industry

20.4.1 Future Demand Trends of Oil and Gas

Since the 1980s, a large number of oil-producing countries and oil companies have operated under the assumption that the advanced industrial world will eventually run out of its readily available oil supplies and become more dependent on oil supplied by OPEC, particularly the substantial Middle East reserves. This long-standing mindset, which existed from the 1980s until recently, maintained that the oil cartel only needed to wait for the day when OPEC's petro-power would increase over time. In the 2000s and up until recently, OPEC followed a revenue-focused strategy, presuming that the world was now oil-constrained and that oil was more desired beneath than on the market (Inkpen & Moffett, 2011).

It is becoming more obvious that the world is moving faster toward sustainability and away from fossil fuels to run the various segments of national economies. In its 2021 decision, the Conference of the Parties to the United Nations Framework Convention on Climate Change (COP26) for the first time specifically resolved a move away from coal and the gradual elimination of fossil fuel subsidies, even though governments, investors, and consumers all over the world are indicating plans for a quicker move away from fossil fuels. According to McKinsey's 'current trajectory' energy transition scenario, world gas demand could peak in 2040 and oil demand could peak in 2027. The transition might happen even more quickly if leading nations implement focused strategies to meet their net-zero commitments. The world oil demand might peak as early as 2024 under this 'achieved commitments' scenario, whereas the global gas demand could peak around 2030.

This worldview led oil corporations and other market players to adopt a business strategy that focused on storing expensive assets and accumulating as much reserves as possible on their balance sheets.

But the US shale boom and other sustainability issues have altered the expectations for the future use and demand of oil and gas. Producers and consumers of oil and gas are beginning to realise that oil under the earth would perhaps eventually be less valued as compared to oil consumed in the upcoming years. This stems from the fact that industrialised nations, particularly the United States of America, China, and Europe, are vigorously trying to shift from fossil fuels produced from shale and other types of rocks including traditional sources despite dwindling costs due to technological advancement. In essence, opinions have shifted from thinking an oil supply peak was feasible to thinking an oil demand peak is probable over the coming decades. As stuck high-cost oil and gas assets are held, some investors are also worried that oil and gas firm shares may be overvalued. The operational environment for oil and gas in the future is being altered as a result of this significant shift in expectations. Furthermore, new initiatives are required if the world is to prevent serious global warming brought on by the build-up of greenhouse gases in the atmosphere. Oil use may remain largely stable in a world where fossil fuel consumption is constrained to keep global warming to 2°C as recommended by scientists.

As a result of this shift, authorities and stakeholders are putting further pressure on the oil and gas industry. The IEA has emphasised that in order for the global energy industry to reach net zero by 2050, a major decrease in the use of hydrocarbons must be made by 2040, including the phasing out of all unabated coal and oil power plants. The IEA further predicts that within the next 30 years, despite significant advancements in energy efficiency, there will be a significant increase in the consumption of oil and gas due to the need to support the global economy for a growing middle class in developing countries. The industry expects to maintain its current business strategies despite the natural decline that occurs with running the oil and gas assets that are now active around the globe. Accordingly, oil demand will rise by 14% from 90.6 million barrels per day in 2014 to 103.5 million barrels per day in 2040.

However, the majority of the energy needed to power economic activity in the global economy will still be provided by oil and natural gas, with fossil fuels contributing nearly 75% of all primary energy needs in 2040. In light of the evolving global economic shifts, technological advancement, and a changing demographic structure, this prognosis becomes more uncertain. For instance, in the near future, a brief peak in the demand for oil for transportation could be achieved due to a number of new factors including efficient and improved technologies in vehicle manufacturing, logistics planning and freight, urbanisation and its effect on transport requirements that limit personal vehicle demands to reduce congestion, and slower than anticipated economic prospects in major developed nations across the globe. Without significant policy changes, population growth and expanding income effects will gradually outpace these advancements, causing oil demand in the transport sector to increase from 52 million barrel per day in 2015 to 55 to 60 million barrels per day by the 2040s. This prediction contrasts with ExxonMobil's 2015 base forecast of around 69 million barrel per day by 2040 and the IEA Current Policies Scenario of 75 million barrel per day for transport oil demand by 2040.

20.4.2 Shifting Strategies in the Oil and Gas Industry

A shift in capitalisation and production strategies is expected to drive private businesses and within the OPEC body, if the sector and markets grow more certain to peak and smoothen. This implies that even if oil markets tighten in the near future, market players will still have to consider the long-term effects of postponing the development and production of reserves. The decision as to whether to take into account the remaining 'carbon budget' for global oil exploration in determining how much, and when, to invest to monetise existing reserve holdings will only be made by parties who have no other option (huge capital requirement, geopolitical barriers, low expertise, bureaucratic failures, etc.).

The oil and gas industry should build a value narrative that is in tandem with its primary output not increasing in this potential scenario since total set production levels may not be achieved by all operators. Quality assurance, frequent monitoring, cost-effective solutions, and manufacturing procedures and mechanisms will undoubtedly play a vital role in lowering costs and boosting margins in order to offer bottom-line value growth with stable top-line production. This will be influenced in part by industry consolidation, competitive forces, and collaboration between the industry and its suppliers. By this move, a significant shift in the industry would be occasioned.

A leaner and more efficient industry is needed in both execution and operation to balance cost issues against the potential requirement for new reserves. Though prices may remain low and carbon externalities priced more properly, businesses will need to be ready to deliver substantial volumes of oil and gas at competitive returns. With much-increased degrees of automation, artificial intelligence, and remote operation, the sector will see a new technological revolution. The new leaner environment will have a detrimental effect on national revenues available from the oil sector directed toward customised solutions to seek competitive advantage as well as on the supply industry, including local content in host nations.

20.4.3 Trust Challenges in the Oil and Gas Industry

To demonstrate that it can sustain the future growth hypothesis for speculators in the era of rising uncertainties, the petroleum industry requires strategies that can create value in any circumstance, such as cutting project durations, reducing product defects (such as biogas spills), and intensifying a circular economy of factors of production like water, heat, and steel. Such strategies move business toward technological developments that will interest the entire population.

But essentially, the oil and gas sector must address the significant trust issues brought about by the failings of its lowest ranks if it is to be recognised as a contributor in energy solutions and economic growth rather than a cause of environmental devastation and a catalyst for sectarian war. Despite the central role of energy in daily life, the oil and gas business was regarded as the least trusted sector in a 2013 Gallop poll, tied for last place with the tobacco sector. The industry's contributions to unwarranted lobbying and legal actions against climate change policies and other environmental and safety standards have exacerbated this loss of trust. The industry typically views improved technical communication as the solution.

The implications for resolving beyond-ground hazards that impede resource development are raised by the more difficult climate for oil and gas investment. Oil will continue to be the predominant transportation fuel for the next 20–30 years, even with stricter environmental restrictions that seek to protect its integrity. However, the oil and gas sectors frequently encounter strong opposition in many communities across the world, particularly in those that have suffered the detrimental environmental, socioeconomic, and geopolitical effects of oil and gas exploration and production. While oil and gas companies have created expectations among their stakeholders that they can operate without having a harmful impact on the environment, actual performance has frequently fallen short of these expectations.

The oil and gas sector is often plagued by occurrences and claims of corrupt activities. The notion of a corrupt oil and gas business is pervasive throughout the world, and significant scandals like the Petrobras and Nigerian government scandals continue to make headlines. Because of the public's lack of confidence in the sector, it is more difficult to undertake projects and it is riskier for governments to approve large infrastructure projects. But corruption affects more than just public confidence. It is a very expensive issue that causes operational and supply chain inefficiencies, can lead to astronomical fines and compliance costs following a scandal, and negatively affects the wealth distribution in some nations by connecting economic harm and political instability to the oil and gas industry. In many places, there are still issues with mistrust, tense relationships, and disputes with the local communities that host oil and gas explorations. Accordingly, stakeholder-related risks constitute the single biggest problem, accounting for close to half of all non-technical project hazards.

The oil and gas industry's poor reputation makes it difficult for the sector to hire the best workers in some places and hinders its ability to obtain capital from institutional investors who frequently view the industry as highly speculative and hazardous. Additionally, consumers would like to switch to cleaner energy sources because they wonder if oil and gas will continue to be a reliable source of fuel. Companies that overlook these issues run the danger of having their balance sheet assets becoming frozen over time. The industry will be able to guarantee market value and source funding for oil and gas in an orderly transition to reflect the shifting demand if these concerns are systematically resolved.

20.5 Conclusion

Due to the reduction in public trust and confidence in the oil and gas sector, job creation, investments, and the sale of energy products are no longer sufficient to guarantee stakeholder satisfaction. It will be necessary to make a concerted effort to increase accountability, transparency, improved management, and efficiency across the entire value chain in the sector in order to confront the mounting challenges to its operations. Industry and society will benefit from setting up an institutional structure that sets a standard for moral behaviour. This kind of framework can encourage transparency and give investors and the general public more assurance that businesses can depend on oil and gas as required, as the energy system changes over the coming decades.

Players who wish to keep their market position in the energy sector must eventually determine whether it is more beneficial for shareholders to create lucrative, low-carbon energy sources as supplemental, and ultimately replacement revenue sources for oil and gas. The way oil and gas investors think will need to change as a result of this. For instance, Shell and BP have started investing hugely in renewable energy and other market players should follow suit to meet the dictates of the energy consumer market. The oil and gas industry may discover new opportunities to expand this second leg of its operations by tackling the technological issues posed by the many renewable energy sources, as well as how to combine large-scale energy storage and transit solutions in a society with a lot of fluctuating renewable energy. The adoption of environment-friendly technologies will do the trick for countries and firms that will still depend on oil and gas in the next decades in order to remain competitive in the global energy mix market.

References

Conference of the Parties to the United Nations Framework Convention on Climate Change Report. (2021). https://enb.iisd.org/glasgow-climate-change-conference-cop26/summary-report

Congressional Research Service. (2020). *Intergovernmental panel on climate change report*. Report Number R47082.

Inkpen, A. C., & Moffett, M. H. (2011). *The global oil & gas industry: Management, strategy & finance*. PennWell Books.

International Energy Agency (IEA). (2018a). *Transport sector CO_2 emissions by mode in the sustainable development scenario, 2000-2030*. Paris. https://www.iea.org/data-and-statistics/charts/transport-sector-co2-emissions-by-mode-in-the-sustainable-development-scenario-2000-2030

International Energy Agency (IEA). (2018b). *Global EV outlook 2018*. Paris. https://www.iea.org/reports/global-ev-outlook-2018

International Energy Agency (IEA). (2019). *CO_2 emission from fuel combustion*. https://iea.blob.core.windows.net/assets/eb3b2e8d-28e0-47fd-a8ba-160f7ed42bc3/CO2_Emissions_from_Fuel_Combustion_2019_Highlights.pdf

International Energy Agency (IEA). (2021). *Renewables 2021*. Paris https://www.iea.org/reports/renewables-2021

Mcclay, R. (2022). How oil and gas sector works. https://www.investopedia.com/investing/oil-gas-industry-overview/

Rozenberg, J., & Hallegatte, S. (2015). The impacts of climate change on poverty in 2030 and the potential from rapid, inclusive, and climate-informed development (Tech.

Rep. No. WPS7483). The World Bank. Retrieved August 03, 2016, from http://documents.worldbank.org/curated/en/2015/11/25257367/impacts-climate-change-poverty-2030-potential-rapid-inclusive-climate-informed-development

Scott, A., & Picard, S. (2020). Oil and gas, poverty, the environment and human rights. https://odi.org/en/about/our-work/climate-and-sustainability/faq-3-oil-and-gas-poverty-the-environment-and-human-rights/

World Economic Forum. (2016). 46th World Economic Forum annual meeting 2016: Mastering the fourth Industrial Revolution, Davos-Klosters, Switzerland. https//www.weforum.org/reports-2016

Index

Note: Page references in *italics* denote figures, in **bold** tables and with "n" endnotes.

3D printing 86, 91

Ablo, A. D. 114
Abugre, J. B. 112, 210
Act of Parliament 32, 57
Addis Ababa Action Agenda of the Third International Conference on Financing for Development 269, 272
Africa: capacity factor analysis 36–38, *37*; crude oil processing 63–64; crude oil production 30; CSR of oil-based MNCs in 214–215; determinants of refinery location 31; future of refinery projects in 41–43; impediments to CSR in oil industry in 215–216; import volumes of petroleum products in *37*; natural resources 30; oil and gas infrastructure 32–33; oil and gas pipelines 67, **67**; oil and gas refinery supply chain 31–32; oil demand in *37*; oil production in *224*; oil refineries in **39**; oil refining in 30–45; overview of oil and gas industry in 223–224; product demand analysis 36; product pricing analysis 38–41; recruitment and selection of oil industry employees 112
African Union: Organisation for Standardisation (ARSO) 161
Agbonifoh, B. 200
agency theory 139–140
Aghaji, M. 192
Aguilera-Caracuel, J. 214
Ahmad, S. A. 75–76, 82
Amadu-Kannike, A. 115
Amanam, U. U. 251
Amenshiah, A. K. 115
Amoako-Tuffour, J. 250

Analoui, F. 115
analytical hierarchy process (AHP) 183, 186n3; framework in petroleum industry **184**
Angola 116, 202, 215, 217–218, 219n1, 240, 245, **248**, 250, 252, 267–268
Anil, A. P. 169
Anlesinya, A. 210
annual objectives 133
Anstätt, K. 210
appraising personnel in O&G sector 120
approaches to performance management 176–178
Arbatli, E. 251
Arctic Council 231
Armah, S. E. 113
aromatics 256, 263
artificial intelligence (AI) 7, 86, 88–89
artificial neural networks (ANNs) 88, 89
association of oil marketing companies (AOMCs) 50
Astron Energy Cape Town refinery 38
Azikel Refinery 64

Babatunde, A. O. 225
balanced score card (BSC) 8, 177–178, 183–185, 185n2; PM framework in petroleum industry **184**
Bank of Ghana 32–33
Barbosa, F. 99
Bayer Crop Science Model Village Project 213
benchmark/benchmarking: imports parity price (IPP) 56; in oil and gas (O&G) industry 8–9
benchmarking 182–183
Benson, C. 192, 199

Berrone, P. 225
big data analytics 7, 86, 89
biological health hazards 194
Bischoff, C. 117
Bitcoin 90
blockchain technology 89–90
Bondy, K. 215
British Petroleum (BP) 3, 117, 159, 287, 292
Bruton, G. D. 211
bulk-distribution companies (BDCs) 56
Bulk Oil Storage and Transportation (BOST) Company Limited 6, 15, 17, 32; overview 22; responsible for Ghana's SPR 19–20; role of 21; storage capacity of Ghana's 23
bulk road vehicle (BRV) tracking system 63
Burrell, G. 175
business-level strategy 134

capability approach 211–212
Chakamera, C. 210
chemical health hazard 194
Chevron 117
Chief Fidelis A. Oguru 218
child labour and human rights abuses by MNEs 208–209, 214, 216
China 3, 5, 43, 102, 197, 232, 234, 245–246, 258, 260, 263, 281, 285, 289
China National Offshore Oil Corporation (CNOOC) 67, 233
Claus method 31
committed leadership 167
Compagnie Française des Pétroles 102
compensation: in O&G industry 119–120; trends in developing countries 120
competition 48, 50, 80, 130, 159, 163, 175
competitive advantage, and TQM 169
Conference of the Parties to the United Nations Framework Convention on Climate Change (COP26) 288
Congressional Budget Office 20
ConocoPhillips 117
Constitution of the Federal Republic of Nigeria, 1999 197
continuous improvement 168–169
contract: for manpower in O&G industry 113–114; -related risks 76
Convention on Occupational Health Services (No. 161) 196
convergent technologies 92–93
Cooperation on Marine Oil Pollution Preparedness and Response 231
Copenhagen Agreement (1971) 231
core values 133–134

corporate environmentalism: greening oil and gas sector in EDCs 233–234; in oil and gas industry 231–234
corporate governance: concepts 139–141; impact of 151–154, *153*, *154*; and level of operation 214–215; mechanisms 151, 154–155, 225; in O&G industry 138–155; overview 138–139; policy implications 154–155; principles and challenges 148–151, *149*; theories 139–141
corporate reputation 215
corporate social responsibility (CSR): across Sub-Saharan Africa 213–214; capability approach 211–212; contextual overview 213; European Commission definition of 209; impact and socio-economic performance of 216; impediments to, in Africa 215–216; importance for MNCs in oil & gas sector 210; initiatives from MNCs globally 213–214; institutional theory 210–211; and local communities 210–213; of multinational corporations 208–219; of oil-based MNCs in Africa 214–215; socio-economic well-being 212–213; stakeholder theory 211; theoretical underpinnings of 210–213
corruption 10, 42, 76, 112, 146, 150, 153–155, 200, 202, 208–209, 216
COVID-19 pandemic 44, 86, 99, 269, 272
Crane, A. 127
critical management studies (CMSs) 176
Crude Distillation Unit (CDU) 38
crude oil: final products and usage *62*; production in Africa 30; refineries in emerging economies 63–64
customer-based approaches 167
customer power 130–131
customer satisfaction, and TQM 169–170
Cybernetix 95
Cybersecurity Act 2020 93

Dangote, Aliko 43
Dangote Group 63–64
Daouda, Y. H. 209–210
D'Arcy, Shell 30
Darkwah, A. 114
data analytics 7, 86, 89
Data Protection Act 2012 93
David, F. 126
deferrals 20, 21
demand of refine products 6–7, 31, 41–44, 45

Deming, Edwards 162, 169
developing countries: natural-resource-endowed 3; oil and gas project management in 106; sustainability challenges in oil and gas industry in 224–225; technology transfer in oil and gas sector 116–118; TQM in 8; *see also* emerging and developing countries (EDCs); emerging economies
devlopment, of O&G employees 114–115
digital privacy 95
digital technologies 96; challenges and opportunities of 94–95; in oil and gas (O&G) industry 86–96; overview 86–87
Diodorus 100
direct (principal) stakeholders 56–57
distribution: exclusive 55; intensity 55; intensive 55; as marketing factor in downstream 54–55; selective 55
domestic revenue mobilisation (DRM) 272
Dooh, Barizaa 218
downstream sector 6, 7, 33, 40–41, 43, 287–288; in Ghana 48–58; Kenya 53; marketing factors 53–58; Nigeria 51, 53; overview 48–49, *49*
drivers of future of oil and gas 281–285; emerging technologies 284–285; environment 281–283; food security and safety 283–284
drone technology 86, 92

'Earth Summit' 1992 268
ecological influence, and strategic management 129
Economic Community of West African States (ECOWAS) 233
economic influence, and strategic management 128
economic well-being 212
Efanga, Alali 218
efficiency/efficiencies: organisational 79; supply chain 79–81
efficient communication 168
Ejikeme, U. 197
Ekong, C. N. 228
Elder Friday Alfred Akpan 218
electric vehicles (EVs) 285
electronic monitoring 91–92
elemental sulphur 34
emerging and developing countries (EDCs) 4–5, 247–248, 253–254; crude oil refineries in 63–64; demand for O&G resources 5; drivers of future of oil and gas 281–285; energy transition and prospects in 288–291; future of oil and gas industry in 280–292; greening oil and gas sector in 233–234; market players in oil and gas industry 285–288; NG and LNG sector in 247–249; O&G industry importance for 60; political instability in 65; strategic posture of O&G firms in 132–134; *see also* developing countries
emerging economies 15, 19; consumption of natural gas in **244**; crude oil refineries in 63–64; downstream petroleum marketing in 6, 48; fiscal and governance challenges 251–252; fiscal and institutional framework 250–251; LNG resource management in 249–253; natural gas and natural liquefied revenue 252–253; natural gas market dynamics in 242–245; NG and LNG sector in world economy 241–247; NG resource management in 249–253; O&G storage infrastructure in 6; petrochemical products and market in 258–262; petroleum industry in 50–53; production of natural gas in **243**; quality of oil and gas products in 62–63; risk management in petrochemical industries 264–265; *see also* developing countries
emerging technologies 284–285
employees: recruitment and selection of 111–112; strategic training and development of 114–115; *see also* personnel
Employee's Compensation Act, 2010 197
empowerment of personnel 115–118, 168
encryption 90
energy carriers 34
Energy Policy and Conservation (EPCA) 16
energy security: defined 18; managing 18–19
energy transition: future demand trends 288–289; prospects of 288–291; shifting strategies 290; trust challenges in industry 290–291
Engen 38
enterprise resource planning (ERP) 69
Enumah, J. 192
environmental, social, and governance (ESG) outcomes, and MNCs 209–210
environmental ethics 227–229
environmental governance 225–229
environmental impacts: of activities of MNEs 209–210; management in oil and gas industry 229–231

Environmental Protection Agency, 1994 (Act 490) 197
environment/sustainability management: corporate environmentalism 231–234; as driver of future of oil and gas 281–283; environmental ethics 225–229; environmental governance 225–229; environmental impacts, managing 229–231; overview 223–224; sustainability challenges in developing countries 224–225
EPA Act 1994 (Act 490) 24
Escolano, J. 251
Etemire, U. 228
Ethereum 90
ethics: environmental 227–229; inter-generational 228; in the oil and gas industry 225–229
European Commission 209
European Parliament 217
European Union 17, 62, 226
exclusive distribution 55
exploration and production (E&P) firms 286
Extractive Industries Transparency Initiative (EITI) 216
ExxonMobil 117, 289

Factories, Offices and Shops Act 1970 (Act 328) 196
Factories Act (CAP 1 LFN 2004) 197
feedstock 256
Fierro Hernandez, D. 79
FIFO schedules 201
financing: innovative 19, 28; project 19; strategic petroleum reserves, in Ghana 19–21; sustainable development 271–272
firms: health and performance KPIs *179*; mission 165; strategic plan 165; total quality infrastructure 165; total quality management plan 165; vision 165
Fluid Catalytic Cracking (FCC) 38
food security and safety 283–284
foreign direct investment (FDI) 160, 218, 267, 272–273
Frank, A. 200
Friends of the Earth Netherlands 218
functional level strategy 134
future of oil and gas industry 280–292

gap analysis 131–132
gas-to-gas competition 251
Ghana 10, 273–274; deferrals 21; direct purchase of oil and gas 20; downstream sector in 48–58; going public with SPR 20–21; IPR, development of 21; liquefied petroleum gas (LPG) programme in 25–28; local content policy of 113; management of oil and gas storage and terminals in 22–24; natural gas and natural liquefied revenue 252–253, *253*; oil and gas contribution to sectoral development in 274; oil and gas storage in 21–25; oil and gas strategic reserves, financing 19–21; oil production fields in 32; OMC Market Share Statistics *50*; petroleum policies 57–58; Petroleum Revenue Management Act, 2011 (PRMA) 252, 273; public capitalisation of SPR 20–21; royalty-in-kind-transfers, of oil and gas 20; SPRs financing in 19–21; storage tank inspection, audit, and calibration in 24–25
Ghana Cylinder Manufacturing Company (GCMC) 26, 27
Ghana Gas Company 242
Ghana Health Service and Teaching Hospitals Act, 1999 (Act 526) 196
Ghana Heritage Fund (GHF) 252, 273
Ghana Labour Act, 2003 (Act 651) 196
Ghana National Fire Service 25
Ghana National Petroleum Commission (GNPC) 32
Ghana National Petroleum Corporation Act, 1983 (PNDCL 64) 197
Ghana National Petroleum Corporation Law (GNPC) 115
Ghana Oil Company Limited (GOIL) 32, 50
Ghana Petroleum Funds (GPF) 273
Ghana Stabilisation Fund (GSF) 252, 273
Ghana Standard Authority (GSA) 25
Ghisel, R. G. 225
Global Development Goals (GDGs) 271
globalisation: and competitive advantage 169; oil and gas industry 162–163
Global LPG Partnership 26
global refining business 43–44
Global South: oil and gas resources for SD 273–275; SD and financing challenges 271–273; sustainable development in 267–277
Gomez-Mejia, L. R. 225
Government of Ghana (GoG) 20
Green Climate Fund 272
Gregory, K. 230
Gulf Cooperation Council (GCC) 263

Haddud, A. 79
Hague Court of Appeals 218
Hallegatte, S. 282
Handfield, R. 170
health and safety issues in oil and gas sector 4–5, 191–204
Health and Safety of Employees (ILO) 191
health hazards: biological 194; chemical 194; mechanical/ergonomic 194–195; physical 193–194; psychosocial 195
Henry Hub in Louisiana 245
Heritage Fund 10
Herodotus 100
Hong, Z. 75, 78
human resource management (HRM) practices: in O&G industry 7, 111–121; recruitment and selection of employees 111–112
Hunger, J. D. 126
Hurricane Katrina 16
Hurricane Rita 16

Imobighe, T. A. 225
imports parity price (IPP) benchmark 56
inclusiveness: oil and gas industry 164; and workforce diversity 164
India 3, 5, 43, 213, 234, 246, 258, 281
indirect (secondary) stakeholders 56, 57
Indonesia 170, **248**; feed-in tariffs 233; Green Building Code 233
Indorama Eleme Petrochemicals Limited 53
industrialisation 3, 43, 106, 191, 208, 250, 254, 264, 274
Industrial Petroleum Reserve (IPR) 21
Industrial Revolution 280
innovations: in oil and gas (O&G) industry 86–96; overview 86–87; strategies 92–93
innovative financing 19, 28
input-output of oil refinery *34*, 34–36, *35*
inspection, maintenance, repair (IMR) system 95
institutional arrangements, in O&G sector 145–148
institutional theory 140–141, 210–211
intensive distribution 55
inter-generational ethics 228
International Energy Agency (IEA) 18, 96, 231, 281, 285, 289
International Labour Organization (ILO) 191, 195, 196, **197**, 200–201
international labour standards and legal frameworks 195–197
International Monetary Fund (IMF) 272–273

International Organisation for Standardisation (ISO) 161
Internet of Things (IoT) 90–92, 163
intra-generational equity 228
Ishikawa, K. 165
ISO 14001 standards 161, 217
ISO 29001 standards 161
Iyer, A. 169

Janus, B. 82
Jensen, M. 139–140
job role localisation (JRL) 114
Johnsen, T. E. 75
Johnson, G. 126, 133, 135
Johnson, H. T. 175
just-in-time (JIT) 182

Kaplan, R. S. 175, 177
Kassem, M. 76
Kaur, M. 170
KBR Inc. 53
Kenya: downstream petroleum market 53, *54*; petroleum pricing 55
knowledge transfer 116–118
Kolk, A. 211
Kosmos Energy 32
Kühn, A. L. 211, 214

lean production 181–182
Ledesma, D. 250
Lenfant, F. 211
Leonard, D. K. 202
Liang, R. 69
Limbe refinery 38
liquefied natural gas (LNG) 9, 247–249; demand, and supply 241–242; emerging economies 241–247; policy 250; proven reserves of 241–242; resource management in emerging economies 249–253; trade 246–247; in world economy 241–247
liquefied petroleum gas (LPG) 103–104; programme in Ghana 25–28
Liu, Z. 69
local content for manpower in O&G industry 113–114
Longoni, A. 227
long-term objectives 133
Lott, M. C. 230
low-carbon economy 4
Luanda oil refinery 217
Lui, S. 192
Luiz, J. M. 215
Lynch, M. C. 19

Major Oil Marketers Association of Nigeria (MOMAN) 51
Manuj, I. 80
marketing in downstream oil and gas industry 6, 53–58; distribution 54–55; policy 57–58; pricing 55–56; product 53–54; stakeholders 56–57
market players 285–288; downstream segment market 287–288; exploration and production 285–286; midstream segment market 287; upstream segment market 285–286
Martins, F. 229
material living conditions 212
Mayer, C. 139
Mcclay, R. 280
McCreery, J. 184
McKinsey 163, 288
mechanical/ergonomic health hazards 194–195
Meckling, W. 139–140
Mentzer, J.T. 80
methanol 256
Middle East 112
Midoil Refining & Petrochemicals Company Limited 53
midstream sector 7, 33, 287
millennium development goals (MDGs) 269, **270**
mission, of firm 165
mission statement 133
Modarress, B. 77
Mohammed, A. M. 170
Mohan, A. M. 230
monitoring 166–167
Morgan, G. 175
Morgenroth, A. 215
Mozambique 43, 65, 202, 241, 245–247, **248**, 250
Muchlinski, P. T. 216
Müller, R. 102
multinational corporations (MNCs) 118; autonomy and managerial discretion of subsidiaries 215; comparing CSR initiatives from 213–214; corporate social responsibility of 208–219; empirical evidence 213–218; environmental outcomes 209; governance outcomes 209; government and local culture 215; linking activities to ESG outcomes 209–210; overview 208–210; pressure groups 215; socio-economic outcomes 209; theoretical underpinnings of CSR 210–213; well-being of local communities 210–213

Murphy, H. 82
MYA Energy 43

Naghi Beiranvand, D. 82
Nakhle, C. 250–251
Nasere, D. 112
National Oil Company (NOC), Ghana 252–253
National Oil Corporation of Kenya 53
National Petroleum Authority (NPA) 32, 63
National Petroleum Corporation (NNPC) 53
natural gas (NG) 9, 15, 247–249; demand, and supply 241–242; employment and GDP contribution 248–249; exports and foreign currency 247–248, **248**; export trade value for top 20 exporting countries **248**; final products from *62*; global proven reserves of *241*; market dynamics in emerging economies 242–245; policy 250; pricing 10, 251; proven reserves of 241–242; resource management in emerging economies 249–253; revenues of 252–253; storage 17; strategic reserves 16–17; in world economy 241–247
Natural Resource Governance Institute (NRGI) 251
natural resources: Africa 30; high dependence on 3–4
NDEP PLC 53
Ndu, O. A. 200
Negi, S. 80
netback from final product 251
new/emerging risks 201
New York Mercantile Exchange 245
Nigeria 10, 30, 250, 275; capacity factor analysis 36; downstream petroleum activities 51, 53; Mineral Oils Regulation, 1962 197; oil and gas contribution to development in 276; petroleum consumption in *52*; petroleum industry bill (PIB) 51; petroleum pricing 55; Petroleum Regulations, 1969 197; product demand analysis 36; refineries under construction in 64
Nigeria Infrastructure Fund (NIF) 275
Nigerian Farmers v. Shell Petroleum Company case 218
Nigerian National Petroleum Corporation (NNPC) 36, 51, 63
Nigerian Sovereign Investment Authority (NSIA) 275

300   Index

Nigerian Sovereign Wealth Fund (NSWF) 275
Nigeria Pipeline and Storage Company Limited (NPSC) 17
Nobel, Ludvig 101
Norouzi, N. 99
Norton, D. P. 177
Nwachukwu, P. I. 69

Obeidat, S. M. 180
occupational hazards: associated with oil and gas industry 193–195; biological health hazards 194; categories of 193–195; chemical health hazard 194; mechanical/ergonomic health hazards 194–195; physical health hazards 193–194; psychosocial health hazards 195
occupational health and safety (OHS): challenges of 198–202; context of 192–193; corruption 202; dealing with challenges of 202, **203–204**; international labour standards and legal frameworks 195–197; new and emerging risks 201; occupational hazards 193–195; off-shore workers 200–201; in O&G industry 9, 191–204; overview 191–192; personal protective equipment and clothing 202; women workers 201; work schedule arrangements 201
occupational health and safety management frameworks (OHSMFs) 192
Occupational Health Services Convention, 1985 (No. 161) 196
Occupational Safety and Health Convention, 1981 (No. 155) 196–197
occupational 'stressors' 198
Odion-Obomhense, A. A. 197
off-shore workers 200–201
Ogbele Refinery 64
O&G resources: and EDCs 5; and global economy 5
oil and gas (O&G) industry 285–288; in Africa 215–216, 223–224; benchmarking in 8–9; compensation and reward methods in 119–120; contracting and local content for manpower in 113–114; corporate governance in 138–155; digital technology in 86–96; empowerment of personnel in 115–118; firm's mission/vision/strategic plan 165; firm's total quality infrastructure 165; firm's total quality management plan 165; future demand trends of 288–289; globalisation 162–163; governance practice in 141–145, *142*, **143**, *143*, **145**; HRM practices in 7, 111–121; importance for EDCs 60; innovations in 86–96; manage process quality 166; monitor, review, and control 166–167; OHS in 9; OTLM in 6, 60–61; petrochemical resource management 10; publicise, communicate, and celebrate successes 166; quality in 160–164; rewarding and compensating personnel in 119–120; shareholder governance framework 145–148; shifting strategies in 290; strategic management in 8, 124–135; strategic training and development of employees 114–115; sustainability management in 3–11, 164; technological advancement 163; and technological transfer 115–118; technological trends in 87–92; TQM in 160–162, 164–167, 169–170; training 165–166; trust challenges in 290–291; value chain of 75; workforce diversity and inclusiveness 164; *see also* strategic petroleum reserves (SPRs)
oil and gas infrastructure 19, 32–33
oil and gas projects: features of 103–104; history of 100–102; management 99–108; overview 99–100; project management of 104–106
oil and gas storage management 15–28; case study 21–25; overview 15
oil and gas supply chain 31–32, 183–184; management 73–83; nature of 73–74; state of technology in 64–65; sustainability practices in 81–82
oil marketing companies (OMCs) 32, 48, 55; downstream sector in Ghana 50; Market Share Statistics in Ghana *50*
oil price volatility: causes of 17–18; defined 17; and strategic petroleum reserves 17–18
oil refinery/ies: demand *vs.* capacity 36–41; in emerging economies 63–64; and environmental considerations 44–45; and health considerations 44–45; input-output of *34*, 34–36, *35*; margins 41; out-of-service 38; and profit margin 38–40; and safety considerations 44–45; *see also specific refineries*
Okeke, A. 232–233
OLA Energy 53
olefins 256
Olson, E. M. 134
operations, transportation, and logistics management (OTLM) *61*, 68–70;

Index   301

enterprise resource planning 69; exploration phase 61; in O&G industry 6, 60–61; pipelines 66–67, **67**; production phase 61; RFID technology 69; and technology 64–65; transformation phase 61; trucks 67–68; vessels 68
opportunities, digital technology in oil and gas industry 95
Organisation for Standardisation (ARSO) 161
Organization for Economic Cooperation and Development (OECD) 3, 16, 212, 284
Organization of Petroleum Exporting Countries (OPEC) 288, 290
OSPAR commission 231
Osundina, O. 262
Owusu-Ayim, J. 250

Pagell, M. 81
Palmer, C. 227
Paris Climate Accord 272
Pearce, J. A. 126, 133–134, 135
peer-to-peer transmission 90
performance improvement process 181–183; benchmarking 182–183; lean production 181–182
performance indicator 180–181
performance management: approaches to 176–178; in oil and gas industry 174–185; in oil and gas industry supply chain 183–184; overview 174–175; performance improvement process 181–183; selecting performance indicator 180–181; structure 178–180; theory and practice 175–176
performance management structure 178–180
personal protective equipment and clothing 202
personnel: empowerment of 115–118; rewarding and compensating 119–120; *see also* employees
PESTLE analysis 128–131; ecological influence 129; economic influence 128; political and/or legal influence 128; social cultural influence 128–129; technology influence 129
Peter I, Russian Tsar 101
Petrobras 291
petrochemical fertilisers 259
petrochemical industry: fundamentals of 257–258; risk management in 264–265; value chain of 257, 259
petrochemical products and markets 258–262

petrochemical resource management 256–265; fundamentals of petrochemical industry 257–258; overview 256–257; petrochemical products and markets 258–262; refinery and petrochemical synergy benefits 262–263; risk management in petrochemical industries 264–265
Petrofina 101–102
Petroleum (Exploration and Production) Act 919 115
Petroleum Commission Act, 2011 (Act 821) 197
Petroleum Exploration and Production Law (Act 919) 251
Petroleum Holding Fund (PHF) 273
petroleum industry: AHP, implementing **184**; BSC PM framework in **184**
petroleum product marking scheme (PPMS) 63
Petroleum Products Pricing and Regulatory Agency (PPPRA) 51, 55
Petroleum Revenue Management Act, 2011 (PRMA) 252–253, 273
Pfeffer, J. 140
physical health hazards 193–194
physical inactivity 199
Picard, S. 281, 282
pipelines, for oil transport 66–67, **67**
policy 92–93; liquefied natural gas 250; as marketing factor in downstream sector 57–58; natural gas 250; on renewable energy 234
political and/or legal influence, and strategic management 128
pollution prevention: international framework 231; in oil and gas industry 231
Prabhakar, G. P. 102
pressure groups 215
Prevention of Major Industrial accidents Convention, 1993 (No. 174) 196
Price Stabilisation and Recovery Levies (PSRL) 57
pricing: as marketing factor in downstream sector 55–56; natural gas 10, 251; petroleum 55–56
printing technology 91
process automation 86
process management 167–168
process quality: managing 166; oil and gas industry 166
procurement: as critical risk factor in oil and gas projects 75–77; defined 75; in oil and gas industry 7, 73–83; overview 73

procurement risks: classification of 76; contract-related risks 76; defined 76; management 77–79, 78; negative consequences of 76–77; tendering risks 76
products (petroleum) 53–54
programme management 102–103
project financing 19
project management 102–103; of oil and gas projects 104–106
Project Management Institute (PMI) 99, 102–103
Promotional Framework for Occupational Safety and Health Convention, 2006 (No. 187) 196
Protection of the Arctic Marine Environment (PAME) Working Group 231
psychosocial health hazards 195
public-private partnerships (PPPs) 19
'Publish What You Pay' initiative 252
PUMA Energy Distribution Ghana Limited 50

Quaigrain, R. A. 193
quality: assurance 162; management 162–164; in oil and gas industry 160–162
quality management system (QMS) 159
quality of life 212

radio frequency identification (RFID) technology 69
Ras Lanuf oil refinery 38
recruitment and selection of employees: in oil and gas industry 111–112; practices in developed and developing oil countries 111–112
refinery and petrochemical synergy benefits 262–263
refinery yields 61, 260
refining margins 41, *42*
remote sensing 90–91
REN21 Renewable Energy Policy Database 233
renewable energy 4, 288, 292; policies on 234; sustainable 233; transition 10, 247, 264, 280–281, 286
requirement management (RMP) 105–106
'resource curse' phenomenon 3–4
resource dependency theory 140
Resource Governance Index (RGI) 141, **143**, 144–145, **145**, 251
reward(s): methods in O&G industry 119–120; trends in O&G industry 120

risk(s): management 125; management in petrochemical industries 257, 264–265; new and emerging 201
Robinson, R. B. 126, 133–134
robotic process automation (RPA) 88–89
robotics 86
Rodriguez, M. R. 251
Royal Dutch Shell Plc 102, 218
Rozenberg, J. 282
Rural LPG (RLP) promotion program 26
Rusali, R. 199
Russia-Ukraine conflict 275

Sahoo, S. 168, 170
Salancik, G. R. 140
Satish, K. P. 169
Saturday, E. G. 170
Saudi Arabia 16
Scott, A. 281, 282
selective distribution 55
Sen, Amartya 211–212
Senoo, J. E. 113
shareholder governance framework 145–148
shareholder rights index 155n1
Shell 117, 159, 292
Shell Petroleum Development Company (SPDC) 218
Shevchenko, A. 81
Shqairat, A. 74
Sigma Gas Ghana 27
situational analysis 126–131; external analysis 127–131; internal analysis 126–127
small- and medium-sized enterprises (SMEs) 74
Smith, Adam 140
social cultural influence, and strategic management 128–129
socio-economic performance of CSR activities 216
socio-economic well-being 210–213; CSR and 210–213; of local communities 210–213
Socony Mobil 102
Sonangol 217
South Africa 5, 17, 30; future refinery projects 43; refineries in 38
Sovereign Wealth Fund 10
sovereign wealth funds (SWF) 240, 267–268
staff: empowerment of 168; involvement of 168
stakeholders 56–57; direct (principal) 56–57; indirect (secondary) 56, 57
stakeholder theory 140, 211

Standard Oil of California 101
Starkey, K. 215
strategic fuel fund (SFF) 17
strategic goals 133
strategic management: defined 124; gap analysis 131–132; in O&G industry 124–135; overview 125; process 125–131; selection of strategies 134; situational analysis 126–131; strategy control 135; strategy implementation 134–135; SWOT analysis (matrix) 131–132; threat of competition among rival firms 130; threat of customer power 130–131; threat of potential new entrants 130; threat of supplier power 131; threats of substitution 131
strategic petroleum reserves (SPRs) 15, 16; evolution of 16–17; financing in Ghana 19–21; managing 18–19; and oil price volatility 17–18; public capitalisation of 20–21; role in price moderation 18; *see also* oil and gas (O&G) industry
strategic plan, of firm 165
strategic posture: annual objectives 133; components 132–134; core values 133–134; long-term objectives 133; mission statement 133; of O&G firms in EDCs 132–134; strategic goals 133; vision statement 133
strategic training, of O&G employees 114–115
strategy/ies: control 135; defined 134; implementation 134–135; selection of 134
strategy map 178, *178*, 185
Strotmann, H. 213
Sub-Saharan Africa (SSA) 196, 208–219
substitution 131
Sumbal, M. S. 114
Sundarakani, B. 74
supplier power 131
supplier risk intelligence 77
supply chain efficiencies 79–81, *81*
supply chain management: objective of 74; oil and gas industry 73–83; overview 73; supply chain efficiencies 79–81
supply chain risks: management 77–79; supply market intelligence 77
supply market intelligence 77
Suslick, S. B. 251
sustainability: challenges in oil and gas industry 224–225; defined 223; oil and gas industry 164; of socio-economic and natural systems 212

sustainability management: in oil and gas industry 3–11; in oil and gas supply chains 81–82
sustainable development: defined 223; and financing challenges 271–273; in Global South 267–277; Leveraging oil and gas resources for 273–275
Sustainable Development Goals (SDGs) 10, 182–183, 268–271, **270**
SWIMMER 95
SWOT analysis (matrix) 131–132, **132**
synthetic rubber 258

Tadesse, S. 197
talent acquisition 94
TechLink 117
technological transfer 115–118, *118*
technology: AI 88–89; big data analytics 89; blockchain technology 89–90; convergence 92–93; drone 92; influence and strategic management 129; Internet of Things 90–92; in oil and gas supply chain 64–65; printing technology 91; robotic process automation 88–89
Tema Oil Refinery (TOR) 22, 32, 38, 63
tendering risks 76
Texaco 117
threats: of competition among rival firms 130; of customer power 130–131; of oil and gas industry in emerging markets 69; of potential new entrants 130; of substitution 131; of supplier power 131
Tingbani, I. 225
Tolley, G. S. 19
Total Energy 53
Total Fina 217
Total Ghana Limited 32
Total Kenya 53
Total Petroleum Ghana Limited 50
total quality management (TQM) 8, 161–162, 182; committed leadership 167; competitive advantage 169; continuous improvement 168–169; critical success factors for implementation 167–169; customer-based approaches 167; customer satisfaction 169–170; efficient communication 168; empowerment and involvement of staff 168; implementing 170–171; in oil and gas industry 159–171; process management 167–168; productivity 169; profitability 170
TransCanada Albert System 245
transparency and accountability index *252*

Index

Transparency International 252
trucks, for oil transport 67–68
trust challenges in oil and gas industry 290–291
Tullow Ghana Limited 32
Turner, J. R. 102

UN Global Compact 216
Unified Petroleum Price Fund (UPPF) 56
United Nations (UN): Conference on sustainable development (SD) 268–269; Sustainable Development Goals (SDGs) 182–183, 268–271, **270**, 275
United States: Department of Energy (DOE) 16; Energy Information Administration 34; price of natural gas 10; recruitment and selection of oil industry employees 111–112
Universal Declaration of Human Rights 216
upstream sector 7, 33

Varma, S. 179, 183
VEB 43
Venezuela 3, 30, 267
vessels, for oil transport 68
vision statement 133
visual PM (VPM) system 177–178
Vivo Energy 53
VIVO Energy Ghana Limited 50
Volkert, J. 210

Voskoboinikov, Nikolai Ivanovich 101

weak institutions 4, 147, 154–155, 211
well-being: economic 212; socio-economic 210–213
West Africa Gas Pipeline (WAGP) 33, 67, 242, 245–246
Wheelen, T. L. 126
Wilman, J. D. 19
women workers 201
Wood, G. 117
Worika, I. L. 228
workforce diversity 164
Workmen's Compensation Act, 1987 (PNDCL 187) 196
work schedule arrangements 201
World Bank 145–146, 149, 240
World Bank Governance Indicators 141
World Health Organization (WHO) 191, 193; healthy workplace model *198*; and safe working environment 202
Wu, X. 232

Yadav, S. 168, 170
Yang, T. 227
Yang, Y. 197
Yom Kippur War 16
Yusuf, Y. 184

ZEN Petroleum Limited 50

Printed in the USA
CPSIA information can be obtained
at www.ICGtesting.com
LVHW020812170924
791295LV00003B/237